A CULTURAL HISTORY
OF GARDENS

VOLUME 1

A Cultural History of Gardens

General Editors: Michael Leslie and John Dixon Hunt

Volume 1
A Cultural History of Gardens in Antiquity
Edited by Kathryn Gleason

Volume 2
A Cultural History of Gardens in the Medieval Age
Edited by Michael Leslie

Volume 3
A Cultural History of Gardens in the Renaissance
Edited by Elizabeth Hyde

Volume 4
A Cultural History of Gardens in the Age of Enlightenment
Edited by Stephen Bending

Volume 5
A Cultural History of Gardens in the Age of Empire
Edited by Sonja Dümpelmann

Volume 6
A Cultural History of Gardens in the Modern Age
Edited by John Dixon Hunt

A CULTURAL HISTORY
OF GARDENS
IN ANTIQUITY

Edited by Kathryn Gleason

Bloomsbury Academic
An imprint of Bloomsbury Publishing Plc

B L O O M S B U R Y
LONDON · OXFORD · NEW YORK · NEW DELHI · SYDNEY

Bloomsbury Academic
An imprint of Bloomsbury Publishing Plc

50 Bedford Square	1385 Broadway
London	New York
WC1B 3DP	NY 10018
UK	USA

www.bloomsbury.com

BLOOMSBURY and the Diana logo are trademarks of Bloomsbury
Publishing Plc

Hardback edition first published in 2013 by Bloomsbury Academic
Paperback edition first published in 2016 by Bloomsbury Academic

British Library Cataloguing-in-Publication Data
A catalogue record for this book is available from the British Library.

ISBN: 978-0-8578-5029-4 (HB)
978-1-8478-8265-3 (HB set)
978-1-3500-0986-8 (PB)
978-1-3500-0995-0 (PB set)

Library of Congress Cataloging-in-Publication Data
A catalog record for this book is available from the Library of Congress.

Series: The Cultural Histories Series

Typeset by Apex CoVantage, LLC, Madison, WI, USA
Printed and bound in Great Britain

CONTENTS

ILLUSTRATIONS

INTRODUCTION

CHAPTER 1

CHAPTER 2

CHAPTER 3

CHAPTER 4

CHAPTER 7

CHAPTER 8

GENERAL EDITORS' PREFACE

The volumes of this series explore the cultural world of the garden from antiquity to the present day in six particular periods. Each volume addresses the same eight topics, determined by the general editors for their relevance to garden history across different times and cultures. Thus a reader interested more, say, in planting or in types of gardens could read through the chapters devoted to those issues in successive volumes. Contrariwise, either of those interests might be contextualized by a volume's discussion of other aspects of the garden in a given period. There is therefore both a horizontal and a vertical way of using these volumes. Further, each volume includes both its editor's introduction, which rather than abstracting or summarizing the other contributions, surveys the period from a fresh vantage point, and a bibliography, which encompasses references from all the eight chapters augmented with that editor's additional readings.

HISTORY

These volumes are a historical enquiry and not an encyclopedia. They do not pretend to be comprehensive, either geographically or chronologically. The authors of the individual chapters have been encouraged to foreground what seem to be the most significant episodes and examples of their particular topic, leaving it to the reader to envisage how other sites that he or she knows better might further illustrate, challenge, or qualify the given analyses. But in every instance, we intend there to be some narrative of one particular theme as it exists, unfolds, or develops during a particular historical period. The definitions of these historical eras must be taken with some caution and elasticity, since a chronology of garden making does not always fit the divisions of time devised for and endorsed by other histories: André Le Notre did his work after 1650 but is arguably more usefully considered in a volume focused on the Renaissance than on the Enlightenment; similarly, Gertrude Jekyll and William Robinson were designing before 1920, but we understand their work better within the cultural content of the modern age.

CULTURAL HISTORY

There are of course many modes of history that have developed over the centuries. A relatively new one addresses the cultural context of human activity. "Culture" derives from the Latin *colere,* which has as some of its meanings "to inhabit," "to respect," "to pay attention to"; it emerges also in our words "colony" and "cultivation." Gardens, then, must be considered as driven by and evidence of a whole congeries of human concerns; they are not, above all, to be examined in terms of their merely visual appearance, materials, or stylistic histories. The diversity and density of human involvements with those sites we call gardens mean that the discipline of garden history draws upon adjacent disciplines such as anthropology, sociology, economic, and political history, along with histories of the arts with which the garden has been involved. So three large questions are posed: why were gardens created? How were they used or visited (there being no handy term for the "consumption" of gardens)? And how does their representation in different arts express the position and value of the garden within its culture in diverse periods? Regretfully, we were unable to extend the range of these volumes to include the garden making of China and Japan among other Eastern cultures, although inevitably the rich examples of such gardens have been invoked on occasion.

GARDENS

The range of places that can be envisaged within this category is enormous and various, and it changes from place to place, and from time to time. Yet this diversity does not wholly inhibit us from knowing what it is we what to discuss when we speak of the garden. Yet the garden is typically a place of paradox, being the work of men and women, yet created from the elements of nature; just as it is often acknowledged to be a "total environment," a place may be physically separated from other zones but answering and displaying connections with larger environments and concerns. Gardens, too, are often created, and subsequently experienced, as commentary and response: a focus of speculations, propositions, and negotiations concerning what it is to live in the world. Both the physical gardens and the ideas that drive them are cultural constructions, and their history is the topic of these six volumes.

John Dixon Hunt, University of Pennsylvania

Michael Leslie, Rhodes College

Introduction

KATHRYN GLEASON

The subject of this volume, antiquity, falls into the centuries traditionally defined as classical antiquity. It begins with the sixth century B.C.E. and the "real,
genuine Greece, where politeness, learning and even agriculture itself, are supposed to have arisen," (Pliny the Younger, *Letters* 8.24.1–5). During this time,
the rhetoric of the wars with Persia (499–449 B.C.E.) set Greek culture in opposition to that Asian monarchy; this echoed through the Roman era and
formed the foundation of "Occident-Orient" views that exist to this day. The
Hellenistic and Roman periods are the core of this period, through the third
century C.E.,[1] with a vaguely defined terminus in Western Roman Empire in the
sixth century C.E. and the Arab conquests of the seventh century in the East.[2]
In garden history, the period stretches from the construction of the Hanging Gardens of Babylon (c. 600 B.C.E.) to the palace gardens of Kashyapa at
Sigiriya, Sri Lanka (c. 477–95 C.E.), or of the Ummayad caliph Ibn Hisham
(724–42 C.E.) at Rusafa, Syria.

The Asian origin of the garden examples that bracket this volume alerts us
to the complexity of the Greco-Roman genealogy currently under critique in the
other arts: the kinds of gardens for which the Romans are most famous seem
not to be Greek, or, at least, it was rhetorically important to suggest so. The
contributions to ancient garden history come from a broad diversity of cultures:
the territories of the Greeks, Minoans, Etruscans, Romans, Gauls, Britons, and
other European cultures; Persians, Lydians, Syrians, Judaeans, Nabataeans,

and Asian cultures stretching on to India, Sri Lanka, and China at the edge of the known world; and Egyptians, Libyans, Carthaginians, and other North Africans. The ancient foundations of the European garden are a *histoire croisée*, an "entangled history" of cultural encounters—particularly during the fourth through the first centuries B.C.E.—that shaped Mediterranean landscapes in ways that we have yet to successfully nationalize.[3]

Yet the contribution of the Greeks is, nonetheless, foundational: their texts imbued gardens with a set of *values* that still govern discourses about gardens and other designed landscapes to this day. Gardens were used as rhetorical devices, defining Greek versus Persian characteristics, beginning with the Greco-Persian wars.[4] Greek gardens were portrayed as simple plots: abundant vegetable gardens and orchards, sacred temple groves, and open athletic grounds. The male figures in this landscape were sundrenched and strong, morally as well as physically. In contrast, the gardens of the Persian and other Asian kings were scented and luxuriant pleasure grounds filled with collections of exotic plants, and perfumed, pale figures who preferred shade.[5] These gardens, to the Greeks, expressed the luxurious nature and decadence of the Asian character. The Romans, in adopting this legacy during their own wars with the Persians, further developed the dialectics of public versus private, pleasure versus utility (*amoenitas versus utilitas*), recreation versus work (*otium versus negotium*), urban versus rural (*urbe versus rus*). Western landscape tradition continues to define designed landscapes in accordance with these values.

By contrast, the Asian garden tradition conveys no such message. The Persian garden, *paradeisos*, appears in texts to range from crops to the luxurious royal gardens portrayed by the Greeks, celebrated as the right and natural expression of divine favor. In fact, monarchies depended on such favor to sustain their hegemony, and few places were more powerful than gardens to express control of natural forces, display the resources expanded by conquest, and evoke the divine in a setting of peace and abundance. See, for example, Bedal, L.-A., and J. G. Schryver. "Nabataean Landscape and Power: Evidence from the Petra Garden and Pool Complex." Crossing Jordan: North American Contributions to the Archaeology of Jordan. Ed. T. E. Levy, et al. London: Equinox. 2007. 375–383.

Thus gardens, in particular, fall squarely on one of the "cultural fault lines" between East and West,[6] and we must read the ancient descriptions, particularly those of the classical world, for their rhetorical value as much as for their descriptions of real gardens.

ANTIQUITY

Scholars today study ancient cultures using methods that might be used in any time period to study people and their culture, interrogating older methods in the process. Nonetheless, antiquity remains a useful concept in surveying garden history, bounding, for now, a body of diffuse and emerging evidence, while designating a time in which classical culture was seen as the preeminent authority in European culture. Possessing, in Erwin Panofsky's words, "a physiognomy that is as difficult to pin down exactly as the description of a human individual"[7] antiquity captures that comfortable familiarity that is so often shaken by forgotten or never before suspected traits. This is particularly true of garden history, where any new discovery of material remains astounds—what could be left after two millennia? students and audiences inevitably ask, and, in fact, it seems that each new archaeological discovery challenges our historical notions. Nonetheless, for many, the ancient garden remains a largely mythical place, rather than a body of real evidence for past practices of a garden culture. This volume seeks to change that perspective with a range of contemporary scholarship.

Antiquity, always a perspective from the present, suggests an epoch of origins, of golden ages, and of mythical events, and to the contemporary reader and designer, it is not continuous with the present. The absence of physical remains of gardens has left it out of landscape architectural theory almost completely. As Norman Newton explains in his thirteen pages of text on antiquity in *Design on the Land*, which has been the primary history text on landscape architectural history for decades:

> From a designer's point of view . . . modern knowledge of the landscape architecture of man's earliest ages is necessarily for the most part conjectural; there is little remaining physical evidence from which to reconstruct the historic actuality in visible form . . . and so for so visual a field as landscape architecture, physical remains are of the utmost importance, verbal descriptions are not enough.[8]

However, it is also possible that the lacuna of writing on antiquity since the early twentieth century is symptomatic of the larger tendency of theorists to focus upon the Age of Enlightenment, in part because of the focus on the modern professions, but also based upon the assumed absence of an industrialized society in the distant past which might have generated similar landscape values. Contemporary work is showing this to be an unhistorical notion, that while "the Enlightenment may indeed have been marked by great discursive and institutional change . . . to claim that modern societal institutions and modern formulations of many affective states have their first appearances, even their discovery here is to misrepresent history."[9] This volume considers the expected traditional range of ancient classical gardens, from small subsistence vegetable plots to luxury villas. But classical gardens, and particularly those of the Roman era, can now be seen to include urban public parks and suburban and villa gardens that provided refuge from overcrowded cities, whose dynamic economies were, made possible by industrialized agriculture and international trade and wars. To the modern student, educated in ideas of progress and evolution, it is inconceivable that ancient Rome was an early industrialized society, yet archaeological discoveries of water-powered factories for mass production, vast latifundia (industrial-scale agriculture), air pollution, central heating, analog computers, and even a tradition of the Grand Tour.[10]

To explore the ancient garden, we begin with the archetypal symbol of antiquity: paradise as a quadripartite or cruciform garden, transmitted to Islamic gardens as the *charbagh*. In its definitive form, the garden is bounded within the ideal geometry of a square or a rectangle of ideal proportions and subdivided by paths and channels cross-axially dividing the square. These elements lead the visitor through the four rivers of Eden and the tree of life, the four directions, the four seasons, the four elements, the four corners of the earth, and are linked to the mandala.[11] In architectural theory, the quadripartite garden is conceptually unified in its genesis with the first acts of rational city planning and architectural design. The ancient garden, in this view, is an ideal geometry, centering humankind within a finite and knowable universe.[12]

Images of the quadripartite gardens of antiquity were most prolifically created for garden history books during the period of the École des Beaux Arts, when a popular exercise for architecture students was the interpretation of the letters of Pliny the Younger describing his villas at Tuscanum and Laurentium, room by room, garden by garden.[13] As neither villa had been found archaeologically, reconstruction depended upon a close reading of the text and comparison with known Roman villas and ideas of ancient gardens known from the Renaissance. In the same periods, dozens of young architects receiving the Prix de Rome documented archaeological excavations, then prepared elaborate reconstructions. In the absence of garden archaeology, the open areas of the gardens were reconstructed according to Renaissance interpretations of ancient geometry, with discoveries of pools, fountains, and art deftly worked into the arrangement. These beautiful drawings have been used to illustrate the textbooks of garden history that remain in use today.[14] Most ancient gardens,

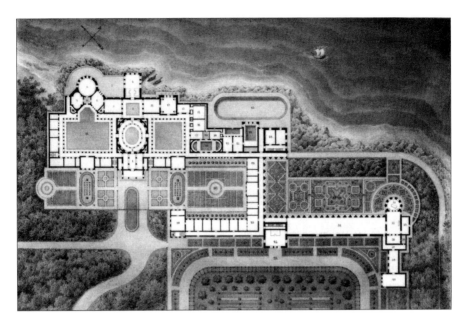

FIGURE 0.1: The maritime villa of Pliny the Younger at Laurentium as imagined by Schinkel (1820).

reconstructed either on paper, in models, or on archaeological sites, are portrayed as this timeless form, particularly within courtyards and other architecturally bounded spaces.

Despite this rich history of the quadripartite garden's transmission, there is, as yet, *no evidence for the quadripartite garden in antiquity*, either archaeologically or in other sources. No Egyptian tomb painting depicts one, nor do any Assyrian reliefs. Stronach's later reconstructions of a charbagh at Pasargadae, while accurate analyses of viewing, were not cruciform in construction, based upon a recent reexamination of the water channels.[15] The Gardens of the Roman Empire project, recording over 1,500 gardens at the full extent of the Roman empire under Trajan, offers no archaeological evidence of gardens with geometrically laid out cruciform walks and beds. Some historians see ancient precedents for the quadripartite garden in rural villa courtyards with paths that casually cross within an enclosure, in a large vineyard a Pompeii, and in cruciform pools, without associated paths, notably at Herculaneum.[16]

Of course, a lack of evidence now does not mean the quadripartite form will not be found in the future; however, its striking absence in antiquity does suggest that we step away from this single iconic form of ancient garden design. This is not an easy proposition, as a vetting of this topic among colleagues and the general public has shown. For many, the paradise garden of this design is nostalgic, in the sense of "a painful desire to return" to a time of symbolic or spiritual unity from the fragmentation of the modern age.[17] The term "nostalgia" has given way, as Susan Alcock points out, to more sophisticated memory studies. She writes, "Far from automatically being deemed negative or at best neutral developments, today[such reversions to the past] are investigated as active strategies."[18] From this perspective, the quadripartite garden has proven a remarkably flexible form over the *longue durée* from the eighth century to the present, offering a frame through which to explore the truly ancient ideas of paradise. Perhaps most compelling today is the role of the ancient quadripartite garden in mediating the divide in Western and Middle Eastern cultures through a sense of shared form and meaning.[19] The quadripartite garden has become a lieude *mémoires,* a place for depositing these desires. The mediating role of the garden is not lost by dispensing with the quadripartite form: the constancy of ancient Oriental-Occidental relations is best illuminated by gently setting aside the symbolism of Antiquity and reexamining the complex and interconnected relationships of the Mediterranean cultures over time.

Throughout this volume, we will see the garden history of antiquity through two lenses: the way we imagine ancient gardens after hundreds of years of tradition about antiquity, transmitted primarily in literature and art, and, secondly, through the vast, recently emerging body of new archaeological evidence on gardens in the broader cultural landscapes. The physical remains are allowing us to critically reread associated texts and iconography. Gardens, as a form of landscape, are particularly dense in their capacity to transmit "patterns in commemoration and forgetfulness."[20] The newly discovered archaeological remains surprise us with forgotten forms and technologies and plant aesthetics and choices, as well as unexpectedly early manifestations of gardens and plants thought to have circulated in global culture only much later. As Alcock notes, this emerging "material evidence can help us watch for phantoms of otherwise invisible memory, and thus can prevent overly tidy versions of the past."[21]

Designed landscapes are particularly interesting in classical archaeology in the absence of a Greek landscape architectural or garden tradition parallel to that of Greek art, theater, literature, philosophy, or architecture. There is a very different legacy of classical design form and garden culture that scholars have yet to fully articulate. Peregrine Horden and Nicholas Purcell discern that the garden was more important than the field in much of the Mediterranean as a locus of productivity,[22] but as Robin Osborne notes, the Greeks neither discussed nor represented the cultivated countryside in their art and literature, almost as if it were unremarkable.[23] Tuplin, in examining Persian gardens, also notes an absence of representation of gardens in Achaemenid sources, despite more ample documentation by cultures within their empire. This may have led to an emphasis on luxury in the definition of paradeisos.[24]

Literature describing this luxury has generally led garden historians to the idea that Roman imperial gardens, and thus much of subsequent landscape architectural history, finds its origins in Egypt and Asia.[25] Did the classical Greeks really have such a simple garden culture? Or was the simple country garden so important in the rhetorical definition of Greek values—and those of the Roman republic—that we cannot conceive of the alternatives? It is the stated absence of a developed Greek garden tradition that sets up the moral dialectics that shaped the Roman garden and continue to shape Western gardens today. Archaeologists have yet to contribute synthetically to the subject: the peristyle courts of Greece houses are largely paved and the larger open areas largely avoided during fieldwork.

The dearth of evidence for classical Greek gardens has had the salutary effect of allowing us to see the distinctly non-Hellenic, Asian, and Egyptian forces that shaped the garden, and thus the larger Hellenistic period. While the arts have struggled to temper the common notion that Greek culture dominated the Mediterranean, then Rome copied it, landscape historians have had little choice but to study the Persian, Egyptian, and Anatolian royal gardens to understand the great landscape projects of antiquity, particularly those of Alexander the Great, and his Hellenistic successors.[26] Rome's luxury gardeners with their Greek names either allude to a reality of gardening in Greece that has yet to be fully explored, or it reflects the assimilation of Asian garden craft into the Hellenistic kingdoms. Recent scholarship explores the roles of contact with India and China, as well.

Even in the absence of archaeological evidence, the literature contributes three important and interrelated dialectics that underlie discourse in Western garden culture today: pleasure versus utility, public versus private, and informal versus formal. None are universal.

PLEASURE VERSUS UTILITY; PUBLIC VERSUS PRIVATE

These two dialectics have a related history and three brief passages from classical texts define them. The first is the oft-repeated story of the Spartan general Lysander visiting the Persian satrap Cyrus the Younger at Sardis, in Lydia (a territory long famous for luxury before the Achaemenid era).[27] The Spartan is astonished that a man who reclines in the shade among perfumed plants is personally responsible for laying out and planting the finely ordered rows of trees. Repeated in Latin by Cicero *De Senectute*, 17, this passage defines luxury versus utility as an recurring theme of Western garden culture. Yet in this passage we see that the gulf is immediately bridged: acts of cultivation, we are told by Xenophon and later authors, are an activity that prepared Persians for war.[28] The two men admiring the fine ordering of trees in straight ranks, much like well-disciplined soldiers, and, by extension, a well-ordered society, articulate a critical moment in garden history, a kind of horticultural détente, in which the Greeks found common values with the Persians in a setting that otherwise expressed everything that the Greeks had represented as antithetical to their identity.[29] Tuplin, however, sees a more measured response in this passage suggesting that the passage might simply mean that the Greeks had not adopted ordered rows of trees at that point and found them noteworthy. (Achaemenid Studies, 126).[30]

A second text complements this story and introduces a second critical concept in landscape architectural history: public versus private in gardens and parks. In this story by Plutarch Cimon 2.13, a Greek writing in Rome in the first century C.E., the victorious Greek general Cimon has returned rich from his campaigns in Persia. How does this Greek citizen handle extraordinary wealth? He makes the public gift of (Cimon 2.13) shade and water to the agora and the gymnasium. Plutarch sets the life of Cimon in contrast to that of *Lucullus* (*Luc.* 39.3), the Roman general famed for returning victorious from his Asian wars and abandoning public life for his fabulously luxurious *horti*, or private lands, on the Esquiline. Using his wealth to blast through mountains to bring sea water to his estates and to make land out of the sea for his villa on the Bay of Naples, he was living like "Xerxes in a toga" (like the Persian king in Roman garb) Plutarch Luc. 39.3; Velleius Paterculus 2.33. Cimon, in addition to his contribution to public space, opens up his (well-endowed) estates to the citizens so they may have food in a time of famine. Stories such as these, kept alive in the classical writings, have an embedded dialectic transmitted across Western history, between public and private, luxury and utility, which is much explored in this volume.

Of course, as we know today, such concerns reflect not an actual eschewing of pleasure by the Greeks or Romans, but the concern for the kind of unpredicted change that "barbarian" or new and foreign practices can bring to a collective identity. It is from the Greeks, and more tangibly from the late Republican Romans, that we have the concept of the public park and gardens.[31] Pompey gave his horti over to the populace during his lifetime, while Julius Caesar and Marcus Agrippa did so on their death. Augustus, as emperor, built the Campus Martius as a vast public park, outdoing the great basilaea, or royal quarter of Alexandria. Yet over time, the nature of these gifts faded, so that the tradition of the Roman public park was lost until the texts were explored again by Rudolfo Lanciani and Pierre Grimal in the twentieth century.[32]

THE FORMAL AND THE INFORMAL

In the popular discourse on gardens today, design is divided into the formal and informal (or naturalistic). This is simultaneously a superficial distinction and yet one also deeply grounded in Western culture, dating back to Cain and Abel and the tension between the agricultural and the pastoral (Genesis 4:1–8).

As popularly sketched, the design of gardens in southern Europe and western Asia is geometric, while naturalistic forms of designs are thought to be rooted in the ancient concept of the pastoral but appear only as a predominant design form in relatively modern times in the English landscape garden, as a cultural and political counterpoint to geometric design. Few examples have been found from antiquity to contradict the notion.[33]

This view can be contrasted with the Chinese garden tradition, which traces naturalistic design traditions back to at least the first century B.C.E. and archaeological remains confirm this. This form is seen archaeologically as early as 90 B.C.E. in a palace complex of the Nanyue Kingdom, discovered in modern downtown Guangzhou. Initially identified as a shipyard, Hongxun Yang noted the fine materials and proposed that the site was a garden and pavilions.[34] The design is organized around a meandering artificial creek leading from a pond. The channel features shaped stone edging and is lined with a variety of stones that varied the appearance and sound of the water. Planting holes suggest a non-geometric layout of the vegetation, and tortoise shells indicate the keeping of ornamental animals. The garden was viewed, like pictures popular in the day, from a pavilion set into its midst. This is but one site representing Chinese garden archaeology from the first millennium B.C., all of which is based upon similar principles.

The literary pastoral is highly developed in ancient classical literature, as well as in art, as is discussed in the following chapters.[35] Bergmann defines the pastoral as "a meaningful and harmonious representation of a confused or conflict-ridden reality" and has explored the genre of "sacro-idyllic" wall paintings within this definition.[36] These scenes of sacred groves and daily life in the rural landscape of the first centuries B.C.E. and C.E. contrast with the realities of the Italian countryside surveyed into a vast geometry of slave-run latifundia. Yet this rural organization is observed only in plan or map view.

"Ancient viewers," Bergmann observes, "reported that in looking into the distance the eye jumped over separate buildings on hills and along waterways, just as it does over the spatial units in scattered landscape compositions [of pastoral paintings]."[37] She emphasizes that, while the kind of groupings of shrines and groves that evoked the pastoral landscape aesthetics in Roman wall paintings are difficult to define archaeologically out in the wider landscape, the role of the view from windows into the distant landscape can be tested on many sites. Visitors to the so-called Villa of Horace at Licenza, for example, could view shrines and temples on the surrounding hillsides, and, although the hills today have been reforested, obstructing many of the ancient monuments, it is possible to envision Horace's descriptions from the remains of the villa today.[38]

Although we tend to look at architecturally enclosed gardens around temples as internally focused features, the paintings of the Roman pastoral depict a number of temples and porticoes with associated trees, viewed from a distance in a wider landscape composition. The theater-temple complex at Gabii, for example, may have appeared within the larger landscape much like the quadriporticus painted in a fresco on the atrium wall of the House of the Menander 1.10.4 in Pompeii. Similarly, the Tropeum of Augustus, with its surrounding garden arrangement and siting on the upper slopes of a small mountain, may have appeared in the landscape, looking up from the harbor, much like a pastoral shrine in a sacro-idyllic painting.[39]

Of the two forms, geometry is most clearly preserved in the record of antiquity, perhaps because it is inherently a tool of the educated elite. Geometry, in moving from land measurement to the highest levels of the academy, became a philosophy of the human place in nature, the very definition of human nature itself. Vitruvius opens his sixth book on architecture with the story of the philosopher Aristippus, who found himself shipwrecked off the coast of Rhodes. Swimming to shore with other survivors, he sees geometric figures scratched in the sand, and declares to his companions that they have reached civilization and should proceed to the agora to discuss philosophy. We will see that that ancient design was grounded in geometry, that principles of proportion, beauty, harmony, and balance in all of the arts are achieved through its application.

The Greeks and Romans, beginning with Herodotus (*Histories* 2.109.3a), attributed the origins of geometry to the Egyptians, who developed it to re-survey agricultural land after the annual flooding of the Nile.[40] Illustrations of Egyptian fields show this application; in fact, Mediterranean and Near Eastern gardens of all kinds, from the earliest times, show geometric calculations as the basis of their design. The land surveyor Agennius Urbicus writes at the end of this period:

> Of all distinguished arts, which are either practiced in conformity with nature, or arranged in imitation of nature, geometry has as its substance the art of reasoning . . . geometry is in all arts and, or that all arts arise from geometry.[41]

That said, geometry lacked the symbolism that would come later in Western garden history. These geometries governed beauty and decor but were an ordering system primarily. The lush verdency of the garden would disguise the underlying geometric lines much the way that figural mosaics animated the simple geometries drafted on to the underlying bedding. These issues are discussed in Chapter One, on design.

It is important to note, however, that both pastoral and geometric ways of enclosing land and handling water existed at the same time in many places in antiquity: irrigated gardens might coexist with larger parks and properties laid out according ancient bounds that responded to topography and landmarks. The English landscape garden, which much later embodies this aesthetic, may also have its resonance in the ancient perambulations of forest bounds with their landmarks, haws, and earthworks and the contrast between the rows of fields and the forest or pasture. Such contrasts in territory existed elsewhere in the ancient world, between the pastoral and the agricultural, but particularly between centuriated land and the *arcifinius*, the land not contained in any survey.[42] The dialogue is not vernacular; rather, it one that is active and politically charged in all times in which the two views of landscape and design coexist.

Ancient design was grounded in geometry, and principles of proportion, beauty, harmony, and balance in all of the arts are achieved through its application. However, our modern habit of dividing gardens into "formal" (or geometric) and "informal" is too rigid, obscuring the varied, hybrid forms and experiences of ancient garden design.

THE MATERIAL EVIDENCE FOR ANCIENT GARDENS

Gardens have a different transmission than literature, art, and architecture, and this is particularly true of the ancient world. Written descriptions and inscriptions, sculpture and painting, and physical garden remains have not created a comprehensible corpus of evidence for ancient landscape architecture.

Rather, it is a dense palimpsest with more scraping than deposition during the
Middle Ages. Much ornament went into lime kiln, while the scrolls of ancient
books were separated and bound into unrelated compilations. Eleventh century Arnold of Regensberg writes:

> Not only is it proper for the new things to change the old ones, but even
> if the olds are disordered, they should be entirely thrown away, or if,
> however, they conform to the proper order of things but are of little use,
> they should be buried with reverence.[43]

For centuries, archaeologists have assumed that the lack of evidence for plants
means the gardens are not possible to know through excavation. The gardens
of the most famous architectural complexes of the ancient world, for the most
part, lie unexplored. Yet the soil, the main artifact of archaeological investigation, is highly manipulated in gardens and preserves the evidence of ancient
garden design. Scientific evidence in the form of soil description and analysis,
environmental evidence, and an ecological framework within which to interpret remains is being used in tandem with classical texts, art, and architectural
remains to illuminate the artifact of the garden itself. Archaeology adds the
critical knowledge of design, construction, and the three-dimensional experience of the garden space, unavailable in any other way.[44]

An important exception to this neglect of garden archaeology is in the region buried by Mt. Vesuvius in 79 C.E. In the nineteenth century, when Michele
Ruggiero developed the technique of pouring gesso into the roots of garden
plants buried by the eruption of Mt. Vesuvius, the importance of actual garden
ruins slowly began to be recognized.[45] Wilhelmina Jashemski, creating the first
systematic methodology for the excavation and study of the Vesuvian gardens,
used her discoveries to address a poorly known topic: daily life in Pompeii. She
focused her work on the afterlife of the gardens—who owned them over time,
how life took place there, and the activities and economies of cultivation. The
material evidence from gardens, as much as the materiality of the garden itself, illuminated and enriched the textual evidence for daily life. In Jashemski's
work, the layout of the plantings was carefully noted, but, as she often said,
none of the gardens at Pompeii were replanted as they had been discovered.
Assessment of art and architecture in the original setting of the garden has
recently been conducted by Stephano de Caro, Bettina Bergmann, John R.
Clarke, Andrew Wallace-Hadrill and other archaeologists working on Vesuvian sites.[46] The work of this author has focused on what the remains tell us of
the original design intention.[47]

At less well-preserved classical sites around the ancient world, a surprising number of garden excavations during the twentieth century were also successful: the Temple of Hephaistos in Athens (1932), Fishbourne Roman villa (1968), the villas of Conimbriga, Portugal (1972), and the palaces of Herod the Great in Judaea (1979–90). More recently, due to these successes and the very active encouragement of Jashemski, the public spaces of central Rome (1990–2005), the villa of Livia at Prima Porta, Horace's villa, and many smaller sites around the Mediterranean are convincing archaeologists to explore the interface of architecture and the designed landscape. Many gardens have been identified, if not excavated in the Gardens of the Roman Empire, and while over half are in the region of Vesuvian, the hundreds more from France, Spain, Britain, Germany, and around the Mediterranean basin suggest that many more will emerge in future years.[48]

These new discoveries are revealing the framework of gardens designs: terraces, walks, planting beds, tree pits, planting pots, root cavities, statue bases, water features, and environmental evidence of the degree of shade/sun. Identification of specific garden plants remains difficult; however, paleobotanists are steadily recording Roman remains throughout the empire, and together with knowledge of plants from ancient literature, papyri, and art, we are building a corpus of plants from which we can better assess the plants cultivated in

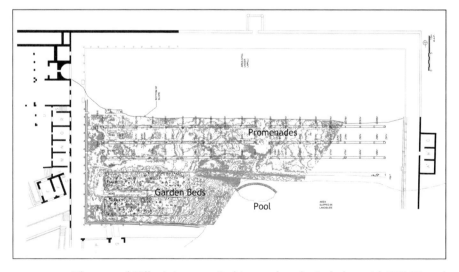

FIGURE 0.2: The coastal Villa Arianna at Stabiae, archaeological plan with LiDAR and excavated features (2011). (Courtesy: Restoring Ancient Stabiae Foundation)

gardens and their meanings.[49] For the moment, that is excellent progress, and such knowledge will aid future paleobotanical developments. We are now able to interpret representations in art with a fresh eye. Overall, the recovery of ancient gardens is giving us the means to more fully interpret the experience of them than has hitherto been possible.

As will be evident in this volume, the limitations of archaeological method have resulted in a focus on gardens within defined architectural spaces. However, large gardens and parks set away from architectural complexes are known in literature from all periods. Advances in the recording of landforms using field survey, LiDAR, and other remote-sensing techniques together with Google Earth and GPS systems will certainly change this picture in the coming years.

CONCLUSION

It is our hope that this volume presents new definitions of antiquity, a perspective akin to the view from Mount Ventoux (Petrarch, *Epistolae familiars* IV.1). Petrarch urged an abandonment of medieval compilers and commentators and a return to the original texts.[50] In the case of garden history, we are coming to this principle quite late. In many ways, we are still on the climb, but already the view of the landscape is exhilarating. Current study of the ancient landscape holds the promise of discovering the inventive landscapes of classical cultures whose values and discourses shaped our own but whose designs have been lost practice replaced by a single mythic form. The real lesson of Mt. Ventroux, however, is the inward view. How we take this abundance of new information, the concepts and design forms that are *not* part of the long European discourse on classical gardens, to create a foundational cultural history of gardens is of great consequence for the contemporary landscape theory and history today.

CHAPTER ONE

Design

KATHRYN GLEASON

The architectural treatise *De architectura libri decem*, the *Ten Books on Architecture*, by Marcus Vitruvius Pollio (c. 75–15 B.C.E.) is our only comprehensive work on ancient design. The books focus primarily on architecture but also on healthful siting, water systems, decorative programs, and machines. From the time of the rediscovery of its manuscript in 1414 and careful transcription by Fra Giovanni Giocondo a century later, to its widespread dissemination by Leon Battista Alberti in his *De re aedificatoria* (c. 1750), the treatise's clear exposition of the Greek orders, the design of temples, public buildings, and villas, as well as details of construction and machinery, has provided the foundation for knowledge and invention in classical architecture.[1] In modern times, Vitruvius's discussion of the healthful siting of cities and buildings and of villa design has given the treatise a valuable place in the history of garden design and landscape architecture, as well. Similarly, *De architectura* continues to structure our knowledge of ancient architecture and our interpretation of archaeological remains, albeit with a more critical reading. The treatise, unfortunately, has long been notable for the writer's scant reference to gardens and other designed landscapes, much lamented in the absence of any surviving treatises on garden design or gardening from antiquity. R. Taylor, 245. The new translation of Vitruvius by Ingrid Rowland and Thomas Noble Howe considers the text of Vitruvius in light of modern archaeological understanding and offers a foundation for reconsidering the landscape terminology.

While Vitruvius does not provide a treatise on gardens or landscapes, he is, in fact, quite specific about his terms for designed landscapes. Recent examination of gardens in ancient texts together with new archaeological discoveries are allowing us to better understand the distinctions he is making as he assesses the integration of new forms of garden in the years between 30 and 20 B.C.E., the nascent years of the Roman luxury garden.[2] This essay suggests that Vitruvius is less concerned with gardens in the sense of the traditional *hortus* and more concerned with types of complex gardens and parks that fall into the scope of work we call landscape architecture today. Vitruvius is discussing their origins and weighing their value to architecture of Rome. As Howe and Rowland have suggested, Vitruvius is advocating the creation of these new design forms, despite the admonitions of conservative philosophers, by pointing out their qualities that conform to Repubican tradition.[3]

This chapter examines the design processes set out in *De architectura*, examining how they pertain to gardens. In the process, we will explore garden forms that have endured through time, as well as forms that we are rediscovering again after 2,000 years.[4]

The first difficulty with the text of *De architectura* is that Vitruvius does not systematically use the most familiar words for Roman gardens or parks (hortus or *paradeisos*). He employs terms that have received generic translation over the centuries: such as *porticus* (portico), *viridia* (greenery), *silvae* (woods), and *ambulationes* or *xysti* (walks). Careful work on the transmission of texts through medieval manuscripts and a close scrutiny of landscape terms in inscriptions, tombs, and papyri by classical scholars has shown that modern translations of Latin and Greek landscape terms have been too limited.[5] Now we can define Vitruvius's use of terms in De architectura as follows:

> Hortus: the traditional vegetable garden with some fruit- or nut-bearing trees. Vitruvius uses hortus in connection with the irrigation of fields, vineyards, and gardens in the region of Hieropolis (8.3.10) and for watering gardens with a tympanum (10.4.2). In both passages, he clearly means an agricultural garden.
>
> Porticus: a walkway covered by a roof supported by a wall on one side and columns on the other, or columns on both sides. It can be affixed to a building or be a freestanding structure. Three or four porticoes arranged around a courtyard, affording a continuous walk, is a peristyle or *peristyla quadrata* (5.9.1, 5.11.3) The common use of porticus in the first centuries B.C.E. and C.E., however, often simply referred to a full quadriportico with an interior garden. The use of "porch" in the

popular Morris Hickey Morgan translation is too limiting: the image of a porticus as being an appendage on another building precludes any accurate image from forming in the reader's mind.[6]

Silvae: this word, together with *nemus*, denotes a plantation and came to mean a luxury plantation.[7] Vitruvius uses silvae in connection with the walks of palaestrae (5.12.4) and in the luxurious walks of elite villas (6.5.2).

Topia: generally translated as landscape gardening, but here we must be careful. This is the realm of *ars topiaria*, not the art of clipping plants into shapes, but the art of arranging plants and other elements to evoke places, an activity that includes the clipping of the plants.[8] This is how Vitruvius uses the term (5.7.9, 7.5.2). As Landgren shows below, all words having to do with ars topiaria are contemporary with the arrival of viridia and, thus, refer to a new form of gardening in Rome during the first century B.C.E.

Viridia: not a generic term for greenery, but specifically a novel display of well-arranged plants, particularly those that are imported, skillfully pruned, or propagated.[9] Viridia are the types of gardens viewed from a luxurious form of dining hall, the Cyzicene oecus (6.3.10). This is also the type of monumental arrangement of plants to be provided in the public colonnades of Rome (5.9.5). A *virid[i]arium* is a collection of viridia.[10]

Xysta/Xystos: well-built walks. Vitruvius (5.11.1) says that in Greek, xystos is a building and *paradromides* are the open walks of a palaestra (exercise yard), while in Latin the xysta are open garden walks. Both terms are so closely associated with gardens and plantations that, as with porticus and peristyle, they seem to have evoked both the built structure and the plantings in common usage.

Did Vitruvius consider the design of these gardens as the work of the architect? It is difficult to work out the different roles with certainty. While Vitruvius uses terms for designed landscapes with specificity, but perhaps because they are well-known to his readers, he describes in detail only the parts of the design that concern the architect. Landgren suggests that *architectus* may have worked together with the *topiarius*, a skilled horticulturalist *and* designer. The *topiarii* had formed *collegia*, or guilds, and appear to have been of comparable social standing to architects.[11] The topiarius clearly designed and inventively manipulated plants (including through propagation) to achieve the desired effects in viridia. Cicero and his brother, Quintus, made use of an architect and a topiarius who collaborated in some fashion on two of Quintus's properties with results that impressed Cicero (*ad Quintum fratrem* 3.1.5). From Vitruvius's descriptions, together with Cicero's, it appears that the role of the architect lay in the structural design—walks, terraces, water systems—while the topiarius handled the treatment of plants. The nature of the collaboration remains a matter of speculation but may have come in the design and planning of the terracing and water systems required to display and sustain the plantings, as well as in the choreography of laying out a program of plants, art, and water features to create an exciting design.

Textual sources, even collectively analyzed, are insufficient for visualizing the design of ancient gardens and landscape architecture, as is clear from their varied interpretations across garden history.[12] Garden archaeology is most valuable in recovering evidence of design, of the framework of an ancient garden or designed landscape. These remains provide a full three-dimensional, volumetric understanding, impossible to gain in any other form of ancient evidence.[13] Recent archaeological discoveries are illuminating the kinds of building projects described by ancient writers. The composite understanding of archaeological remains together with the reassessment of texts, and ancient art, is allowing us to better understand what Vitruvius is discussing: new forms of design in Rome. The treatise touches upon all of the major types, and by their inclusion, Vitruvius implies that they fall within the body of work to be considered in a design treatise, despite being beyond the general knowledge Vitruvius asserts is required for an architect.

This chapter focuses on the process of design as Vitruvius organizes it and how his discourse may apply to landscapes. Vitruvius begins with a didactic discussion of the education of the architect and the overall organization of the design process. Then he turns to each type of project (temples, palaestrae, private residences, machines, etc.) to provide details. This is where we encounter his discussions of landscape features. He does not explicitly set forth how design leads into construction. I provide a summary of the basic steps of landscape architectural construction in order to deepen our reading of Vitruvius and allow us to begin to gauge the division of responsibility in the design and implementation of large garden and park projects.[14]

THE DESIGN PROCESS

De architectura libri decem was a set of ten scrolls. In this first of these, Vitruvius lays out the requirements for the education of the architect, arguing for a liberal education. The aspects of this training that would be needed for landscape architectural projects include *drafting*, in order to "use illustrated examples at will to represent the appearance of the work"; *geometry*, "which enables the on-site layout of the plan" (1.1.4); and *optics*, which he later describes as perspective (7.praef.11). The required knowledge related to water was far more extensive than that gained by design students today: *physiology*, to deal with water pressure in aqueducts (1.1.7); *climates*, to be able to judge healthful sites (1.1.10); *music*, to design water organs and other decorative water features (1.1.9); and *law*, to know the legal issues in water supply and cost, as well as to avoid creating hazards on the property of others that might result in litigation (1.1.10). The knowledge of astronomy is necessary to understand the gnomon, or sundial, both for siting sundials and for using them to set up a land survey. There is no discussion of knowledge about botany or plants, but in Book 2 we see that Vitruvius advocates knowledge of trees and their habitat, gained from the writings of Theophrastus, for sourcing the correct types of lumber for construction. Elsewhere, the value of horticultural knowledge is seen in details about pollarding and preference for certain trees. In general, however, we will see that his references to planting design are brief, as if, perhaps, it is the role of another craftsman.

Vitruvius advocates a broad knowledge so that the architect can be informed in working with other disciplines, but he does not specify the delegation of design work.[15] He is specific about the kinds of landscapes that he includes in his discussion of design: walks and plantings within public place, such as the courtyards of theaters and palaestrae, and those of the public areas of private houses of high-ranking individuals. While he is clearly less interested in planting, he concerns himself with all of the aspects that landscape architects would consider today: well-designed layout, the adaptation of the design to suit the site, well-built water supply, appropriate site engineering, and circulation. The basic steps that a landscape architect would take to design and implement a large project today are reflected in Vitruvius' treatise.

Vitruvius is specific about the process of design, although as Howe and Rowland note, "none of Vitruvius' prescriptions constitute what could be called a full design . . . [they] seem to carry the act of design only up to a point, after which it seems that the final business of design is left until the time of execution, possibly to other artisans."[16] The process has been difficult for scholars to interpret. J. J. Coulton in the 1970s explored the extent to which Greeks had designed their temples in advance of their construction. The almost formulaic proportions of these buildings had previously led to a common belief that they were like kits that everyone just knew how to build.[17] Coulton discussed the ways in which advanced design and planning were required,

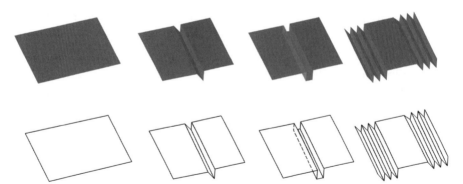

FIGURE 1.1: Simple planar surfaces created by terracing simplified calculations for construction and water supply. (Courtesy: K. Gleason and K. Wilczak)

and other architectural historians have continued the study of design into the Roman era.[18]

Howe and Rowland point out that even in Vitruvius's day, there was only a discipline of architecture, not a profession, and many people undertook ambitious architectural ventures with inadequate training. Vitruvius is writing his treatise for Augustus in part because of the need to elevate architecture so that only well-trained individuals would practice it.[19] Regardless of who undertakes the work, however, the demands of labor, quarrying, transport, and assemblage necessitated design work for any major building projects. Scholars have continued to investigate and elucidate this process.[20]

Vitruvius breaks down the process of creating a building complex into the tasks of ordering, design, shapeliness, symmetry, correctness, and allocation. The definition of the terms are obtuse, even bewildering. Mark Wilson-Jones provides a helpful summary.[21]

The following adds to the discussion by reflecting upon the applicability of the terms to the process of designing a landscape.

Ordering

Ordering (*ordinatio, taxis*) refers to establishing the proportion of the elements to the whole, achieved through modules, agreeably executed (given the requirements of the site). Here one imagines the process has begun with the choice of a healthful site, laid out in Book 1.2, the acquisition of the property and the surveying of its bounds to create the basis for a plan. Large architectural projects, including gardens and parks, are built out on terraces or podia and enclosed with walls, porticoes, or terrace walls with balustrades. The use of terracing creates a simple plane out of a complex natural slope and allows the designers to calculate surface areas, water supply, and layouts, as on the tablet or two-dimensional surface on which they were designed. Vitruvius generally directs architects to rest the foundations of their major buildings directly on solid ground, but then to extend out with compacted fill from that point (3.4.1). He stops short of describing the podia or terraces, but this is what we find archaeologically.

Setting up the geometry of the whole to allow for well-proportioned elements is both an ideal and a practical first step for drawing and for setting the actual limits of the site. This process would be the same for a large garden as for a building, as most of our known examples of ancient gardens are within rectilinear precincts, enclosed with buildings, porticoes, and walls.

Design

Design (disposatio, diathesis), according to Vitruvius, is the apt placement of things and the elegant effect obtained by their arrangement. Vitruvius suggests that analysis and invention are used to create designs; *analysis* being vigilant attention to the execution of the project (1.2.1–2) and *invention*, the clever solving of the specific problems to produce new principles within the traditional framework of what is known. In this passage, Vitruvius is talking about making drawings, and it is clear that ancient designers used many of the tools of design that we use today. The types of design drawings are *ichnography* (plan), scale drawings using compass and rule that will allow the design to be surveyed onto the land; *orthography* (elevation), the frontal image drawn to scale and rendered to guide the work; and *scenography* (perspective, optics), a shaded rendering of the front showing how the sides recede and converge to a point.[22]

The use of scaled drawings is far more ancient than Roman times. A statue of Gudea of Lagash from Tello (c. 2200 B.C.E.) shows the ruler seated with a board, stylus, and ruler.[23] The board shows a plan of E-Ninnu, a temple to the god, presumably drawn to scale. Egyptian building projects were also drawn to scale, as in a papyrus fragment from the Tomb of Ramses IV (twelfth century) that can be compared to the actual building.[24] Egyptians used a variety of media, including papyrus, plaster-coated wooden boards, pot shards, and stone.[25] These ancient plans also lay out the plants and other features of the tomb gardens. Excavations at Deir el Bahri revealed a marble fragment measuring out the plantings of the tomb of Mentuhotep. Fig. 1 The plan can be compared to the excavated remains of the layout of the tomb with its processional way and flanking plantings.[26] Coulton initially surmised that the Greeks relied on a system of conventions and calculations that appeared

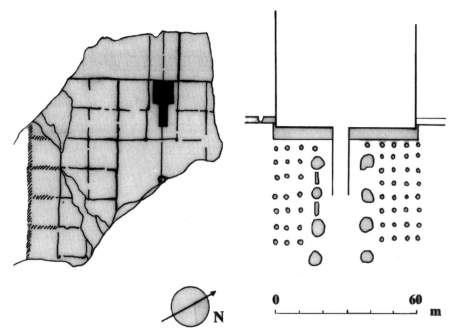

FIGURE 1.2: Stone plan of the tomb area of Mentuhotep paired with plan of the excavated garden remains. (Courtesy: K. Gleason after A. Badawy)

to make minimal use of plans.[27] In 1983, Lothar Haselberger found working drawings finely etched into the walls of the unfinished fourth century B.C.E. temple to Apollo at Didyma, after which archaeologists found many other examples around the Mediterranean.[28] Wilson-Jones provides a fine account of these and other known architectural plans and models of the Roman period in his *Principles of Roman Architecture*.[29]

A range of "as built" garden and landscape plans from the Roman era, serving a variety of purposes, are helpful in suggesting some of the conventions used. The stone plan of a garden tomb (*cepotaphion*) near Rome, exhibited at Urbino, Italy (Figure 2.10), appears to offer conventions for boundaries, vineyards, and planting beds. The great Forma Urbis Romae, a 1:240 plan of the entire city of Rome dated to 210 C.E. (see Figure 4.3), records numerous public and private gardens around the city, discussed below. It was drawn on marble slabs from tracings of accurately surveyed cadastral documents, possibly as a decoration of the hall in which the documents were stored.[30] Many of the conventions used to represent architectural elements are similar to those used today, but the landscape features are cryptic and have required archaeological investigation to accurately interpret them.

From these plans, we can see that the emphasis is on the layout of walks, alleys of trees, trellises, and water features such as canals or fountains. Shrubs are rarely shown, although we now know from archaeological remains that many linear features shown on the Forma Urbis may be planting beds in which shrubs and some herbaceous plants were arranged. This focus on the built infrastructure of the garden correlates well with the aspects of gardens that Vitruvius describes.

Shapeliness

Shapeliness (*eurythmia*) is the attractive appearance achieved in the composition of elements in terms of dimensions. The distinction between eurythmy and symmetry has been a much debated one. It seems that Vitruvius puts it third because it is the extension of the plan and elevation into three dimensions, what we would call "massing" today: the preliminary effort of working out the best dimensions for the individual program elements, first in plan and elevation, then arranging them into volumes that "fit" in a balanced "well-formed" composition, as the name signifies.[31] The concept makes as much sense for the arrangement of building elements on a site as for parts within a building. A simple geometric study of the elements of Pompey's great complex on the Campus Martius suggests that the theater and porticus were conceived as paired units, with the temple and senate house falling within smaller spaces associated with these two zones.[32] The proportions and volumes of the latter buildings then followed.

Symmetry

Symmetry is the correspondence of the proportions of the elements to the whole. In this step, the designer refines the massing of the buildings and open areas into mathematic proportions that allow for the continued design of the building down to its details. Howe and Rowland note that, prior to the use of Arabic numerals, mathematical calculations were cumbersome, so that it was more efficient to use proportional systems and geometry in the design and surveying phases, rather than general dimensioning via mathematics, even though trigonometry was well understood.[33]

Both of these stages, eurythmia and symmetry, happen first as drawings, although models are very helpful, particularly to clients for whom proportions and geometric figures meant little. While Vitruvius does not list models among the representations used in design, he later refers to one created by Callias, an architect from Arados, who presented a design for a fortification wall to the people of Rhodes that was so effective that they fired the government architect, Diognetus, and offered the position to Callias (10.16.3).[34]

Correctness

Correctness (decor) is the refined appearance of a project, achieved with respect to its function, tradition, or nature, in the sense of "decorous" rather than "decorative." Function refers to the right design for the use—temples of different types, for example. Tradition refers to the cultural associations a people make about architectural elements; an architect might create confusion if he mixed them up. Nature refers to the healthful siting of rooms and elements, as well as what is in the correct nature of things.

Much of Vitruvius's discussion of viridia and silvae fall into the category of decor, their appropriateness for different architectural settings, and their appropriateness for Rome. He offers the Porticus and Theater of Pompey in Rome as a case in point. First, Cicero sets the context, writing:

Posterity grants us greater gratitude for our public improvements. Out of Pompey's memory, I am rather diffident about expressing any criticism of theaters, colonnades, and new temples; and yet the greatest philosophers do not approve of them. (De officiis 2.60)

The poets of the time make it clear that the offending characteristics include luxury, idleness, and cruising for sex. Catullus (in 55 B.C.E.) encounters a group of whores in the gardens and asks them where he might find his friend, Camerius. Ann Kuttner writes, "This teasing poem is a panegyric tribute to Pompey's new dedication, saluting both its serious purpose and its character as a *locus amoenus* with authors and girls in many guises to attract poets."[35]

Propertius, a contemporary of Vitruvius, c. 24 B.C.E. (2.32.7–16), provides a vivid description of the physical setting of the Porticus, emphasizing the delightful qualities that made it a popular venue:

Pompey's colonnade with its shady columns brightly hung with gold-embroidered curtains [from Pergamon], the avenue thickly planted with plane trees rising in trim rows, the waters flowing from Maro's slumbering form [that] run babbling through their circuit until they vanish in the Triton's mouth.

And yet, perhaps in defense of these innovations in Rome's landscape, Vitruvius (5.9.1-5) speaks of them approvingly and makes the case that these luxurious facilities with their useless plane trees[36] really are quite practical, possessing the correct decorum for a good Roman:

> Behind the scene building [of the theater] set up porticoes so that when sudden rains interrupt the performances, the audience has a place to gather . . . the central spaces should be adorned with viridia because open air walks have a great benefit to health . . . in times of siege, such walks are thrown open and wood is distributed to each citizen . . . such buildings are firstly a place of health in peacetime and, secondly, of safety in time of war.

Rome's varied uses of its public and private gardens are explored by Macaulay Lewis below, but in terms of design, we see Vitruvius's role in advocating for these new forms, which his patron, Augustus, is energetically building on the Campus Martius (1.1.2). He describes their foreign origins but makes them Roman by asserting this notion of correctness and linking them to traditional values.

Allocation

Finally, allocation (*oikonomia*) is "the efficient management of resources and site, and the frugal, principled supervision of working expenses." Vitruvius (6.5.2) explains that different resources occur in different places and people of different rank and growing status need to have a design that accommodates their activities. He enlarges on this point in his famous passage in Book 6, discussed below, about the walks and gardens to be laid out in the public areas of private houses owned by the highest officials.

The economics of building materials and labor have been closely studied by Janet Delaine for the baths of Caracalla and more generally for Rome by Rabun Taylor. This kind of study has yet to be done for a monumental garden project, but models are available for similar scales of design from other periods in garden history. Mark Leone, for example, has looked closely at the role of slave labor in landscape designs of Tidewater Maryland and Virginia.[37]

CONSTRUCTING GARDEN COMPLEXES

So little remains of ancient plans and drawings used in this process of designing gardens (or buildings) that we must turn to archaeology and work

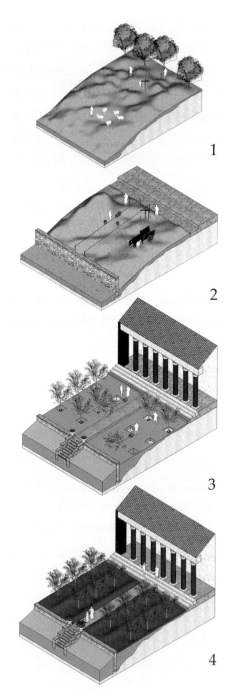

FIGURE 1.3: Sequence of construction of a large garden or park: (1) surveying the area of the terrace; (2) building the terrace wall, grading the terrace, and laying out the design; (3) bringing in topsoil and installing footings and larger plants; (4) finish grading and installation of decorative features. (Courtesy: M. Palmer)

backward from the as-built remains to find the original conception. As Wilson-Jones notes, "The onus on modern scholarship is to distinguish the historically probable from the historically improbable. The prime arbiter in this endeavor is archaeological evidence of a technical nature, which must be taken into account even if it goes against accepted wisdom."[38] For an understanding of the basic "bones" of a garden, designed before the garden was built, we must work from the archaeological remains, including water systems and any environmental evidence, to an ecological reconstruction in light of a careful reading of textual sources, as seen in Chapter Three.

Vitruvius does not lay out uniform steps in architectural projects once the design phase is complete and implementation begins. These can be determined from his discussions in the following books.[39] For landscape projects, we can combine the basic requirements of any built project with references throughout the treatise to put together a set of steps that underlie the different kinds of garden design Fig. 2.[40]

1. In a series of stages, the site is surveyed and the well-proportioned boundaries of the design staked out on the ground (1.1.4; 5.1.3–5).

2. Retaining walls are constructed and leveling fills are brought in to create both the podium for buildings and the terrace area for the temple grove, gymnasium, forum, or garden (3.4.1–2). These fills are typically not suitable for cultivation (3.4.2). Archaeological evidence indicates that garden courtyards are first used as working yards during the construction of the surrounding architecture, then installation of the garden proceeds.[41] These fills are then surveyed and more finely graded for the water system (piping and subsurface drainage) and for the careful levels required in the construction of surrounding architecture.

3. At this stage, landscape architectural features are built—colonnades, trellises, statue and fountain footings, and foundations. In some gardens, walks may be laid out and paved at this point. Permanent masonry triclinia, or dining couches, may be created. On sites with high bedrock, tree pits and water channels are cut. Then the trees and shrubs are installed in their pits.

4. Finally, topsoil is brought in, the beds are shaped for surface water distribution and finished effect, fountains are plumbed and fitted, and decorative fences installed. The setting is now ready for the final decor: fine statuary is set on the bases, the ivy is drawn around the columns, the water is turned on, and curtains and garlands are hung between the columns of the colonnades.

THE TYPES OR "DIVISIONS" OF DESIGN

Vitruvius then lays out the divisions, or main areas, of architecture: *construction*, the focus of this discussion; *gnomonics*, the making of sundials, which is of interest in terms of both the initial survey of a site, whose orientation is determined by a gnomon, and the locating of ornamental sundials of different sorts within a project; and *mechanics*, which includes the important topic of water-lifting devices, as well as the equipment for building walks and transporting heavy elements.

He divides construction into two parts, public and private, and discusses all of the main types of large gardens within both. He notes that private houses contain places, including gardens and walks that are open to the public (6.5.2). Among public works, the placement of city walls and other issues of defense are of less concern in this discussion of gardens, though for the broader field of landscape architecture they are of importance. The landscape of religion, also under public works, receives little discussion in *De architectura*, which focuses on the design of the temple building itself. Service is the central category under which Vitruvius talks about designed landscapes. He defines service as the design of public places for common use and includes *fora*, porticoes, and promenades, terms that signal the public gardens of the Roman world (1.3.1). The absence of discussion of temple landscapes is likely due to the building of new temples in large architectural complexes along with fora, basilicas, theaters, baths, markets, and government buildings. Many (cf. Saepta Iulia, Diribitorium, Stagnum, etc.) of the great complexes of late Repubican and early Imperial Rome were consecrated as *templa* and offered colonnades and open walks, as had been popular in Italy for over a century at that point (Diodorus Siculus 2.10; Strabo, *Geographies*, 16.1.5; *Scriptores Rerum Alexandrii Magni*).

In the following discussion, rather than following *De architectura* point by point, we will examine three types of designs popular in antiquity, illuminated by Vitruvius' treatise. The first are hanging gardens, which Vitruvius does not mention by this name. They are basically extensive substructures with villas or horti perched on their level terraces. In Vitruvius's day, they were mainly the creations of generals and private individuals, and so he discusses them under private buildings. The plantings are silvae. The second topic is promenades, about which Vitruvius has much to say in his sections on both public and private buildings. The third is viridia, a particular sort of garden, long translated as "greenery" but now understood to be much more complex and specific, occuring in both public and private buildings.

Opus Pensile: "Work that Hangs"

One of the most nearly mythological ancient gardens, the Hanging Gardens of Babylon, was, in fact, a popular design form in antiquity, as well as being the subject of one of the most detailed accounts of a designed landscape in ancient texts. In the absence of assured archaeological remains, it has become one of the great design puzzles of Western and Middle Eastern cultures. According to ancient sources,[42] the gardens were the creation of the Babylonian King Nebuchadnezzar II in 600 B.C.E. for his wife, Amytis, who was homesick for the hills of Media. The resulting artificial terrace garden was considered one of the seven wonders of the ancient world, though its remains have eluded definitive identification by archaeologists. Stephanie Dalley has concluded that it was not built by Nebuchadnezzar at Babylon at all, but by Sennacherib at Nimrud about a century earlier.[43] Julian Reade, in tracking the final days of Alexander the Great, provides a very careful inspection of all of the accounts of the Hanging Gardens, their construction and location, as well their history, and concludes that the site lay across the river from Babylon.[44] Whatever the reality, the texts record a complex form and construction that went on to influence later garden design. Diodorus Siculus (2.10) writes in the first century B.C.E.

> The Garden was 100 feet (30 m) long by 100 ft wide and built up in tiers so that it resembled a theatre. Vaults had been constructed under the ascending terraces which carried the entire weight of the planted garden; the uppermost vault, which was seventy-five feet high, was the highest part of the garden, which, at this point, was on the same level as the city walls. The roofs of the vaults which supported the garden were constructed of stone beams some sixteen feet long, and over these were laid first a layer of reeds set in thick tar, then two courses of baked brick bonded by cement, and finally a covering of lead to prevent the moisture in the soil penetrating the roof. On top of this roof enough topsoil was heaped to allow the biggest trees to take root. The earth was leveled off and thickly planted with every kind of tree. And since the galleries projected one beyond the other, where they were sunlit, they contained conduits for the water which was raised by pumps in great abundance from the river, though no one outside could see it being done.

This garden and its romantic story captured the Roman imagination to become one of the important types of garden design. The literary concept of *opus pensile*, or "work that hangs," was among the many introductions that conservative Roman philosophers felt went against the natural order of things.[45]

In Vitruvius's day, the prestigious real estate on Rome's hilltops was rapidly being extended out by means of such vaulted terraces. Pliny the Elder, by the first century C.E., would see Rome as a vision of hanging gardens and buildings (Pliny, *Historia naturalis* 3.67; Seneca, *Epistulae morales* 122.8, and *Controversiae* 2.2).[46] This radical change was unsettling. Seneca the Seneca the Younger writes, "Do they not live at odds with nature, those who sow orchards at the tops of towers" or who "[make] on the highest roofs false copses and harbor-sized swimming pools?"[47] Chapter 8 to the construction of

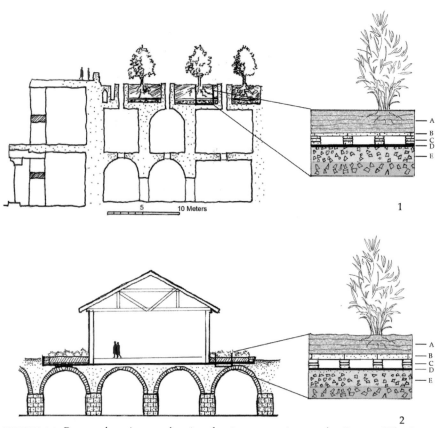

FIGURE 1.4: Roman hanging garden (rooftop) construction at the Domus Tiberiana, Palatine Hill Rome, and the Byzantine Praetorium, Caesarea Maritima, Israel. (Courtesy: M. Bolton after L. Lancaster and J. Patrich)

relieving arches, substructures, and retaining walls for underground rooms. Recent excavations have uncovered Augustus's hanging garden at Prima Porta, a grove appearing atop a massive retaining wall, high above the approach road from Rome (Pliny, *HN* 15.47).[48] Again, we see that Vitruvius, in his way, is embracing innovation while emphasizing the wisdom in tradition.

Surprisingly, we now have two archaeological examples of roof gardens that preserve details of construction that follow the basic principles laid out above. Figure 1.3 Nero built a garden over the vaulted substructures of his palace on the northwest corner of the Palatine. A palatial building for Byzantine officials at Caesarea Maritima in Israel appears to be the conversion of a pool built on top of masonry vaults to a garden suspended on ceramic tiles. In both gardens, the vaults are protected from the moisture of the garden by a waterproof coating of bitumen or *opus signinum*. Then a drainage space is created with *suspensurae*, stacks of tiles holding up a suspended tile floor. The garden soil is spread over this floor and the plantings are installed. These are the ancestors of the roof gardens that are popular today. Pliny the Elder even had suggestions for plants, such as jujube and tuber, that would do well in such settings.[49]

Traditional terraces built into slopes also evoked hanging gardens. Herod the Great's monumental sunken garden at Jericho featured a theater-like hemicycle

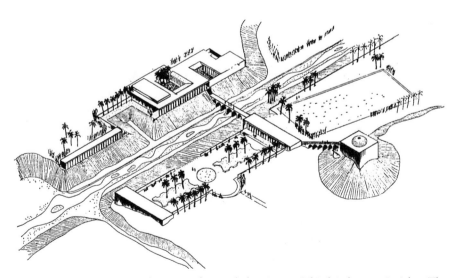

FIGURE 1.5: Axonometric drawing of Herod the Great's Third Palace at Jericho. The large sunken garden featured a theater, whose cavea was found with potted plants rather than seats. (Courtesy: E. Netzer)

in which the seats were actually occupied by potted plants. Fig. 1.4 Similar effects may have been created in the Auditorium of Maecenas in Rome and the hippodrome garden of Hadrian's villa.

Thus we see a textual connection between these forms of design and the Hanging Gardens, but we also see from the archaeological evidence that the form evolves to be independent of the original configuration of its model.

Xystos, Xysta, and Paradroimides

In every city that has had conscientious architects, there are porticoes and walkways around theaters (5.9.1).

For the most prominent citizens, those who should carry out their duties to the citizenry by holding honorific titles [should be provided with]. . . lush gardens and broad walkways refined as properly befits their dignity (6.5.2).

A probable reason for the absence of the quadripartite form in antiquity, discussed above, is the singular importance of walking, certainly in Greek and Roman culture, and quite probably in Asia and Egypt as well. Peripatetic walking was a philosophical practice that became synonymous with cultured conversation. Strolling, exercising, and parading require unimpeded movement for two or more abreast, allowing for unconstrained gesture and discourse. Vitruvius devotes considerable discussion to creating serviceable walks for varied uses within public building complexes. Perhaps because the philosophers stroll such paths themselves, Vitruvius's discussion is open and detailed, without the veneer of justification we see for viridia.

The importance of "les promenades" in the landscape architecture of ancient Rome was recognized by Pierre Grimal in his 1947 publication *Les Jardins Romains*,[50] but it has not received the attention it deserves. Recent scholarship has begun to address the issue. Timothy O'Sullivan has shown the profound role of movement in the Greek and Roman landscape.[51] Strolling was a central activity in all dimensions of a civic life, from school days in the academy or gymnasium to business in the *agora* or forum, to leisured gatherings at one's villa with learned companions.

A variety of architectural and open-air layouts for strolling were often combined: circuits around a quadriporticus or peristyle, for example, might be continued along straight open-air promenades. Figure 1.5 Vitruvius (5.11.1) recommends that porticoes provide a stroll of two stadia. The design typically allows the viewer, with companions, to ambulate (on foot, in a litter, on horseback) without impediment along a straight path across the middle of a courtyard or enclosure, encountering a sequence of views and elements ahead or off to the side. Cross axes are visual only, not perambulated, as changes in direction appear to be of little interest until the space available demands such a turn, as at the end of the spina on a race track. In fact, the kinds of plantings associated with these walks are in linear beds of three basic kinds. The first is grids of trees with space for the walks, the second is thin spina-like beds with a single row of trees or shrubs, of one or mixed species, while the third kind is the thicker linear beds designed to be seen in layers (foreground, middle ground).

Most of the ancient gardens for which we have evidence are processional in nature. The royal garden at Pasargadae places Achaemenid royalty and guests in a raised pavilion observing a procession of visitors moving across the garden before them, made permanent in the triumphal processions depicted on the reliefs of the East Stairway of the Apadana at Persepolis, Here, tribute bearers in their native dress paraded between even ranks of trees and art brought from conquered lands.[52] In the first millennia B.C.E., Greeks and Romans shared with Persians an aesthetic in which orderly ranks of trees were admired as an analogue to processions of figures or to the disciplined order of troops (Xenophon, *Oeconomicus* 4.20 ff., repeated by Cicero, *de senectute* 59). Large gardens of the Roman period featured a central avenue running the length of a courtyard rather than the width. For example, the *porticus* of Pompey the Great in Rome engaged its visitors as participants in a regal or religious procession observed by Pompey's protectress, Venus Victrix, as they moved from the senate house, through a lushly planted grove ornamented with art and fountains, toward her temple atop the theater. The great plane trees of this complex must have been impressive not only because they were relatively new to the Italian continent, but also because of the difficulty in acquiring hundreds of matched specimens required for such a regular effect in the absence of large plant nurseries at that time. Later, such nurseries developed to meet the need for imported plants, and the fascination shifts to varied displays of skillfully pruned or propagated specimens, each one different from the other.

We see also that the design of a single central axis flanked by wide planting beds shifts to multiple parallel walks, separated by linear planting displays, which increase the area available for strolling. In Rome, these are seen in the Templum Pacis, the Claudianum, and a new set of gardens on the Palatine[53] and near Pompeii at the Villa Arianna, Stabiae. The archaeological

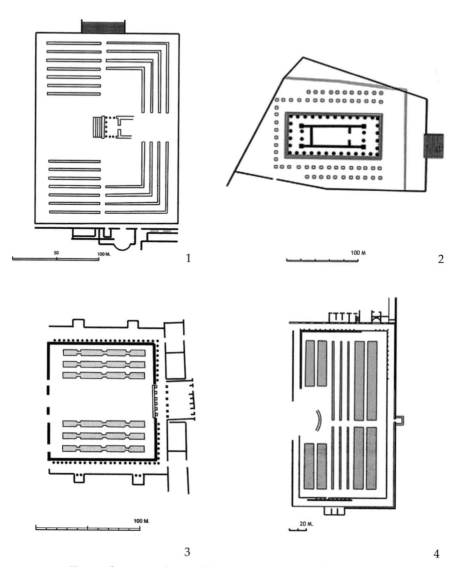

FIGURE 1.6: Types of promenades (ambulationes) 1) Temple of the Divine Claudius in Rome, 2) Temple of Hephaistos in Athens, 3) Forum of Vespasian (Templum Pacis), Rome, 4) Villa Arianna, Stabiae. (Courtesy: M. Bolton)

evidence from these sites also suggests a transition from ordered ranks of single specimens (Porticus of Pompey) to more novelty plantings. The interpretation remains spectulative, but excavated remains suggest a great variety of plants trained into unusual forms or imported from distant lands and propagated into new forms—trees to vines, for example. The handling of plants in Roman gardens is addressed by Lena Landgren in Chapter 3.

These experiences of "visiting" recall the itineraries along linear representations of landscape, such as that preserved in the twenty-two-foot-long scroll of
the Peutinger Atlas and mosaics such as the Madaba mosaic. Figure 1.6 These
show routes along roads and coasts as linear routes marked by notable landmarks and features, omitting much of the interior dimension of the landscape
or sea. Both examples were large and physically took the viewer on a kind of
stroll or a journey across the known world.

Scholarship in this area is suggesting that the viewer perceived groupings
that would prompt learned conversation, according to the function of the
portico, rather than a continuous narrative sequence, but much remains unknown.[54] The linear plantings of diverse specimens seen at the Villa Arianna in
Stabiae and the Temple of Elagabalus on the Palatine suggest that the viewers
would admire each individual plant as they strolled. Presumably, each would
evoke an association or prompt observation and discussion. Although we
cannot determine the specific plants or their treatment through archaeology,
evidence from art and literature suggests that exotic plants, new varieties, and
ingenious ways of training, grafting, or pruning vegetation were the focus of
these displays.

FIGURE 1.7: The Peutinger Atlas displayed at eye-level for viewers strolling along a wall.
(Courtesy: M. Bolton)

Viridia: Innovation and Display

*The central spaces between the porticoes and open to the sky should
be adorned with gardens (viridia) because open air walkways are of
great benefit to health . . . I think there is no doubt that spacious and
ornate walkways should be set up in cities outdoors and in the open
air (5.9.5-6).*

*There are rooms (oeci) which the Greeks call Cyzicene, although
they are not an Italian custom. They face north to open upon gardens
(viridia) . . . they hold two couches facing each other with room to walk
around the back. From the dining couches there are views through the
windows onto the gardens (viridia) (6.3.10).*

If Vitruvius is enthusiastic about any form of landscape architecture, it is the
combination of walks with viridia, collections of plants, or silvae, plantations.
The expression of lush verdancy was a highly desirable aspect of the planting
beds of gardens, particularly during the long dry summers. (We see little sign of
excitement about xeriscaping, celebrating deserts or other fascinatingly barren
places.) Themes of an eternal spring garden, the evocation of the green summer landscapes of the mountain pastures, or the well-watered conquered lands
in temperate climates may have inspired the design of these lush plantings in
ancient gardens. Abundant water and good soil, together with skillful planting
arrangments, is required to achieve this effect.

Our most important representation of verdancy in a garden is that of Livia
at Prima Porta. Scholars extol

> an impossibly utopian mixture of bright flowers beside laden fruit trees,
> tidy shrubs before a receding woodland vista, planned garden display
> within a surround of Italian trees, as if in their natural habitat. It is an ex-
> ercise in blue and green. And a celebration of naturalistic technique . . .
> But this is not nature reproduced; instead, a world specially made for
> us—yet made to do without us. Beyond the balustrade, as no wild birds
> ever could, these pay not the slightest attention to anyone in the room,
> impossibly ignoring our proximity. Emblematized by the songbird in its
> golden cage, art here *creates* nature, beyond anything you could find in
> the real world.[55]

Until recently, we had no archaeological remains that could be paired with
Vitruvius's passage and garden paintings. Even in the area of Vesuvius, which
featured many garden paintings in houses great and modest, scant evidence

has been found over the years to suggest that such an apparently imaginary arrangement was a specific type of garden. Our understanding has changed recently with the discovery of a small courtyard garden at the House of the Chaste Lovers in which the remains of a reed fence clearly contain a small garden of the sort seen in paintings.[56] In 2007, a new excavation at the Villa Arianna at Stabiae, also preserved by the eruption of Vesuvius, has revealed garden beds with planting cavities that more fully illuminate the garden paintings.[57] The layout of the root cavities in these beds creates the same effect as seen in the Prima Porta and other garden paintings. In this garden, we can now see a type of garden design that combined linear arrangements of different species of plants and statuary against evergreen backdrops that give exactly the effect of garden paintings. Work on the original find spots of the great sculptural groups from the horti in Rome and sculpture framed by plantings in the gardens buried by Vesuvius allow us to see additional relationships between the painted image and the archaeological remains.[58]

A careful examination of the composition of garden paintings also hints at design principles—their artless appearance is deceiving. Most of the paintings are given foreground and middle-ground compositions that include symmetry. Between a study of these paintings and the new archaeological remains, it is now possible to argue that garden paintings depict a kind of garden that Romans actually planted. As Mary Beard and John Henderson suggest, the utopian dimension is the ability of the artist to manipulate time: to depict a diversity of plants each in its full seasonal glory accompanied by a great variety of birds gathering in a single moment that, occurring in real life, might either be a portentous moment, a naturalist's fantasy, or *delectatio*.[59] This is not incompatible with the garden's form being possible to create; in fact, the composition can

FIGURE 1.8: Garden trees seen in villa paintings signal the presence of irrigated gardens. (Courtesy: M. Bolton, line drawing after fresco in House of M. Lucretius Fronto)

FIGURE 1.9: Garden Painting from the so-called "Villa of Livia," Primaporta, Rome, c. 20 B.C.E. (fresco) appears to depict the exuberance of nature, but close examination shows a carefully pruned and cultivated effect. (Courtesy: Museo Nazionale Romano, Rome, Italy/Bridgeman Art Library)

only add to the meanings that have been attributed to this type of painting by art historians.[60]

A little-studied aspect of these paintings is the degree to which the plants were manipulated. A careful examination of the known garden paintings fails to reveal the slightest interest in depicting unrestrained nature. Most of the plants are depicted as heavily pruned, not only in their shape but also with carefully depicted cut marks. Only the spruces and firs, which do not respond well to pruning, retain their natural habit. We see orchard trees with their interiors pruned out, leaving the fruit appealingly ripened in large clusters at the ends of the branches, as if offering refreshment to a passerby. Shrubs are cut back to the ground, allowing only single shoots to emerge as drifts of color and texture in the composition. The focal point of many of the garden paintings is the dwarfed trees. The evidence that these are dwarfed, rather than downsized by the artist, is discussed by Langren (Chapter 3) who shows that this is the work of the the topiarius.

The containment of gardens appears to have been of considerable interest to the Romans. Lush gardens held back by fragile woven reed fences were depicted in many paintings and appear in the archaeological record. Fig. 1.9

An odd trend is the depiction of only the fences in small relief panels in wall paintings. Fig 1.10 The enclosed spaces contain only a few plants if any at all. A related painting style depicts simple beds, with only a few shrubs or small trees, outlined in fencing or hedges in the foreground of villa facades.

It has been difficult to detect specific geometric patterns of the sort long imagined for ancient gardens. Garden remains before and during Vitruvius's day are remarkably linear with no preserved patterning. By the first through third centuries C.E., we do have examples of patterned layouts of beds or water features in peristyle gardens of various sizes, such as the gardens of the Domus Augustana on the Palatine Hill, the main walk at Fishbourne Roman Villa, and the water gardens of Conimbriga, among many more examples. These designs are surrounded by walks or colonnades, allowing the viewer to look in at the pattern or down from rooms raised up above the height of the garden. Sometimes a single walk runs through the middle, but rarely, if ever, does the viewer move through the full pattern.

CONCLUSION

Whether evoking a distant landscape or a local one, the garden forms of Vitruvius's Rome—silvae, *ambulationes*, *opus pensile*, and *viridaria*—offered well-designed displays of abundance and ordered control central to the image of the capital of its empire. Vitruvius's *De architectura* allows us to see these new introductions to the Roman cultural landscape as correct decor, despite the supposedly corrupting potential of their luxurious appointments and the culture of idleness they fostered in the citizenry. The value of the garden and park lay in the expression of resources, from those displayed as cultural relics from conquered territories to the wise investment in aqueducts

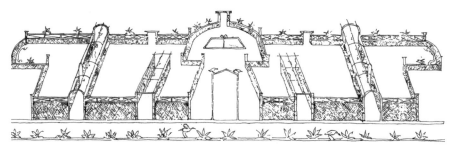

FIGURE 1.10: Garden fence fresco from the House of the Cupids, Pompeii, Italy. (Line drawing by K. Wilczak)

and water systems. While a fountain might display water at a nymphaeum or other single source point, or along a channel, these displays had to be appreciated on-site. Gardens and parks, by contrast, could be seen across a plain or a city. The horti of the Palatine, Caelian, and Esquiline offered gardens that created verdant landmarks of their properties. Those of the villas on the Bay of Naples and of the harbors of Alexandria or Caesarea could be seen from the sea. To a world in which water equaled wealth, the visible presence of tall trees and the enjoyment of the plant collections beneath complemented the architectural monuments Vitruvius describes. To an audience already enthralled with the new gardens around Rome, he needed only to signal their important place in Roman architecture.

CHAPTER TWO

Types of Gardens

INGE NIELSEN

Gardens have always formed a very important part of human culture and society, and the many garden traditions of antiquity are no exception, as has long been known from written and iconographical sources.[1] In recent years, our knowledge has been considerably augmented by the discovery of preserved gardens, made possible by improved excavation techniques and an increasing use of scientific disciplines such as agronomy and botany. Thus, gardens have been excavated in a wide range of localities and time periods, primarily in the area around the Vesuvius, where the possibilities are especially favorable on account of the unique circumstances of the destruction of this area in 79 C.E.

In antiquity in general, and according to the archaeological material, we may basically distinguish between three different types of gardens.[2] Type one is a large park-like garden surrounding structures of various kinds; type two defines a garden area attached to a structure and more intensively planted than the first one; type three is the garden found inside an architectural structure, typically a courtyard, often surrounded by columns. These three types may in certain cases be designated with an ancient term, but since the ancient terminology is far from unambiguous in all languages, only the most common ancient terms for each of the three garden types are presented. The discussion thus refers to the types by numbers rather than ancient designations.

Within the three basic types of gardens, ownership is used as the point of departure for discussion: (1) religious gardens (including sacred groves, temple-gardens); (2) palatial gardens (including peristyle gardens, parks, hippodrome gardens); (3) "public" gardens (including gymnasium gardens, thermal gardens); (4) private gardens (including recreational and/or utility gardens); and (5) funeral gardens. Other garden forms are included where appropriate.

THE FIRST GARDEN TYPE

This garden type represents the great expansive park, into which may have been set structures of various kinds. These parks could be designated *paradeisos* or *alsos*.[3] They are especially characteristic of palatial settings and villa gardens of the elite. They were filled with trees and bushes, some of which might be utilitarian or semi-utilitarian in character. Flowers are very seldom mentioned in this context.[4] Some are set beside rivers and lakes, while in other locations there were often great pools for swimming. These parks were almost exclusively recreational and intended for promenades, dining, and so on, and recreation in *diatai* or pavilions. But also, tombs, altars, and temples could form part of such royal parks. Most were used officially, for meetings, dinner parties, or receptions so great that there was no place for them in the palace itself.[5]

Royal Palaces and Villas of the Elite

Although none have been excavated, the royal palaces of the pharaohs were furnished with gardens of this kind.[6] Examples include the palace complex called Malkata, built by Amenotep III in Thebes, and the great palace complex in Tell el-Amarna, belonging to Ank Aten (mid-fourteenth century B.C.E.). The palace of Apries in Memphis was the only palace extant in the early Hellenistic period and was surrounded by parks and lakes. The palace itself was used by Alexander and the first Ptolemy, and the park formed part of the new garden-filled palace built by the later Ptolemies there.[7]

Parks of palaces are also attested in the Near East, although again, unexcavated. For example, parks were attached to the Assyrian palaces and often depicted on reliefs.[8] Whether the famous Hanging Gardens traditionally constructed by Nebukadnezer II (604–562 B.C.E.) belonged to this type, and whether they were situated in Babylon or Nineveh, is uncertain, but their royal context is beyond discussion, as is the prestige combined with the effort to introduce a mountainous landscape into the river lowlands. There was also a great park with a variation of trees on the other side of the river in Babylon, in Sittake, which Xenophon visited. Arrian later reports that Alexander the Great, falling ill in Babylon, rested in a small garden house with a pool in a paradeisos across the river from the palaces, which must be this one.[9]

We have better evidence for the paradeisoi belonging to Achaemenid palaces, some of which were known or even reused by the Seleucids.[10] The park in Pasargadae, comprising palatial buildings, pavilions, a sanctuary, water installations, and the tomb of Cyrus the Great, has been partly excavated.[11] In Susa, the capital of the Achaemenid kingdom, a paradeisos surrounded the palace of Artaxerxes II below the palace of Dareios.[12] The well-watered plain below the main palace of Persepolis, with its many palatial structures, water channels in terracotta, and collecting basins indicates the presence of gardens.[13]

Outside the Achaemenid heartland, paradeisoi formed part of satrapal palaces in Kelainai and Daskyleion in Anatolia. In Syria, the client kings of Sidon and the satrap Belyses possessed such parks in association with their palaces. Near Jerusalem there was a royal *paradeisos* belonging to the Persian

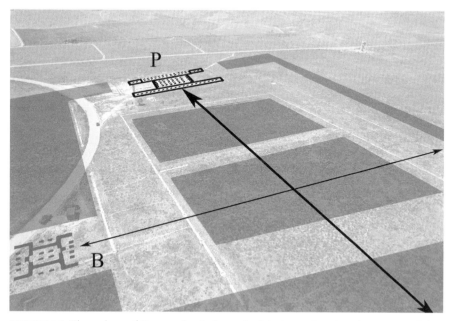

FIGURE 2.1: The palace of Pasargadae in Iran. Aerial photo showing the excavated formal garden with garden paths flanked by channels, related to Palace P and Pavilions A and B. (Courtesy: K. Wilczak. Photo by R. Boucharlat and D. Stronach 1989, Figure 3)

king, from which timber for the rebuilding of Jerusalem was to come. Archaeological garden remains have recently been discovered at Ramat Rachel around a palace/fortress dating to this period. Finally, further east, ancient authors mention *nemora* or *saltus* with walls and hunting towers in Bazaira in Sogdiana, where Alexander hunted down a lion and 4,000 animals, then held a banquet.[14]

In the Greek period, Herodotus (Histories 8.138) mentions a rose garden called the garden of Midas, which existed in Macedonia from an early period. And this kingdom, according to Polybius, later included a game reserve (Polybius 31.29.1–8). It is possible that the old Macedonian kings had such parks, as their culture was inspired in many ways by the Persian presence in Asia Minor. In addition, parks are referred to by the ancient authors in connection with the palaces of the tyrants in the Greek colonies of Sicily. Thus Gelon's great pool with fish and birds lay in a park. Plato indicates that Dionysius I in Syracuse laid out a walled garden with many promenades, as well as a paradeisos with plane trees in Rhegion.[15] These were probably inspired by the Achaemenid gardens and parks, as well as Egyptian ones.

In the Hellenistic period, few parks of the first type have actually been excavated, but royal gardens are increasingly attested in written sources. These gardens could have been built from scratch or taken over from the predecessors of the new Hellenistic monarchs following the conquests of Alexander the Great. The example par excellence is the great *basileia* district of Alexandria. This palace precinct is not preserved, but the descriptions of Strabo and Polybius are detailed. Official and private buildings, were spread in a huge park called *alsos*. These included pavilions, a *palaestra*, the *maiandros*, a water channel or pool of some kind, the *sema* with the tomb of Alexander and the Ptolemies, the *museion* with the famous library, and various temples and sanctuaries. This park was apparently laid out orthogonally, with wide promenades connecting the various parts.[16]

Less well-known is the royal palace of the Seleucids in Antioch, situated on an island in the river Orontes.[17] Later sources suggest that the Roman emperors continued to use the palace with its huge, regularly laid out and well-watered park. Further, we hear of gardens and parks flanking the road to garden-filled Daphne, and Syrians were also later famous for their gardens and gardeners.[18]

This palace may have inspired the far-away palace of Ai Khanoum in Afghanistan, built as a Seleucid governor's palace around 300 B.C.E., then transformed into a royal palace by an independent local dynasty in the middle of the second century B.C.E.[19] The main palace consisted of several buildings and to the west, limited by the river, was land undoubtedly laid out as a park. In it were placed a huge swimming pool as well as a "gymnasium," among other features.

As was the case with the Achaemenid palace gardens, this custom was thus also in the Hellenistic period reflected in the palaces of governors and especially of client kings. The second-century B.C.E. palace of Hyrcanus the Tobiad in Transjordania was probably inspired by the basileia, or royal precincts, of Antioch and Alexandria, where Hyrcanus had served as an official. This huge park included cliff-side dining halls, columbaria, and a well-excavated lion pavilion set into a lake, or *baris*. From this palace, there was a marvelous view to the park, the lake, and the agricultural valley below.[20]

This palace has a certain affinity to the great palace complex built by the Jewish Hasmonean dynasty in the late second century B.C.E. in nearby Jericho. This palace was placed in a fenced park in connection with a very prosperous

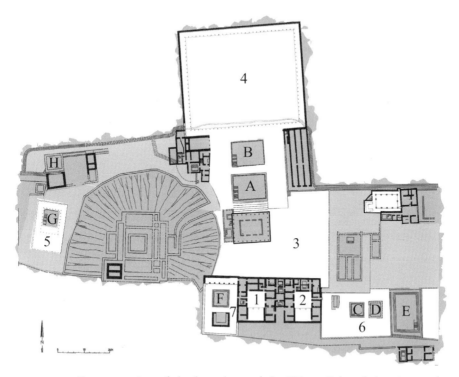

FIGURE 2.2: Reconstruction of the last phase of the Winter Palace belonging to the Hasmonean dynasty in Jericho. Nos. 1–2 are courtyard gardens of the third type, and nos. 3–7 are gardens of the second type. Nos. A–H are swimming pools. (Courtesy: M. Bolton after E. Netzer 1990, Figure 1)

oasis, both natural and irrigated, constituting the royal domain.[21] This palace, which was enlarged continuously during a century of existence, included a great many swimming pools surrounded by gardens and also a fine pavilion. The linear combination between pools and pavilions is a typical feature of

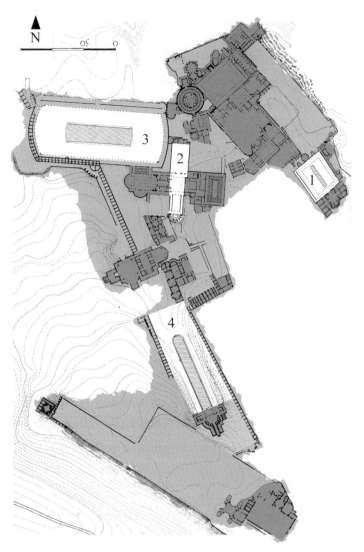

FIGURE 2.3: A plan of the emperor Hadrian´s Villa at Tivoli. The villa is placed in a great park (light grey on the plan). No. 1 is the peristyle garden of Piazza d'Oro of the first type, no. 2 is the Stadium garden; no. 3, the Poikile garden; and no. 4, the Canopus garden; the latter three are all of the second type. (Courtesy: K. Wilczak after W. Jashemski and E. Salza Prina Ricotti 1992, Figure 1)

Egyptian gardens. This tradition was continued by Herod the Great who built huge palace complexes of that kind, in Caesarea, Jericho, and Herodion.[22] A newly discovered garden and pool complex at Petra, Jordan, contemporary with Herod the Great's projects, also features pavilions, water channels, and planting pots on a terrace below a large pool and pavilion similar to that at Herodion.[23]

In Italy, we have evidence of parks from the Hellenistic period as well, although here, we should rather use the term republican period. As mentioned, Sicilian tyrants of the archaic and classical period laid out such parks in connection with their palaces. In the second through first centuries B.C.E., Italian gardens are prolific, including also this park-like kind. Villas in a park-like environment are often depicted in miniature wall paintings, according to which they had pavilions and were often placed by the sea or by rivers. In Rome, the aristocracy laid out suburban villas with parks around the center of the city, and these luxurious *horti* were taken over by the emperors in the first century C.E.[24]

During the Roman Empire, the emperors continued to develop these large parks, even in urban contexts. In Rome itself, although the Roman emperors of the Julio-Claudian dynasty soon took over the luxurious horti from the Roman elite, Nero was the first to build a palace complex surrounded by a huge park of the first type in the center of Rome. This Domus Aurea constituted a pleasure villa in the middle of the city, and, as such, it created outrage among the citizenry. The Flavian emperors returned this land to the public, building the amphitheater (Colosseum) and baths. Owing to the limited space on the old Palatine hill, even Domitian had to limit his garden ambitions, but he compensated at his great villas at Albano and in Campania. Hadrian's villa at Tivoli constituted a culmination of this trend—placed, as it is, in a huge park.[25]

THE SECOND GARDEN TYPE

The second type of garden is closely related to the first one and could be a subarea of it. It was typically smaller and of regular, usually rectilinear, form, enclosed by a wall or porticoes. This second type was carefully laid out and contained bushes and trees of various kinds, among them plane trees and fruit trees, planted regularly. This type is associated with various types of buildings, but is especially characteristic of the public gardens and sacred gardens, where it was used for promenades and religious festivals respectively. It could be designated *kepos* or alsos, *nemus* and *lucus* but also *gymnasion* or palaestra, thus taking its name from the garden-filled Greek gymnasium used for sports and philosophical discussions. If this type of garden was present in palaces and villas, it was used for promenades, private dining, recreation, and as a focus of views from the parts of the palace/villa facing it. This form of garden appears in commercial and funeral contexts, as well. A subtype of this kind of garden is the specialized garden: botanical and zoological gardens, aviaries, and fish pools in the royal palaces and luxurious villas of the elite.[26] The exotic displays in this kind of garden had a special significance for the ruling classes as a microcosm of the empire ruled by their owner.

Sacred Gardens

In Greece, the sacred groves described by the ancient authors (*alsoi*) should probably be included in this second type of garden as well.[27] In the *Odyssey* (6.293ff), Homer mentions a sanctuary of Athena, with a garden and trees, a meadow and a spring, in Scheria, the land of the Phaiakes. Sappho (c. 600 B.C.E.) mentions a sanctuary of the Cyprian Aphrodite on Lesbos with apple trees, meadows, and a spring (33–44 Fgt. 2),[28] and such gardens formed part of her sanctuaries in Cyprus and in Athens, where her sanctuary below the Acropolis belonged to "Aphrodite in the Gardens." The garden flanking the Hephaisteion in Athens has been excavated and produced forty-eight rock-cut pits with planting pots. The size of these cavities suggests shrubs, and laurel and pomegranate were selected by the excavators for the replanting. The plants were watered by means of channels.[29] Further archaeological remains of temple gardens are found in the Corinthian Asklepieion and in the Sanctuary of Zeus in Nemea, southeast of the temple. Strabo (8.6.22) refers to straight lines of plane trees in the Isthmian sanctuary. Of the aforementioned sanctuaries, only in that of Nemea are the trees not placed in precise, straight lines.[30]

Sanctuaries could also be surrounded by external parks or vineyards and plantations. In Cyprus, we hear of an extended park belonging to, but not included in, the sanctuary of Apollo Hylates ("of the wood"), which contained wild animals, especially red deer. Although the references to this park are rather late, the god's epithet indicates that woodlands belonged to this sanctuary from the beginning—that is, the seventh century B.C.E. (Pausanias, *Description of Greece* 2.15.2; Aelianus, *De natura animalium* 11.7).[31] In the city of Rhodes, extensive parks on the Acropolis surrounded various sanctuaries, including nymphaia. Whether the park in the Rhodini area, flanking a ravine south of the town, had a religious connotation is unknown, but likely. (In Italy, there was a park of the same character in Tibur.) A garden that could be leased out, and had a utilitarian character with trees, is known in the sanctuary of Heracles on Thasos.[32] And we know of vineyards with 20,000 grapevines at Rheneia on an area of seventy-eight hectares and fruit gardens on Mykonos owned by the Temple of Apollo on Delos.[33]

In Italy, such sacred groves, called nemus and lucus are known from an early period as well; for example, the grove of Diana in Nemi. At Gabii, the Temple of Juno Gabina was excavated and found to be surrounded by trees set into rock-cut pits on the temple terrace, dating, like the temple itself, to the early second century B.C.E.[34] In Campania, a garden was located in connection with the suburban Temple of Dionysos, 700 meters south of the amphitheater in Pompeii. The temple belongs to the Samnitic period (late third through early second century B.C.E.). Two large garden *triclinia* flanking an altar were situated in the temple court, and near them, very old vine plants were excavated by Wilhelmina Jashemski.[35] They formed a pergola and gave shade to the diners. There were also other vine plants in the sanctuary, and perhaps trees as well, flanking a semicircular *schola*.

In Rome, we hear from this same time—that is, the republican period—of gardens surrounding the temples in the early porticus structures, built by the generals back from the East, on the Campus Martius, the Porticus Metelli and Philippi. This tradition was later followed by Pompey, whose luxurious garden

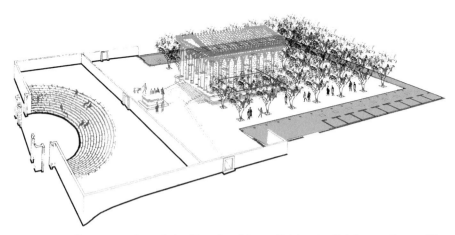

FIGURE 2.4: Reconstruction of the Temple of Juno Gabina in Gabii near Rome. The sacred grove was placed regularly around the temple. (Courtesy: K. Wilczak after M. Almagro-Gorbea 1982, Figure 2)

in connection with his theatre was dedicated to Venus. One may also refer to the early imperial sanctuary of Isis on the Campus Martius, only known from the Forma Urbis Romae (marble plan of Rome dating to c. 200 C.E.), with a row of what looks like big trees flanking a central area with a channel in the northern part of this oblong sanctuary.[36] In the imperial period, such a garden has recently been excavated (and partly also known from the Forma Urbis Romae) in the court of the Templum Pacis. On the Palatine in Rome, and closely related to the imperial palace, an enclosed garden was laid out in the northeastern part called on the Forma Urbis Romae "Adoneia", and dedicated to Adonis and Venus. Recent excavations have revealed the general layout of this garden.[37] The use of such a garden in relation to the Near Eastern god Adonis may also indicate that such sacred gardens formed part of sanctuaries in the Near East.[38]

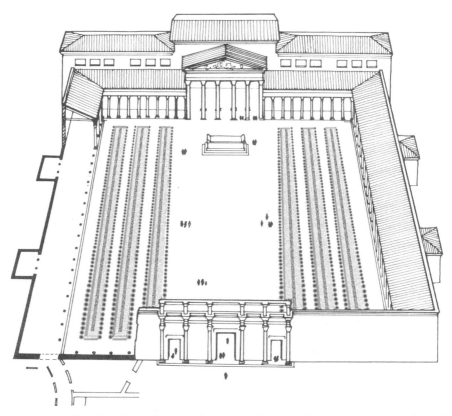

FIGURE 2.5: Templum Pacis showing the proposed garden layout. (Courtesy: Adapted by M. Bolton from A. Meneghini and R. Valenzani, 2007; and J. B. Ward-Perkins 1981, 66)

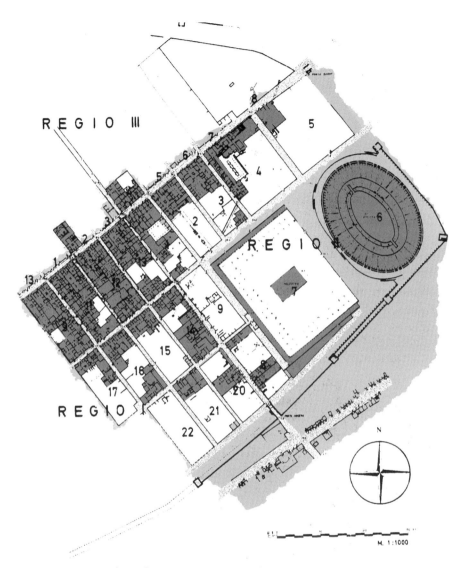

FIGURE 2.6: City plan of Pompeii, Region I dominated by gardens of the second type: no. 7 is the Palaestra with garden surrounding a swimming pool, flanked by plantings around the amphitheater (no. 6). On the west and north side of the Palaestra are insulae with commercial gardens (nos. 3–9, 15–17, 20–22). No. 4 is the Restaurant garden of Julia Felix with the attached vineyard, and no. 2 is the House of Octavio Quartio with a luxurious Egyptianizing garden. Inside the houses court-yard and peristyle gardens of the third type are seen. (Courtesy: K. Wilczak after S. Jashemski)

In the Roman provinces, we have few references to sacred gardens, although in the eastern provinces such gardens continued to exist as they had always done (for example, in Cyprus and Rhodes). Again, few have been excavated, but among them are a small part of a temple garden in the *temenos* of the East Temple in Thurburbo Maius in Tunisia. The garden flanked the temple and an area in front of it paved with mosaics. The whole was surrounded by a portico and a wall. It dates to the second century C.E. Only a one-meter-wide strip was excavated, and only one linear row of six root cavities, fifteen centimeters (approximately six inches) in diameter and fifty to seventy centimeters (approximately twenty to twenty-seven inches) apart, was found; all the same, this suggests a formal planting of the court. Jashemski[39] suggests that trees or large shrubs, perhaps laurel, were planted there. She compares this with depictions of such formal gardens on the Forma Urbis Romae. In Spain, the recent investigations of the monumental sanctuary of Munigua have revealed a series of holes for trees on the temple platform.[40] In Britain, the Temple of Divus Claudius in Colchester probably imitated the temple of this emperor on the Caelian Hill in Rome and had surrounding gardens as well.[41]

Public Gardens

In Greece, old gymnasia were normally built around *heroa* (for example, the Academy in Athens). These early (archaic and classical) gymnasia were situated on the outskirts of town, in tree-filled areas near streams and rivers and sometimes meadows and consisted not only of a sports area, but also of enclosed gardens for promenades, according to the ancient authors. Best known in this context are the three old gymnasia of Athens: the Academia, the Lykeion, and the Kynosarges, which were probably all founded in the sixth century B.C.E.[42] Plane trees were typical of these gardens, and Plutarch mentions that Cimon (*Cim.* 13.7. 487c) planted plane trees, elms, poplars, and olive trees in the Academy *alsoi*. Although the most famous of these gymnasia were situated in Athens, they were far from limited to that city. Thus, there was one with plane trees in Sparta, the famous round *platanistas* gymnasium mentioned by Pausanias (3.14.8–11), and probably also one, likewise on the outskirts of the city, in Corinth, the Old Gymnasium, likewise mentioned by Pausanias (2.4.5), near the Lerna spring. Such gardens probably existed on the upper terrace of the fourth century B.C.E. gymnasium in Delphi and on the middle and upper terraces (where later the East Baths were built) of the huge gymnasium of Pergamon.[43]

From the fourth century B.C.E., these gardens were used by philosophers for teaching. The evolutions of parks for recreation into philosophical gardens took place in Athens, where Plato first moved his school from the Academy proper into his own house with a garden furnished with *exedra* and museion (Diogenes Laertius 4.1). A generation later, Epicurus bought a plot inside the city walls, probably near the Dipylon gate, and planted a garden for his own use and for that of his pupils (Pliny, *Historia Naturalis* 19.4.19). At the same time, Theophrastus bequeathed his garden, including the museion therein, to the Lykeion gymnasion (Diog. Laert. 5.52). It has been suggested that it was a botanical garden (Gotheim 1909, 130f). Pliny (*HN* 19.4.19) sees this gymnasion garden as a model for the gardens of the Roman upper class.

In the republican and Roman imperial period, *gymnasia* could also, synonymously, be called palaestrae. This is, for example, the case as regards the Latin ancient sources; thus, Vitruvius mentions a garden with groves (*silvae*) of plane trees between the colonnades, or *xysta*, and paths paved with cement (*opus signinum*) outside, but connected to, the building he describes as a palaestra (5.11.4). It has been much discussed where this palaestra of his was situated; it may have been an ideal type, but a building of that kind would certainly be at home in Campania in Italy. Regarding this connection, it is important to remember that the Roman aristocracy could also name gardens in their rural villas after famous Greek gymnasia. Thus, Cicero called two gardens in his villa in Tusculum after the Academy and the Lyceum of Athens, respectively (Cicero, *Tusculanae Disputationes* 2.9), and he also boasted a palaestra, undoubtedly a garden, in his house on the Palatine (Cicero, *Epistulae ad Atticum* 2.4.7).[44]

This transition in the meaning of the gymnasium inspired the public gymnasia of the Campanian cities of Pompeii and Herculaneum as well, for the palaestrae belonging to these towns included plane trees and swimming pools in their huge courts, which were recovered during garden excavations. In the Great Palaestra in Pompeii, in the center of which was a large swimming pool (34.55 by 22.25 m; approximately 113 by 73 ft), two rows of root cavities at a distance of eight meters (approximately 26 ft 3 in) were located; they were probably the popular plane trees. A likewise park-like character is documented for the less well-preserved Great Palaestra in Herculaneum, with two pools.[45]

The Roman *thermae*, whose recreational areas were originally taken over from the Greek gymnasia, represent a radical change of function from hard sports to pleasure garden for strolling and light sports. When the gymnasium part was added to the public baths in Rome by Agrippa, thus creating the

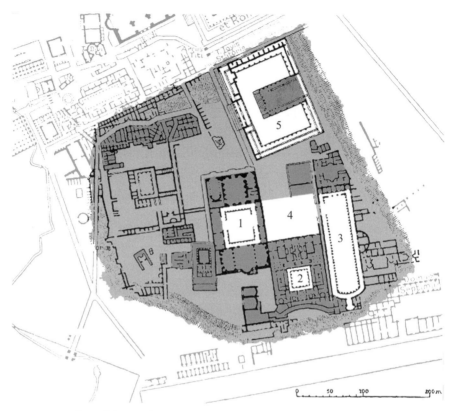

FIGURE 2.7: Plan of the gardens on the eastern part of the Palatine hill in Rome. Nos. 1–2 are peristyle gardens of the third type in the Palace of Domitian, and to the same palace belong also the Hippodrome garden (no. 3) and entrance garden (no. 4) of the second type. Finally, the religious Garden of Adonis (No. 5) to the north of Domitian's Palace is of the second type as well. (Courtesy: M. Bolton after Jashemski, 1979, based on map by Hans Eschebach).

Roman thermae, it was of a royal gymnasion pleasure garden type.[46] Agrippa's gardens and thermae, with their huge swimming pool, *stagnum*, in the Campus Martius may have been inspired by the royal palaces of the Hasmoneans and those of Agrippa's contemporary, Herod the Great, with whom he had regular contact.[47] In the imperial period, this kind of garden was then taken over, especially by the great imperial thermae. For example, the thermae of Caracalla in Rome were surrounded by green spaces limited by monumental enclosure walls with various rooms. The same general idea of classical Greek functions turned into Roman luxury gardens certainly lay behind the so-called *stadia* and *hippodromes*, which turn up in Roman villas and palaces, the most famous being that of Domitian on the Palatine of Hadrian at Tivoli and the hippodrome garden described by Pliny the Younger at his Tuscan villa.

In the Roman provinces, a palaestra garden has been found in the Trajanic Thermae in Conimbriga.[48] In the apses of this large open space, *caissons* for plants with water spouts in the center were found, and along the northern wall there were water spouts, too, indicating gardens here flanking the great staircase, and probably an alley between the apses.

Another public building that should be included under the gardens of type two is the "public" portico garden. This kind of building seems to be a Roman invention, reflecting the Romans' imperial wealth and love of displaying it in gardens. Such public gardens are especially typical of the late republic and the early imperial period in Rome. It is not always possible to differentiate these gardens from the portico gardens that surrounded temples, as the Romans did not make such a distinction themselves. Public gardens can be said to be those connected with types of buildings that were given to the public by private individuals, in the republican tradition. The Porticus Metelli and Philippi or the Templum Pacis all seem to have multiple functions. Similarly, the great garden in the Porticus behind the theatre and temple of Pompey on the Campus Martius in Rome, known from the Forma Urbis Romae, may be regarded as a sanctuary garden for Venus Victrix, as a theatre garden for strolling in the intervals, and as a popular public garden as we might conceive of one today (see Chapter Three, this volume).[49] An example of a library garden is the Library of Hadrian at Athens.[50] There was an old tradition to combine a library with a garden in the palaces, especially that of Alexandria with the *museion*. But at least in the Porticus Liviae built by Augustus on the Esquiline hill in Rome, the garden was the main thing.[51]

Palace Gardens

In the Near East and in Egypt, such Type Two gardens did undoubtedly exist in connection with the palaces, but they are difficult to trace. In Persia, gardens of this second type in a palace context are more recreational than utilitarian. In Pasargadae, a formally laid out garden of this type has been excavated. It belonged to Palace P, was divided in two parts with paths flanked by channels and pools, and was probably surrounded by a wall and entered through the Propylon R.[52] Also at Susa, such a palace garden has been found albeit not excavated, namely the one belonging to the palace of Artaxerxes on the plain. Here, there is an internal area between two wings which has been restored as a garden by the excavators.[53] Another probable garden was included in the great

paradeisos and palace by Takht-i-Rustam—a walled area of 210 by 170 meters (689 by 558 ft), which equals 3.5 hectares (8.6 acres), embracing both the
palace and the tomb surrounded it.[54] Finally, on the terrace of Persepolis, there
were probably, in the first phase, areas with gardens, while in the late period,
there was only room for one, in front of Dareios's *tachara*.[55]

In Greece, such gardens existed, according to Homer, already in the
Mycenean period, but again, we should probably rather see here a reflection
of his own period. Thus, Homer's description of a garden outside the court in
Alcinous's palace should perhaps rather be taken as a reflection of the chieftain
palaces of the *basileis* of Homer's own time; in any case, the garden described
was utilitarian rather than exclusively recreational in character. Another example is Homer's description of the estate of Laertes, where the fruit and vine garden was surrounded by a wall and watered with channels. In general, Homer
uses the word kepos for a fruit and vegetable garden.[56]

In the Hellenistic period, we see that the kings took over this kind of garden, probably primarily from their Achaemenid predecessors, including them
in their palaces, which, in addition, drew several originally public Greek *polis*
institutions, such as the theatre and the gymnasium/palaestra (and, to a certain extent, also the library), into the orbit of their palaces. In connection to
this, one may mention the Alexandrian *basileia*, where a palaestra is mentioned close to the *maiandros* (see n. 16). Since there was a huge gymnasium
in the center of the city, this palaestra was surely not primarily used for sports,
rather, it was a garden. Also the *museion*, which included *peripatoi*—that is,
promenades—might have had a garden of this type (see n. 16). At least its
models, the famous gymnasia in Athens, had *museia* in their gardens, and
Aristotle's school in the Lykeion in fact took its name from such peripatoi.
That the Seleucids, too, included such gardens in their palaces is indicated
by the description of the palace that Seleucus II placed at the disposal of
Demetrius Poliorchetes; in it were *peripatoi basilikoi* and a *dromos*, both giving associations to the gymnasium (Plutarch, *Demetrius* 50.1–2). Such peripatoi, with beds flanking them, are in fact mentioned together with a gymnasion
and a garden in connection with the huge royal bark, called Syracusia, built
by Hieron II of Syracuse as a present to Ptolemy IV of Egypt (see Athenaeus
5.206d ff [cit. Moschion]). In relation to this garden was a dining hall-cum-
temple for the garden-loving Aphrodite as well as a library, evidently a kind of
museion. Also, two pools are mentioned, one of them for fish.

A preserved example of such a garden has probably been found in Ai
Khanoum, since a building called gymnasion, which was added to the park
of the palace in the middle of the second century B.C.E.—that is, after this

palace had been taken over by a local dynast—probably belonged to this type. It was situated near the huge swimming pool and constituted a closed courtyard with water channels, surrounded by porticoes and furnished with only a few and strangely formed rooms.[57] One may compare this with the later Roman palaestrae in Pompeii and Herculaneum. It was certainly rather a garden than a Greek style palaestra for sports, but unfortunately it has not been excavated.

A similar enclosed garden has been found in the Hasmonean palace of Jericho, in the area just north of the main swimming pools.[58] A huge fenced garden, probably with partly utilitarian trees and perhaps surrounded by a portico and reached from the recreational area, have been ascertained. Later, this garden was opened up and an entrance portico was added, making it possible to get a view of it from the dining hall facing the swimming pools. This happened during the reign of Alexandra, widow of the former king Alexander Jannaeus, and it was also she who built the so-called twin palaces. Both had closed courts with swimming pools and, surely, gardens, and in one of them a Roman-style open-air *triclinium* was found, showing that this kind of dining was popular already in this period in Palestine, but it may have been inspired by similar dining arrangements in Alexandria.[59] In the third winter palace built by Herod the Great in the same locality, this kind of garden had been further elaborated; thus a huge, elongated sunken garden was placed on the south side of the wadi Qelt, facing the main palace and surrounded by walls and porticos with exedras. It was, again, situated near an enormous pool and a pavilion.[60]

The Roman imperial palaces followed this trend. An early example of this is the recently excavated Villa at Prima Porta near Rome, which belonged to the empress Livia[61] and in which the famous garden paintings were found. On a garden terrace (74 by 74 m; approximately 243 by 243 ft), which was enclosed by porticoes with garden paintings, fragmented garden pots and traces of roots and sticks were found, indicating that the terrace was (perhaps formally) planted. Behind the northern portico were niches, probably containing beds since *ollae perforatae* were found there. Along them ran a two-meter-wide (6 ft 6 in) *euripus*, which was later transformed into a bed. The niches were cut into the slope of the hill and were interpreted as a hanging garden by the excavators. A garden of the second type was also found in connection with the Palace of Domitian on the Palatine.[62] This garden was formed like a stadion or hippodrome but used only for recreation. Also in the imperial villas, such as Domitian's villa in Albano[63] and Hadrian's villa in Tivoli, such gardens were included. In the latter, garden investigations were carried out in the 1980s by Jashemski and Eugenia Salza Prina Ricotti in the so-called Stadion Garden with its pools and apsidal nymphaeum, as well as in the Canopus Garden.[64]

Villa Gardens of the Elite

Only a few villas with gardens of this second type have been found in the Greek area; the same is the case in the Near East, Persia, and in Egypt. Rather, these luxurious *otium* villas are a phenomenon of the Italic and Roman elites. We know such villas from several ancient authors, among them Pliny the Younger, who described two of his recreation villas, one in Tusculum, one in Laurentum, in detail, including also the gardens there.[65]

In Italy, we are fortunate to have an example of an excavated villa of this kind, namely the Oplontis villa in Campania. This villa was investigated by Jashemski,[66] who found no less than thirteen gardens, among them not only peristyle and courtyard gardens of the third type (see below) but also, which is rather seldom, gardens surrounding the villa and thus belonging to type two. The villa was first built in the middle of the first century B.C.E.

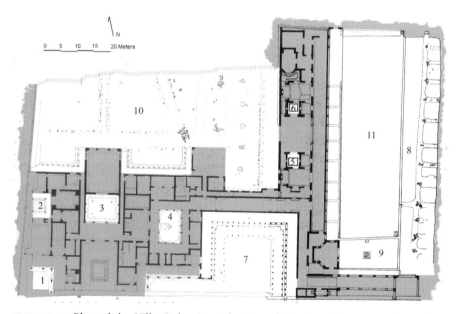

FIGURE 2.8: Plan of the Villa Oplontis at the Bay of Naples with excavated gardens. Nos. 1–6 are peristyle gardens of the third type, gardens nos. 7–10 are gardens of the second type, and 11 is the swimming pool (Courtesy: M. Bolton after S. Jashemski)

as a compact villa, but what interests us in this context is its enlargement toward the east between 50 and 70 C.E. The new great swimming pool (60 by 17 m; approximately 197 by 56 ft) was flanked to the south and east by gardens. The eastern garden was decorated with numerous garden sculptures, and had a promenade flanked by at least thirteen trees, some of them probably plane trees, with smaller oleander and lemon trees in between, with a statue base in front of each.[67] Behind the villa to the north was a park laid out in the Augustan period, reflecting the plan of the villa itself. Following the main axis through the atrium, central garden, and main hall, a garden path continued the view. This promenade, as well as the other garden paths, was flanked by trees or bushes, among them box. Toward the east was a row of very old and huge plane trees leading to the new wing. Four built-up bases for marble busts were found by the diagonal path in this northern park.

Also in the Roman provinces, villa gardens of this second type have been ascertained but very seldom excavated. However, villas with second type gardens have been found in Libya: Salza Prina Ricotti (1970–71) excavated two such seaside villas at Silin near Leptis Magna, which were built by rich ship owners, and Luisa Musso excavated a third one. Behind these villas, empty areas indicate gardens that were protected from the wind that came off the sea. The seaside Villa of the Maritime Odeon is especially interesting in that it had a stone garden by the sea front that was partly formed as a theatre. In the other villa investigated by Prina Ricotti, the Villa of the Little Circus, there was at the extreme west of this huge villa, a long, narrow enclosure shaped as a circus, eighty-five by fifteen meters (approximately 279 by 49 ft), with a *spina* in the center, measuring sixty by six meters (approximately 197 by 20 ft) and containing a flowerbed with two apsidal pools at the ends and a square basin dividing the bed into two unequal parts. One may compare the garden at Villa of the Little Circus with hippodrome gardens such as the one in Pliny the Younger's Tuscan villa (5.6.32–40), the stadium in Domitian's palace on the Palatine (mentioned above) and in his Villa Albana, and finally with the so-called stadium in Hadrian's villa in Tivoli. The third maritime villa in this Silin area was excavated in the 1970s and 1980s.

This preference for gardens in North Africa is also reflected in the mosaics decorating the villas and houses of the elite. In this area, garden mosaics showing villas surrounded by gardens are well-known from the first century C.E. (Zliten) and into late antiquity. Of the great number of garden mosaics from this period, one may mention the mosaic of Dominus Iulius from Carthage, dating to the fourth century C.E., and the mosaic from Tabarka, circa 400 C.E.

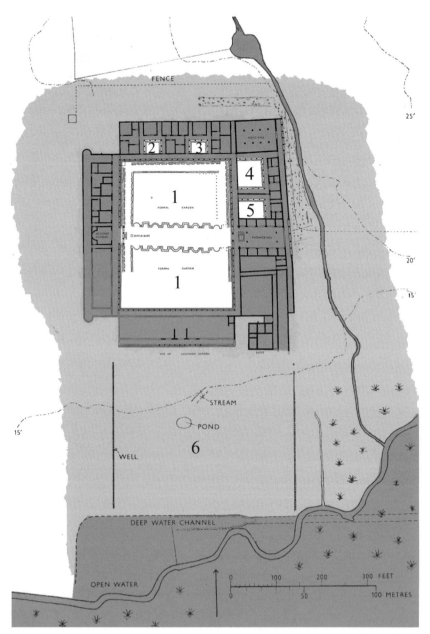

FIGURE 2.9: Plan of the provincial palace of Fishbourne in southern England with the excavated garden in the courtyard of the second type (No. 1) and several peristyle gardens inside the palace (nos. 2–5). To the south of the palace was a great park (no. 6) (Courtesy: M. Bolton after B. Cunliffe 1971, vol. 1, Figure 21)

We are even better off in Britan. Here, the courtyard garden in the unique Flavian palatial residence in Fishbourne,[68] perhaps built by a Roman client king, has been excavated. The design of the villa was imported, as was the garden model, probably from Rome via Gaul. While the five peristyle gardens in the north and east wings, the kitchen garden to the northwest, and a less formal, natural garden on the southern terrace could not be excavated, it was fortunately possible to excavate the great courtyard garden. Here, bedding trenches twenty to twenty-five centimeters (eight to ten inches) wide and up to forty centimeters (sixteen inches) deep filled with humus (artificial fill) were found cut into the infertile clay and gravel of the courtyard; undoubtedly they had been planted with bushes and hedges. The whole court, except for the pathways, was then covered by a layer of topsoil ten to fifteen centimeters (four to six inches) thick. The layout of the hedges was regular; those flanking the path from the entrance to the east wing with the audience chamber had recesses in alternately semicircular and rectangular form. Another pathway ran around the garden along the columns. A cavity for a tree was found in the northwest corner. Inside the path on the northeast sides were stone-packed postholes alternating with bedding pits filled with loamy soil. The area inside the hedges does not show pits and was probably grassed. The water came from a tank in the northwest corner and was led to the various parts of the garden by means of clay pipes that probably went to basins.

Utility Gardens Belonging to Private Houses

In most cultures, it was normal for people living in houses to have a garden inside a fenced area. Of course, farms outside the cities had always utility gardens of this kind, but we have very little evidence for them. There were, however, also sometimes gardens related to the houses inside the towns and cities (see Isae 5.11).[69]

The houses of the Greek area are mostly known from a time when houses were situated in closely built-up sites inside the city walls. In this case, they are very seldom furnished with gardens, and these were never situated in the central courtyard. But it is obvious that in the early towns, especially in the colonies, there was still room for a small garden around the house bounded by a wall. Such early plots have, for example, been traced in the early strata of the colonies in Sicily and are well documented especially in Megara Hyblaea, founded in the late eighth century B.C.E.[70]

As for the early Roman houses, the atrium, if present, was never planted with a garden either. Such gardens, called *hortus/i* in Latin, were normally placed behind the house, as is seen in the almost identical houses of the early Latin colony of Cosa founded 274 B.C.E.[71] as well as in the early houses in Pompeii, such as the first phase of the House of Polybius. Later, the richer houses were normally furnished with an often formal peristyle garden (Type Three, which was added to the back of the house, where earlier the utilitarian hortus was to be found.

Commercial Gardens

In the Greek area, where, at least in the fully constructed towns, there was room for no private gardens, these were planted outside the city walls in a green belt. They could be owned by one person or by a group. In Italy, such commercially used utility gardens are mentioned by Cato the Elder in 160 B.C.E. (*De Agricultura* 9.10), who recommended that such suburban gardens should include flowers for religious use, onions, myrtle for weddings, laurels, and nut trees. Such gardens have been found in relation to several houses in Pompeii and been investigated by Jashemski.[72]

One was laid out at two levels and situated behind the House of the Ship Europa.[73] In the lower part, two vegetable gardens were found, which were regularly laid out. The northern one had six beds divided by furrows, the southern one had five beds. Thirty-one root cavities were located in this garden, indicating that small fruit trees were planted there in a haphazard way. The main part of the lower garden was planted with grapevines. A central pathway led to the various parts. The small ramps along the side walls were flanked by trees, too. Here twenty-eight garden pots in terracotta were found as well. Since the aqueduct did not reach this area, water from the roof was used.

A commercial flower garden was connected to the small House of Hercules (II.7.6)[74] near the Great Palaestra. A pathway led from the house to a garden triclinium in connection with an altar and a shrine at the eastern wall. This garden was divided into several beds, among which water channels led the rather great amount of water necessary to the beds from reservoirs near the house. Also eleven root cavities were found, the biggest one containing an old olive tree. Also here, terracotta pots were found along the walls. The fertile area around Vesuvius was known for the growth of flowers, which were mostly used for garlands.

Also, a vine garden has been excavated in Pompeii by Jashemski,[75] it was situated north of the Amphitheatre and included also installations for vine production. The vine yard was regularly laid out and divided into four parts by two garden paths crossing at right angles and flanked by posts carrying a pergola, which was also recommended by the agrarian authors like Cato and Columella. Two thousand fourteen vine plants and supporting sticks for them were found at a distance of four Roman feet and between every second were traces of waterholes. Also, fifty-eight root cavities for trees were found. The presence of a garden triclinium and of animal bones shows that also this garden was used for recreational eating.

This function was also served by the gardens that in Roman times were often found in connection with restaurants (*cauponae*). Especially is this the case in Pompeii, where one of them was excavated by Jashemski.[76] It belonged to a certain Euxinus and was situated near the Amphitheatre. The garden had two small garden rooms, but the guests could also eat at tables under the trees. Thus root cavities for two trees were found, together with thirty-two for wine plants, probably producing the house wine. A *lararium* stood in an *aedicula* with an altar in front of it by the eastern garden wall, and another altar was found in its northeastern part.

Funeral Gardens

The *Iliad* (6.419f) mentions sacred groves surrounding hero tombs, and as we have seen, some of these developed into gymnasia. In Asia Minor, we know of such gardens from the fourth century B.C.E. surrounding the Heroa in Kalydon and Trysa in an enclosure, a kind of sacred grove, in fact. They are also well-known from the Hellenistic period (for example in Halikarnassos, Larissa, Kos, and Alexandria), where we hear that they could be leased out, as was the case with the temple gardens. In a royal context, the tombs of the monarchs were often situated in the palatial park, as was the case with the tomb of Cyrus in Pasargadae in Persia, which was surrounded by its own garden as well. We know that Alexander the Great visited this tomb, and eventually he was himself buried in similar surroundings, in the Basileia of Alexandria. In Rome, Augustus was the first to plant a garden surrounding his Etruscan-inspired mausoleum on the Campus Martius in Rome (Strabo, *Geographia* 5.3.8; Suetonius, *Divus Augustus* 100).

But also, normal (rich) people could be buried in a garden setting. Plato (*Nomoi* 12.947) in fact in his ideal state suggested tombs in groves for famous people. Such gardens were probably also present in the Keramkei necropolis in Athens, inside the larger tomb enclosures.[77] Finally, we may mention one of the very rare documentations for a funeral garden in an Italic context from the Vesuvian area, in Scafati.[78] The walled grave area in question is triangular in form and flanks a road. Six large root cavities were found inside the walls, two

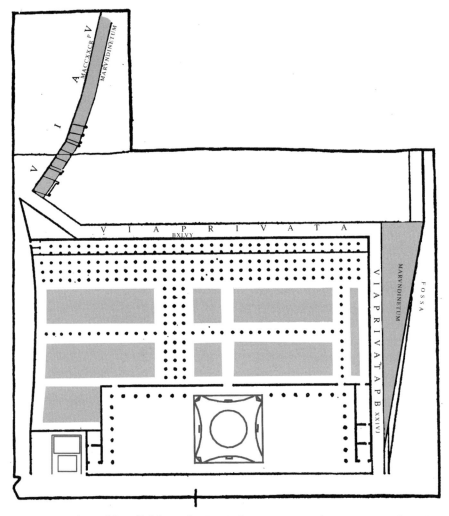

FIGURE 2.10: A marble relief from the Via Labicana, Rome, depicting a tomb with a garden including flowerbeds and trees. (Courtesy: K. Wilczak after W. Jashemski II, 223)

behind the tomb, four in front of it, surrounding an *ustrina*—that is, the area used for cremation. The appearance of such gardens may also be elucidated by means of engraved marble slabs depicting tombs with gardens.[79]

THE THIRD GARDEN TYPE

The third type of garden was placed within the structure itself, in a court-yard, and normally surrounded by a peristyle. This kind of garden could be called kepos in Greek and *viridarium* or hortus in Latin and was normally only present in royal palaces and the rich houses and villas of the elite of the Hellenistic and Roman period. These courtyard-gardens were, in comparison to the above-mentioned garden types, rather limited in size. They invariably had rooms facing them on several or all sides, and thus the garden constituted a focus for views from these rooms, many of them used for dining.[80] These internal gardens typically displayed water in ornate basins and pools with fountains. The courtyards frequently featured regularly laid out flowerbeds and shrubs. The plants typical of these formal gardens are ivy, box, laurel, myrtle, acanthus, rosemary, and various flowers, primarily roses, as well as small trees. The larger examples of this type could be used for short promenades.

Palatial Gardens

This third garden type is characteristic of private and palatial architecture from far back in time. In ancient Egypt, such gardens have been ascertained from an early period, both iconographically and archaeologically, placed in the courts of the royal palaces as well as in the houses of the elite.[81] These enclosed gardens centered on a pavilion and a large rectangular pool with fish and ducks. The pools were deeply set to reach the ground water and were flanked by beds and trees. In the palace of Tell el-Amarna, from the middle of the fourteenth century B.C.E. gardens furnished with peristyles and surrounded by rooms have been found. Gardens of this type, albeit without peristyle, also existed in Ugarit in Syria at the same time. Here, the palace featured a courtyard (20–25 by 40 m; approximately 66–85 by 131 ft) with a pavilion that opened onto a garden (12–15 by 21 m; 39–49 by 69 ft), which was enclosed by a low stone wall and watered by a channel from a well with a small basin. A reception hall with two columns *in antis* flanked the garden. Unfortunately, we do not know what grew in it.[82] Neither in the Minoan palaces, nor in the Mycenaean ones, have courtyard gardens been ascertained. On the contrary, all the courts in these palaces seem to have been paved.

In the Greek area including the Hellenistic kingdoms, this type of garden has been much discussed. Although it is generally believed that the peristyle court is a Greek invention (which, however, is far from proven),[83] no garden has, as mentioned, been found in any Greek private urban house courtyards, which are found normally paved or furnished with a hard earthen floor. Based on the examples of these small courtyards, it has been doubted that peristyle gardens existed in the Hellenistic palaces, although this would make their sudden appearance in the rich houses of the Vesuvian area during the second century B.C.E. difficult to explain.[84] In fact, Graeme Clarke has recently located proof of Hellenistic peristyle gardens at the early Hellenistic governor's palace in Jebel Khalid by the Euphrates in Syria. The eighty centimeters (31.5 inches) wide and up to one meter (approximately three feet) deep border along the peristyle filled with loose nitrogenous soil does, indeed, indicate that a garden decorated at least part of this main court. This means that although this palace was placed on a bedrock formation in an arid climate, it was regarded as very important to have some kind of a garden in the court.[85]

Since this early Hellenistic palace was owned by a Macedonian governor, it would not be surprising to find such gardens in the palaces belonging to the kings of Macedonia, too. There might well have been a garden in the main official peristyle of the royal palace at Pella, but in the absence of excavation this cannot be proven.[86] However, water installations and the absence of pavement suggest that garden archaeology is warranted here and in other preserved palaces of the Macedonian kings in Aigai and Demetrias. It is difficult to envisage a plain earth courtyard in these luxurious palaces, offering barren views from the dining rooms surrounding it.

Similar gardens undoubtedly decorated the main peristyle of the Ptolemaic governor's palace of Ptolemais in Cyrenaica,[87] since this oblong peristyle had an ornamental pool in the center and room for promenades along the colonnades. This oblong court has clear affinities to the gardens of the old Egyptian palaces such as Tell el Amarna, with the palace of Alexandria as a "missing link."

With gardens present in two governor's palaces of both the Seleucid and the Ptolemaic dynasty, royal palaces of the kings in Alexandria and in Antioch certainly also featured such gardens. One may mention the flowers and bushes placed in the court of the *akra* in the Alexandrian *basileia* when the dining pavilion of Ptolemy II was raised.[88] Comparison may be made with the marquee, which the Persian king had raised and used for banquets for the people of Susa, which was set up in a large square in front of the park by the palace.[89] In Judea, a royal context of peristyle gardens is attested by Josephus, who describes connected peristyles with gardens, together with trees and promenades flanked by channels and basins, in Herod the Great's palace in Jerusalem (see Josephus, *Bellum Judaicum* 1.21.1 [401–2]).[90]

These features are evident in the archaeological excavations of a garden in Herod's winter palace in Jericho (see Chapter One in this volume). This garden, which was situated in the official part of the palace, with an apsidal hall facing it, was surrounded by a both a colonnade and a paved walk outside the columns, and measured twenty by twenty-one meters (approximately 66 by 69 ft).[91] Seven straight rows of garden pots and planting pits were found dug into the plaster of the construction surface of the courtyard (c). Evidence of the original contouring of the fertilized garden soil showed the pattern of irrigation of the rows. The planting pits, for trees, flanked the apsidal space. It has not been possible to identify the plants archaeologically, but Kathryn Gleason suggests that the two famous plants of the area featured in literary sources grew here: palms in the deep pits and balsam in the pots. At Caesarea, the lower palace situated on a peninsula was furnished with a swimming pool surrounded by a peristyle, between the columns of which were beds for flowers and so on cut into the rock.[92]

The Roman emperors, the heirs to these Hellenistic kingdoms, quickly introduced these luxurious gardens into their residences as well. In Italy, these gardens already decorated the peristyles of the late republican elite, as we shall see.[93] The first emperor, Augustus, included such gardens in his palace on the Palatine.[94] This palace included two peristyles flanking the temple of Apollo, of which the Portico of the Danaids had a garden filled with statues. The so-called Domus Tiberiana built by Nero on the Palatine probably also included a garden in its huge peristylar court.[95] In the famous Domus Aurea built by Nero, there was at least one great peristyle court in the western part which undoubtedly had a garden.[96] A preserved example has further been found associated with Domitian's palace on the Palatine, in the official peristyle court, to which there was a view from the main dining hall. Another faced the "private" wing of this palace. Recently, it has even been suggested that the Farnesine gardens on the northwestern corner of the Palatine reflect the garden in the Neronian Domus Tiberiana, in whose courtyard it was later planted.[97] At Hadrian's Villa, the garden in the Piazza D'Oro was excavated in the 1980s.[98] A shallow euripus crossed the center of the garden and was flanked by two beds. Since there was only a thin layer of earth, the architect had to cut pits into the (tufa) and fill them with garden soil. A double row of large pits contained trees along the edge of the garden. On the west side of the euripus, a complex irrigation system for the beds as well as smaller planting holes was cut into the tuff.

A late example of a palatial peristyle garden is to be found in the Agora of Athens. This great complex was earlier interpreted as a gymnasium (Gymnasium of the Giants) but is now convincingly identified with an official residence for the imperial court and high-ranking Roman officials (Palace of the

Giants).[99] Two of the three inner courtyards were not paved, and the building was directly supplied from the late Roman aqueduct. In the great northern court (29 by 38 m; 95 by 125 ft), statues standing in a row were found. There is no direct evidence for gardens here, but their presence is highly likely in this representative structure.

Gardens in the Private Houses of the Elite

As mentioned, gardens are seldom found in Greek private houses. Exceptions may lie in the unexcavated, rich houses in Pella in Macedonia (second half of the fourth century B.C.E.). These feature several courtyards, one or more of which were probably furnished with gardens, as was the case in the Macedonian palaces, but again, none have been excavated. But in general, gardens in this setting are basically a Roman phenomenon.

In Italy, we are, as mentioned above, in a privileged situation when it comes to excavated gardens of this kind, thanks to the detailed garden investigations in the area around Vesuvius, where some three hundred peristyle gardens have been documented in this area.[100] The following discussion concentrates on the courtyard gardens of Pompeii. Although the peristyle garden dominated in the late phase of the houses, archaeology is rarely undertaken below the 79 C.E. levels. There is some limited evidence that their precursors were the utilitarian hortus behind the old atrium house, and some gardens were still planted in plain courtyards or in courts with porticoes on only one, two, or three sides. Jashemski excavated seven peristyle courts in Pompeii, of which six had been informally planted and contained big trees. Only one was planted formally with shrubs.

In the House of Polybius in Pompeii,[101] the peristyle garden, a former hortus, was not formally laid out, and it not only included shrubs but also trees of an impressive size, some of them fruit trees, reminding us that the Roman appreciated productivity together with pleasure (see Chapter Six in this volume). There was a cistern for watering the garden in the peristyle, and the outline of a high ladder used for picking fruits was found. Along the west wall, soil formations in the shape of sombreros were found—in fact, the center contained a root surrounded by a channel, for young plants. Planting pots were excavated, too, as was the case in other gardens.[102] In the wall above, nail holes show that the trees had been espaliered. A possibility is that lemon trees were planted here (cf. Pliny, *HN* 12.16). In the peristyle area, several bigger roots were investigated, in the northwest of a fig tree, in the northeast, a fruit tree, perhaps a cherry or pear; that on the south side was a young olive tree.

Another two tree roots were traced but could not be identified. The smaller cavities along the east wall and the south edge were probably those of shrubs. Jashemski suggests myrtle and ivy bushes, often seen in the Pompeian wall-paintings. The soil in the garden was analyzed, too, and was very fertile and contained large quantities of small pumice pieces, which were porous and could keep moisture.

Another courtyard garden (House I.16.2), with porticoes on two sides, contained seventeen root cavities with a mean diameter of seven centimeters placed in three irregular rows, with two roots in a fourth row.[103] They could not be precisely identified but were roots of nut and fruit trees. The peristyle garden in the House of the Ship Europa (I.16.3) was damaged from earlier excavations, but root cavities were, allS the same, found, showing an informal pattern.[104] Almost all roots were situated on the edges of the garden, and a tree was planted in each of three corners, and there may have been one in the fourth corner, too. Nine smaller cavities belonged probably to grapevines.

While the gardens described above were rather informally laid out and dominated by fruit trees, the garden in a small house (I.12.11), which had a portico on three sides, was strictly formal in character and planted with small shrubs. In the center was a statue base surrounded by evergreens, probably clipped box. This luxurious model was a result of the introduction of the aqueduct during the reign of Augustus; now it was possible to plant also greens that needed much water, and to fill the gardens with pools and fountains. A very popular new focus of the now formal gardens became the pool, the size of which varied greatly,[105] thus leaving more or less space for the garden itself. Another focus was garden sculpture. This wealth of statues is best illustrated in the garden of the House of the Vettii (VI.15.1), which included evergreen bushes and a lot of fountains and basins. This new type of luxury garden is also well-known from wall paintings. Such garden paintings were also often found in the gardens themselves, thus making an illusion of a larger garden.[106] Such garden paintings were of course especially useful in small houses without room for a big garden. A good example is the little house (I.12.16) where a garden painting dominates a very small garden of 0.5 by 2 meters (1 ft 8 in by 6 ft 7 in).[107] The wild animals depicted on some of these paintings reflect the great estates, with paradeisoi owned by the elite. Recently, another formal peristyle garden was excavated in the Casa degli Epigrammi Greci (V.1.18) in Pompeii, dating to the first century C.E.[108] A fountain was situated in the center of the garden, and in the southwestern quadrant, seventeen flowerpots and pits with not-local earth and planted in a grit pattern were found, indicating the positions of ornamental, probably evergreen, plants.

Throughout the Roman provinces, peristyle gardens have been identified in
the richer houses and villas, although few have been excavated. Jashemski[109]
examined part of two inner gardens with semicircular pools in the House
of Bacchus and Ariadne in Thurburbo Maius in Tunisia. She felt that many
of the houses had such gardens, but no further study has taken place. One of
these inner gardens was a peristyle garden in the private part of the complex,
with a triclinium facing it. She found a row of trees along the southwestern
edge. The other garden, placed in a courtyard without columns in the representative or more public part of the house, faced a large and luxurious triclinium
that was reached from the garden by three steps. This garden, fully excavated,
was abundantly planted with great fruit-bearing trees, probably olive, fig, and
apricot trees. Smaller root cavities indicated the presence of shrubs of various
kinds. The forty-five cavities suggest that the garden was overplanted.

In Conimbriga in Portugal, gardens are seen in four great *domus*.[110] All
houses are laid out with only one court, each a garden peristyle, and decorated
with numerous mosaics of high quality. The Maison aux Jets d'eau features a
peristyle that was taken up entirely with a pool (179.52 sq m; 1932 sq ft), in
which six *caissons* in intricately curved shapes were built, giving it a baroque
character. The caissons were filled with earth for plants, shrubs, and/or flowers. The pool was furnished with no less than 400 water spouts with lead pipes.
The contemporary Maison de Cantaber featured a similar but simpler layout,
its pool (161.28 sq m; 1736 sq ft) offering only four caissons. Smaller yet was
the pool (80 sq m; 861 sq ft) in the peristyle of the Maison aux Swastikas,
built in the third century C.E., again with four caissons. Finally, the Maison des
Squelettes had a peristyle layout of another type, probably owing to its earlier
date, the second century C.E. The pool is a simple channel surrounding the
garden with a kind of platform.[111]

In Gaul, recent excavations have revealed Romanized gardens found in
some great city houses of the elite.[112] In Vaison, an unpaved surface in the second peristyle of the Maison du Buste en argent, from circa 100 C.E., adjacent
to a bath building, included a garden. Especially interesting are the houses of
Vienne, situated in the Saint-Romain-en-Gaul quarter of the town.[113] Typical of these houses, dating from the first through second century C.E., is a
very large peristyle court featuring a large, centrally placed U-shaped pool
set into an earthen surface that was probably planted. Paintings with plants
and birds are found on the surrounding walls. In some houses, a smaller
peristyle with a basin taking the place of the atrium was present as well. A
good example is the axially planned Maison no. 2 in Vienne. In this large

(7,200 sq m; 77,500 sq ft) house, the great peristyle with *oeci* flanking it covered alone 2,800 square meters (30,139 sq ft). At the Maison des dieux-Océan (no. 3), a rectangular basin in the great peristyle was surrounded by a garden as evidenced by garden pots found from the fourth phase of this house.[114] The smaller peristyles of these houses were probably laid out as very ornamental gardens. The situation of these huge houses near the harbor and in a quarter of merchants and industries negates, in the opinion of Le Glay,[115] a rich suburb character, and they were probably owned by rich merchants and manufacturers.

In Greece, a domus with peristyle gardens of the Roman period has been found at the foot of the Acropolis of the city of Rhodes, built in the late Hellenistic period.[116] It included three courtyards in the eastern part of the building and a large open area in the western part with a semi-circular pool (15.30 by 17.30 m; approximately 50 by 56 ft). It is uncertain whether the three courts were ever paved. At least in the Roman period, where various renovations was made before the late second century C.E., two of them included decorative pools and accordingly probably also formal gardens. The western area was never paved, and since garden sculpture was found there, it was likely a garden as well. Finally, in Athens, an early Roman house on the northwest shoulder of the Areopagos had a large peristyle courtyard, in the middle of which was a rectangular basin with apsidal ends surrounded by an unpaved area, which may well have included a garden.[117]

Villa Gardens

In the luxurious villas of the elite outside the towns we find various types of gardens and parks, and also, these villa courtyard gardens belong to the late republican and Roman imperial period. Jashemski has delivered the best evidence in her garden excavations in the villa of Poppaea in Oplontis (see above), where no less than thirteen gardens were found, some of them courtyard and peristyle gardens.[118] In the oldest, republican, part of the villa, in the southeast peristyle with its massive fountain, a large root from a chestnut tree was found, which would have shaded the entire garden. In the courtyard along the main axis behind the atrium lay a garden with walls decorated with garden paintings. A large tree stood in each of three corners. In the eastern part of the villa, built in the early imperial period, two small courtyard gardens flanked a large central room. Another villa with a garden is the suburban Villa of the Papyri (L. Calpurnius Piso) at Herculaneum,[119] where abundant garden sculpture was found, now exhibited in the Museum of Naples. This garden has been reconstructed by J. Paul Getty at Malibu. We know very little of the flowers grown in Roman gardens, but the rose, the lily, and the violet are most frequently mentioned by the ancient authors (Pliny, *HN* 21.131).[120]

In the Roman provinces, several such villa gardens have been found. In Greece, the second century B.C.E. villa on Samos[121] had two peristyle courts. When the villa was rebuilt in the early first century C.E., if not before, the courts were furnished with designed gardens, as indicated by water installations. In the northern court, a broad channel fed by piped water ran around the inside of the peristyle, while the southern court (20.58 by 14.70 m; 67 ft 6 in by 48 ft 3 in) was planned with a central part with semicircular and rectangular niches and a more elaborate water system. The garden was divided in two parts by a channel, and in the middle was a diamond-shaped pool with a central fountain in marble, fed by a pressure pipe. By the end of inhabitation in second through third century C.E., this water system had undergone many restorations. The newly excavated villa of Herodes Atticus near Astros on the Peloponnese featured exciting garden sculpture. The center of this great villa of imperial quality focused on an enormous peristyle garden with water basins surrounded by luxurious halls. Built in the second century C.E., it was still in use in the third and fourth centuries C.E.[122]

Undoubtedly, many of the villas built in late antiquity throughout the Roman Empire were furnished with gardens, but few have been examined. The villa in Piazza Armerina in Sicily was initially identified as an imperial villa due to its great size and beautiful mosaics, but as many such villas have been found in the provinces, we should perhaps see a private owner here. The great central peristyle with its elegantly formed pool may be a candidate for garden archaeology. This garden could then be viewed from the great audience hall. Formally laid out beds and plantations should be envisaged here. Another important villa is that of Montmaurin in France, at which several peristyle and courtyard gardens have been excavated.[123]

Courtyard Gardens in a Non-Private Context

Only rarely do we find such peristyle gardens outside a private recreational context. Of special interest is the sacred garden in the House of the Sibyl (II.1.12) at Pompeii, where Zeus Sabazius was worshipped by a religious group[124] and where a row of trees were found. Also, the sanctuary of Zeus in Olympia featured a row of guesthouses along the limit of the Altis during the Roman imperial period. These structures imitated to some extent rich private houses, and all of them were furnished with peristyle courts with water installations, indicating their use as recreational gardens for the rich pilgrims. The earliest of these belonged to the so-called House of Nero.[125] Its peristyle court (14 by 17 m; 46 ft by 55 ft 9 in) was surrounded by a water channel one meter wide inside the stylobate, with bridges on four sides. This feature is also seen in the Roman rebuilding of the huge guest house Leonideion. Built originally in the fourth century B.C.E., its court was transformed into a water garden in second century C.E.[126] This consisted of a quatrefoil island surrounded by water with beds and sculptures in each of the four protrusions. In the center of the island was a circular channel encircling a fountain. Such an island surrounded by channels was also present in a guest house (House I) built circa 170 C.E. east of the Kladeos baths.[127] The last guest house (House II) was built in the vicinity in 220–230 C.E., with a similar courtyard.

The finest of the fifth century C.E. houses (House C) north of the Acropolis in Athens featured ornamented peristyle courtyards with water installations, while the others had courtyards with wells. These houses, although rather "private" in character, have been interpreted as philosophical schools belonging to the Neoplatonists, in which the directors lived and the students were instructed.[128]

CONCLUSIONS

The three types of ancient gardens presented basically had their origins in royal or religious garden architecture as we know it from the old Egyptian and Near Eastern cultures. While the first and second type of garden were found both in sanctuaries and palaces, the third type is more closely related to residential architecture. The gardens found in a city context also took their models from religious and palatial gardens. Thus, the Greek gymnasia had their origin in shrines for heroes, but were eventually secularized in the form of Roman thermae. The libraries were first found in the palaces of the kings before they became public property in the cities. The close relationship between garden and water was also first evident in the sanctuaries and palaces.

The palaces, which were eventually built by the Hellenistic kings, took their inspiration from the Persian palatial paradeisos, the Egyptian palatial courtyard garden, and the Greek gymnasium garden. These Hellenistic palace gardens again served as inspirations for the rich aristocracy of late republican Italy, as well as for the Roman Emperors and the provincial elites in the imperial period, when they were to build their palaces, rich townhouses, and villas. Thus the monarch, with his palaces, gardens, and luxurious lifestyle, has always inspired an ambitious elite, just as this elite in its turn, served as the model for the bourgeoisie, as we see so clearly in Pompeii. The royal gardens' function as pleasure garden, with carefully planned views and collections of plants, animals, art, and water installations, created a symbol of the prestige of the king. The landscape space needed for this dimension of palace life shaped architectural development.

In late antiquity, the sacred gardens gradually lost their importance with the introduction of Christianity, but the palace gardens kept their role as models for the elite gardens for a long time, at least in Constantinople.

CHAPTER THREE

Plantings

LENA LANDGREN

Written and artistic sources suggest that a tour through an ancient garden gave an aesthetic experience, in part through associations conveyed
by particular plants, their treatments, or their particular arrangements in
relation to other garden features. These plants were chosen with care and
used with deliberation, serving myriad purposes, often simultaneously. An
understanding of the role and management of plants in ancient gardens requires a close reading evidence from texts to archaeobotany, to the culture
and ecologies of a region. The diverse and fragmentary evidence for ancient
plant use cannot yet be distilled across the broad time frame and many cultures of antiquity. The focus of this discussion is on Roman practices, due
to the relative abundance of textual material, the preservation of gardens
and plants in the region of Mt. Vesuvius, and their influence on later garden
history. Based on a study of Latin terms in light of recent archaeological evidence, this article presents exciting new evidence for plants, horticulture, and
gardeners.[1]

If the garden of the emperor Gordianus III, reigning from 238 C.E. to
his death in 244, had ever been laid out, the citizens of Rome certainly
would have been both delighted and impressed. The emperor planned a
public garden in the Campus Martius, in the centre of the city. According
to his biographer:

There are no public works of Gordian now in existence in Rome save a few fountains and baths. And these baths were built for commoners and were therefore correspondingly equipped. He had projected, however, a portico on the Campus Martius, just under the hill, a thousand feet long, intending to erect another of equal length opposite to it with a space of five hundred feet stretching evenly between. In this space there were to be pleasure-parks on both sides, filled with laurel, myrtle, and box-trees, and down the middle a mosaic walk a thousand feet long with short columns and statuettes placed on either side. This was to be a promenade, and at the end there was to be a basilica five hundred feet long. Besides this, he had planned with Timesitheus to erect summer-baths, named after himself, behind the basilica, and to put winter-baths at the entrance to the porticos, in order that the pleasure-parks and porticos might not be without some practical use. But all this is now occupied by the estates and gardens and dwellings of private persons. (Historia Augusta, *Gordianus* 32.6, trans. Loeb)

In this spacious garden, the visitors would have enjoyed evergreen plantings, perhaps shaped into fanciful topiary figures. The choice of laurel, myrtle, and box is not surprising; non-deciduous plants are among the plants most often mentioned by Latin authors when referring to Roman gardens, public as well as private. The mosaic walk would have gleamed in the sun, as well as when wet from rain, and was probably to be laid out in a straight line, judging from other public gardens of Rome. Through its controlled and well-defined space, the garden would have given visitors experience of both art and nature—an experience to which the Romans were accustomed from centuries of other gardens. This garden of Gordianus is the last detailed literary evidence we have on the public garden in Rome, and it reflects a tradition begun in the first centuries B.C.E. that developed over time in ways we are just beginning to explore.

EVIDENCE FOR PLANTS AND PLANT USE

Evidence of plants in public as well as in private gardens of the Roman antiquity is manifold, the description of the gardens of Gordianus III with its evergreens being but one. Accounts of specific gardens with plants and other features are found in Latin literature from the late republic age onward. Pliny the Younger's descriptions of his country estates in the Apennine Mountains (the so-called Tusci) and on the shore outside Rome (Laurentinum) stand out as being particularly detailed when it comes to garden planning and planting.[2] His descriptions of the grounds of his Tuscan villa, with the *xystus* (a terrace) and the *hippodromus* (a horse racing–shaped ground), furnish us with valuable details regarding plants and their disposition. These are enriched by study of the works of his uncle, the Elder Pliny, whose *Natural History* describes more than 80 percent of the plant material attested in texts of his time in Italy and around the Empire.[3] He gives a number of notices on garden plants, their treatments, and importation, as well as inventors of horticultural novelties. The poets Propertius, Ovid, and Martial, among others, also dwell on matters regarding gardens, as do the agricultural writers Columella and Varro. References to public gardens are of special importance, providing some of the scant evidence we possess about this area of landscape architecture. Also significant are various remarks about luxury estates and their formal plantings.

The archaeological record, primarily from Pompeii and environs, provides new evidence of how the plants were arranged in the gardens and of some specific plants known to the Romans.[4] The eruption of Mt. Vesuvius in 79 C.E. created unique conditions for identifying plants that once grew in the gardens. More importantly, the archaeological record also furnishes us with records of plant types (shrub, vine, tree, herbaceous plants) and planting

FIGURE 3.1: Traces of plants and their overall design at the Villa of Poppaea, Oplontis during excavations, 1975. (Courtesy: The Wilhelmina and Stanley Jashemski Trust)

FIGURE 3.2: Garden painting as an extension of garden, House of the Menander (I.10.4), Pompeii. (Courtesy: The Wilhelmina and Stanley Jashemski Trust)

patterns in the form of root cavities from plants. The gardens of the Villa of Poppaea at Oplontis stand out; traces of plants and of how they were integrated into the villa clearly show how they formed part of the overall design of the complex.[5] These features of the Campanian gardens are rarely preserved on garden sites elsewhere. Generally, archaeologists can locate tree pits, buried flower pots, and the shape of planting beds, but rarely the plants' remains or their root cavities.[6]

In addition to the archaeological record, wall paintings, which represent all kinds of plants, are found in abundance in the Campanian houses and elsewhere. They form a genre known as "garden paintings." As representations of the plant material known by the Romans, these paintings are important to the study of Roman garden plants. However, they are complex subjects for botanical study. Wilhelmina Jashemski has noted how some paintings created the illusion of—or an extension of—actual gardens. Recent scholarship analyses them simply as "manipulations of nature by artist and patron,"[7] fantastic creations with less bearing on real gardens.[8] New evidence from the Villa Arianna at ancient Stabiae, buried by Vesuvius, reveals gardens full of plant cavities and fence posts that appear to create garden effects very like the paintings. Kathryn Gleason now suspects that while garden paintings are not of specific gardens, and have agendas of their own, they reflect planting styles and effects sought in actual gardens of the time.[9]

When taken as a whole, the evidence indicates that the Roman garden must have been well planned, its design based on well-defined ideas about how to work with the plant material that was an important element of its composition.

GROWING GARDEN PLANTS

Out of all plants referred to by Latin writers, some twenty-five deciduous trees, evergreens, fruit trees, shrubs, and flowers are referred to as growing in gardens or used in a garden context.[10] In addition, the evidence also shows that plants were employed to express ideas and sentiments through various kinds of manipulation. Literature about the Roman garden indicates manipulation of its plant material in order to change its natural growth and appearance through training and shaping. An example of this is topiary—that is, the cutting and shaping of evergreen plants into geometrical or figurative representations. In addition to such manipulation, the Romans put efforts into various techniques of forcing flowers and fruits to bloom and mature outside the natural season. One of the methods to make plants mature out of season involved exposure to heat. This could be achieved by covering the plants with various materials, such as thin sections of what was called *lapis specularis*[11] or cast glass, in the forms referred to as *vitrum* or *gemma*. Some descriptions certainly suggest constructions similar to greenhouses. These matters were obviously not only of relevance in a didactic horticultural context but seem to be rather more generally known, since not only Pliny the Elder but also the poets dwell on these matters. These interventions, resulting in a change of the natural order of maturing and rate of growth, testify to the strong involvement Romans had in the lives of their gardens. Thus, we become aware of the way the Roman garden and its plants were used as objects of influence.

DESIGNERS AND GARDENERS

Testimonies of the professionals working in the Roman gardens, known as the *topiarii*, help us to put some life into the gardens. From references to the occupational title *topiarius* in epigraphy and literature, we know of Roman gardeners by their names and in some instances also their social status and their places of work.[12] We also get some insight into their daily tasks.

In the literary record, topiarius is referred to eight times between the times of Cicero and that of the legal writer Marcianus in the third century. However, the evidence is unevenly distributed in time; in the period between Cicero and Pliny the Elder, no references are found. Further, the texts mention topiarii only in relation to matters referring to Italy. The dating, however, is more even in the epigraphical record, such as inscriptions in stone, and epitaphs on tombs. Most of the inscriptions come from the first century C.E. Except for one, they are all from the Italian peninsula, and the majority are from Rome.

Of the fifty or so individuals known to us, many are referred to in epitaphs, in which the gardener is commemorated by his relatives or in which he is commemorating a family member himself. Some of these inscriptions refer to gardeners who were members of so-called *collegia*.[13] These were "clubs" or guilds made up of individuals working in various fields in the same household, so-called domestic collegia.[14] In our cases, the gardeners were slaves or freedmen who had been employed in the imperial household or in other prominent families.

In two inscriptions referring to gardeners, apprentices (*discentes*) are mentioned (*Corpus Inscriptionum Latinarum* V 5316 and XIII 5708). In the agricultural sphere, evidence for apprenticeship is scarce. There must have been training in this field, but the testimonies are elusive.[15] This makes the discentes referred to in the area of gardening even more interesting, as they nominally testify to some kind of professional instruction. However, the specific nature of the training evades us.

In connection to the term topiarius it is of interest to discuss two other terms with some bearing, namely *viridia* and *viridarium*, which refer to plant materials and their locality respectively, since the literary and epigraphical testimonies of all the terms show a contemporary emergence in the late republic or early Augustan time.[16]

Even though the terms *viridia* and *viridarium* are scattered in time and place, they introduce us to some principal characteristics of the practice of Roman gardening in the late republic and imperial period. The aforementioned garden of Emperor Gordianus III in Rome is referred to as a viridarium, which gives us a hint as to what kind of structure the term denotes. Unlike *silva*, or wood, for example, viridarium is never used in the Roman literature to indicate a natural plantation. Instead, viridarium seems endowed with more technical and specific connotations than are other terms.

It is obvious from both literature and epigraphy that viridia were present as components in both private and public designed landscapes. In the earliest evidence, the term viridia may refer to greenery in a general way. By the end of the first century C.E., viridia refer specifically to sculpted evergreens. Thus, the development of this word might be understood in terms of a growing complexity in Roman garden art, where special items such as topiary figures played a significant part.

Thus, the common chronology and subject matter regarding the three terms cannot be a pure coincidence. Rather, the formation of a new terminology suggests a specialization and professionalization in the field of gardening and garden design, which is visible at least from the end of the first century B.C.E.

The development in Roman gardening by this time was of great significance. *Ars topiaria*, this art of gardening, made up the foundation for what we meet later in the garden of Gordianus III in Rome, and it has served as the foundation for gardening in the Western tradition ever since.

ARCHITECTURAL USE OF PLANTS

Plants should not be studied as isolated features. In the Roman garden, the work of the topiarius was to employ plants and other elements to create complex design effects and establish the setting of the garden. The following section incorporates an analysis of a close reading of texts and of material remains in order to establish how plants interacted with other components, such as architectural structures and freestanding objects in a design framework.

FIGURE 3.3: Trained ivy at the Villa of Poppaea, Oplontis. (Courtesy: Wilhelmina and Stanley Jashemski Trust)

Plants "Clothing" Walls and Climbing Columns

In a letter to Quintus, dated to 54 B.C.E., Cicero discusses his brother's villa. He states that the topiarius, the gardener

> has so clothed everything with ivy, not only the foundation wall of the villa, but also the spaces between the columns of the portico, that the statues seem to be making garden art, and to be advertising ivy.[17]

Without doubt, the gardener arranges the ivy so as to climb walls and cover them with its green boughs, as in the mural from Oplontis. The choice of the word *convestire* in the letter shows the "clothing" aspect of the plant.[18] Furthermore, ivy is arranged between the columns and in some way also in connection with statues in the portico.[19]

The pictorial as well as the considerable archaeological record shows that foundation walls are prominent parts of the Roman villa complexes.[20] Cicero's description testifies to an incipient trend in Roman garden design, in which garden plants were applied in an architectural fashion. Cicero's description of the use of ivy certainly raised questions of what was built of stone and what was not. The employment of ivy in this way might further be looked upon as a 'play' with different kinds of materials; the soft green leaves of ivy covered the wall, giving it a green appearance. In addition, the choice of an evergreen kept the wall in Quintus' villa constantly green. Thus, the gardener's work could be appreciated throughout the year.

Cicero's letter is the only text describing the application of ivy to cover walls, apart from two short notes by Pliny the Elder, who states that ivy can "damage

FIGURE 3.4: Plantings along wall at the garden of Julius Polybius (IX.13.1–3), Pompeii (Courtesy: Wilhelmina and Stanley Jashemski trust)

tombs and walls," and that the branches of the white ivy "embrace things on either side, this being the case even on walls" (Pliny, *HN*. 16.144, 16.152). These statements testify to the growth, natural or trained, of ivy on walls. However, there are examples of other plants in relation to walls in domestic context. As an illustration of the vitality of the vine, Pliny the Elder records that a single plant could encircle entire country houses and mansions with its shoots and clinging tendrils.[21] Further, we learn that a climbing vine was shadowing Pliny the Younger's so-called *zothecula*, a recess in his garden parlour in the Tuscan villa.[22]

From the discovery of root cavities below walls in Pompeian gardens, a pattern of trained plants has been identified. In the garden of the House of the Chaste Lovers (IX.12.6–7), cavities of roots as well as stakes along the eastern garden wall are identified as traces of trained vine, which once concealed the wall.[23] Furthermore, in the House of C. Julius Polybius (IX.13.1–3), root cavities along the western garden wall are interpreted as remnants of lemon or citrus trees, possibly espaliered because of the large number of nail holes in the wall above the roots.[24]

The ways in which different plants were used in relation to surrounding architecture produced diverse results. Thus, ivy covering a wall in unrelieved green, vines trained up a garden wall, or fruit trees with their branches espaliered against a wall invited different experiences. The architectural impact given by an ivy "cloth" wall has already been commented on. In agricultural cultivation, vines were trained in a variety of ways.[25] If the root cavities are indeed evidence of vines concealing the wall in the House of the Chaste Lovers in Pompeii, we could be dealing with quite another kind of training; apart from providing grapes, the vine may have been taken inside the garden for additional, ornamental use. Further, a fruit tree espaliered against the wall was functional as well as decorative, and the very mastering of the tree could be a topic of conversation. The choice of plant is also significant; fruit trees and vine shed their leaves, resulting in bare branches in wintertime, while the ivy stays green all year round.

The topiarius in the garden of Quintus also made the ivy grow between the columns in the portico. In order to dress these spaces, the plants ought to have been set at the foot of the structures, since ivy requires some kind of support onto which it can fasten its roots.[26] Parallels for plants used as climbers on columns are found in the archaeological record. In the House of the Centenary (IX.8.6) in Pompeii, root cavities were found in front of each column in the peristyle.[27] Further, small root cavities in pots found in the ground in front of nearly every column in the large peristyle garden (59) at Oplontis are believed to indicate climbing plants once growing in the pots. Because of the limited number of climbers available for use in Roman gardens, the Cicero text just discussed has formed the basis for the interpretation that ivy was once climbing the columns.[28] Additionally, columns are found at Oplontis with their lower parts painted with climbing ivy and birds[29] as well as those carved with climbing plants that have some similarity to ivy.[30] At Oplontis, soil finds and artistic representations show similar use of ivy, described by Bettina Bergmann as "multimedia variations" on a horticultural theme.[31] This is a good example of what becomes evident from Bergmann's study on the Oplontis villa; it clearly shows how the villa's architecture, sculpture, wall paintings, and garden plantings fuse into a unified visual arrangement.[32] Variety in media and motif provide the residents and visitors with visual and physical experiences in the villa and its garden. Here the plantings constituted an integrated part in the arrangements. This site furnishes us with many illustrations for the discussion of the use of plants in Roman garden design.

Another use of climbing ivy, in this case not on columns but on trees, is also attested to; climbing ivy "dresses" (vestire) the trunks of the plane trees, "borrowing its green to the trunks," along the farther side of the hippodrome in Pliny the Younger's Tuscan villa (Pliny, *Epistulae* 5.6.32). The trees thereby almost take on the appearance of columns. The application of the various materials creates a green wall surrounding the hippodromus all year round, certainly giving experiences of "green architecture."[33]

Hedges

In the archaeological record, hedges are not ubiquitous, as might be imagined from recreated gardens in books and at archaeological sites. However, there are some examples of design and planting conditions that tell of the existence of hedges. Again, the Oplontis villa furnishes us with examples. Root cavities were found on both sides along the paths in the north garden. The location as well as the size of the cavities makes up the basis for the interpretation of them as remnants of hedges bordering the paths. Unfortunately, traces of any remaining plant material have not been recorded to allow us to know the plant used in the hedge. Based on the size of the cavities, as well as the literary descriptions of Roman authors, a hedge made out of *buxus* is the generally accepted interpretation.[34]

It is reasonable enough to presume that the hedge was not free growing but cut. The nature of hedges in such planned environments as the Oplontis garden includes shaping of the plants. Since the cavities are found in what seems to be a fairly straight line, we can assume it was cut in a linear shape.

The hedges emphasize the order implied by paths and walkways. The hedge-lined paths in the garden certainly once gave an impression of order and control. Trimmed hedges were certainly experienced as structural elements, giving the sensation of defined spaces.

This interpretation also applied to the well-known garden of the Fishbourne villa in Sussex, England. Along a central path in the main garden, trenches were cut down into the ground so as to furnish good planting conditions.[35] These trenches show what the hedge once growing there must have looked like; it was planted and shaped to the geometric pattern indicated by the trenches. The excavators suggest box as a possible plant.[36] Whatever the plant, it must have been cut in the shape of the meander-like trenches.

One of the very few accounts for a plant as hedge is given by Pliny the Elder when describing the cypress. He states that "nowadays the cypress is clipped and made into thick walls."[37] The cypress hedge is here referred to as *paries*, literally "a wall," not being among the ordinary terms for enclosures in a horticultural setting.[38]

The height of hedges is of importance in a garden design. A low hedge, bordering a path, does not give the same impression as a higher hedge, closing off or hiding away a special area. The *ambulatio* in Pliny's Tuscan villa is

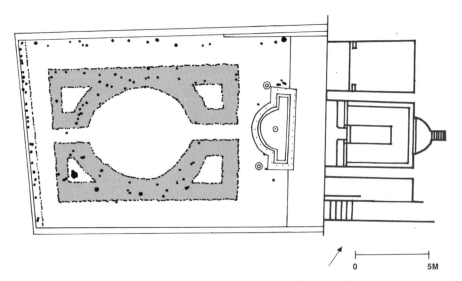

FIGURE 3.5: Plan of the garden at House of the Golden Bracelet, Pompeii. (Courtesy: K. Wilczak after S. Jashemski/Jashemski Trust)

further fenced in by a wall masked by a box hedge, shaped into tiers (Pliny, *Ep.* 5.6.17), suggesting that it reached quite a height (Pliny, *HN.* 16.140). In addition to cypress and box, rosemary is referred to as a hedge plant in Pliny the Younger's Laurentine villa (Pliny, *Ep.* 2.17.14). Myrtle is planted in ordered rows in the gardens of Bassus, referred to by Martial, in an arrangement that might be interpreted as hedges (Mart. 3.58). Thus we see a range of plants available for edging and hedges.

A finding in Pompeii has not been given the attention that it possibly deserves. In the House of the Gold Bracelet (VI, insula occidentalis 42), traces of root cavities indicate a hedge-like use of some plant, making a geometric pattern similar to a knot garden.[39] In post-Roman times, a knot refers to an arrangement of plants, often evergreen species such as box or santolina, shaped to create a more or less intricate knot pattern. Such a design has a purely ornamental aim. The planting pattern in this particular Pompeian garden does not seem complex, but the very fact that the design is more intricate than just a bordering of a garden bed is highly interesting, testifying to an inventive employment of plants.

MANIPULATED PLANTS

The following section delves into the phenomenon of some of the horticultural methods attested in the literature used to cut, restrict growth, and shape to create representations such as the hunting scenes or fleets of ships mentioned by Pliny the Elder, as well as the forming of letters in the name of master and gardener out of box, found in Pliny the Younger's garden. We will also look at the phenomenon of the *chamaeplatanus*, tightly pruned plane trees.

Topiary

The common way to denote figurative topiary in Latin literature is by way of the adjective *tonsilis* (and in one instance *tonsus*), from *tondere*, to clip or shear, together with the object of the cutting, greenery as well as specified plants.[40] Box is the plant most often mentioned in this context, but there are also references to the cypress, myrtle, spruce, and *Iovis barba*, identified with the silver-leafed Jupiter's beard, as are various words denoting "greenery."[41] However, there are also descriptions of topiary without the explicit indication of the action of cutting (Pliny, *Ep.* 5.6.16–17). Pliny the Elder writes that "trimmed shrubberies were invented within the last 80 years by a member of the Equestrian order named C. Matius, a friend of the late Augustus."[42]

Since many phenomena in the *Historia Naturalis* are assigned to various inventors,[43] Pliny need not be taken literally. However, the assignment to an *eques*, the lower of the two aristocratic classes of Rome, as well as the given date, is not altogether unlikely in the light of the general development of garden art and its main players in early imperial times.

A need to protect oneself from wind and sun, or a wish to obtain a fitting frame for the gardens of rulers and nobles, has been proposed as an explanation for the origin of the cut hedge and, by extension, of figurative topiary.[44] Such a usage of suitable plants must certainly have been present in all parts of the ancient world in order to protect or enhance a garden area for various reasons. However, to my knowledge, evidence of figural topiary cuttings does not exist before the Romans. It has been suggested that we "might reasonably assume that others elsewhere had already set a precedent," since from the invention of topiary to the mature examples concerning cypresses recorded by Pliny the Elder, it would not have been possible to develop such a technique without predecessors.[45]

Nevertheless, there are good reasons to believe that the Romans could have invented a practice such as figurative topiary. Chronologically, the literary testimonies to topiary all date to the first century C.E. and beyond, suiting the notion of Pliny on the date of its invention by C. Matius. This is a time both of the widespread importation of plants and ideas, accompanied by great experimentation and invention.

Whatever the truth of the role of the eques C. Matius (*Realencyclopädie der Classischen Altertumswissenschaft* XIV:2 [1930], s.v. "Matius" 2, 2210 [Stein]), also mentioned by Pliny as the inventor of a new apple, the *malus matianus*, as well as the author of fancy cooking books,[46] in the development of topiary,[47] horticultural fascination and knowledge seem to have been present among his fellows, in view of their activities in plant production and in import of foreign plants. Thus, we learn that another Roman eques, a certain Corellius, developed the so-called *Corelliana*, a variety of the chestnut tree (Pliny, *HN.* 17.122). Further, both the azarole (*tubur*) and the jujube (*ziziphus*) were imported into Italy from abroad by the consul in 36 C.E., Sextus Papinius Allenius. Pliny the Elder, who describes the import, also describes how the consul had grown the fruit-trees in his military camp (Pliny, *HN.* 15.47).

Pliny the Elder presents several examples of topiary made out of specified plants. Iovis barba is named as a plant used for topiary, in that it was cut into a round shape (Pliny, *HN.* 16.76). In addition, in Pliny's days the spruce is found in garden design inside the houses because it is easily shaped (Pliny *HN.* 16.40). This is an interesting reference, as spruce does not lend itself well to clipping, but rather to pruning techniques, such as bonzai, in which shapes are achieved both by constraining and trimming the roots as well as the branches, as will be discussed below.

As we already have seen, Pliny the Elder discusses cut cypress as a hedge. He also says that "nowadays the cypress is even made to provide representations of ornamental gardening, arraying hunting scenes or fleets of ships and imitations of real objects."[48] Could this complex scene be interpreted as a wish to exploit the technique to its maximum?

Box is the plant most frequently referred to as being used for topiary. Pliny the Elder states that what he thinks is a cultivated variety of the wild box is evergreen and clipped (Pliny, *HN.* 16.70). In the epigram to Bassus, Martial takes among other things clipped box as an example of the addressee's unfruitful farm (Mart. 3.58).[49]

In the description of the *xystus* in the Tuscan villa, Pliny the Younger mentions various examples of topiary, all made from *buxus*: there are box plants "clipped into different shapes"[50] on the terrace, and below, the topiary arrangements continue with figures of animals as well as box in multiple form.[51] In the *hippodromus*, box is used in several ways, including being clipped into different shapes—even those of letters.[52] That letters were part of topiary shapes is of interest, not only for the cutting itself but because of the fact that the letters reproduced the name of the gardener, here referred to as *artifex*, who through his very name was visible in the garden.

In the *Apologia* of Apuleius, when relating a visit to the house of a sculptor, here called artifex, the narrator mentions that he saw "many geometrical forms of box."[53] These are generally considered to refer to "simple models of circles, squares, triangles, and the like" made out of boxwood.[54] However, it might be that the artifex was creating topiary figures out of the plant. It would certainly be possible for a sculptor to work also in a living material. This is an interesting parallel to how Pliny the Younger refers to his gardener in the passage just mentioned.

The only specified locality where cut hedges and topiary are found, according to the sources, is the private villa garden; there are no references to public locations in connection with topiary. However, the instances in Martial of buxus in the *Porticus Europae* (Mart. 2.14, 3.20) are of relevance when trying to comprehend the design of plantings in public places. Since it was argued that the hedges in the Oplontis garden were cut to match the overall design, it also seems possible that the box plantings in public porticoes in Rome were cut, although we are not told whether these were figurative or not. In such a planned environment, we must certainly expect nature inside to be controlled and shaped. Considering the description of the planned garden by Gordianus III, this is certainly what comes to mind.

There are two ways to make topiary figures. The figure can be cut directly from the plant, so that the bush or tree itself constitutes the body. As the plant grows, it is trimmed and shaped according to the desired stature. Descriptions of the various kinds of topiary shapes from the ancient records—figures, both representative and geometric, as well as letters—are quite informative. In his Tuscan garden, Pliny the Younger refers to eight different topiary shapes, all out of box, among which there were also *multiformae*. Compared with topiary work from the Renaissance, which survives through literary descriptions and in illustrations in the form of woodcuts and paintings,[55] it is highly likely that the ancient descriptions represent some kind of reality. Also, even though we do not know how detailed they were, we must remember that in the Renaissance there were no more tools available than those present in antiquity for cutting plants and trees to topiary shapes.[56] Thus, there were no technical obstacles when it came to topiary shapes.

It is also possible to make topiary figures with a frame, into which plants are placed and then trained and cut so as to achieve the shape of the frame. Of course, a combination of the two methods, such as training part of a figure on top of a hedge with the help of a wire or cane, is plausible.

In Roman garden paintings, mounds of ivy, trained around a stake to form an upright shape, are depicted occasionally. Found in Pompeii, Oplontis, and Prima Porta, these mounds are often represented on the lower register, but in some cases also "within" the painting itself, always in the bottom register. One especially nice representation is found in the House of the Vettii (VI.15.1) in Pompeii, where the stake is clearly shown. These representations might be viewed as a kind of topiary—in modern literature they are occasionally called "topiary mounds."[57] Some mounds are depicted alongside shrubberies with spreading branches, so as to further stress their shaped and controlled form.[58]

Stunted Trees: The Case of Chamaeplatanus

The tree most often referred to in Roman literature is the plane tree, *platanus* (*Platanus orientalis* L.). Many references deal with the shading properties of the tree.[59] This goes well with Pliny the Elder's remark that the plane was imported to Italy only because of its shade (Pliny, *HN.* 12.6). The plane is one of the few tree species referred to as planted in public gardens. Thus, Propertius

comments on the orderly plane trees in Pompey's Portico in Rome, inaugu-
rated in 55 B.C.E. (Prop. 2.32.13). Close by Pompey's portico was the so-called
Hecatostylon, also a portico and also planted with plane trees, according to
Martial (Mart. 3.19.2). Further, references to the platanus as *sterilis*, *vidua*, or
caelebs, widowed, are found among some writers.[60] These references to "widowed" are to be understood as allusions to the fact that the tree, with its big
and shadowing crown, was not used as a support for climbing vines, a method
practiced with other trees.[61] Thus, the tree was of only ornamental and no
practical use and therefore scorned. Horace mentions widowed planes that
will drive out the elm—the tree most often associated with the vine[62]—as a sign
of invasion of luxury (Horace, *Carmina* 2.15.4), and Martial takes widowed
planes as examples of what can be found in villas of his days, characterized by
artificiality and unfruitfulness (Mart. 3.58.3).

Out of twenty-five different plants with the prefix *chamae* or *chame* referred
to in Latin literature, the majority denote shrubs characterised by their small size
or a creeping appearance.[63] Chamaeplatanus, on the other hand, is recognized
as an artificially low-kept variety of the ordinary plane tree (*Platanus orientalis*).
The identification is based on a description in the *Natural History*, which is the
only reference to this specific designation of the phenomenon.[64] In the twelfth
book, Pliny the Elder discusses the plane, including famous exemplars from different parts of the Mediterranean world as well as various odd varieties of the
tree, such as one that never sheds its leaves (Pliny, *HN*. 12.6–12). He continues:

And these monstrosities from abroad still last on in Italy also, in addition, that is, to those which Italy has devised for herself. For there is also
the variety called the *chamaeplatanus*, stunted in height—since we have
discovered the art of producing abortions even in trees, and consequently
even in the tree class we shall have to speak of the unhappy subject of
dwarfs. The *chamaeplatanus* is produced by a method of planting and of
pruning.[65]

The phenomenon as such is described as invented by *ipsa Italia*—that is, the
Romans themselves. Thus, the phenomenon of stunted trees is yet another independent invention of the Romans in the horticultural area, according to Pliny.

The stunted planes are described as *coactae brevitatis*. The use of *cogere*
is of importance to note, since this is the verb used in descriptions of various other instances of forcing—for example, the shaping of cucumbers into a
serpent-like form, referred to by Pliny the Elder (Pliny, *HN*. 19.17).[66] Thus, as
with other plants, the trees were forced to adopt their small size.[67]

The method of stunting is briefly explained by Pliny as gained by "planting as well as by pruning," (*et serere et . . . recidere*). With all certainty, *serere* must be understood in its sense of "planting," not "sowing."[68] Unfortunately, this does not help us to comprehend how the trees were produced. Commenting on what sort of planting could affect the growth, a possible cultivation in containers has been suggested. With such a method, the growth of the tree was diminished, since the walls of the container prevented the roots from expanding.[69] But serere can also in some instances mean "transplanting."[70] Such an interpretation opens up the possibility that Pliny might be referring to root pruning; the trees were "transplanted,"—that is, taken out of the ground on a regular basis, with the aim of cutting the roots.

With the choice of the word *recidere*, Pliny emphasizes the heavy pruning required to shape a fast-growing and vigorous tree such as the plane.[71] The branches of the crown might have been quite extensively pruned, giving the appearance similar to pollarded trees. Recidere was obviously not one of the more normal words for pruning, *deputare* and *putare* being more frequent.[72] From this follows that the kind of pruning denoted was not one of the more commonly practiced, but of another, and rarer, kind.

The plane is naturally a vigorous tree. If only the crown was stunted, the tree still ought to have been quite ample in size. If the pruning included the roots as well, the size of the whole tree was affected more efficiently. However, since detailed evidence is lacking for how the chamaeplatani were produced, no conjectures can be made for the ways in which sizes were achieved.

Two passages in Pliny the Younger's *Tusci* letter are relevant in the context of tree stunting. In describing the hippodromus, Pliny mentions an area where small plane trees, *breves platani*, are growing in the middle of an arrangement of topiary and fruit trees, bringing about a sophisticated mixture of artifice and nature (Pliny, *Ep.* 5.6.35). Pliny is quite brief in his account, but concluding that he is describing the phenomenon of the chamaeplatanus, albeit in less specific words than his uncle's description, seems reasonable. It is indeed the same tree and further, we should note that *brevis* is used by both writers to describe the characteristics of the plane trees.[73]

Early on in the same letter, Pliny writes about "low growing and small forced trees"[74] found on the terrace in front of the house together with topiary figures cut out of box.[75] The trees are not specified as to kind.[76] The forcing action is here emphasized with the use of *manu*, applied to work done by humans in contrast to something "natural."[77] Obviously, Pliny wants to underline that the trees are not naturally small, but made so. Without doubt, here is yet another reference to stunted trees. Gleason suspects these may be the sorts of

FIGURE 3.6: Garden painting with chamaeplatanus at House of the Golden Bracelet, Pompeii. (Line drawing by K. Wilczak)

trees depicted in garden paintings, where they are often the focal point behind an urn or fountain, as in the House of the Golden Bracelet.[78]

According to Grimal, the reason for the invention of these "arbres nains" may have been the ability to grow the same kind of trees as in the grand parks, such as the Portico of Pompey in Rome with its plane trees, but in a much more confined area, such as a private garden.[79] The popularity of the plane tree in Roman gardens is indeed familiar. In the Oplontis villa, root cavities from a row of plane trees were found, arranged in a mounded bed along the eastern side of the north garden,[80] and in the Stabian San Marco villa, the excavations have revealed two rows of root cavities identified as plane trees.[81]

However, it does not seem very plausible that Pliny the Younger, for example, would have incorporated dwarf trees in his big hippodromus for such a motive. With all certainty, there were other reasons for his choice. Thus, the phenomenon of chamaeplatani must certainly be seen as yet another example of a wish to change the natural progression of a tree's growth. If this practice was also applied to other species, it is not known. It might be that it was restricted to this very tree, since pollarded planes have an additional characteristic— that is, a distinctive and sculptural look. Their knotty branches, highly attractive and also visible when dressed in leaves, were certainly recognized. Further, the plane was among the largest trees available; the involvement of man would be even more visible and impressive if this particular species were heavily treated.

CONTRASTIVE EFFECTS IN THE GARDEN

The available evidence indicates that garden plants and trees were arranged so that all their characteristics, including the shapes of leaf and the colours of flowers and fruits, were exploited, obviously often for contrasting effects. Preparation and treatment were of significance; cut (shaped) evergreens and freely growing (not shaped) plants were used together in order to create deliberate excitement and tension. There are also descriptions of how other garden features, such as objects of stone, were used in the same way.

Pliny the Elder discusses varieties of the cultivated myrtle, produced by a topiarius, a gardener. The work of the topiarius resulted in myrtles with different kinds of leaves, broad, small, and thick ones respectively (Pliny, *HN*. 15.122). For some reason, there was a demand for a variety of leaves when it came to myrtle.

To my knowledge, no other popular garden plant is referred to as an object for plant breeding. There are various kinds of box, laurel, and cypress described in Latin literature, but it is only in relation with the myrtle that the topiarius effectuated some kind of breeding. However, the practice of breeding with myrtle suggests that other plants may have been manipulated as well, and certainly fruit trees and other productive plants also used in pleasure gardens were bred. Pliny writes that the famous balsam shrub, from the famous plantations of along the Dead Sea, was propagated into the form of a vine (Pliny, *HN*. 13.67).

If, as we have suggested above, the plants along the paths in the north garden at Oplontis were cut, forming a tight hedge, this arrangement would contrast nicely to the oleander thickets found in various places in close relation to the laid-out paths. Perhaps they were included because they were flowering bushes. It seems certain that they were free growing, since the flowers disappear if the plant is cut. The contrast of the lush oleander, growing freely and flowering in pink, purple, or white against a tightly shaped evergreen hedge may have been intentional, offering a similar effect to garden paintings, in which lush vegetation is held back from the space of the viewer by low fencing.

The xystus area and part of the hippodromus in the Tuscan villa of Pliny the Younger might illustrate a design of contrasting plants, both cut and free growing. The terrace and the nearby bank were planted with figures cut out of box, and the area close by, with acanthus, described as *mollis* and *liquidus* (Pliny, *Ep.* 5.6.16). In the hippodromus, "sinuous" and "winding" acanthus was grown together with cut box in many shapes (Pliny, *Ep.* 5.6.36). The acanthus was grown freely with its moving leaves, while the box was trained and mastered. In this part of the garden, the contrasting was even more apparent with, as it seems, a closer spatial relationship between the two species. With its distinctive leaf of high ornamental quality, the acanthus was one of the very few plants described as *herba topiaria*, probably because of its merits for garden art.[82]

The ornamental value of acanthus leaves was appreciated not only in architecture and other media, but also in garden art. The use of this plant's bold leaves complements our picture of the propagated varieties of myrtle handled by the topiarius, as caused by a demand for various leaf sizes and textures. Leaves were looked upon as a material that could be used for various aims, some purely ornamental in themselves, like the acanthus, but some also to be contrasted with other plants.

In the middle of Pliny's Tuscan hippodromus, with its topiaried box plants, "here and there little obelisks rise intermixed alternately with fruit-trees."[83] There are different interpretations of this passage.[84] From the text itself, it is not possible to decide whether Pliny refers to objects made out of stone and natural trees respectively, or if rather he alludes to topiary plants. In trying to understand the display from a garden design point of view, there are different possibilities. If the *metulae* and *poma* were cut out of box they would mix together with all the other topiary plants and would not stand out, in the way suggested by Pliny. Instead, an arrangement with metulae out of stone and poma being real fruit trees would be more attractive.[85] Man-made objects like the metulae as well as "natural" trees together with topiary would create an exciting design, full of contrasting effects. Additionally, the fact that the trees were not ornamental, like the planes, but were instead fruit-trees might have heightened the contrast between *ars* and *natura*. A further argument that supports this interpretation must be put forward. A passage in Pliny the Elder that attests to the use of items such as marble or stone metulae in a garden context has not been read together with the actual description by his nephew. According to Pliny the Elder, in the *horti Serviliani* in Rome there were, apart from the Greek statues mentioned above, also two turning posts, *campterae*, on either side of a seated Vesta (Pliny, *HN.* 36.25). Pliny uses here *camptera*, which corresponds to *meta* in its sense of turning post in racing courses (*Oxford Latin Dictionary*, s.v. "cam(p)ter," 263). Pliny also informs us that there were two replicas of the *campterae* in the collection of Asinius Pollio in Rome.[86] Thus, it would not be surprising if Pliny chose to put up metulae in his garden, as an allusion to items in famous collections in the capital.[87] There are many examples of how copies of sculptures from public collections were used in private ones with the aim of showing the education and the cultural level of the owner.[88]

If we return to Pliny the Younger and his description of the hippodrome, the contrast theme is further emphasized. Pliny writes: *et in opere urbanissimo subita velut illati ruris imitatio*—that is, he states that there is a sudden rural touch in the middle of the highly urban work (Pliny, *Ep.* 5.6.35). This rustic touch, seemingly represented by *poma*, would not be very clearly expressed if the fruit trees also were cut out of box, but was emphasized with an old and knotty fruit-bearing tree.[89] The stone *metulae* would emphasize the urbanity of the scene, certainly also alluding to the shape of the hippodromus.[90] It might be argued that the contrast would be all the more effective if these were the only examples of stone elements, apart from fountains, in the garden. Finally, Pliny's use of *subita*, sudden, might show the surprising effect of the contrasts, certainly consciously sought for.

CONCLUSION

Conscious design and planning governed the selection and placement of plants in Roman gardens. The formulation of these garden design theories is still unknown; literary sources reveal little; Vitruvius, for example, mentions gardens in passing, such as the *viridarium* behind the Pompey's theatre, but offers no guidance on their design. However, a careful review and analysis of the extant literature on plants and their appearance is bringing into focus the first contours of the working theories employed by Roman designers and gardeners.

Experienced as green architecture, occasionally used in order to create a sensation of defined space by way of tight hedges, garden vegetation was exploited for a three-dimensional design. Further, as a medium of aesthetic appreciation, variety in color, form, and structure of the plants was exploited. Effects were produced through particular combinations: cut plants (topiary) in gardens where there were also free-growing ones are particularly interesting as it bears on the Roman discourse of culture (*cultura*), or art (ars), against nature (natura). It is a discourse that continues today. In other cases, vegetation contrasted and created tensions in regard to sculptures. Box topiary together with stone pillars and fruit trees embodied excitement in the design of a garden, while playing off the contrasts of cultura and natura.

Throughout this study, the intensity of horticultural manipulation of plants has been noted. The examples given of techniques used are both numerous and varied. Some have an air of experimentation, of something tested for the possibility of getting an exciting result rather than a useful product. The fact that all kinds of flora are found as objects of the various methods—in forcing vegetables, flowers, and vines as well as fruit trees and ornamental trees—confirms the broad spectrum of these activities.

It is difficult to understand from the available sources the exact use to which the forced specimens were put in every case. There is, however, information that such items could be gifts, as illustrated by some epigrams by Martial that dealt with gifts given at the Saturnalia feast. The forced plants, whether flowers or vegetables, whether grown in greenhouses or not, and whether planted in pots or not, must have belonged to the garden environment. In particular, a forcing house, made of expensive glass (in one instance denoted *gemma*, literally "jewel"), was not to be hidden away, inconspicuous. We may compare this to the conservatories of later times that made up an integral part of a manor garden.

The obvious interest and activity of the Romans in this area of manipulating the form and forcing the growth of plants are further seen in the claim that some methods were, in fact, invented by Romans. Pliny the Elder's account of the invention of topiary, his naming of an individual, the *eques* C. Matius, as the inventor, and his dating of the event does not have to be taken as historical truth but can well be considered as a proposal for historical truth that would have rested on the general acknowledgement of really good technical capacity in the field. Other possible examples of Roman invention in the areas of horticulture are also found, such as the *chamaeplatani*, stunted plane trees and forcing of plants. These techniques occur in the sources in early imperial times, coevally with Matius's alleged invention.

Thus, a pattern starts to emerge: the evidence seems to indicate that there was a certain period of creativity when several techniques of importance for horticulture had reached a point where they attracted a strong and convergent interest for Roman writers, making them stand out in the literature of the age. These indications point uniformly toward early imperial times as that specific period. Further, it seems clear that prestige and economic value were among the motivating factors behind this trend: this is seen in the examples of greenhouses and expensive gifts cited above. Gardening had developed into a niche in which one could flaunt both one's capacity to invest and one's interest in the latest vogue.

This study has shown how Roman gardens, their design, and the treatments of their plants can be understood in terms of a discourse on ars and natura. Like gardens in all societies, the Roman garden not only mirrored the culture's relationship to nature but actively explored it. Instances of control of natura, the involvement of humans in the natural order of growing things through treatments of plants, made up a crucial part of the Roman garden and its contribution to garden history.

CHAPTER FOUR

Use and Reception

ELIZABETH MACAULAY-LEWIS

Many studies of gardens focus on the original design and intention of the landscape architect or patron. In antiquity, no evidence survives of celebrity garden designers such as Andre La Nôtre or Lancelot "Capability" Brown or of designer-patrons, such as Henry Hoare II of Stourhead or Thomas Jefferson. Cicero praises his brother's unnamed *topiarius*, a gardener or landscape architect, who skillfully designed and managed his brother's garden (*Epistulae ad Quintum fratrem* 3.1.2); Pliny the Younger, too, had a gardener who created animal-shaped box hedges in the gardens of his Tuscan villa.[1] We know the name of the architect and engineer team Severus and Celer, who were responsible for the architectural and landscape design and construction of the *Domus Aurea* (Tacitus, *Annales* 15.40), but little else. There are no surviving treatises about ancient garden design,[2] and few plans can be connected with actual garden sites, and none of these were made prior to the garden's construction. We are left only with the archaeological remains of the gardens themselves—botanical, hydraulic, sculptural, artistic, architectural—and, in certain cases, a rich record of ancient sources and wall paintings from which to reconstruct the designer's aims and the garden's use. While in principle it is possible to identify the original garden design, the archaeological record presents us with a garden as it was used and altered over time.

In the best of our ancient sources, we can see that there were multiple experiences in a single garden, depending upon the individual, and that this experience changed and evolved through time. This essay examines the inter-section between design and use. Both archaeological evidence and the historical record favor this perspective.

In the Greek, Hellenistic, and Roman worlds, two types of gardens, villa or palace gardens and the public park, are particularly well-attested. These types of gardens were intertwined in an ongoing dialogue about public and private, luxury and utility, providing two different but complementary windows into ancient gardens, allowing us to understand the user's obedient or disobedient experience of designed space from classical Athens to late antique Rome. Our preserved sources generally have an embedded political message in this regard and set the stage for modern discussions about the values of gardens and parks.

CIMON'S FARM: OPEN FOR ALL

Throughout antiquity, large farms and estates near or within ancient cities were the main private residences for important figures.[3] The agricultural estate of the wealthy fifth century B.C.E. Athenian general and statesman Cimon is particularly iconic, held up as a model for future aristocrats and rulers by the early imperial Roman author Plutarch, whose work *The Lives* pairs significant figures in history for instructive comparison. Plutarch sets up Cimon, his estate gardens, and their use as an amenity to be shared with the public, in contrast to the gardens of Lucullus, who kept his wealth to himself. The role of the gardens in each case is discussed below.

We gather from Plutarch's description that Cimon's farm was a typical ag-ricultural operation, with fields, olive trees, and perhaps other fruit trees, al-though Cimon himself had certainly become quite wealthy from his exploits in the Eastern kingdoms. Cimon opened his farm, removing its fences, to the poor and needy of Athens, and gave a simple daily dinner to anyone who visited him (*Vitae Parallelae Cimon* 10.1; 10.2).[4] He even allowed the general population to take the best and ripest fruit from his country estates. He also opened his urban residence to the Athenians (Plut. *Vit. Cim.* 10.6).

These actions, by the owner himself, initiated an alternative function for the garden and transformed his farm solely from being a functioning agricultural realm to a political space. As the location for such public dinners, the garden became a space that earned Cimon the gratitude and undoubtedly political support of those who tasted the farm's free bounty. Thus, the "simple" farm became a political tool. The Greek divisions of ancient space into private and public were blurred: Cimon's farm—whatever its original design—became a public garden. Its evolution from a private realm to a public one with overt or semi-overt political overtones connotes a distinction in the use of private estate-cum-garden between Athenian Greeks and Eastern monarchs. The opening of his gardens and fields, as well as his sharing of his crops, marked Cimon as a man of the people, a demagogue to his detractors (Plut. *Vit. Cim.* 10.7). He could not be accused of enjoying private luxury and wealth while fellow Athenian citizens suffered.

From his expeditions in the East, Cimon clearly brought elements of private luxury to the citizens of Athens, notably by planting plane trees in the Agora and a grove of trees (*alsos*) in the Academy, where he also established shady running tracks (Plut. *Vit. Cim.* 13.8). The similarity of this linear form of planting with Xenophon's description of Cyrus the Younger's garden at Sardis is striking, yet the audience receives a very different message from this royal Achaemenid garden (Xenophon, *Oeconomicus* 4.16–20). In the Achaemenid garden, the trees, planted in a *quincunx* pattern, also cast shade. Lysander, the visiting Spartan, expressed surprise at the plantings, so masculine and sensible, and asked Cyrus who was responsible for their layout. Cyrus replied that he had designed the garden and planted the trees himself. Cyrus's garden testified to his potency, power, and wealth; it also was a realm for him and those he invited in. While similar in form and muscularity, Cimon's planting of trees in the Agora provided a benefit for the Athenian community. Plane trees bore no useful fruit, but they provided shade, appropriate in Greek culture for philosophical schools and public spaces, if not for productive agricultural estates and their farmer/soldiers. These trees introduced an element of leisure and luxury into the Agora, giving the citizens a pleasant place to stop and rest from the heat of Athens in the summer. Likewise, Cimon transformed the Academy, which was to become one of Athens' renowned philosophical schools, from a dry, hot location to one with a well-irrigated grove, shady walks, and running tracks. Cimon's selective use of Persian elements—otherwise viewed by the Greeks as luxurious and decadent—created additional uses and afterlives for his farm, the Agora, and the Academy. Although no contemporary Greek descriptions of the Academy survive, Diogenes Laertius's *Lives of the Philosophers*, written in the second century C.E., suggests that trees and walks had become fundamental parts of landscapes of the Academy and Athens' other philosophical schools. Plato reportedly perched in a tree while engaged in philosophical debates in the Academy (Diogenes Laertius 3.7). Polemo, another philosopher, disputed while walking on the Academy's paths (Diog. Laert. 2.130). Artistotle strolled with students in the tree-lined walks of the Lyceum (Diog. Laert. 5.2). Theophrastus, Aristotle's chosen successor, left his gardens and walks to his friends in his will so that they could continue their discussions (Diog. Laet. 5.52–3). Such walks remained popular with the philosophers and the citizens of Athens long after Cimon.

THE GARDENS OF ROME'S HORTI AND VILLAS: DESIGN AND AFTERLIFE IN LATE REPUBLICAN AND EARLY IMPERIAL ROME

The leading men of the late republic and early Empire transformed their *horti*, estates located around the city of Rome, from simple republican villas or agricultural properties to monumental private *villae suburbanae* in the manner of the Hellenistic and Persian palaces encountered in their campaigns. The ancient writers employ horti to explore the impact of imperial wealth, from creating vast realms of private luxury to following traditional republican values in the provision of public amenities,[5] by examining the role of these estates as political stages on which important public events were set or plots were enacted, often to the detriment of the patron. Originating in the second century B.C.E., the horti were known for their innovative architecture and extensive gardens.[6] The general Lucullus set the example for opulent horti as a private retreat from the public life of Rome, where civic and political business was traditionally played out in the forum. Nonetheless, the close proximity of the horti to Rome soon made Lucullus's ideal for behind-the-scenes political intrigues.[7] Unlike Cimon, Lucullus never opened his horti to the public; in this private, luxurious abode, he demonstrated an extravagant lifestyle and dining habits supported and inspired by the cultures of his military conquests in the eastern Mediterranean. His concession to the public was that he opened his extensive libraries to all, even the Greeks (Plutarch, *Vitae Parallelae Lucullus* 42.1–4). While this suggests some sense of republican civic duty, libraries were not used by large parts of the population and did not curry him extra political favor. Later, by contrast, both Julius Caesar and Pompey used their horti to enjoy private luxury, yet provide for public activities in keeping with the republican tradition of using private resources for the public good.

Pompey used his horti on the Campus Martius as a location for staging his political machinations. Here, in 61 B.C.E., he bribed voters in the election of Afranius as consul (Plutarch, *Vitae Parallelae Pompeius* 44.3). This was the first mentioned instance of the *plebs urbana* being invited en masse into a private horti.[8] Pompey, as discussed below, also constructed a series of public works, including a theater and Rome's first public park, the Porticus Pompei, on his private land. Such actions, typical of the rivalry between Julius Caesar and Pompey, were the first indication that these private gardens could have a very active political afterlife in Rome.

Julius Caesar's Horti trans Tiberim was used in a public, political capacity.[9] This horti was his private residence on the far side of the Tiber, in the region now known as Monteverde. Designed as his personal residence, it soon became a political zone, used to greet heads of state and to woo the urban masses. In 46 B.C.E., Caesar held a public feast, the *epulum publicum*, for the plebs urbana to celebrate his Spanish triumph in his horti rather than in a public venue (Valerius Maximus 9.15.1).[10] This innovation was quite remarkable on several levels. While Pompey had bribed voters in his horti, and set aside the Opera Pompeiana for public use, he never hosted another public function within the horti proper (Plut., *Vit. Pomp.* 44). Caesar did not hold back on the meal either; he offered the best wines, Chian and Falernian, to the plebs (Pliny the Elder, *Historia Naturalis* 114.97). Such an action altered the use of Rome's horti from locations where elite rivalries played out into quasi-public spaces where political events transpired. Caesar used this feast to further his support with the plebs, providing him with another power base within the city. He stood in one of the intercolumniations of a portico in his horti and greeted the plebs directly. Caesar was not the only one to capitalize on his generosity for political gain; Herophilus, who pretended to be the grandson of Marius, spoke to the plebs at the same time in the adjacent intercolumniation (Val. Max. 9.15.1).[11] Such actions confirm that Caesar's horti, its gardens, and its architecture were no longer just used by Caesar in a private capacity, but they had become a public space. Whether this is afterlife or an estate that demanded the ongoing efforts of a talented designer is hard to say, but clearly the challenges of political life are expressed in the uses of these horti. Here, for example, Caesar received Cleopatra in 44 B.C.E.[12] By this time, Caesar was the undisputed ruler of Rome, and so it is unsurprising that his residence was used in place of the Roman Forum or other traditional public venues. Yet his residence during his lifetime was essentially private. The political, public afterlife of his Horti trans Tiberim is confirmed by Caesar's final act of leaving his horti to become public land, in a sense making his home the plebs' home.[13]

The horti's original function as the luxurious and private retreats of Rome's elite, used for dining and walking, persisted throughout the imperial era. The horti continued to be built and employed innovative horticultural and architectural forms. Yet from this time onwards, the gardens of these estates were home to official political business as well as darker political machinations. Caligula, for example, also received an embassy from the Alexandrian Jews in the Horti Lamiani in 38 C.E., following the violence between the Greek and Jewish populations of Alexandria.[14] Rather than greeting them in a reception hall, the embassy was shuttled in and out of various porticos, gardens, and other corridors (Philo Judaeus, *Legatio ad Gaium* 359).[15] From Philo's perspective, the legation was not accorded political respect in this manner; however, as Caligula marched them through portico after peristyle after garden, he was demonstrating his power over his surroundings, his ability to modify these surroundings at a whim; by extension, Alexandria and her people were subject to his desires.[16] Clearly, these horti had a political function in addition to being a luxurious residence, full of marble-decked halls and lavish gardens.[17]

Two rather infamous events highlight how potent this political afterlife of Rome's gardens had become by the first century C.E. The first occurred during the reign of Claudius and relates to his wife, Messalina. Not only did she force Valerius Asiaticus to commit suicide so that she could gain control of his horti, in another of the horti, she married her lover, C. Silius, whom she hoped to make emperor in place of Claudius through a mock marriage ceremony (Tac. *Ann.* 11.1.1; 11.27–37; 11.31). Upon learning of her treachery, Claudius sentenced her to death and she, weeping, committed suicide in this horti as well (Tac. *Ann.* 11.37–8). Unsurprisingly, events such as this helped to further the consolidation of horti in imperial hands; as spaces, they were politically too dangerous to be left to private individuals, or even to the wives of emperors.

The second example of a garden in a horti having a bizarre and dark afterlife is the stuff of legends. The Horti Maecenatiani was constructed in the late first century B.C.E. by the emperor Augustus's confidant Maecenas. Built on the Esquiline hill, the complex was filled with impressive and innovative architecture, including the so-called Auditorium, which was built over a section of the republican city walls. This complex featured commanding and uninterrupted views over the Roman countryside toward the Apennines.[18] In addition to this, a tall belvedere was also constructed which looked back over the city. Maecenas was a man known for his patronage of literature and the arts. Such views were a topic of conversation suitable to cultured and learned Maecenas and his guests to discuss and enjoy during their walks in the garden.[19] The tower over the city was reportedly the location where Nero watched the burning of Rome in 64 C.E. (Suetonius, *Nero* 38.2). While scholars debate whether this event actually transpired, viewing Rome while conflagration overwhelmed it was not what one was supposed to do. One was meant to admire a view and to be seen by those within the realm of the view. Here Nero inverted the proper use of the view and a garden, as he would in his Domus Aurea, which was a suburban villa located in the heart of Rome (Tac., *Ann.* 15.42; Suet., *Ner.* 31). By not doing anything to stop the fire but admiring the blaze, Nero affirmed his power and tyranny over the city.

Through their blurring of public and private and their gradual politicization, the horti continued the tradition that began with Cimon's farm. The use of horti for staging public feasts and receiving embassies affirmed that they had other functions in addition to their intended uses as private residences. The extreme examples of Messalina's marriage and suicide and Nero's viewing of the burning of Rome in 64 c.e. demonstrate just how far the use of a garden could deviate from its original design and purpose.

Many of the gardens of Rome's horti were used over the course of numerous centuries, had various owners, and, thus, inevitably had many afterlives as their design, use, and function changed with the times. Not all the afterlives and uses of ancient gardens were political; sometimes the design of a garden and the owner's perception or use of a garden could vary. The divergence between garden design and the conceptualization of a garden and the reality of a garden can also be seen in the rural villa gardens of republican and imperial Rome. The writings of certain authors, such as the poet Horace, portray their villas and gardens as belonging to a life of simple rural *otium*, or leisure, rather than luxury (Pliny *HN* 19.52; 19.53–5). Horace, whose work was patronized by the statesman Maecenas, wrote in the late republic and early empire. A theme that dominated Horace's writing and that was extremely popular with many Roman writers was the contrast between rural and urban life.[20] Discussed at length in his poetry, Horace paints a specific picture of his Sabine villa and its garden,[21] as one of rural simplicity, in sharp contrast with the residences of many of his contemporaries.[22]

In Satire 2.6, Horace describes his Sabine residence, emphasizing that it is not an extensive estate, but a simple one with a garden, a natural spring, and woodlands nearby. He does not desire more but only hopes to enjoy such blessings for the rest of his life. This satire also tells the tale of the town and country mice; the country mouse that welcomed his city cousin to the serenity of his humble home and shared his dried raisin and bacon. When the country mouse visited his city cousin, the food and nibbles from the tables of the wealthy were far richer, but hounds chased them from the couches. The country mouse, like Horace, says that he prefers the simplicity and safety of the country over the chaos and hazards of the city.

In *Ode* 2.18, Horace compares his Sabine residence to the luxurious estate of some unknown rival. His villa is unlike that of his unnamed nemesis; it lacks ivory (*ebur*) and golden panels (*aurum*), and it has no beams of Hymettian marble that rest on marble columns from distant Africa (*non trabes Hymettiae / premunt columnas ultima recisas Africa*); he even states explicitly that he is not the owner of a palace (*regiam*). His rival, on the verge of death, has not built a tomb, but rather has continued to expand his residence on the coast of Baiae out into the sea (2.18.–20), and it greedily devours the lands of his neighbors, driving them out of their homes (2.23–28). By contrast, Horace, like his Sabine estate, is humble. Horace describes himself as poor (*pauper*) but faithful (*fides*), ingenious (*ingeniosus*), and one asks the gods and his powerful friends for nothing (*nihil supra /deos lacesso nec potentem amicum / largiora flagito*, 2.11–13). His simple Sabine residence is enough for him (*satis beatus unicis Sabinis*, 2.14). *Ode* 3.1 continues this theme; again, Horace's Sabine residence and the lifestyle associated with it are compared to that of an affluent, social, and acquisitive man. Horace, by contrast, does not hunger for more than what he has. He reiterates that he is pleased with his Sabine farm; he does not need the burden of Phrygian or purple marble— which might be a reference to porphyry[23]—nor the challenge of erecting a modern atrium (3.1.41–48).

While his garden (*hortus*) is only directly mentioned in Satire 2.6, it is clear that like the architecture of his villa, his garden is simple. Several of his other poems describe the larger landscape, praising it for its natural spring, the *fons Bandusia*, woodlands, idyllically grazing sheep and cattle, and shy wolves (*Epistulae* 1.16; *Odes* 1.22; 2.13; 2.17; 3.4; 3.8; 3.13; 3.18; 3.23; 3.29). These descriptions further Horace's vision of his villa as a simple, rustic abode. Scholars, aware of his descriptions, have long located Horace's villa in the Sabine hills to the east of Rome in Lazio. Based upon the close correlation between the site and location of various landmarks in the surrounding landscape, the most likely candidate is the villa located near Licenza.[24] Horace does not discuss the specifics, but describes at great length the natural topographic and the rustic setting of his Sabine villa. The villa was ideally located in the landscape between several hills to provide it with a spectacular setting that created specific views from the garden to the north and the south for its owner, marking it out as a "view villa," popular in the first centuries B.C.E. and C.E.[25]

The results of archaeological excavation challenge the image of rural simplicity presented by Horace in his poetry. While the visible remains are now known to be of a rebuilding of the first century C.E., archaeologists[26] have located first-century B.C.E. levels of architecture and gardens.[27]

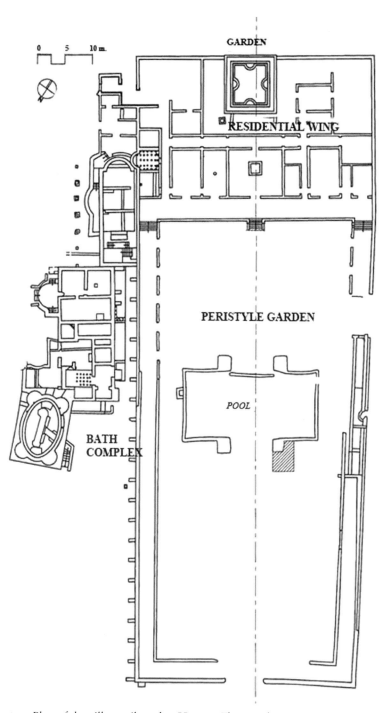

FIGURE 4.1: Plan of the villa attributed to Horace; Flavian phase. (Courtesy: K. Gleason)

In reality, his villa was carefully placed to take advantage of the natural contours of the land.[28] It is quite possible that gardens, in addition to those located within the villa, might have been created around the villa to allow the kind of visual experiences he describes in his poems.[29] Preliminary archaeological evidence and the position of the villa indicate that Horace's simple villa and garden were probably not as unassuming as his writings suggest.

The villa was constructed on an interesting site, a kind of saddle between two steep hills on the east and west, dropping down into valleys on the north and south. This dramatic topography left a limited precinct for the architecture of the residence. While we cannot fully reconstruct the early plan, the distribution of remains suggests that the building and associated gardens probably occupied its full extent. While a building of this size is not among the more extravagant known from this period, neither can it be placed among the more modest residences preserved at Pompeii, for example.

Horace's garden encapsulates the many lives and experiences that a single garden could generate. First, there is Horace's perception of his garden and villa as simple, rustic structures far removed from the grandeur of many other elite residences. His villa was less ostentatious than the most grand and luxurious villas known from the Bay of Naples or Rome's horti, but it was not the lowly farm that Horace presents. It had an atrium, was well positioned in the landscape, and had a large garden that was not used for agricultural purposes. Horace's understanding or presentation of his garden and villa as a simple place allowed him to have a specific experience of his garden as a rural retreat, even if the remains of the estate do not confirm what he envisaged.

In addition to the poetic afterlife of Horace's garden, the garden itself had another afterlife of its own. Ancient gardens, like modern gardens, were often reinvented as owners changed and fashions evolved. Horace left his garden to Augustus, who came into possession of so many properties that it appears he did not make use of this one. However, Bernard Frischer theorizes that the site once again came to life under the patronage of the Flavians, whose ancestral lands were in this region. Water pipes with the name of Ti. Claudius Burrus, the father of Domitian's assassin, may connect the site with an owner known to have been a patron of poets himself.[30] Perhaps the home of Horace had particular appeal. The *quadriporticus* garden at Horace's Villa was remodelled according to the horticultural and architectural tastes of the Flavian age (late first century C.E.). The level of the original garden was raised, and there were new plantings, attested by the presence of purpose-made planting pots and an amphora reused as a planter.[31] A central walk,

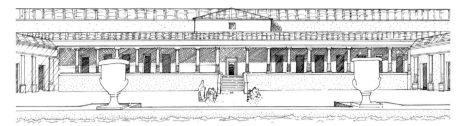

FIGURE 4.2: The peristyle of Horace's Villa. Perspective from the central pool look-ing north along the central axis of the garden, lined with potted plants and statuary. The distant hill at Civitella is possibly framed through the doorways of the *domus*. (Courtesy: K. Gleason and E. Clemence Chan)

leading from the residence down into the garden, was probably added at this point, and it may have been bordered by a light wooden or reed fence or feature.[32] The garden was laid out in axial arrangement,[33] aligned to take advantage of views of the nearby hills, but further work is required to flesh out further details.[34]

The garden clearly enjoyed another life under these new owners who re-designed the garden to suit their needs—whether this was enjoying looking at the garden from the residence, strolling in the porticos or in the garden itself, or looking out over the very landmarks on the hills described by Horace himself.

THE PUBLIC PARKS OF ANCIENT ROME

Since the foundation of Rome, private gardens were a fundamental, but—the sources would have us believe—modest aspect of Roman life.[35] During the triumvirate of Julius Caesar, Pompeius Magnus (Pompey the Great), and Marcus Licinius Crassus, Pompey took a very different approach to his horti from that discussed for Julius Caesar above. He gave large areas of his horti over to public use during his lifetime in his bid to gain public support, follow-ing the republican tradition of private wealth benefitting the public good. With the erection of the Porticus Pompei as his victory monument in the mid-first century B.C.E. on his private land, public parks became an important feature of Rome's urban landscape.

The Porticus Pompei offers an unusually rich combination of archaeo-logical, art historical, and literary evidence for examining the afterlife of a design. Completed in 55 B.C.E., the Porticus Pompei was Rome's first public park[36] and a key element of the Opera Pompeiana, a series of public works and parks, which included a theatre and temple to Venus Victrix, on the Campus

Martius.[37] The Porticus Pompei, its art collections, plants, and design represented and celebrated the power and glory Pompey the Great had acquired in the East. Study of these elements helps us to establish the intentions of Pompey and his designer and the uses that they envisioned for the complex. At the same time, the poetry of Catullus, Ovid, Martial, and Propertius discuss the use of public porticos and gardens in Rome and suggest that many of the highly complex and politically charged messages of the complex were a bit too highbrow for some of the clientele. While it is problematic to base our interpretation of the use of the Porticus Pompei and Rome's other public parks on the poets, there seems to be enough repetition in their poetry and stories to suggest several common experiences in Rome's public parks, in addition to those intended by Pompey.

In the Porticus Pompei, Pompey utilized plants and a curated program of sculpture by artists from Pergamon, the cult of Venus, as well as the architecture and design of the portico to advertise his eastern successes and promote his political ambitions.[38] The central space of the portico was a *nemus duplex* (Martial 2.14.10), double grove of laurel, dedicated to Venus Victrix, Pompey's protector and the goddess of gardens.[39] The laurel grove, which was the symbol of victory, was presumably a constant reminder

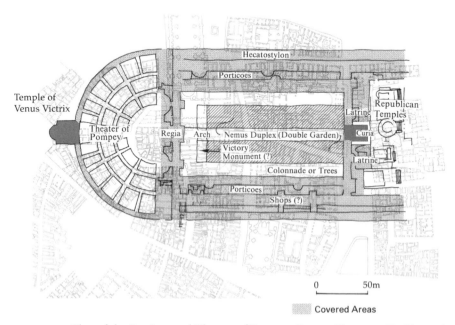

FIGURE 4.3: Plan of the Porticus and Theater of Pompey, Rome. (Courtesy: K. Gleason)

of Pompey's military feats. The rows of towering plane trees (Propertius 2.32.13) planted along the central axis that culminated in the theater-temple complex dedicated to Venus Victrix recalled, in Gleason's words, "the even ranks of troops or the procession of the military triumph."[40] This military emphasis and Venus Victrix's support of Pompey were also reinforced by the art of the complex, discussed below, and the visual relationship between the theatre and the garden.

The Romans enjoyed this potent garden en masse as a locus of leisure, giving it a second intended use. The fountains in the garden, as well as the plantings, especially the plane trees, and the works of art made this space extremely pleasant. Plane trees bore neither edible fruits nor useful wood products and so were considered luxurious by conservative philosophers, but they did provide outstanding shade for those in the garden (Pliny *HN* 12.3.4). The ornamental garden and water features, coupled with the outstanding sculptural and painting collection, made this complex an ideal location for leisured walking. At least six semi-circular and rectangle *exedrae* on the northern, eastern, and southern sides of the complex probably allowed for attractive sculptural displays, and served as locations where one could pause, rest, and perhaps sit.

Many of Rome's citizens went to stroll in the porticos to relax and enjoy the shade and tranquility of this garden and others on the Campus Martius. The first-century C.E. poet Martial chided Canius Rufus, a Roman of independent means, for misusing his *otium*. Rather than writing a history or translating works from the Greek, the lazy, dissolute Canius Rufus spent his day strolling slothfully in the wide colonnades of the Porticus Argonautarum or walking or sitting carefree in the Porticus Europae (Martial 3.20.10–14). One can imagine him ambling from the shade of one portico and alley of trees to another when he grew bored. His strolling is not an exceptional activity. The Saepta Iulia, also located in Rome's Campus Martius, had originally served as a voting precinct, but gradually became a location for leisure activities, including browsing, strolling, and looking at outstanding pieces of art (Pliny *HN* 36.29; Mart. 2.14.6).[41]

One wonders if Canius Rufus and other gentlemen of leisure thought about the politicized nature of the parks and porticos in which they strolled, or were they also just content to walk in such pleasant spaces, ignoring one of the most important aspects of the design? Many of the ancient authors take considerable interest in which works of art were displayed, suggesting that these works were important. These objects, taken from the east, were a testament to the military achievements of Rome and her cultural equality, if not superiority to Greece. The Porticus Pompei was host to an elaborate display of politicized art, selected from Pompey's spoils from the East: female representations of the fourteen eastern nations that he had defeated (Pliny, *HN* 36.41; Suet., *Ner.* 46).[42] Another sculptural series represented the founders of the Hellenistic dynasties.[43] Sculptures of famous Greek women, poets, and *hetairai* were also present (Pliny *HN* 7.34).[44] Pompey's inclusion of a painting of Alexander the Great also more overtly advanced a model of Hellenistic kingship in the portico (Pliny *HN* 35.132).[45] The gardens showcased the cultural treasures of Asia, which Rome's military superiority, and specifically Pompey, had rescued and preserved.[46] Through these works of art, especially those that alluded to or were of eastern monarchs and Alexander the Great, Pompey presented a cultural inspiration for Rome and a form of government—monarchy.[47] While many visitors to the park may have been aware of these lofty allusions, others were not.

The inclusion of the *hetairai*, the famed courtesans of the Greek world, inadvertently alluded to another popular use of Rome's public parks: sex and love. The famous first-century B.C.E. poet Catullus had a run in with several saucy prostitutes in the Porticus Pompei in poem 55 when he was searching for his friend Camerius (Catullus 55.1–12).[48] Bemoaning that he could not find his friend anywhere in Rome, the Campus Martius, or the Circus Flaminius, he stopped in the portico of Pompey and asked the prostitutes if they have seen Camerius (Catull. 55.1–10). They responded with taunts, and one of the more racy ladies exposed her breasts to Catullus, joking that Catullus will find Camerius here among her nipples (Catull. 55.10–12). This entertaining passage highlights an afterlife of the portico that Pompey probably did not intend: the use of the portico as place for soliciting prostitutes. A Roman could go here, or, no doubt, to another one of the porticos on the Campus Martius, the heart of Rome's leisure activities,[49] in search of sex, rather than to be educated by the political art, gardens, and architecture of each portico. This afterlife began almost as soon as the park was created, suggesting an early divergence between intent and use.

One did not only go in search of politics and sex in the porticos; true love was also to be found here as one strolled.[50] Ovid, the famous Augustan poet wrote about lovers strolling—specifically women looking for new lovers—in Rome's porticos. Ovid mentions the Porticus Pompei, Porticus Octaviae, Porticus Liviae, and Porticus of the Danaids, associated with the Temple of Apollo on the Palatine, as locations where women often strolled, seeking new paramours (Ovid, *Amores* 2.2.3–4; *Ars amatoria* 1.67–74; *Tristia* 2.1.285–6).

Ovid even warns jilted lovers to avoid the places where they might find their former lovers walking seductively (*Remedia amoris* 627–8). The shade of the porticos and tree-lined alleys, skillfully designed to evoke military triumph, were also perfectly suited to a romantic interlude. When one was free from work, one could stroll in one of Rome's spacious public porticos to find a new lover (Ov., *Ars am.* 1.491–2). The Roman garden also belonged to the realm of Venus, and this garden in particular was in the protection of Venus (Pliny, *HN* 19.50). Thus, it is unsurprising that this garden had associations of sex and love. Rome's public parks were spaces where the sexes could mix and different social classes interacted; it offered freedom and a chance to break some of Rome's strict social rules.

Propertius, a first century B.C.E. poet, often wrote on similar topics and specifically about his lover Cynthia and her journeys through Rome's public porticos. In his poem 2.23, he recalls following Cynthia and trying to please her. Propertius reports that he used slaves to pass messages to his mistress to find out which portico or park she was walking in that day (Prop. 2.23.3–6). This passage confirms that Cynthia, a woman of leisure, spent her time in the public porticos of Rome. Here she could be found walking or perhaps sitting. The wide range of evocative works of art in the Porticus Pompei brought the empire home to Rome. Propertius urges Cynthia to return home in his poem 2.32 since she can see everything the world has to offer here and be with him. So even the wide-ranging subject of the works, which many visitors to the Porticus Pompei ignored, were not lost on all.

It is interesting to note that a slave was sent to find her and convey Propertius's message. This episode also suggests another experience of the garden. The slave does not have time to stroll leisurely in the tree-lined avenues or the spacious colonnades or admire the works of art; rather he was there on business. One can imagine leisurely strollers accompanied by or followed by slaves, who scurried about attending to the needs of their owners.

In addition to strolling for leisure, window-shopping, and picking up lovers or prostitutes, walking in the porticos was a way to find a dinner invitation. Dining was an important social ritual, especially for elite Romans;[51] it was a way of forming social alliances and conducting business, as well as relaxing and socializing.[52] Martial's scathing poem 2.14 recalls the tale of a social parasite, Selius, who desperately sought a dinner invitation in the public porticos on the Campus Martius in Flavian Rome.[53] In his quest to avoid dining at home, he visited the Porticus Melaegri and the Porticus Europae, which may have actually been the Porticus Vipsania,[54] all in search of a dinner invitation.

He then visited the Saepta, as Martial mockingly reports, to see if the son of Philyra was there (Mart. 2.14.5–6). The son of Philyra was not an individual but rather Chiron the Centaur, a statue of which was on display in the Saepta. This fun little jab hints that Selius in his mad dash to find an invitation has completely ignored not just the political works of art, but all works of art. For him, the use and experience of Rome's public parks had a social purpose; it was closely related to his social status, and his attempts to find an invitation demonstrated the importance of dining in Roman society. Since his visit to the Saepta was unsuccessful, he then headed off to Porticus Argonautarum, determined as ever to find a dinner invitation. He then visited the Temple of Isis and the Hecatostylon; not seeing anyone hanging about who would invite him to supper, he then made for the Porticus Pompei (Mart. 2.14.9–10). The whole poem suggested that there were people walking or hanging out in the porticos, their gardens, and exedrae, engaged in a variety of social activities.[55] Since Selius failed to find any invitations in the public parks, he departed for the baths, a sensible idea since many Romans went bathing before dining.[56] However, again these visits were unsuccessful and so he returned to the Porticus Vipsania to renew his search there (Mart. 2.14.14–18); the poem concluded with Martial mocking Selius and suggesting that he ask some of the personified art for a dinner invitation (Mart. 2.14.14–18). This witty poem underscores another experience or afterlife of the Roman public park. Selius uses Rome's public parks as places to seek dinner invitations, a place of social networking; he misses the political, artistic, and even pleasurable experiences of the gardens.

While Pompey's lofty aspirations of education and political persuasion were lost on many of those who used his portico as a location of leisure, the sophisticated political meanings and aims of the complex did not necessarily have to influence Rome's population directly for the space to be politically effective. Rather, the park as a public amenity cultivated support from Rome's masses, making Pompey the bringer of luxury and leisure to all and currying favor with the mob that often played a key role in Rome's politics. This use or afterlife was probably intended from the earliest days of this complex. While the bulk of Rome's urban populace did not focus on the militaristic and political ideologies embodied in the art, plants, and architecture of the complex, the leading politicians of Pompey's day and of future generations understood his political ideas and aims clearly. Pompey was locked in a battle for control of the political center of Rome with his archrival Julius Caesar. By constructing a theater-temple and grove to Venus, Pompey attempted to monopolize her publicly and win her away from Caesar, who also claimed her as a patron goddess and as an ancestor. Pompey politicized his portico by placing a *curia*, or senate house, within his portico: architecturally, the senate had come to him. As Kathryn Gleason observed, "His aims with the complex appear more ambitious: the unified form of the garden and buildings makes a powerful reference to Italic *fora*, suggesting a politically aggressive attempt to shift the focus of the city west from the Forum Romanum."[57] The senate began to use the curia as the regular location for its meetings, as the curia in the Roman Forum was under construction. Pompey attempted to realign Roman political power around his agenda, shifting the political landscape of Rome westward. It is clear that the elite of Rome understood this, including Caesar himself. In 54 B.C.E., Julius Caesar begun to purchase land for the construction on his own forum, later known as the Forum Iulium, which was to border the Forum Romanum (Cicero, *Epistulae ad Atticum* 4.16.9).[58] This building project, beginning a year after the completion of Pompey's portico-theater complex, seems a direct response to Pompey's actions. Furthermore, the political nature of the Porticus Pompei was confirmed by the infamous act that occurred within the complex. On the Ides of March 44 B.C.E., Caesar was murdered at the foot of Pompey's statue in the *porticus* (Cicero, *De divinatione* 2.23; Suetonius, *Divus Iulius* 88; Plutarch, *Vitae Parallelae Caesar* 66). One can imagine the conspirators awaiting Caesar in the garden just before the fateful moment, knives tucked away in togas and ready to be drawn.[59] While the public may have ignored the original, political overtones of the park, they were certainly not lost on the leading Romans of the late republic.

Augustus, Caesar's adopted son, avenged his father and in doing so became Rome's first emperor. His reign, lasting from 31 B.C.E. to 14 C.E., saw the transformation of Rome, her temples, civic buildings, and spaces from places that expressed the political ambitions of competing generals to one of peace and the security of Augustus's reign. These projects included "demolition" work on the Porticus Pompei (Suetonius, *Divus Augustus* 31). Augustus's alterations to the complex acknowledged the political power inherent in design and art of the portico. He erected a permanent *scaenae frons* that blocked the central axis, thereby destroying the powerful visual line to the temple of Venus Victrix.[60] The monumental statue of Pompey was removed from the curia, and the senate house was transformed into a latrine (Dio Cassius 47.19.1). Augustus confirmed the political nature of the garden by modifying the garden and architectural features to make the design of the complex less overtly political and militaristic and more about his own agenda (Suet., *Aug.* 31).

FIGURE 4.4: Perspective along the central axis from the senate house to the temple of Venus Victrix atop the theater, assuming a temporary (though elaborate) stage building. Elements depicted are those known from literary sources and the Forma Urbis Romae. (Courtesy: L. Cockerham Catalano)

FIGURE 4.5: The view along the central axis from the senate house to the temple of Venus Victrix atop the theater, after the construction of a permanent stage building by Augustus. The gardens would have been elaborately furnished. (Courtesy: L. Cockerham Catalano)

The life of the complex extended for generations. Domitian restored it after a fire in 80 C.E.; at this point, the grove may have been replaced with a roofed colonnade, one interpretation of the symbols on the Severan Marble Plan, the Forma Urbis Romae.[61] Such a renovation would have profoundly changed the experience of the space and begun its transformation from a public open space to the residential street it became by late antiquity (Scriptores Historiae Augustae, *Carinus* 19; *Corpus Inscriptionum Latinarum* 6.25–256 (= *Inscriptiones latinae Selectae* 621–22); Chronography of 354 C.E. 148: *porticus II*). Clearly, the garden, or at least the use of the space for promenades, continued into the late third and early fourth century and many of Rome's other porticos were also still in use until this period or even later.[62] Walking also remained a popular leisure activity into late antiquity,[63] so it is likely that the use of parks for walking remained, even if the original political agendas of these spaces were lost on later audiences.

The example of Pompey's porticus-theater complex and Rome's other public parks not only reminds us of the afterlives of public spaces, but also of our own habit of overly simple categorization. We tend to see specific buildings or spaces as needing to have one defined use: a theatre for theatrical events, a temple for religious services, and so on. But in the Roman world, these boundaries were not nearly as well defined or as rigid as scholars sometimes think. The spatial design and artistic program of the porticus did reflect Pompey's political achievements, but it was also a sacred precinct with temples, an art museum, a place for theatergoers to take shelter in the rain or to clear one's eyes from air pollutants, as well as an extremely pleasant park with ambulatories and porticos for walking and exedrae for sitting, whether for business or to find an invitation to dinner. The works of art,[64] decorative materials, plantings, and water features of the portico created an atmosphere of delight (*amoenitas*) for both business and leisure, enjoyed by Romans.[65] Rome's other public parks, for example—the Porticus Liviae and the landscape setting for the Mausoleum of Augustus—also were highly politicized spaces where the senate could meet or religious activities could take place, and whose elements both conveyed Augustus' political agenda and also made these public parks the *loci* of leisure in the city of Rome.[66]

CONCLUSION

In garden history, design and use are often seen as two divergent approaches, in conflict with each other. The palatial and elite gardens of ancient Greece and Rome demonstrate different values around public and private, luxury and utility, and the expression of civic values. The forms of garden design, seen commonly across these gardens over time—colonnades, water displays, plants, and art—are imbued with specific meanings that are different over time, gleaned from combined study of the original forms and intentions together with evidence of their subsequent use. Only when this combination of form and use are studied over time as complementary can the specific cultural history of a garden be understood.

CHAPTER FIVE

Meaning

KATHARINE T. VON STACKELBERG

*And the Lord God formed man of the dust of the ground, and breathed
into his nostrils the breath of life; and man became a living soul. And the
Lord God planted a garden eastward in Eden.*

—Genesis 2:7

Where did gardens start? When? Most importantly, why? In the Judaeo-
Christian tradition, the Garden of Eden marks the beginning of human history.
This garden is the first meaningful place to be associated with human activity;
language, sex, and knowledge are all rooted here. The planting of the garden
is not an arbitrary quirk of Biblical tradition; it reflects and transmits a specific
set of cultural meanings. Yet how did meaning accrete to gardens, and why?
Students of garden history interested in the material origins and antecedents of
ancient gardens find plentiful evidence for their development in the art, archaeology, and literature of the ancient Mediterranean. Yet the process whereby
the ancient garden grew to be more than the sum of its parts, from a source
of agricultural surplus to a medium for cultural communication, is less readily
determined.

Garden histories of the nineteenth and twentieth centuries traced a linear progression from East to West, via a series of conquests.[1] This model articulated the cultural dynamics of conquest as a process in which the rude
conquerors inevitably adopted civilized customs of the conquered. This is

a well-established trope found in antiquity from Herodotus to Horace.[2] Although war was an important vector for cultural exchange, considering the garden itself as a trophy passed from the Assyrians to the Persians, the Greeks to the Romans, misrepresents the evolution of garden meaning. Better, perhaps, to consider a grain of pollen as synecdochical for the emergence and evolution of garden meaning. Just as the hybrid results of pollination may in turn fertilize the parent plant, so the garden's evolution of a complex and multilayered set of meanings represents a dialogue between cultures of the ancient Mediterranean.

The first intimation of such a dialogue can be detected in Mesopotamia, Egypt, and the Aegean during the Bronze Age. The period from the third to second millennia B.C.E. was one of sustained interaction through trade, diplomacy, and military campaigns. It is during this exchange of ideas and artifacts that gardens emerge as distinctly meaningful spaces. The emergence of garden meaning developed in tandem with its process of evolution. To create a garden, a space must be cultivated, a labor-intensive and time-consuming activity. An enclosure is subsequently erected to deter pests; this visually segregates the area under cultivation from the surrounding landscape. Since the contents of the space are valuable, desirable, and perishable, they are often best guarded by being in close proximity to an inhabited space. A garden is therefore the product of a cultivated space, distinguished from the surrounding landscape by a visual indication of spatial transition, that is contiguous to, or in the vicinity of, a man-made structure. Each stage in this process of development from field or grove to garden transmits new levels of meaning to the garden.

SAFETY, SEPARATION, HABITATION

The initial accretion of meaning begins with the transition from surrounding landscape to discrete space. Our earliest evidence for this process of spatial segregation is from a Sumerian hymn, the *Lugale*, recounting the deeds of the hero Ninurta.[3] In one episode, the fresh water of the earth, instead of flowing into the Tigris and watering the fields, flows uselessly into the *kur*. Written with a sign that has its roots in the pictograph for mountain, kur (or *q'ur*) signifies a wilderness or inimical land.[4] Ninurta's dealings with the kur signify a re-categorization of landscape space, a moment of transition from wilderness to civilization. The hero enters the kur, conquers the monstrous Asag, and piles the stones of the kur into mountains that enclose Sumer. Blocked by this dam, the waters return to their regular courses, irrigating farms, and creating gardens and groves.[5] Finally, Ninurta blesses the artificial mountain in the kur:

> Its valleys shall be verdant with vegetation for you,
> Its slopes shall produce honey and wine for you,
> Shall produce for you cedar, cypress, *zabalum*-trees[6] and boxwood on its
>   terraces,
> Shall be adorned with fruit for you like a garden.[7]

The Sumerian word for garden is $kiri_6$, a combination of the noun *ki* (place) and the verb ru_5 (to send forth shoots, buds, or blossoms). The Sumerian $kiri_6$ was probably the root of the Assyrian *kirû* (garden, grove, or tree plantation) and *kirimāhu* (pleasure garden). Phonetic closeness and semantic associations suggest a relationship between the Assyrian *kirû* and the Hebrew *kar* (pasture, enclosed pasture), *karmel* (plantation), and *kerem* (vineyard), all of which derive from the root verb *khr*, "to dig."[8] From its origin as a wild and inimical space, the kur is transformed into a useful, fruitful, and secure place for humanity.

The import of Ninuta's *ur*-garden lies in its concretization of his suprahuman ability to overcome chaos and create a safe habitat for his people. Gardening and the creation of gardens subsequently became a subject of royal encomia among cultures of the ancient Near East (see p. XX). Related Biblical tradition also situated human existence in a protected garden space away from the surrounding wilderness (Gen. 2:7). Yet although the early garden is secure, the process of separation, cultivation, and re-categorization that create it also mark it indelibly as "other" space. The garden is familiar in that it is formed from the surrounding local landscape, but its difference from that landscape makes it also alien. It is related, but not integrated. This "otherness" is reflected in the earliest pictorial representations of garden space from frescoes of Minoan Crete and Thera.

ALIEN TERRITORIES, INDIVIDUAL POWER

Landscape frescoes of the Bronze Age Aegean depicting animals frolicking in stylized mountain or river landscapes collectively span a period from 1700 B.C.E. to 1450 B.C.E.[9] Although most of these scenes appear to represent the local habitat, with particular emphasis on lily[10] and crocus, both the Miniature

Frieze from the West House in Akrotiri on Thera and the Birds and Monkeys Frieze from the House of the Frescoes at Knossos on Crete depict landscapes that disaccord with their native environment. The Miniature Frieze depicts a combination of Orientalizing elements and non-native plant species as deer, cats, ducks, and griffins move among palms and papyrus by a water channel. Although this scene suggests Nilotic wetlands, its divergence from contemporary Egyptian representations indicates an Aegean landscape deliberately cultivated to evoke a wild Egyptian landscape. Instead of the dense, man-high thickets present in Egyptian paintings, each papyrus appears as a single individual plant. Moreover, the papyrus is growing in a rocky location where it would not normally be found, among sedges that are native to Crete, not Egypt.[11] Deer are absent from Egyptian wetland scenes (it is not their normal habitat), but are present in Crete and suited to the rocky and wooded terrain depicted in the landscape frieze.[12] In the stylistically similar Birds and Monkeys Frieze, a similar mix of native and exotic can be seen. Egyptian papyrus and Cretan sedge grow together by a meandering stream in a rocky landscape. A monkey, probably imported as a pet from Egypt, sits in this controlled habitat eating a bird's egg.[13]

The significance of both friezes lie in their reflection of a desire to control and change the environment through the introduction of foreign flora and fauna. In 1992, frescoes executed in a "Minoan" style and dateable to 1500–1450 B.C.E. were discovered in Egypt at Tell el-Dab'a (Avaris). Their discovery confirmed a nexus of sustained cultural dialogue and exchange between Thera, Crete, and Egypt.[14] During this period, Pharaohs Hatshepsut and Tuthmosis III both exercised their divine control over their environment through the introduction of foreign species. Their intervention not only demonstrated temporal power, but also showcased the new resources available to their subjects.

The garden that Hatshepsut (c. 1475–1458 B.C.E.) built at her temple to Amun at the rocky and inhospitable site at Deir el-Bahari is remarkable not only for its scale, but also for the enormous difficulty and expense Hatshepsut took to import incense trees from Punt. Their inclusion made her garden a physical manifestation of Egypt's power over distant territories and validated Amun's divine approval of her reign:

> Trees were taken up in God's Land, and set in the ground in Egypt . . .
> for the king of the gods. They were brought bearing incense therein
> for (giving of themselves) ointment for the divine limbs, which I owed
> to the Lord of the Gods . . . he commanded me to establish for him a

Punt in his house, to plant trees of God's Land beside his temple, in his garden.[15]

As Hatsheptut's proclamation notes, incense was essential for religious observances and therefore a valuable commodity in the ancient world; this project had economic value in addition to spiritual. Hatshepsut's appropriation and introduction of alien flora was emulated by her successor Tuthmosis III (c. 1479–1425 B.C.E.).[16] The reign of Tuthmosis III was marked by extended military campaigns in Palestine and Syria. In celebration of his victories, he built the Festival Hall at the Temple of Amun at Karnak. A list of conquered settlements in Syria, Palestine, and Lebanon was carved on the pylon that marked the entrance to the Festival Hall. At the rear of this hall was a T-shaped area with a low-relief frieze of plants on the walls. Here, iris, arum, and calanchoe native to Palestine and Syria were depicted among the native botanic repertoire of date palm, sycamore fig, vine, and lotus.[17] Their inclusion among the Egyptian plants is a visual reaffirmation of Tuthmosis's subjugation of their native habitat and their new availability to the Egyptian economy as both valued flower and medicine.

This compound use of gardens and garden elements to demonstrate regal power is also demonstrated in gardens of the ancient Near East. The tradition of Sargon I (c. 2333–2279 B.C.E.), founder of the Akkadian dynasty, being the son of a gardener may have had set a model for an association between kings and horticulture. The 900-year evidential lacuna that followed the destruction of Mari by Hammurabi in 1759 B.C.E. obstructs definite conclusions. However, when evidence for garden culture does resurface in the reign of Tiglath Pileser I (1115–1076 B.C.E.), the connection between the royal heritage, divine approval, expeditionary success, and foreign trees demonstrated by Hatshepsut and Tuthmosis is replicated:

I took cedar, box-tree, and Kanish oak from the lands over which I had gained dominion—such trees as none of the previous kings, my forefathers, had ever planted—and I planted [them] in the orchards of my land. I took rare orchard fruit which is not in my land [and therewith] filled the orchards of Assyria.[18]

This transplantation of exotic tree specimens from subject lands was a core feature of later Assyrian palace complexes. The aggressive and expansionist outlook of Assurnasirpal II (883–859 B.C.E.), Sargon II (721–704 B.C.E.), and Sennacherib (704–681 B.C.E.) encouraged the development of specimen

gardens that demonstrated royal power over the environment. A royal proclamation issued by Assurnasirpal celebrating the gardens (kirû) created at Kalhu
gives a long list of exotic specimens culled from his campaigns:

> I dug out a canal from the Upper Zab, cutting through the mountain
> peak and called it Abundance Canal. I watered the meadows of the Tigris
> and planted orchards with all kinds of fruit in the vicinity. I planted seeds
> and plants that I had found in all the countries through which I had
> marched and in the highlands I had crossed: Pines of different kinds, cy-
> presses and junipers of different kinds, almonds, dates, ebony, rosewood,
> olive, oak, tamarisk, walnut, terebinth and ash, fir, pomegranate, pear,
> quince, fig, grapevine.[19]

Trees were not the only garden feature to evoke these associations. In the
royal gardens of his new capital at Dur-Sharrukin, northeast of Nineveh,
Sargon II embarked on a major landscaping project that explicitly recalled his
campaigns against Hatti (Northern Syria and Anatolia). The topography and
architecture of the region were conjured by its artificial mountain and pillared
pavilion (*bitanu*), transforming this garden into an overt display of territorial
wealth and far-reaching power.[20]

Sargon II referred to his achievement as a new type of garden, a *kirimāhu*
(pleasure garden), yet his interest in gardening was rooted in political as
well as aesthetic concerns. His kirimāhu represented the Assyrian inheritance
of Akkadian glory; a horticultural legacy that connected his dynastic and
military successes with those of Sargon the Great, the gardener's son.[21] Sennacherib, Sargon II's successor, reiterated his own legitimacy by planting a
kirimāhu at Nineveh. Surpassing his forbears, Sennacherib not only transplanted subjugated trees, but he also reproduced the entire foreign ecosystem
of a subjugated territory, the marshes of southern Babylonia, complete with
reed beds, herons, waterfowl, and wild boar.[22] This use of garden space to
represent subject territory reaches its literary acme with the Hanging Gardens of Babylon, allegedly built by Nebuchadnezzar in the sixth century
B.C.E. to please a Persian wife who missed the hilly landscape of her home-
land (Diodorus Siculus 2.10.1–2). Conceptually, the process of enclosure and
cultivation initially documented in the Deed of Ninurta evolves into a statement of territoriality, standing in opposition to what was before. The garden
takes on a sense not only of being a place of ensured security, but can also be
adapted to representing another land. Autocratic power guides this transfer-
ence of meaning originally hinted at in the Theran frescoes and reiterated in

the gardens of Hatshepsut, Tuthmosis, Tiglath Pileser, and his successors, and on to the *horti* of Imperial Rome and beyond. In arid Jericho, Herod the Great constructed a tiered garden of potted plants in emulation of the gardens of the Julio-Claudian dynasty on the Palatine.[23] The garden emerges from its pre-classical origins as a vehicle of personal, political, and cultural appropriation.

SACRED SPACE

Physically, the garden represents human control over nature. Ancient nature is divine, yet gardens are human creations. Where human and divine meet is therefore a space of tension, and also epiphany. Gardens of the ancient world are therefore conceived as a meeting place between man and god. The most abundant archaeological and inscriptional evidence for ancient gardens comes from Egypt between the eighteenth and twentieth dynasties (1550–1070 B.C.E.). The New Kingdom tombs of officials and artisans are decorated with garden scenes representing the concept of an afterlife. Coffin texts, funerary rituals inscribed on coffin lids, repeatedly declare that the way to prepare for the afterlife is to "build a domain in the west, dig pools and plant sycomores."[24] This "garden of the west" was not only the habitat of the dead, but it was also representative of divine order; one version of Egyptian cosmogony attributed the origin of the universe to the mound of creation, crowned with a tree or lotus that rose from the primeval waters.[25] In their garden, the dead were present at the eternal moment of creation.

The religious connotations of garden space were not only apparent in tomb paintings and coffin texts. Many of the plants grown in Egyptian gardens—acacia, sycomore fig, tamarisk, date and doum palm, poppy, mandrake, lotus, and papyrus—had religious significance as well as practical applications. Lotus and papyrus were used in funerary rituals, the sycomore fig and tamarisk were resting places for the soul, and poppy and mandrake were associated with rebirth. This reflexive dynamic between garden space and sacred space was evident in the gardens of Egyptian temples. The Egyptian temple was both the residence of the god and a concrete manifestation of the mystical landscape inhabited by the god. Temple architecture therefore mirrored garden vegetation, with temple columns fashioned to resemble papyrus. At the temple of Dendera, water lilies carved on the outside wall were reflected in the now-vanished lake that evoked the primeval ocean. The famed "lotus lake" of Hermopolis also stood as a remnant of these primordial waters of creation.[26] Herodotus commented on the lush, obviously mature, plantings around the temples and avenues of Bubastis and the date palms and fruit trees that surrounded the temple of Apollo at Buto (Hdt. 2. 138, 156). Such sacred gardens were also part of Greek temples and were later adopted by Romans on selected sites such as the Temple of Sol Invictus.[27]

Not only did these gardens allude to the afterlife of plenty that would be enjoyed by the just in the land of the dead, but they were also self-supporting agricultural compounds, providing incense and offerings for ritual ceremonies and, in the case of temple cities such as Karnak, food for its priests. Rameses III boasted of the stupendous garden complex he created at the temple of Amun at Heliopolis consisting of fruit trees, date and olive groves, trees that could produce myrrh or scented wood, an orchard of 200 persea trees, vines, flowers, pools filled with waterlilies, and papyrus to provide bouquets for the god.[28] These early iterations of the garden as an alien, even otherworldy, space created by an autonomous individual converge in the most influential description of an ancient garden, Homer's garden of Alcinous.

CROSS-FERTILIZING GARDENS: HOMER

It is one of the paradoxes of garden history that "the first written documentation of gardening in the Aegean" should belong to a fictional site.[29] The Phaeacians of Scheria are a semi-divine people, "otherwordly ferrymen," who inhabit a world far removed from Odysseus's.[30] They are not troubled by war, nor do they fear the sea (Homer, *Od.* 6.200–215, 7.35, 8.557–558).[31] The garden of their king, Alcinous, also appears to be removed from the normative context of the Homeric world:[32]

> Outside the courtyard, fronting the high gates,
> a magnificent orchard stretches four acres deep
> with a strong fence running round it side-to-side.
> Here luxuriant trees are always in their prime,
> pomegranates and pears, and apples glowing red,
> succulent figs and olives swelling sleek and dark.
> And the yield of these trees will never flag nor die,
> neither in winter nor in summer, a harvest all year round
> for the West Wind always breathing through will bring
> some fruits to bud and others warm to ripeness—
> pear mellowing ripe on pear, apple on apple,
> cluster of grapes on cluster, fig crowding fig.

And here is a teeming vineyard planted for the kings,
beyond it an open level bank where the vintage grapes
lie basking to raisins in the sun while pickers gather others;
some they trample down in vats, and here in the front rows
bunches of unripe grapes have hardly shed their blooms
while others under the sunlight slowly darken purple.
And there by the last rows are beds of greens,
bordered and plotted, greens of every kind,
glistening fresh, year in, year out. And last,
there are two springs, one rippling in channels
over the whole orchard—the other, flanking it,
rushes under the palace gates
to bubble up in front of the lofty roofs
where the city people come to draw their water. (Homer, *Od.* 7.112–131,
    Fagles trans.)

The intense fecundity of this garden,[33] impervious to the seasons and bearing perpetual harvest, conceptually links it to other such mythic garden places such as that of the Hesperides and the Elysian fields.[34] If the Phaeacians are gatekeepers to the afterworld, the garden of Alcinous is a gateway. Homer's description of the gardens of Alcinous marks the start of a long-standing literary symbolism that visualizes the transition from life to death as entering a beautiful garden or flowery field.[35]

Yet these associations with the afterlife do not necessarily restrict the garden of Alcinous to the otherworld alone. The Egyptian garden had already established a tradition whereby a physically real garden could also operate on a symbolic level as a place of the afterlife. The gardens of Alcinous, while not demonstrably real in the archaeologically recoverable sense, were not an impossible ideal. They were rooted in the already established garden traditions of the ancient world that tally with traditional Mediterranean farming practices.[36] The abundance of the garden may seem to be magical but can also be the product of careful husbandry. The prevalent west wind is as likely to be the result of its situation as of divine favor. The enclosure shelters the produce from adverse winds. There is harvest all year round, not just because the garden is a utopia sealed off from time, but also because it is carefully planted to produce the maximum yield all year round. The plants named are all typical Mediterranean crops grown in their traditional combinations, pears with apples and figs planted with vines. Even the grapes in different stages of development are not as magical as they first appear:

Odysseus himself fondly remembers that the grapes ripened at different times in his first vineyard, a space that is never presented as being magical (Homer, *Od.* 24. 341–344).

The architectural context of the garden also provides realistic comparanda. Although the palace of Alcinous resembles neither Homeric palaces within the text, nor megaron palaces of the Bronze Age, there is a high level of congruence between Homer's description and the palace and the gardens of Assyria. Both the Phaeacian and Assyrian palaces place monumental gilded statues at the doorway and are richly decorated with bronze, gold, and silver within and without (Homer, *Od.* 7.81–102).[37] The Assyrian palaces were notable for their gardens and praised in terms of their flowing waters and wonderful variety of fruit. Homer's garden of Alcinous is the territory of the "Other," but recognizably based on an already existing, exotic, non-Greek model. Homer identifies the garden with the exotic Other, making it a place where conflicting cultures meet.

A demonstration of how this idea was adapted can be found in the *Argonautica* of Apollonius Rhodius. One of the principle themes in the *Argonautica* is the conflict between Greek and barbarian. Apollonius plays with this conflict, introducing ambiguities between the two. Taking the Homeric account of Odysseus's arrival in Scheria as his model, Apollonius described Jason and his men arriving in Colchis, where they see the garden and palace of Aeetes:

> They stood at the entrance, stunned at the royal enclosure, the wide gates and the columns which rose in ordered lines round the walls: and high up on the palace a coping of stone rested on bronze triglyphs. Silently they crossed the threshold. Close by, garden vines covered in green foliage were in full bloom, lifted high in the air. And beneath them ran four springs, ever-flowing, which Hephaistos had delved out. (Apollonius Rhodius, *Argonautica* 3.215–223)

The palace of Aeetes is a familiar scene in the literary sense, in that it has close parallels with the palace of Alcinous, and also in an architectural sense since the features described by Apollonius can be mentally assembled into a contemporary Hellenistic peristyle palace, surrounded by a garden with watered and cultivated grounds.[38] Referencing Homer, Apollonius uses garden space as a place of transition between conflicting cultures, Hellene and Barbarian.

The gardens of Alcinous were rooted in already established garden traditions of the ancient Near East: supra-human activity, royal power, otherness, the afterlife. Homer's account transmits these associations into the corpus of Greek and Latin literature. Yet cross-fertilization is also a process of evolution, and it is notable that the Greek, and later Roman, conception of garden space differs from ideas established in Egypt and the Near East.

GARDENING AND GOVERNMENT

That the ancient Greeks adapted earlier concepts of gardens to promote alternative meanings is reflected in their transmission of the Persian *paridaiza*. Constructed from *pairi* (around) and *daêza* (wall), the paridaiza was literally the "walled enclosure" of Persian nobility that was to have an enduring legacy in Islamic and Mughal gardens.[39] There were two forms of paridaiza. One was a walled garden with a central water feature and pavilion that mixed productive fruit and vegetable plants with exotic botanical specimens. The other was an enclosed hunting preserve or game park, a successor to Sennacherib's Babylonian marsh.

However, although their government was no less autocratic than the Assyrian and Babylonian regimes that preceded them, Greek sources for paridaiza predominately represent them as a metaphor for good and just government, not territorial expansion or royal privilege. Xenophon promulgated a tradition that explicitly associated the maintenance of *paradēsoi* with competent governance. In the *Oeconomicus*, he ascribes the good governance of the Persian empire to the fact that the Great King paid the same attention to gardening that he did to war:

> In all the districts he resides in and visits he takes care that there are "paradises," as they call them, full of all the good and beautiful things that the earth will produce, and he himself spends most of his time there, except when the season is inclement. (Xenophon, *Oeconomicus* 4.13)

This equation of good governance with good garden maintenance is later reemphasized in an anecdote concerning Lysander's visit to Cyrus the Younger. Cyrus personally showed Lysander around his paradēsos. When Lysander admired the trees in their regular rows and praised the gardeners, Cyrus told him that he had planted them himself and that he never sat down for dinner without first exerting himself at some task of war or agriculture (Xen., *Oec.* 4.20–25). Cyrus's example demonstrates his awareness that good government, like good household management, requires personal commitment and attention to detail, and illustrates his fitness for the throne he ultimately never attained (Xen., *Cyropaedia* 1.3.14, 1.4.5, 8.6.12, *Anabasis* 1.2.7). Cyrus's interest in gardens is an example of the awareness of a *koinē*, connective cultural practices and heritage, shared by later Greeks and Romans in their concept of the antique. Cicero relates the same anecdote in his philosophical dialogue on old age, and to emphasize the cultural authority of the tale, he frames it as a speech from Cato the Elder, who is in turn citing Xenophon. Yet Cicero reworks the anecdote for his own purposes; his Cyrus is engaged in gardening not as a form of government manqué, but as an example of the benefits of old age (Cicero, *De senectute* 17.59–60). It is not that Cicero was unaware of the symbolic association between gardening and government; since he had already alluded to it (Cic., *Sen.* 16.55–56), he acknowledged the tradition, and added to it.

Xenophon's account downplays the physical reality of royal Persian gardens, which were clearly designed to impress the visitor with a luxury that demonstrated the autocratic power of their owner. The garden of Cyrus the Great at Pasargadae, constructed in about 546 B.C.E., was a microcosmic representation of Cyrus's empire and an embodiment of Cyrus's title, "King of the four quarters [of the world]."[40] The persistent importance of trees as both a cultural symbol and symbol of conquest was also maintained, with Europe's rich variety of trees cited as an incentive for Xerxes's invasion of Greece, as well as the Greek attack on Sardis and the burning of its sacred groves provided as one of the *casus belli* (Hdt. 7.5, 7.8b).

In spite of Xenophon's interest, the high demand for agricultural land, urban demographics, and the variety of competing political structures could not accommodate the establishment of autocratic *paradēsoi*. Yet Xenophon's association of garden space with the principles of order and just government is indicative of an Athenian tendency toward discussing philosophy within a garden context.

PHILOSOPHICAL GARDENS

Homeric Greece recognized two main kinds of agricultural planting: the *ampelos* (vineyard) and the *orchatos* (orchard). Subsidiary to these was the *chortos*, signifying an enclosed space that grew leafy greens for fodder or food (Pindar, *Olympian* 13.44; Xen., *An.* 1.5.10).[41] When describing the garden of Alcinous, Homer is careful to distinguish three different parts (the orchard, the vineyard, and vegetable beds) and pointedly refer to the whole as a *kēpos*, the Greek word most commonly associated with gardens (Homer, *Od.* 7.129). The kēpos is differentiated from the related areas of vineyard and orchard both by its mixed production and by its proximity to the palace. The *kēpos* therefore has a distinct relationship to both the architecture and urban situation; the latter introduced a new set of meanings into ancient gardens.

In the fifth century B.C.E., as part of his renovation of Athens, Cimon arranged for shade planting and permanent irrigation of a garden in the Academy (Plutarch, *Cimon* 13; Strabo 9.1.17). Plato, and later Polemo, taught here and established a new level of meaning for gardens as places of contemplation and inquiry (Diogenes Laertius 3.20, 4.19; Aelian 3.19). With each succeeding generation of philosophical inquiry, the methods and conclusions changed, but the perception of the garden as a suitable location for philosophical investigation became entrenched. Another garden of philosophical study was established at Colonus, and Aristotle had a garden at Chalkis (D. L. 3.5, 5.14). Following Aristotle's death, Theophrastus established his own garden school of philosophy, where he founded the study of botany (D. L. 5.39, 5.52). The Stoic Kleanthes married the life of the mind to the health of the body by debating by day and laboring in a garden by night (D. L. 7.168–170).[42] The gardens of Epicurus, established in 306 B.C., were the largest, costliest, and most famous, particularly among the Romans who frequently alluded to them in their own garden literature (D. L. 10.10, 10.17; Athenaeus 13.588B; Pliny, *Historia naturalis* 19.19.51; Cicero, *Epistulae ad Atticum* 12.23.2).[43] Philosophical gardens became tourist attractions for educated Greeks and Romans who found them a connective link between their concept of a classical past and the realities of the imperial present (Cic., *De finibus* 5.2–5). Plutarch, writing his biography of Cimon, frames the politician's horticultural endeavors in a manner readily intelligible to readers living under the imperial authority of Rome. Cimon's euergetism of garden produce to the poor of Athens and his creation of a pleasant public park read as a cultural precedent for the similar largesse of Roman emperors (Plut., *Cim.* 10, 13).

Although these gardens were legally the property of private individuals, they were quasi-public spaces, taking in a large number of people (pupils and antagonists) in their communication of Greek philosophical education. The goals of this education—*eutaxia* (good manners), *euexia* (good physical health), *philoponia* (capacity for hard work), and *polumathia* (general knowledge)—were instilled through the process of exercise, dining, and conversation within a secure garden setting. Aristotle's peripatetics inspired the exploration of the garden as a place for the recreational exercise of body and of mind. With the sole exception of Kleanthes, the gardens of philosophers facilitated a transition of our perception of gardens away from the context of hard labor or despotic privilege and into spaces of intellectual labor and general recreation.[44]

More significantly, philosophers inspired the lasting associative tradition between gardens, classical education, and higher thought that persisted into the
eighteenth century.[45]

GARDENS OF GRATIFICATION

Inevitably, Epicurean and Stoic perceptions of garden space conflicted with
each other, but their conflict did not undermine the overall influence of the
Greek philosophical garden on secularizing previously sacred aspects of garden
space. In part, this may be attributed to the fact that although sacred gardens
were a part of Greek communities, their position was shared with other kinds
of sacred green space.

Kēpos usually refers to a planted temple enclosure. Yet Greek *kēpoi* did
not have the metaphysical association with divinity exhibited by their Egyptian and Near East counterparts. Instead, that aspect of sacred space was concretized in the *alsos* (sacred grove). Sacred groves were unbounded, natural
spaces that nominally existed before the presence of man.[46] They often acted
as wildlife preserves since it was forbidden to cut or graze upon them. The
most famous and most ancient of these groves was the oak grove of Zeus at
Dodona (Hdt. 2.52–57), and many more are attested.[47] In contrast, the kēpos
was man-made, was bounded with walls and hedges, excluded animals, and
was almost invariably urban.[48] Apart from the fact of their existence, Greek
sources reveal little about temple kēpoi; the sacred gardens for which we have
the fullest information are the smallest and most atypical of their kind, the
gardens of Adonis.

This festival of Adonis, held either in early spring or the dog days of summer, commemorated Aphrodite's mourning for her mortal lover.[49] The Adoneia
was an urban festival, but one celebrated in private houses, not public spaces
or sanctuaries. Its most conspicuous celebrants were not citizen wives, but
courtesans (*hetairai*) and metic women. These women gathered on rooftops
decorated with wheat, barley, fennel, and lettuce grown in pots, bowls, vases,
baskets, and wicker trays.[50] Evanescent and sterile, these container gardens
bore no fruit and lasted barely a week, commemorating the spectacular youth
and premature death of Adonis.[51]

Commenting on the Adoneia, Plato unfavorably contrasts the short-lived
pleasure of these roof gardens to the deeper and more profitable pleasure
to be had by the serious farmer. To Plato, the gardens of Adonis are a pas-
time (*paidia*), specifically created for the purpose of short-lived enjoyment

(Plato, *Phaedo* 276B). In this, Plato records a significant shift in garden meaning that saw the emphasis of the garden diverted away from its associations with labor and toward the experience of pleasure. Plato's negative reaction to the somatic delights of the garden can be linked to the tradition of luxury gardens in enemy Persia. In pre-classical antiquity, the pleasurable aspects of the garden were unproblematic to the residents within. Relief scenes of music and banqueting are depicted in Ashurbanipal's garden,[52] and the hymns of tomb owners from New Kingdom Egypt celebrate garden pleasures:

> My heart rejoices on its earth to refresh itself under its sycamore, to walk among his own trees, to take the *ihi*-plants and the lotus, and gather the *hnw*-plants and lotus buds, the dates, the figs and the grapes. My sycamores wave in front of me, they give me bread which is in them, my basin offers water. My heart rests in its freshness.[53]

Yet, despite Plato's dismissal of garden pleasure as trivial *paidia*, his observation recognized that the garden of leisure was no longer the sole privilege of royalty or a benefit of the afterlife. Gardens were a part of private and community life, perceived not simply in terms of productive or sacred space, but as a locus of individual interests and desires.

For the Greeks, gardens communicated not only the values of a philosophical education, but also sexual pleasure. As the Adonia demonstrated, Aphrodite had a special relationship with gardens; her sanctuary at Cnidos was the site of a famous kēpos (Pseudo-Lucian, *Amores* 11–18). *Maniokēpos* described a woman who was "sex-mad," and kēpos was used colloquially to signify female genitalia, an association also transmitted to the Latin *hortus* or *hortulus* (Anacreon 158; D.L. 2.116).[54] This eroticization of the garden was assimilated into Latin literature. When Calpurnius Siculus writes of two young men, a shepherd and a gardener, wooing a girl, it is the gardener who wins her with a lush description of the pleasures his hortus can offer her senses (Calpurnius Siculus, *Eclogues* 2.32–35). As with the educational import of Greek philosophical gardens, the correlation between garden space and sexual or sensual gratification persisted long after the garden's antiquity. The Vauxhall Gardens of seventeenth century London and the Bois de Boulogne of twentieth century Paris trace their roots to assignations in the gardens of Pompey, and to Pyrrha clasping her lover in a grotto among the roses (Hor., *Od.* 1.5.1–3, 1.9.18).[55]

CONCLUSION

To create a garden is to set a space apart from its context, to cultivate and alter its appearance making it both familiar and strange. Ninurta's segregation and cultivation of the kur created a secure proto-Eden for his people, and the essential recognition of the garden as a safe habitat persisted throughout ancient history. Yet the garden is also defined by its fundamental opposition to what was there before it and by seasonal change, creating a disjunction of perception, a dynamic tension between past and present, real and ideal, that is manifested in its associations with sacred space, divine power, and the afterlife.

Meaning is mutable, and sacred power legitimizes secular power. The association between autonomy and control, gardening and government, is reiterated throughout the gardens of the ancient Mediterranean, and not only among expansionist monarchs. The gardener's desire to have control over the environment can translate into the territory of the mind and body. Garden life can paradoxically encompass both intellectual exploration and sensual gratification. In the cross-fertilizations of garden meanings, the serpent of Eden takes the form of ithyphallic Priapus to guard the apples of the Hesperides (Tibullus 1.1.17–18; Propertius 4.2. 41–44).

The gardens of the ancient Mediterranean occupied an interstitial niche between productive orchard and immanent grove. As discrete space, the garden communicates on two levels, through physical locale and metaphysical association. The former is both site and culturally specific, the latter mutable and transferable. Physically, the gardens of Pompeii, the Villa d'Este, Stowe, Villandry, and Dungeness are independent and distinct garden sites, each communicating diverse values, aspirations, and tensions. Metaphysically, they are connected by the cross-fertilization of meanings originally established among the gardens of the ancient Mediterranean and Near East.

CHAPTER SIX

Verbal Representations

ANTONY R. LITTLEWOOD AND
KATHARINE T. VON STACKELBERG

The garden sites of the Greco-Roman world have long been abandoned, over-grown, and built over. Yet their literary representation has survived to inspire European garden traditions that range from the monastic walled garden to Ian Hamilton Finlay's Little Sparta. This chapter addresses the representation of gardens in the principal genres of Greek and Latin literature from the years 500 B.C.E. to 500 C.E. This is not an exhaustive analysis of all garden sources in Greco-Roman antiquity; gardens were the subject of written accounts before this period and continued to appear long afterward. Yet this millennial span includes the most influential literary genres and periods of the ancient Mediterranean: classical and Hellenistic Greek, Gold and Silver Age Latin, and the writings of the early Christian Fathers. The transmission of these texts in the West through the *soi-disant* dark ages and into the Renaissance had a profound impact on many aspects of European garden culture. In the East, Greek texts in particular became the bedrock of the Byzantines' gardening techniques and landscape architecture.

THE EPIC GARDEN

The most influential literary garden of the ancient world can be found in its oldest identifiable genre, the epic poem known as Homer's *Odyssey*. The garden of Alcinous on the island of Scheria (Homer, *Odyssey* 7.112–131), home of the magical and mysterious Phaeacians, has already been discussed in Chapter 5. Although the date of its composition and redaction fall outside our 1,000 year span, the centrality of Homer to Greco-Roman education ensured that Alcinous's blooming and fruiting palace orchard watered by two springs persisted as a literary model. Its influence can be seen in the Hellenistic epic the *Argonautica* of Apollonius Rhodius.[1] His account of the garden of Aeetes in barbarian Colchis, with its orchard, palace, and multiple springs, has physical parallels with Homer's account and conceptual parallels as a point of transition between Hellene and "Other" (Apoll. Rh., *Arg.* 3.215–223). The garden of Alcinous, as a miraculous and semi-divine garden with features impossible to attain in the real world, influenced descriptions of Elysian and the mystical Orphic-Pythagorean and even Christian paradises, as well as of the gardens in the Byzantine romances;[2] it also assumed a proverbial status, referenced by Martial and Pliny the Elder as ideals of peace and beauty (Martial, *Epigrams* 12. 31, 13. 37; Pliny, *Historia naturalis* 19.49).

The Homeric precedent of a divinely protected, fruitful, peaceful garden scene is echoed by the most influential garden of Latin literature, the *hortus* in Virgil's *Georgics*:

> For I call to mind how under the towers of Oebalia's citadel, where dark Galaesus waters his yellow fields, I saw an old Corycian, who had a few acres of unclaimed land and this, a soil not rich enough for bullocks ploughing, unfitted for the flock and unkindly to the vine. Yet, as he planted herbs here and there among the bushes, with white lilies about, and vervain, and the slender poppy, he matched in contentment the wealth of kings, and returning home in the late evening, would load his boards with unbought dainties. He was the first to pick roses in spring and apples in autumn; and when sullen winter was still cracking rocks with cold, and curbing running waters with ice, he was already culling the soft hyacinth's bloom, reproaching laggard summer and the loitering zephyrs. So he, too, was first to be enriched with mother-bees and a plenteous swarm, the first to gather frothing honey from the squeezed comb. Luxuriant were his limes and wild laurels and all the fruits his bounteous tree donned in its early bloom, full as many it kept in the ripeness of autumn. He, too, planted out in rows elms far-grown, pear trees when quite hard, thorns even now bearing plums, and the plane already yielding to drinkers the service of its shade. (Vir., *Geor.* 4.125–146)

Framed as an epyllion (a little epic), Virgil's account of an elderly man's garden labors (Vir., *Geor.* 4.116–146) drew not only on Hesiod's *Works and*

Days but also from Homer's heroic account of Odysseus's wanderings. The unnamed man's Corycian origin suggests retirement from an Odyssean career of piracy, while the close phonetic relationship with Corcyra (ancient Corfu) and its identification as Homer's Scheria emphasize the intertextual relationship between the two gardens (Thucydides 1.25.4, 3.70.4).[3] Virgil's account serves as a meditation on the workings of time and mortality. Although, like the Phaeacians, the old man occupies the penumbral country between life and death, his life is sustained not by the exceptional favor of the gods, but by his unstinting labor. The old man, his age emphasized by the presence of the hyacinth and its mythological associations with youth, is shown working in a garden, a space particularly vulnerable to the passage of time.[4] Gardens necessarily reflect the evanescence of time by the nature of the changing seasons and the lifespan of their plants, yet man's labor in the hortus structures the passage of time, creating something to offset the transience of nature. So the old Corycian is shown working not only all the hours of the day and into the night, but also over the passage of months and years during which the garden is created. The flowers of spring and early summer are mentioned at the beginning of the passage and are followed by autumn fruits, winter, and then spring again, heralded by the hyacinth and warm winds. The intense fecundity of this garden parallels that of the garden of Alcinous and suggests the *aurea aetas* of Augustan Rome.

Virgil's description of the Corycian's garden as a complete landscape in miniature, with trees, running water, grass, and flowers, corresponds to the poetic *topos* of the *locus amoenus* or "pleasant place." These idyllic landscapes were an idealized hybrid of wild and cultivated spaces, possessing all the appeal of pastoral and rural life without its dangers and discomforts. The perfect peace associated with the locus amoenus extended its association to mythical gardens of the afterlife, the Hesperides and Elysian fields. The locus amoenus of Virgil's garden was to prove influential to the development of later European literature, notably in Jean de Meun's *Le Roman de la Rose*.[5] This tale of courtly love, centering on an encounter within a walled garden, drew on another Roman epic, Ovid's *Metamorphoses*. But whereas Homer's and Virgil's epic gardens were indicative of a positive transition toward home, toward peace, Ovid uses the imagery of garden and locus amoenus in the context of emotional struggles that do not always have a positive outcome. In this story of Polyphemus and Galatea, the unlucky lover compares the beauty of Galatea to a well-watered garden (Ovid, *Met.* 13.797), a simile that makes the nymph doubly unattainable because Polyphemus is a Cyclops, the race that neither plants nor ploughs (Hom., *Od.* 9.105–111). Polyphemus is no more able to woo Galatea successfully than he is able to plant a garden. In contrast to the sunny idealized gardens of Homer and Virgil, Ovid's gardens reflect more nu-anced concepts of struggle, attainment, and loss.

GARDENS OF POETRY

Elegiac and lyric poets of the classical and Hellenistic period did not estab-lish a tradition of songs that celebrated singular gardens, as for the garden of Alcinous. Instead, they focused on individual pastoral features of meadow, stream, orchard, or grove in works where the distinction between natural countryside and cultivated garden is not made clear. However, the emergence of a set of core concepts in garden literature can be traced through a series of intertextual connections between Greek and Latin lyric and elegiac poets. For example, the trope of erotic garden encounters can be traced to Anacreon, whose sixth century poetry inspired an imitative vogue during the Hellenistic period (Anac., *frag* 346.1).[6] Theocritus's seventh *Idyll*, in which the poet and goatherd Lycidas sings in praise of love, was particularly influential. Lycidas is thought to represent the pastoral poet Philitas of Cos, who in turn is thought to be the literary model for the Philetas in Longus's *Daphnis and Chloe*, who informs the protagonists that Eros may be found in his garden.[7] Following these complex, nested allusions, a coherent image emerges of the poetic garden as a secure, idyllic space, nurturing love as well as plants.

Inspired by Hellenistic poets, Latin elegists transmitted this perception of the garden as a secure space for rest, pleasure, and love.[8] For Horace, the value of his garden lay not in its productive capacity as a traditional Roman *hortus* but in the respite it offered from the irritations and concerns of city living (Hor., *odes* 2.3, 2.11, 4.4; *Satirae* 2.6). In his satire describing how a statue of Priapus protected a garden from witches, the garden stands as a symbol of Augustus's urban renewal (Hor., *Sat.* 1.8). Horace's employment of Priapus as a narrator derives from a subgenre of Latin verse, the Priapea, a corpus of roughly eighty anonymous verses in which Priapus, the traditional guardian of the garden, celebrates its fertility while warding away intruders with his phallus.[9] Priapus also appears in the gardens of Horace's contem-poraries Propertius and Tibullus who, in keeping with their sophisticated Callimachean ethos, soften Priapus's sexually aggressive character (Tib. 1.1.17–18; Prop. 4.2. 41–44).[10] Instead of conveying earthy sexuality, Tibullus's Priapus oversees a bucolic romance, watching over apples that recall the garden of the Hesperides, foreshadowing the erotic Elysium of the lovers' consummation in a later poem (Tib. 1.3).[11] Propertius's Priapus is just one of a series of protean but harmless guises adopted by the god Vertumnus in the garden. This theme of Priapus/Vertumnus in the garden appears in Ovid's romance of Pomona and Vertumnus where Vertumnus, disguised as an old woman, couches his declaration of love in a description of a garden filled with fruit and herbs (Prop. 4.2.41–44; Ovid, *Met.* 14.687–691).

The literary associations of gardens with security and pleasure continued in Silver Age Latin verse. Statius's *Silvae* offer vivid depictions of the pleasures of elite villa gardens shaded by ancient trees and cooled by fountains (1.2.153–155, 1.3.38–41, 2.3, 4.4). His garden villas do not stress Elysian or erotic associations, but rather they are places of Epicurean withdrawal from public life. His poetry reflects contemporary enthusiasm for the manipulation of nature,[12] especially in the lengthy description of a millionaire's estate on the Punta della Calcarella at Sorrento, on which hills had been leveled, rocks removed or reshaped, and groves created on previously barren ground (2.2).

Subsequent poetry, with few exceptions, offers more hortulan hints than actual descriptions, indicative of a real decline in the number and extent of gardens in a period of increasing economic troubles and lawlessness. Pentadius's verses on the arrival of spring from the third or fourth century C.E. owe something to the literary tradition of gardens (*Carmina* 2 = *Anthologia Latina* 1.1.235);[13] Reposianus's poem (of a very uncertain date) on the amours of Mars and Venus is set in beautiful grove on a couch of garden flowers (*Anth. Lat.* 1.1.253); Claudian's on the epithalamium of the emperor Honorius and Maria in 398 C.E. includes a terrestrial paradise of Venus, which again owes a debt to real gardens (*Epithalamium* 49–96). Ausonius's famous poem of his journey down the Moselle lists the merits of situations for villas, his preference being for those with broad prospects from their elevation, but he gives only the merest glimpses of gardens, while the poem on his own estate (*De Heriodolo*) describes just a simple farm. The author of an anonymous poem sometimes included with those of Ausonius strolls through a garden glimmering with early morning's hoarfrost and became the inspiration of Herrick's "Gather ye Rosebuds while ye may" (*Anth. Lat.* 1.2.646).

For the fifth century, a few poets attest the survival of villas, but by now these are not so luxurious as before, and some are clearly fortified to some extent, while the actual gardens have shrunk in size. The most important figure is the Gallo-Roman aristocrat from Lyons, Sidonius Apollinaris, appointed city prefect of Rome in 468 C.E. and, shortly after, bishop of the Auvergne. In one lengthy poem, he significantly terms the mansion of Pontius Leontius a *burgus* ("castle") rather than a villa, but it clearly contained open land with grain crops and laurels and a spring with rocks so beautiful that they required no embellishment. The distinction between house and garden, as was often the case on Roman estates, is blurred, with two inlets from a river entering the buildings, one bringing fish right into the dining-room (*Carm.* 22). Another poem (24) mentions secluded gardens, compared to that of Virgil's Corycian, a mock grotto, and many species of lovely flowers.[14] Somewhat earlier in the century (probably in 417), Rutilius Namatianus wrote a poem on his journey by sea from Rome to his estates in Gaul, making many stops en route. In Rome itself, he describes woods with singing birds enclosed within colonnades with paneled ceilings (just painted on to give a semblance of nature?) and a villa garden at Faleria possessed of a wood and extensive fishponds (*De Reditu Suo* 111–114, 377–380). For the sixth century, we have the Christian writer Venantius Fortunatus, who wrote also on secular themes including three different Burgundian villas with fragrant flowers, an elaborate fountain, and a fishpond (*Carm.* 1.18–20).

Finally, the poems of Luxorius provide interesting evidence that under Vandal hegemony many aspects of Roman culture continued in North Africa in the fifth and sixth centuries. One celebrates Eugetus's garden, home of Greek divinities and containing beauteous foliage, balsam, singing birds, delicate fountain, and mossy stream; a second, a pleasure garden's pavilion decorated with a picture of its Vandal owner, Fridamal, piercing a boar's head with his spear; others, fish trained to accept food from human hands, a tame boar fed at table, and a talking magpie (*Carm.* 46; 18; 5; 6; 84 respectively)—all variations on familiar features in Roman gardens.[15]

COMIC GARDENS

In contrast to the images of peaceful stability and romantic pleasure offered by epic, lyric, and elegiac genres, drama and epigram used the garden as a focus for more acerbic social commentary. Gardens are rarely mentioned in Greek drama, but they regularly appear in the Latin comedies of Plautus, always in an urban context and usually with a view to sexual activity. The association between gardens and sexuality is a persistent feature of garden literature, from the ribaldry of the *Priapea* to the satiric eighteenth century didactic poem *A Sketch from the Landscape*, which is leveled against the Priapic studies of gardener, antiquarian, and author Richard Payne Knight.[16]

Plautus's focus on urban or suburban gardens is found also in the poems of Martial and Juvenal. In contrast to the ideal gardens of epic poetry, or the stately villas and mock-wildernesses of Ovid and Statius, the garden of the city is a space of conflicting social mores. Martial may describe his garden in the language of a traditional Roman farm, producing honest, simple fare of mallows, lettuce, beans, and apples (3.58, 10. 48, 10.94), but the very self-sufficiency that the garden is supposed to confer is couched in a social web of reciprocal obligation:

> This wood, these springs, this woven shade of overhanging vine, this ductile stream of flowing water, and the meadows and the rose beds that yield nothing to the twice-flowering rose of Paestum, and the pot-herbs green in January and not frostbitten, and the household eel that swims in closed water, and the white tower that harbors birds as white as itself, these are the gifts of my lady. To me, when I returned after seven lusters, Marcella gave this house, this little realm. If Nausicaa were to offer me her father's gardens, I could say to Alcinous: "I prefer my own." (Mart., *Ep*. 12.31)

Martial's itemization of everything within the garden as the bounty of Marcella undermines the note of proud possession in his final line. If his ownership comes by virtue of Marcella's patronage, how much can we read into his statement of personal preference? Is Martial expressing a preference for the real over the ideal, or is the poem an elegant complement to his benefactress? There is no clear, single answer to these questions.

Martial uses the social desirability of the gardens to play on differences between appearance and reality in contemporary Roman society. For Martial, the garden is subject to the same absurdities and contradictions as any other aspect of Roman life. In one poem, Martial replies to a friend who has asked to stay with him and warns him that his expectation of staying in a luxurious villa with grand gardens is in for a rude surprise; Martial has paid so much for his suburban garden that he cannot afford to furnish house or garden with the appropriate couches for entertaining (5.62). The comic decrepitude of the hortus is matched by its mean and stingy produce (11.18). Martial cannot impress anyone with his garden; it fails both as a status symbol and a larder.

The comic possibilities presented by social desirability of gardens are more barbed in the work of Juvenal. At the start of the second century C.E., Juvenal's poetry articulated the tension between luxury villa gardens as contemporary objects of aspiration and the simple kitchen-gardens of rural tradition. Villa gardens, Juvenal claims, are the visible affirmation of a life of crime and deceit (1.75–76). In his satire on women, Juvenal presents the garden as a once pure space of female chastity, now corrupted by sexual license (6.14–18, 374–376). In denying the verisimilitude of man-made grottos, a popular feature of pleasure gardens, he mocks the conceit of imitating nature (3.17–20); even the seemingly uncomplicated association of the garden with philosophical retreat, encouraged by Epicurus, is presented as a denunciation of urban life (3.223–229; 14. 316–320).

The comic potential of gardens is also apparent in Petronius's *Satyricon*, where its philosophical and Epicurean associations are subverted in a dialogue with a pompous philosopher, and then a symbol of Trimalchio's excess (6, 53). Ancient fiction presents gardens that reflect the dominant tone of the novel. Comic fiction gives comic accounts; romances present a romantic space. So, in Apuleius's *The Golden Ass*, garden roses are the fodder for a scatological scene of entrapment and escape, whereas in Longus's *Daphnis and Chloe* and Achilles Tatius's *Leucippe and Clitophon*, the garden is the site of erotic awakening (Long. 2.3; Ach. Tat. 1.15, 2.10).[17] The latter begins a tradition in which the garden is primarily associated with the heroine and even seems to reflect the extent of her sexuality.[18]

TECHNICAL WRITERS

Varro gives a long list of Greek writers of treatises on agriculture but gives pride of place to the Carthaginian Mago, whose twenty-eight books in Punic on the subject were translated into Greek by Cassius Dionysius (*De re rustica* 1.1.7–11). Although all these works have perished, we have the works of Roman continuators of the tradition who included horticultural sections in their compilations.

Cato, whose treatise is the oldest surviving work of Latin prose, proposes that if an estate is located near a town, the second most important part for its owner, after a vineyard, should be a watered garden for growing vegetables and chaplet flowers (*De agricultura* 1.7, 8.2). It is clear that Cato's intent was entirely commercial despite the Elder Pliny's anachronistically romantic vision of him delighting in sportive nature's varied and delicate blossoms (*HN* 21.1). A little over a century later, Varro wrote a manual for the use by his prospective widow, who had just bought a farm. Amid its sound practical advice, he reflects changed values in admitting that an owner had the twin goals of profit and pleasure (*RR* 1.2.12, 1.4.1–2, 3.3.1). His description of an aviary, fishponds, and tholos housing his ingenious garden dining room on his own estate at Casinum serves as a warning over assuming that the marvelous appurtenances of gardens so regularly decried by writers in many genres are exaggerations (*RR* 3.5.9–17). Although Vitruvius does not deal with gardens per se, he does state that a villa's salubrity is enhanced by greenery (*viridaria*) (*De architectura* 5.9.5), and much of his architectural information was applied in the structures that often formed a part of Roman gardens, such as the colonnade (*De Arch.* 5.11.4). The Elder Pliny devotes no fewer than sixteen books (12–27) out of thirty-seven in his colossal encyclopedia to the vegetal kingdom. Although a major emphasis is on medicinal uses, his comments on many species, allied with information from wall paintings and archaeology, are invaluable in filling in our picture of what was planted in a Roman garden. Of great interest in any history concerning the increasing sophistication of horticulture are his scattered remarks on topiary work, an invention, he claims, of C. Matius in the time of Augustus (*HN* 12.6.13).[19] Also valuable is the only complete book surviving from antiquity that was dedicated entirely to gardens: Book 10, an agricultural treatise by Pliny's contemporary Columella. Unlike the rest of the work, this was written in (very unpoetical) hexameter verse and is a strange compound of mythology and practical wisdom on soil enrichment and pest control.

It is a great pity that the *De Hortis* of Gargilius Martialis from the mid-third century is lost,[20] but its remaining fragment on arboriculture shows a man not only able to cite divergent views of his sources but to also criticize from his own experience and autopsy. He was used by the last known Roman agricultural writer, Palladius (of probably the mid-fifth century), whose work has survived and indeed became the authoritative agricultural text of the Western Middle Ages.[21] Palladius, however, drew also on a fourth century agricultural/horticultural treatise in Greek by Vindonius Anatolius, which, in one form or another after it had passed through Cassianus Bassus in the sixth century, was translated into Syriac, Pahlavi, Arabic, and Armenian. It gave rise also to the *Geoponika*, one part of the encyclopedic enterprise orchestrated by the Byzantine emperor Constantine VII in the first half of the tenth century. Despite its emphasis on agriculture, its date, and a chapter specifically devoted to the planting season in Constantinople, it is probably the most informative text on ancient horticultural techniques,[22] although it must necessarily be used with caution for anachronistic practices (the two allied sciences have been, however, notoriously conservative until the most recent times [and still are in "the third world"]).

GARDENS AND HISTORIOGRAPHY

Gardens (*kēpoi*) are rarely mentioned in Greek historiography, except as the exotic property (*paradeisoi*) of Persian kings and their satraps; this is not to say that they did not exist, for Livy has Perseus of Macedonia climbing the wall of the garden adjoining his residence to flee Samothrace (Livy, 45.6), but rather that only the gardens of notable men were of interest. Cimon's plantation of trees in the Athenian agora would not have attracted comment if it had not been in accordance with his euergetistic persona (Plutarch, *Cimon* 13).

Gardens in Roman historiography are often a barometer of character. In Plutarch's biographical studies of republican generals, Marius is condemned for "the extravagant and effeminate appurtenances" of his expensive estate at Misenum on the Bay of Naples (*Mar.* 34.3), a clear case of an historian with an *idée fixe* since the Elder Pliny reports that it was laid out like an army camp (*HN* 18.7.32; cf. Seneca, *Epistulae* 51.11). Plutarch, however, reserved his most objurgative comments for Lucullus, acting like "a veritable Xerxes in a toga" at his villa on the Bay of Naples.[23] There he suspended hills over underground walkways, surrounded buildings with waterways and channels for breeding fish, and constructed residences "in the sea"; at Tusculum, the same magnate had "observatories, open-air banqueting chambers and colonnades" (*Lucullus* 39.1–4). Plutarch also vouchsafes the fact that a garden could be the excuse for a false accusation during the Sullan proscriptions, adding the sad tale of the inoffensive Q. Aurelius who, upon seeing his name on the dreaded list, said, "Alas, my Alban estate is prosecuting me" (*Sulla* 31.5–6).

As a barometer of character, it is not surprising that gardens appear during the Principate in the context of surfeit and catastrophe since both Tacitus's *Annales* and *Historiae* are concerned with the reigns of the Julio-Claudian dynasty and the Year of the Four Emperors, a ruinous period for Roman *libertas*. Gardens are the focus of forced seizures and judicial murders, places of luxury, sloth, and death (Tac., *Ann.* 11.1, 11.32–37, 12.59, 14.3, 14.52–55, 15.44; *Hist.* 2.92, 3.11, 3.14, 3.36). Tacitus's contemporary also equated imperial gardens with imperial decadence: Suetonius's contemptuous criticism of Caligula emphasizes that he not only wasted money on terrestrial gardens but also, in imitation of the elaborate ship whose construction was supervised by Archimedes for Hiero II of Sicily,[24] had boats transformed into floating gardens with baths, colonnades, dining rooms, and "a great variety of vines and fruit-bearing trees" to delight him and his guests on musical cruises (*Calig.* 37.2–3). The Elder Pliny adds that the emperor also had a dining room, called by him his "nest," in an enormous plane tree that accommodated fifteen guests and their servants (*HN* 12.5.10).[25] This trope of the garden as a sign of noxious character and bad government is emphasized by its relative absence in accounts of the "good emperors"—for example Vespasian and Titus, for whom gardens are alluded to only in the context of two portentous trees on the Flavian estate, an oak and a cypress, that throve and withered according to dynastic fortune (Tac., *Hist.* 2.78.2; Suet., *Vespasian* 5.4, *Domitian* 15.2). Yet Flavian-era gardens provide the most extensive archaeological evidence for the garden in Roman, Italy, belying the paucity of literary evidence.

In the *Historia Augusta*, an account of the lives of emperors from Hadrian to Carinus, gardens continue to be represented as places of imperial excess. For the irredeemable Elagabalus, gardens are decadent retreats in which to indulge in murderous thoughts, to play at racing chariots, or to create artificial mountains (*Elagabalus* 13.5, 14.15). Elagabalus also made his gardens' swimming pools fragrant by the addition of spices and roses (*Elag.* 21.7), wherein he was outdone by Carinus, who swam amid apples and melons (*Carus et Carinus et Numerius* 17.3). The work condemns also Gordian II, who "lived a life of revelry in his gardens, baths and most delightful groves" (*Gordian* 19.5). It can, nevertheless, simply record, possibly even on occasion with approbation, as when it describes the planned magnificent gardens of Gordian III in the Campus Martius (*Gord.* 32.6–8), and the palace with a pool built by Severus Alexander near Baiae, named in honor of his mother, Mamaea (*Alexander Severus* 26.9). Its most positive depiction describes how the grounds of Hadrian's Villa at Tivoli were constructed to recall the famously beautiful Vale of Tempe and other sites of empire (*Hadrian* 26.5). Another indication that the lavish estates with their gardens could be perceived as morally positive environments is afforded by Herodian, who reports (3.13.1) that Septimius Severus deliberately spent most of his time at his suburban properties just outside the capital and on the Campanian coast so that his sons would be removed from life in Rome and could enjoy a "healthy lifestyle," a plan that ended in abysmal failure in the case of his son the future emperor Caracalla.

Since "bad emperors" (such as Claudius) frequently confiscated aristocrats' estates, which virtually always included vast pleasure gardens, for their own delight, and "good emperors" (such as Augustus) made them once more publicly available, these actions are also recorded by historians such as Cassius Dio (68.2.1, 75.8.4) and Herodian (3.8.2). Two passages are particularly notable; Trajan's eulogist, the Younger Pliny, writes:

> You do not embrace in your huge holdings every marsh, every lake and even woodland pasture through dispossession of their former owners; rivers, mountains, seas are not now dedicated to the eyes of just one man; there are things for the emperor to see but not to own; at last dominion of the *princeps* is broader than his personal acres. (*Panegyricus* 50.1–2)

The other occurs in Herodian, who claims that in 193 c.e. the emperor Pertinax decreed that any man who brought back into cultivation any wasteland, even if that was imperial property, would become the legal owner in perpetuity, with immunity from taxation for ten years (2.4.6).

Alongside the tradition of immoral and self-indulgent excess, there was, nonetheless, one that merely recorded imperial interest in gardens. From Hellenistic examples, Roman emperors had inherited a Near Eastern belief that grand gardens were symbols of royal or imperial power (indeed in Assyria and Egypt, destruction of an opponent's garden had been an assertion of superiority).[26] Pompey the Great's establishment of a public grove at the foot of his Temple to Venus Victrix alluded to this belief.[27] Augustus, too, had taken an interest, though much more modestly, in the enhancement of his gardens adorning

> his own villas not so much with decorative statues and pictures as with terraces, groves and objects notable for their age or rarity, such as . . . the colossal bones of monstrous sea creatures (whales ?) and wild beasts . . . and the weapons of heroes. (Suet., *Aug.* 72.3)

Although this bizarre taste seems not to have been imitated, later emperors were often personally involved in the imperial gardens, especially during and increasingly in the Byzantine period, when, for a while, there was even a technological rivalry between the imperial and caliphal courts in the hydraulic automata that graced gardens,[28] and, later, Constantine IX became obsessed, according to Michael Psellos, by landscape architecture and horticultural legerdemain (*Chronographia* 6.173–175).

THE EPISTOLARY GARDEN, FACTUAL
AND FICTIONAL

Much of our evidence for the social desirability of gardens comes from Cicero, who mentions gardens more than any other Latin writer.[29] In almost every case, the hortus is the object of his or another's acquisitive desire,[30] and once acquired it becomes the locus for appropriate displays of educated taste and learning for him and his circle of friends, and of dissipation and luxury for his opponents.[31] Most of the gardens mentioned by Cicero are suburban, although several are clearly attached to villas in parts of Latium and Campania, and all of them are gardens of the Roman elite (Cicero, *Epistulae ad Atticum* 12.40.2; *Epistulae ad Quintum fratrem* 3.1.14).

The perception of gardens as an essential part of elite residences encouraged an association between gardens and *luxuria*. The condemnation of large-scale landscape architecture and showcase gardening was a favorite theme of both Seneca the Elder and Younger, reflecting their own Stoic principles and prejudices (Sen., *Controversiae* 5.5; *De tranquillitate animi* 3.6–8; *Epistulae* 122.8). Seneca the Younger scorned Vatia's villa with its lovely grounds as a place where its master hid from life's responsibilities (Sen., *Ep.* 55.4). In contrast, Pliny the Younger wrote of his gardens not as places of negative *luxuria*, but of positive *otium*. Two letters of Pliny the Younger give detailed descriptions his villa gardens at Laurentinum, near Ostia, and in Tuscany (Pliny, *Ep.* 2.17, 5.6).[32] Constantly alluded to and cited in both popular and specialist books on gardening, these letters were not only seen as the quintessential model against which Roman villas and their gardens as a whole were measured, they also influenced the layout of Italian Renaissance villas.[33] Moreover, they played a part in formulating the principles of seventeenth and eighteenth century landscape gardening. Pliny's letters established the tradition, later drawn upon by Renaissance and Enlightenment humanists, whereby a man of letters should also be interested in the layout and content of his garden.[34] However, the cumulative effect of Pliny's epistolary technique entails the gradual detachment of the reader from clear points of reference and the subjection of the self to Pliny Reading an account of Pliny's garden offers the reader not only an opportunity to see how the villa garden is constructed, but also how the author constructs himself within his wider society.[35]

After Pliny, apart from a few brief notices in Symmachus (*Ep.* 2.26, 5.93, 7.24),[36] there is a long chronological break in surviving epistolary descriptions of gardens in Latin literature until the fifth century when, in prose this time rather than verse, Sidonius Apollinaris proudly expatiates on his own villa at Avitacum (near Clermont-Ferrand). His almost exclusive emphasis upon the mansion itself and the lake suggests that there was little actual garden, but there was a swimming pool fed from a stream above and a ball court shaded by two enormous lime trees. What for us is most notable is Sidonius's delight in aural delights—distant piping of shepherds and bleating of sheep, singing of nightingales, twittering of swallows, crowing of cocks, cawing of rooks, honking of swans and geese, chirruping of cicadas, and vespertine croaking of frogs (*Ep.* 2.2).

Since in later antiquity the eastern half of the Roman Empire was not as subject to military invasion and marauding as the west, it is hardly surprising that the only two surviving descriptions of villas there, both from the second half of the fourth century, have an hortulan component. The emperor Julian recalls the small estate, overlooking the Sea of Marmora and given to him by his grandmother, with its trees, garden springs, and bathhouse. It is where on a summer's day he would lie reading a book on the greensward sweet with smilax, thyme, and roses (*Ep.* 25.426D–428B). The future saint Gregory of

Nyssa gushed over a Christian friend's house and garden in central Anatolia that boasted a chapel (*Ep.* 20).

A completely different type of letter is the fictional, which is often, after Ovid's *Amores*, erotically charged. The most elaborate involving a garden is one by the second or third century sophist Alciphron, whose epistles were imaginarily penned by some Athenians of Plato's day. In this letter, (4.13 Schepers) one courtesan supposedly regales another with an account of a wanton party set in the land surrounding a villa, "the property of an amorous man rather than a farmer." Interspersed between couplings in thickets and a picnic with the ancient equivalent of a Fortnum & Mason's hamper come descriptions of features typical of a Roman pleasure garden—shrubs such as myrtles and laurels, fragrant flowers, singing birds, water dripping from a crag, statues of rustic divinities, and an altar. A similar garden is the setting in one of Aristaenetus's erotic epistles (1.3).

FICTIONAL GARDENS OF THE RHETORICIANS

Allied to the fictional letters are ekphraseis of rhetoricians, such as that (technically an *eikon* or *imago*) by a Philostratus (either L. Flavius or "the Lemnian") of Cupids amorously pelting each other with apples in an orchard with, at the end, certain distinctly hortulan characteristics (*Imagines* 1.6). Ekphraseis of spring are also irrigated by descriptions of gardens, or at least by the locus amoenus. One by Libanius has the unusual feature of an appreciation of not just the sight and fragrance of flowers but also the touch (8.482 Foerster). We may perhaps add to these a brief imaginary (albeit masquerading as factual) description by L. Flavius Philostratus of a little shrine of the sort to be found in Roman gardens that was made by Dionysus in honor of himself on Mount Nysa. This contained an image of the god within a circle of laurels surrounded by ivy and vines which in time grew to form an impervious canopy (*Vita Apollonii* 2.8).

Two ekphraseis, embedded in longer works rather than standing on their own, are of gardens or loci amoeni where the laws of nature are suspended or reversed. Dio Chrysostomus, with tongue in cheek, delivered a speech in Celaenae (Apamea) praising the city and holding it inferior only to India, where rivers run with milk, wine, honey, and oil; shady flowering trees nod their branches to bring fruit within easy reach; seated birds sing more beautifully than musical instruments; and the people hum as they recline on the greensward after swimming in a warm white or blue cold bath (35.17–21). The more elaborate occurs in Lucian's *Vera Historia*, a literary parody in the form of a travelogue that outdoes Raspe's narrative of the adventures of Baron Munchausen. After finding woods and a garden irrigated by a spring in the belly of a whale over 170 miles long (*VH* 1.32–33), he and his comrades escape from their cetaceous prison to discover the island of heroes, who in the Elysian Fields recline on couches of flowers, with further flowers dropped by singing birds in place of garlands, drink wine from cups that grow as fruit on glass trees, and fill themselves of their own accord, while rivers run with water, honey, myrrh, milk, and wine (*VH* 2.5, 12–16).

ETHICAL GARDENS: PHILOSOPHY
AND CHRISTIAN LITERATURE

The philosophical garden traditions of the Academy, and in particular the garden of Epicurus, inspired a long tradition of literary referencing. Cicero's philosophical works are all set in, or mention, the garden of Scipio Africanus Minor (Cic., *De amicitia* 7.25; *De natura deorum* 2.4.11; *De republica* 1.9.14); while he actually called two gymnasia at his Tusculan villa the Lyceum and the Academy (*De divitatione* 1.5.8; *Tusculanae disputationes* 2.3.9), in which practice he was imitated by Hadrian at his Tiburtine extravaganza.

Following Augustine's epiphany in a garden, Christian compositions frame gardens in two principal ways. First, those magnates who flee to their country villas, which always include gardens, to escape aestival urban heat are castigated, especially when they possess an abundance of these properties, as by John Chrysostomos (Homilies, *In Matthew* 61.3, 63.4).[37] Second, they, and sometimes the allied locus amoenus, are used to describe a paradise, either terrestrial or celestial. Prudentius, "the Christian Horace," pictures the righteous where "all the ground is covered by red rose-beds and, moist from running streamlets, it pours forth dense marigolds, soft violets and delicate saffron" as the blessed souls sweetly sing hymns over the grassy sward "and tread the lilies with their white feet" in a garden to which the wicked can come on holiday from hell every Easter Sunday (*Liber Cathemerinon* 5.113–128). Since vegetation is a major part of God's great creation, the whole world could be seen, not only notably in art[38] but also in literature as a garden in homilies on the Hexaemeron (beginning with Basil's) and in, among others, Gregory of Nazianzus's sermon extolling nature on "New Sunday," the first Sunday after Easter (*Hom.* 44).[39]

The Biblical injunctions of Psalm 127(128):2 and Jeremiah 29:5 (= 29:28) to grow one's own food[40] made productive gardening an important part of monastic life and the gardener became the specimen of the ascetic;[41] but the classical tradition, too, had its influence. Basil, whose monastic rules became the model for all subsequent Byzantine typika, had engaged in gardening as a boy and encouraged his monks in this area, but more interestingly his description of the remote retreat he found in Pontus is redolent of a somewhat wild locus amoenus. Although he avers that he is set on higher things than appreciation of "the exhalations from the earth or the breezes from the river . . . the great quantity of the flowers or song-birds . . . and fruit of every sort," he does yet mention these commonly praised ingredients of the literary tradition and gives the game away when he claims superiority for his retreat over the isle of Homer's Calypso (*Ep.* 14).

Briefly, to exceed our time-span, it may be noted that Cassiodorus, who represents the final flowering of Greco-Roman garden culture, went further. When this quondam politician retired in the early 550s, he took his love of gardens[42] to his ancestral estate, Scylacium (Squillace) in Bruttium, which he converted into a monastery that he actually named Viridarium ("Garden"). Having provided the tougher anchorites with an abode on Mount Castellum, he made this site home for their weaker coenobitic brethren. In addition to gardens liberally supplied with irrigation he excavated "within the bowels of the rocks" what he called the "Gates of Neptune." Through these swam "a school of fishes sporting in their free activity," which:

> both refreshes the spirit with amusement and delights the eye with wonder. Eagerly they rush to the hand of man and demand tidbits before they themselves become food: man feeds his darlings[43] and, although he can catch them, frequently when well provided he lets them go. (*Var.* 12.15 and *Inst.* 1.29: cf. *Var.* 8.32)

Basil would have frowned, Sidonius smiled upon this stubborn intrusion of Roman luxury into the lives of men of God.

CONCLUSION

The millennium covered by this chapter witnessed a spectacular flowering of literary expression, both personal and rhetorical. The shared cultural *koinē* of the Greco-Roman world encouraged adaptation and experimentation with literary genres in which gardens were a significant and recurring trope. For this reason, written accounts of gardens should not be taken at face value: consideration of genre must also be taken into account. A garden is more than the sum of its parts; the grassy bank, the rill of water, the fresh-picked apple, the scent of flowers under the shady tree, representations of this locus amoenus are multifarious. It is simultaneously a sensual retreat, a simple *potager*, a haunt of decadence, and the soul's paradise. The final distinction lies in the eye of its literary beholder.

CHAPTER SEVEN

Visual Representations

CATHERINE KEARNS

I associate the visual information presented to me . . . with the generic concept of "garden" because it coincides with remembered images of a "world of gardens."

—Bernard St-Denis[1]

What does it mean to represent a garden visually? The garden, historically a type of mediation of artifice and nature, constitutes an interstitial space full of the ephemeral materials of the earth, such as plants, soil, and water, which tend to challenge pictorial replication. And yet, the garden and broader cultural landscapes can be inherently pictorial, as they frame specific, constructed projections of "nature," a nature that has been in some way appropriated for human needs and desires.[2] In these cultivated spaces reside the tensions between order and unchecked wilderness, which include manipulations such as grafting and irrigation, as well as the contrast of human creativity and the raw, less-handled products of the earth. The portrayal of these tensions, set within a larger narrative of interwoven memories, ideas, and imaginations of landscapes and garden spaces, constitutes one of the earliest modes of artistic endeavor in the ancient world.

Humans have sought to capture the fleeting environments around them for millennia, and their pursuits reveal a number of important characteristics of image creation. One is the relationship between viewer and image, dependent on a situated context and artistic conventions such as perspective, setting, or repetitive patterns. The experience of viewing was active, whether an individual explored a representation while walking or seated; many ancient images conveyed the kinetic, itinerant aspects of gardens, while others framed specific views to recall traditions of scenery, panel paintings, or books.[3] Perspective, in particular, held important resonance in the construction of ancient imagined landscapes for viewing.[4] The physical embedding of an image on a wall, floor, or object also affected the viewer's experience, and a range of interactions between body, eye, and image highlighted the ambiguity of representing these constructions.[5]

Another important element of ancient visual representations was their interaction with social, political, and cultural trajectories, and their resultant multifunctionality. Kings could set metaphors of conquest, authority, and power in designed royal or imperial gardens in order to reinforce and maintain their political ends.[6] Gardens could also be immortalized in funereal imagery, as well as serve as the backdrop for religious and social activities such as dining, dancing, or marriage. The patronage of these types of imagery could project one's authority, wealth and prosperity, and personal taste. The confluence of these varied meanings, while impossible for the modern scholar to obtain, reveals itself in the setting, mechanics, and techniques utilized in specific images and their embedded placements within houses, monumental buildings, or openly accessible and socially significant places.

These various valences, dependent on the ancient viewer and the associated context, also contributed to the historicity of garden imagery, as individuals or groups echoed previous traditions or modified earlier instantiations of these interactions between man and his environment. These representations therefore participated in a larger "world of gardens," as St-Denis has described, establishing a range of meanings, sensibilities, and imaginations that often concentrated on a shared, diachronic vocabulary of styles and arrangements. Different individuals or groups used these images to self-identify with larger trends, to enhance their sociopolitical position within society, or to connect to the social and political potency of distant and exotic ideas and landscapes.[7] The afterlife of the garden thus existed within the realm of the visual as well as the verbal.[8]

This chapter's aim is not the recovery of the specific plants, designs, or features of ancient garden and landscape imagery, nor the composition of a reference guide.[9] What follows is a cross-cultural sampling of those paintings,

mosaics, textiles, objects, and constructed spaces found throughout antiquity, in a broad spatial and temporal survey, that suggest how ancient viewers
wanted to experience gardens. It is not meant to be an exhaustive collection
of every known example, but a selection of both iconic and less well-known
objects and images. While the majority of examples derive from the Roman
world, evidence from earlier and later cultures has been included to show that
throughout the long expanse covered in this volume (500 B.C.E. to 800 C.E.),
and across the Mediterranean and surrounding regions, people created and
employed garden images within their own cultural environments.

A study of the visual economy of the ancient garden cannot ignore the
contextual nature of the evidence. It is important to analyze the placement
of frescoes, mosaics, or sculpture in the three-dimensional spaces in which
they were discovered. Any attempt to understand the function of a particular
example is problematized by the multifunctional nature of many of the spaces
in ancient buildings, as well as the limitations of preservation. The identity of
the viewer(s) also often remains ambiguous, and in reality there were multiple
fluid and mobile identities involved in the production and reception of a given
image or object.

NEAR EASTERN VENATIC LANDSCAPES

Garden design developed as an important statement of regal wealth and
power among the kingdoms of the ancient Near East. These gardens signaled
the ability of the ruling figure to conquer and control nature and his capacity to distribute the earth's gifts to his subjects.[10] They represented iconic
landmarks of the surrounding topography as well as distant, imagined landscapes imbued with the power of the exotic or unknown.[11] Neo-Assyrian
scribes, for example, mention that royal gardens were laid out "in the like-
ness of Mt. Amanus," an important ideological marker on the North Syrian
landscape.[12] Monumental stone reliefs, found at the Neo-Assyrian capitals
of Nimrud, Khorsabad, and Nineveh, visually concretized the royal capacity
for creating the lush garden and reiterated the formations of legitimation
and power.

Reliefs that depicted the constructed spaces of these Neo-Assyrian gardens
emerge especially during the reigns of Sargon II and Ashurbanipal, in the seventh century B.C.E. The king, whether on a hunt, a military triumph, or leisurely enjoying a banquet, is seen positioned within an artificial landscape. In
the North Palace at Nineveh, images of Ashurbanipal in gardens decorated

FIGURE 7.1: The Garden Party relief from the North Palace of Ashurbanipal, Nineveh. (Courtesy: Trustees of the British Museum)

several rooms; one shows the king and his wife reclining amidst an ordered arrangement of trees and plants.[13] Hanging from one tree is the decapitated head of his enemy, reiterating the subjugation of his ecumene, human and nonhuman. The artist has delicately rendered the fruits, flowers, leaves, and vines of the garden to invoke fertility, abundance, and beauty,[14] and the viewer allowed access to these images could imagine the king's control over beast, plant, and water within his territory.

The Achaemenid empire of Iran, in the sixth and fifth centuries B.C.E., established the *pairadaeza* as a combination of hunting park and botanical garden, and a central element of royal built environments.[15] Our understanding of the pairadaeza is severely limited by sparse archaeological evidence and a lack of images that survive to exemplify how imperial figures saw these parks and how they might have projected that conception to their world.[16] Yet the pairadaeza had profound influence on later Mediterranean cultures as the *paradeisos*, a landscaped estate with productive orchards, exotic trees, and/or imported wild game. These conspicuous displays of royal authority and the appropriation of the surrounding landscape were not forgotten by later dynasties in the region, such as the Seleucids and Ptolemies during the Hellenistic period, the Romans, and the later Parthians and Sasanids.[17]

We can see the echoes of these sumptuous green spaces in a Sasanian relief dating to the late fifth century C.E., found at Taq-i Bustan, the Arch of the Garden, in what is now western Iran.[18] Within this royal complex were two grottoes with columns carved as flowering trees; the pairadaeza that would

FIGURE 7.2: Relief of royal boar hunt, Taq-i Bustan. (Courtesy: Taq-i Bustan, Iran/ Bridgeman Art Library)

have extended out from the rock face has disappeared.[19] Two reliefs on the grotto's walls show the king on a hunt in a marshy environment, echoing the Assyrian kings over 1,000 years prior.[20] These scenes clearly derive from the venatic imagery of earlier Mesopotamian cultures and frame the perspective from the grotto, looking out over the park. The viewer could gaze at a celebration of power, fertility, and the provision of nature in a palatial context. The images of royal hunts, banquets, and processions set within a verdant, conquered landscape serve as one extant window into the significance of these designed spaces.

ECONOMIES OF GREEK GARDEN ART

Some of the buildings and ritual spaces of the Aegean islands, principally Crete, Akrotiri, and Melos, were decorated during the second millennium B.C.E. with

FIGURE 7.3: Spring fresco, Room Delta 2, Akrotiri. (Courtesy: National Archaeological Museum at Athens)

polychrome frescoes of marine and vernal landscapes. These frescoes are considered an innovation in the rendering of landscape as an artistic theme, and some examples suggest garden elements.[21] The functions of these images remain obscure, as it has been observed that many of the plants and animals bear religious significance, especially crocuses and lilies, while others imply exotic, foreign milieus. Their placement in less accessible areas of houses also suggests an elite control over images of the constructed landscape and the reinforcement of a dominant social standing.[22] While less frequent and more abstract, elements of nature also appear in the wall frescoes at sites on the Greek mainland, such as a frieze from Pylos that depicts rocks and olive branches.[23] While their roles within domestic or ritual space are still questionable, these vibrant paintings suggest that the physical environment featured as an important backdrop to social and ritual practice.

Although these landscapes had been celebrated in Bronze Age frescoes, in later periods Aegean societies seem to have abbreviated landscapes in their art.[24] In the Archaic period of the mid-first millennium B.C.E., both poetry and art are noticeably frugal with representations of nature, leading some scholars to see a Panhellenic disinterest in landscape.[25] A closer analysis of archaic and classical Greek vases, reliefs, and frescoes suggests that an economical use of nature served to connote a larger surrounding environment. Trees, rocks, vines, and plants were used as narrative props, divine symbols, markers of virtue, and topographic cues that locate the scene within a larger evocative or imaginative landscape.[26] While the focus is consistently on human figures, the isolated tree, stream, or crag in painting or sculpture aroused conceptions of "grove," "field," or "grotto." This minimalist use of landscape is also manifest in the coinage of the Greek world, which rendered single trees to connote temple groves, or a head of grain to symbolize a region's fecundity.[27] The miniaturization of these coin depictions, as well as the medium itself, also contributed to a different sensory experience for representations of constructed landscapes.

The study of gardens in Greek art should therefore not be discounted, despite this economical treatment of nature. Relief sculptures dedicated as votives to gods such as Pan, Dionysos, and Asklepios pictorialized caves and groves to evoke rustic environments.[28] A few examples from vase painting that depict so-called Adonis Garden scenes portray women with potted plants in honor of the vegetation deity Adonis.[29] The connection between Aphrodite, her son Eros, and gardening is also shown in a vase that depicts Eros watering flowers.[30] Gardens certainly existed in ancient Greece, such as the spaces for philosophical discourse at the Academy at Athens, but they do not appear to be a pervasive element in the built environment.[31]

PROTO-ITALIAN LANDSCAPES

The remnants of colorful wall frescoes have survived in the tombs, or *tumuli*, of the Etruscans, the dominant inhabitants of central Italy prior to the emergence of the Romans. The trees, plants, flowers, and animals that were incorporated in many of these frescoes suggest that the Etruscan people saw the environments of the living and the dead as contiguous. Some trees occur repeatedly in tomb paintings because of their associations with gods of the underworld.[32] In scenes of ritual dancing, for example, trees were decorated with garlands, ribbons, and mirrors, a combination of artifice and nature with antecedents in Greek religious practice.[33]

Extant wall frescoes exhibit an artistic development that began with highly stylized decorative renderings of flowers and vegetation and grew to envelop entire scenes within marine or sylvan landscapes. One of the most iconic examples depicts an expansive coastal environment in the Tomb of Hunting and Fishing at Tarquinia, dated to around 510 B.C.E. Here, the natural surroundings

FIGURE 7.4: Fishermen in a boat, from the Tomb of Hunting and Fishing, Tarquinia. (Courtesy: Museo Nazionale Archeologico, Tarquinia/Bridgeman Art Library)

are given precedence over human figures who dive, swim, or carry nets or slings to catch fish and water birds. The wall recedes under the large space of the painted sky, which seems to vibrate with the movement of colorful sea birds. The deceased is compelled to join the swimmers and fishers in this lush, watery panorama.

These frescoes do not reveal the types of gardens the Etruscans had, but the images do capture a living and kinetic nature. The ritual dressing of trees, in particular, indicates a meaningful association between man-made objects and plants. The encompassing landscape paintings converted funereal space into animated views of human and nonhuman afterlives. These tombs fell out of use in the third and second centuries B.C.E., after the Etruscans lost their control of central Italy. Yet elements of Etruscan art continued, and the later chapters of Italian painting that emerge in the Roman period were significantly influenced by this Etruscan appreciation of environments.[34]

THE LANDSCAPES OF THE NILE

Egyptians began portraying gardens in their art in the third millennium B.C.E. In homes, palaces, and temples, gardens provided daily essentials as well as space for leisure and religious activity. Gardens were a prevalent image in funerary art, as peaceful and productive possessions for the afterlife. In the *Book of the Dead*, scenes depicted the deceased in lush and fertile gardens, awaiting divine blessing. Tomb walls were decorated with scenes intended for the deceased in the next world, which included utilitarian and pleasure gardens. Some images show square plots of orchards and cultivable land being watered by slaves.[35] These gardens were often walled and could be planted with trees as well flower beds that circumscribed pools.[36] These walled gardens could also be juxtaposed with paintings of wild, vibrant ecosystems, as in the case of the Tomb of Nebamun.[37]

Some paintings show horizontal lines of evenly spaced trees interspersed with reeds and flowers. Pools are shown from a bird's-eye perspective, projecting out to the viewer. Tall palm trees extend from the corners, as if from the tomb wall, and paths surround the pools, which are active with jagged lines of ripples. The paintings of gardens and vegetation on house floors generated a more dynamic viewing experience.[38] Symmetry is conspicuous in these gardens, a principle inherent in the land management of the Nile as well as Egyptian pictorial conventions, and it had a large influence on later Mediterranean gardens.[39]

The desire to create an accurate depiction of the world developed in the three millennia of pharaonic rule, despite the adherence to a set of established artistic techniques that governed perspective and rendering. A growing interest in botany induced Queen Hatshepsut in the fifteenth century B.C.E. to commission the study and retrieval of plant specimens from Punt, the exotic land south of Nubia. The wall reliefs of her temple near Luxor depict this trading expedition and various trees and plants, especially frankincense, being stored and shipped on the royal barges.[40] These representations signaled the growing extent of her power as well as her ability to transport rooted trees and plants great distances.

The Nile region, with its unique annual flooding and long history of gardens, became a *topos* of fertility and fecundity in later Greek and Roman thought, an exotic land of palm groves and fantastic creatures. In the first century C.E., wealthy Romans began to travel the distant stretches of the Roman Empire, encountering the oases of Egypt and the monumental temple complexes with

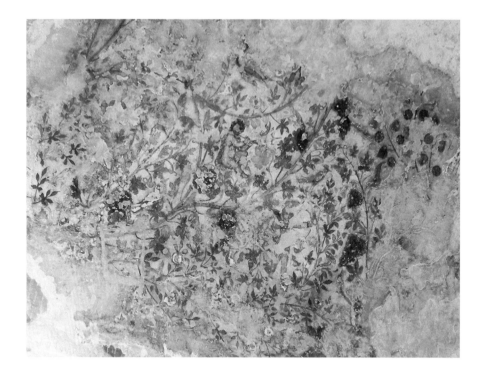

FIGURE 7.5: Dionysiac landscape fresco, Siq el Bared. (Courtesy: K. Gleason).

their sacred gardens.[41] "Egyptianizing" motifs enjoyed a prominence in contemporary Roman art, and gardens incorporated decorative or design features
that symbolized the power of the Nile, its exotica and culture, and the symmetry of Egypt's own garden traditions.[42]

Alexandria, the bustling Ptolemaic city positioned on the Nile delta, was
one of several important Hellenistic nodes in the exchange of ideas in science,
philosophy, and art. From this city, styles and conceptions of gardens and landscape travelled between the peoples of Africa, Asia, and Europe, leading scholars to assign an "Alexandrian style" to potentially unrelated work.[43] At the
site of Siq el Bared outside of Petra in southern Jordan, an area that was once
the capital of the Nabatean Kingdom, a colorful fresco was discovered that depicts a mass of sinuous vines with grape clusters and exotic birds being hunted
by winged children, or *putti*.[44] The fresco decorates a vault in a *biclinium*, a
dining room with two reclining couches, and likely dates to the mid-first century B.C.E. The composition of a painted Dionysiac tangle of vines brought an

FIGURE 7.6: Hanging showing Euthenia in a garden. (Courtesy: Metropolitan Museum of Art/Art Resource)

outdoor ambience to the people dining indoors, enhancing the sensory impact of the experience.

Egyptian art was also receptive to later Greco-Roman conventions, styles, and themes, which began appearing in the second and first centuries B.C.E. One linen painting, which belongs to a long history of decorative Egyptian textiles and likely dates to the first century C.E., depicts Euthenia, a goddess associated with abundance and the flooding of the Nile.[45] The figure is shown reclining and holding a bowl of water, a substitute for her consort Nilos, the personification of the river. Behind her grows a lush garden of ivy, date palms, and possibly vines, inhabited by birds that perch on branches or fly toward her bowl. The illusion of space is created by portraying a thick, dense patch of vegetation behind the languid figure. The similarities of this linen to contemporary Roman garden frescoes are striking, and the trees, plants, and birds all recall the garden images of Italy, as we will see below.

FIGURE 7.7: The Nile Mosaic, detail depicting pergola. (Courtesy: Museo Archeologico Prenestino, Palestrina/ Bridgeman Art Library)

THE HELLENISTIC QUESTION

At the end of the fourth century B.C.E., after the death of the Macedonian conqueror Alexander, the relatively localized phenomena of previous periods exploded onto a global stage. Art produced in this "Hellenistic" setting, the last three centuries B.C.E., was part of a large interactive network extending across the Mediterranean into Asia and Arabia.[46] The exchange of ideas, methods, and trends driven by people in Egypt, Greece, Macedon, and Asia stimulated and engendered a varied, heterogeneous art. At the same time, intellectuals were becoming more and more interested in their ecological surroundings.[47] Combined with the growing interest in actual garden spaces, the principle of leisure, and the acquisition of wealth and luxury, the Hellenistic period was a catalyst for a new, cosmopolitan interpretation of landscape. It is in this period that formal visual descriptions of the landmarks, environments, and peoples of the known world emerge. A larger tradition of cartographic art, in which topographical detail, information on flora and fauna, and distinct features of the landscape were depicted, is mentioned in the literary sources as an Alexandrian innovation.[48] A number of the most iconic objects of Hellenistic art reveal a new focus on continuous spatial panoramas, exotic landscapes, and the visualization of garden culture.[49]

One such work, known as the Nile Mosaic and dating to the end of the second century B.C.E., was found in the Sanctuary of Fortuna in Praeneste in central Italy. The enormous mosaic depicts the Nile River in flood and was placed within an apsed artificial grotto in a large public building.[50] The work takes the viewer on a river tour as it sinuously wanders amongst animals, buildings, and people in various activities; the thin layer of water that would have covered this *nymphaeum* mosaic simulated the flowing river. The conception of nature moves from the foreground of buildings, gardens, and groves into the wild and untamed environment in which men hunt large animals. Toward the bottom of the scene, a reed lattice-work pergola gives shade to reclining figures along the river and is girded with a thick mass of grape vines and lotus flowers. Water flows between the reclining couples on the two sides of the pergola. It is possible that the artist(s) adapted the concept of a riverside garden party for this scene.[51] Whatever its inspiration, the artist(s) drew from the topography of Egypt, and much attention was given to the strange plant, animal, and aquatic life that would populate this landscape.[52]

The Odyssey landscapes from a house from the Esquiline hill in Rome also demonstrate originality in their focus on pictorialized landscape rather than the human figure. These frescoes depict, in continuous narration, a cycle of episodes taken from Homer's *Odyssey*.[53] The works, which have no clear antecedent in Greek art, are suggestive of a two-dimensional *chimaera*, a mixture of elements from Greek, "Hellenistic," and Roman artistic conventions and trends.[54] The mid-first century B.C.E. paintings were framed by painted red pilasters, a Roman innovation that imitated a porticoed walkway, and incited the viewer to contemplate the story while moving. At the same time, the pilasters created a framework through which a viewer could imagine the scene, as if a picture, extending back into continuous horizontal and vertical space. This intellectually motivated movement epitomized philosophy as practice in the Hellenistic period.[55]

ROMAN GARDEN PAINTINGS

A man named Studius (or Ludius) is credited by Vitruvius and Pliny as the inventor of representations of landscapes, *opera topiaria*, in the first century B.C.E.; regardless of authorship, the visual encoding of the Roman garden in painting constituted a subgenre emerging in the mid-first century B.C.E. (Vitruvius, *De Architectura* 7.5.2; Pliny, *Historia naturalis* 35.116).[56] The first extant example of garden painting, and one of the more iconic examples of Roman art, dates to around 25 B.C.E. and covers the four walls of an underground hall at the villa of Livia, the wife of the first emperor Augustus, at Prima Porta, north of Rome.[57] The hall incorporates an immersive style of decoration, continuing the scenery of a unitary landscape across corners and inviting the viewer to walk around the room.[58] As they are painted in a dining room, the images also prompt a more static experience, as if viewing a garden from a seated position within a grotto.[59] The remarkably well preserved frescoes depict a garden full of various types of trees, flowering bushes, and arbors of all seasons, affording a symbolic reading of prosperity and continuous fertility.[60] Only a low marble parapet separates the viewer from the thickly planted garden. The spontaneity of the disordered garden beyond the fence conveys a sense of wildness, opposed to the ordered, formally arranged trees and arbors in front.

A similar example has been uncovered in a house in the city of Ephesus on the coast of ancient Asia Minor, under construction from the first century to the seventh century C.E.[61] Excavations revealed two panels of a vibrantly colored garden painting concealed under a late antique fresco in a courtyard of the house. In the panels, an intricate marble balustrade encloses a garden of apple and pomegranate trees, what appears to be cypress or juniper, and several birds. The two garden paintings form a corner, without a break in the scenery, suggesting that the entire open-air courtyard would have been painted with a continuous garden image.

Some painted garden rooms, such as those in the Villa of Poppaea in Oplontis, incorporated real fountains and plantings, enhancing the ambiguity of the garden space and challenging the eye's recognition of real or painted plants

FIGURE 7.8: Ephesos, Hanghaus 2. Reconstruction of the garden room. Dotted line indicates preserved extent of painting; faded area is reconstructed. (SketchUp and Photoshop model by M. Palmer and M. Bolton)

through a series of windows.[62] Wilhelmina Jashemski noted that the majority of the wall frescoes she examined in the first century C.E. houses destroyed by the eruption of Vesuvius decorated the rear wall of the peristyle garden, often as single panels. She suggested that these garden paintings were employed to extend the garden space, so that a smaller garden might appear larger and lusher.[63] Some Pompeian houses contained just the suggestion of a garden image, perhaps a bird on a trellis or a sketched enclosure.[64] It is indicative of the appreciation for these garden paintings that not only did the majority of houses in Pompeii and Herculaneum have some wall area devoted to garden representations, but that these frescoes were some of the most carefully executed in the house.

Beyond the genre of paintings that were strictly representations of gardens, another first century B.C.E. style consists of "villascapes," frescoes with framed views of large villas, usually along coasts. These paintings explored the dialogue between the villa's architecture and the sea, sky,

FIGURE 7.9: Garden room with yellow ochre painting, Oplontis. (Courtesy: S. Jashemski)

and land around it. They seem to represent views of villas, as if one were encircling or approaching them from a place nearby.[65] The colonnaded *porticus*, a recurring symbol of wealth and luxury, was often shown girded by a formal garden with arranged trees.[66] The varying degrees of bird's-eye views, which emphasize perspective, conveyed the spatial layout of these gardens, and the placement of frescoes within a building afforded different viewing responses. Some were painted with hazier strokes, creating an illusion whose details were less important than the general atmosphere of a constructed landscape setting.

A wealth of examples of garden paintings survive from the Roman period, which belong to a discourse on garden imagery that reveals influences from Etruscan, Persian, and Greek traditions.[67] Roman garden paintings decorated a range of spaces, some cultivated with plants and others more interior. They did not aim to replicate the exact arrangements of their living, ephemeral counterparts in peristyles and backyard garden plots. Instead, they represented a combination of elements—artificial, ecological, spiritual, moral, historical—that accumulated as a visual embodiment of garden and landscape fantasy. Landscape and gardens, in particular, also became key themes in materializing status and wealth.⁶⁸ As people granted more and more space to gardens in their houses during the early empire, the relationship between *ars* and *natura* emerged as a prominent visual project in painting and other media.

ROMAN GARDEN SCULPTURE

In the Roman garden, the selection, placement, and styling of three-dimensional art, such as sculpture and architectural structures, constituted an important facet of the larger experience of viewership.⁶⁹ In the peristyle garden of the House of Venus at Pompeii, a fresco depicting a statue of the god Mars set amidst a garden's lush plants and trees plays with these tensions between surfaces, sculpture, and vegetation.⁷⁰ Objects embedded within the flower beds and shrubs could direct the viewer's gaze, stimulate conversation, and help build the self-image of the owner. An inscription that adorns a marble herm, found in a villa near Frattocchie outside of Rome, addresses the garden visitor with praise for this crafted mixture of plant and marble:

> You look at the monuments of men, worthy of poets in the manner of the ancients, and also vineyards, groves, violet-beds. Lilies, apples, roses, vines and arbors crown the faces of the Greeks and the shrines dedicated to the Muses. The figures suggest enough of the expression and face of Socrates and the vivacious mind of Cato that you know the type.⁷¹

In this garden, the busts of important philosophers and statesmen displayed the owner's intellect, while the surroundings served to locate the viewer in a distinct garden space. A garden's statuary and art pieces had a fundamental role in the identification of that garden space.

Types of Roman garden sculpture range from small statuettes to large-scale figures, but they all tend to belong to a mythic or historic interface with the garden itself. Gods, nymphs, satyrs, centaurs, and Muses were popular themes; the wild, carnal world of Bacchus was also a favorite, for he stimulated leisure and ecstatic movement, as well as tied the garden to the theater. Statues of garden deities such as Venus, the sylvan huntress Diana, or the mischievous woodland god Pan were also prominent. Priapus, guardian of the garden was often represented in herms and figurines.⁷² In the House of Octavius Quartio at Pompeii, paintings of the well-known metamorphoses of Narcissus

FIGURE 7.10: *Symplegma* of Satyr and Hermaphrodite near pool, Oplontis. (Courtesy: S. Jashemski)

FIGURE 7.11: *Symplegma* of Satyr and Hermaphrodite near pool, Oplontis. (SketchUp model Courtesy: M. Palmer)

and Actaeon helped to signal the charged mythic atmosphere.[73] Apart from figural pieces, reliefs carved or painted on stone or wooden panels known as *pinakes* rested on posts, along with herms and elaborately decorated fountains, and *oscilla* with theatrical motifs engraved in stone hung from gables or even tree branches.[74] An example of this deliberate and constructed scene setting is the subject of a garden painting in the House of the Orchard at Pompeii.[75]

A garden's sculptural ensemble was not erratically configured, but curated with specific themes and motifs in mind. At the same time, successful collections were not monotone but incorporated *varietas* and repetition. The relationships that united a sculptural group might involve mortals and gods, animals and humans, kings and conquered, or women and men. In Pompey's Porticus, the garden-temple precinct he designed in Rome in 55 B.C.E., he honored his patron Venus Victrix and the power of the female by gathering sculptural images of female poets, virgins, and infamous women taken from eastern paradigms. Pompey definitively designed his Porticus for the public, ensuring that its symmetrical rows of trees balanced with sculptural collections would be an accessible landmark of the urban environment.[76]

In many Roman gardens, the intertwining of plant and object discouraged a static viewing process, so that one could move around the garden and view sculptures from new angles. Even within sculptural pieces, the twisting and wrenching of bodies implied motion, similar to the arrested flight of birds in garden paintings. The *symplegma* statue type found at the villa of Poppaea at Oplontis, in which a satyr wrestles with a hermaphrodite, is charged with frozen action: arms twist and push, legs entwine, and backs cave. Placed on the edge of a garden pool, the reflection of this mischief in the water further instilled the statuary with movement, which the itinerant viewer could experience.[77] Other statues interacted with the water itself, playing with the balance of water and marble.[78]

TESSELLATED ROMAN GARDENS

The art of mosaic work, using small pieces of stone, glass, and shell to create images, was an additional medium for garden representation found in Roman houses and public buildings, having been developed centuries earlier in Greece and North Africa. Mosaics formed a vast corpus of images that complemented the paintings discussed above, both reimagining popular scenes and introducing new ones through their ability to decorate dining structures, floors and even ceilings. The development of mosaic art on

FIGURE 7.12: Mosaic of gardens, detail of fence with foliage, Massa Lubrense. (Courtesy: K. Gleason)

walls is a genre distinct from floor mosaics and is currently thought to be a Roman invention of the late Republic and early Empire, used in the decoration of grottos and cave-like structures in luxury villas.[79] The close connection between images of vegetation and geometry, prominent in mosaics but

FIGURE 7.13: "Silenus Bound" mosaic, Thysdrus. (Courtesy: A.-A. Malek/CNRS)

also apparent in early garden art, counters other stylistic goals of realism or naturalism.

Water shrines, known as *nymphaea* or *musaea* for their devotion to the divine gallery of nymphs and Muses, were often positioned near or within gardens. The inclusion of bits of Egyptian blue glass and volcanic rock, pumice, and entire marine shells further played with the representations of landscape and water. The inspiration behind the motifs composed with these materials was the garden painting of the period, and some *nymphaea* were complemented by garden frescoes on nearby walls.[80] A beautiful example of a large *nymphaeum* with multiple niches and *exedrae* covered in gardenscapes has been found at Massa Lubrense on the Bay of Naples.[81] In several recesses in the wall, a trellis fence is depicted in the mosaic to separate the viewer from the pine trees and bushes of the garden, and the open background, made of striking blue glass, is broken by the flight of several birds. This polychromatic series of enclosed images, combined with the variation in texture, enhances the depicted plants, birds, and water.

In Roman Africa, the popular motif of branches and vines emerging from craters was employed by craftsmen on floor mosaics that played with perspective and the viewer's experience in different ways than wall ornamentation. The visual dynamic of looking onto a landscape from above, while possible in aerial panoramas in paintings, was physically achieved through floor pavements and the garden walks that they recreated.[82] At Thysdrus, in Tunisia, the four corners of an immense floor mosaic of a private house are occupied by large craters, from which the thick tendrils of vines extend toward the center.[83] The white background of the composition is almost completely covered by a woven configuration of leaves, grape clusters, animals, and even human figures, such as shepherds and diminutive cupids. This efficacious mosaic immersed the viewer in a tangled, Dionysiac landscape by angling the vines so that they appear to grow upward, toward the viewer, from the four corners.[84]

CLASSICAL CONTINUITY INTO LATE ANTIQUITY

In the dynamic period following the rise of Constantine the Great in the fourth century C.E. and the emergence of Christianity in the Roman world, some of the earliest churches across the Mediterranean grappled with the interrelationship of nature and monotheistic religion. The methods for incorporating landscape imagery in Christian art, however, drew heavily on the classical representations of these environments seen in villas and buildings of earlier periods. Mosaicists working to depict biblical stories and allegories used the same pictorial markers that had been recurring in landscape art since the early Hellenistic period. The widely recognized ancient

FIGURE 7.14: Ambulatory of Santa Costanza, detail of flowers and birds, Rome. (Courtesy: Santa Costanza, Rome/Bridgeman Art Library)

scene of birds perched on the rim of a water-filled basin, for example, appears in a depiction of two apostles in the fifth century C.E. Mausoleum of Galla Placidia at Ravenna.[85] Here, the water basin placed on a green swatch of earth serves as a metonym for an entire paradisal garden. The artistic conceptions of the pastoral identity of Christ as a shepherd and the Garden of Eden also utilized and echoed landscape elements from earlier periods.[86]

At the same time, some churches, basilicas, and even tombs explored non-Christian depictions of landscapes.[87] A series of mosaics that cover the vaults of the ambulatory, or walkway, in the fifth century C.E. mausoleum of Santa Costanza in Rome utilized a Dionysiac theme with dense jumbles of vegetation. Satyrs and maenads, panthers, and masses of tangled grapevines occupy nearly all of the space.[88] Sectioned stems and branches of trees, bushes, and

vines appear to float against a white background, and birds, vessels, and fountains are interspersed among the foliage and fruits. With these images above,
people could walk beneath the swirling, ecstatic vegetation, as if under a vine-
covered trellis.[89] Although Christ had identified himself as the "True Vine,"
these ambulatory mosaics show that late antique garden imagery was often
ambivalent and was not understood as entirely "religious" or "secular," perhaps in an appeal to a plurality of viewer identities.[90]

An additional late antique example shows the return to a classical garden
motif, that of outdoor feasting, seen earlier in the pergola section of the Nile
mosaic. On a large silver plate belonging to the fourth or fifth century C.E.
Sevso treasure, the central medallion is decorated with an aristocratic picnic
and hunt.[91] In the center, four men and a woman recline on a *stibadium* in
front of a small table under a canopy in a sylvan setting, with attendants
in various states of procuring, cooking, or serving food. The stibadium was
the semicircular dining couch used in Roman gardens. Dozens of rosettes
fill the space surrounding the picnic. Despite the presence of Christ's mono-
gram on the rim's inscription, the scene lacks any overt Christian motifs,
celebrating instead the wooded world encircling the hunt and the amenities
of the host's estate.[92]

When Arabs conquered the Sasanian city of Ctesiphon in Mesopotamia
in 637 C.E., they encountered an enormous carpet dating to the reign of the
sixth century king Chosroe I in the royal palace. Literary records from Arab
historians describe the astonishing treasure, reportedly 450 feet long and
90 feet wide, as depicting the spring *paradeisos* of the king.[93] This textile garden was full of colorful fruit trees, paths, and watercourses and was enclosed
by a flowery border running along the edges. The background consisted
of gold thread, while the water was made of crystals; gemstones and shiny
jewels were woven into the fabric for the buds and petals of the flowers. One
could theoretically move above this enclosed "garden" and view the varied
plants and landscape elements portrayed.[94] The work, as well as the monumental Sasanian reliefs at Taq-i Bustan mentioned earlier, was not function-
ally limited to capturing an eternal landscape. By recalling the long tradition
of palatial *paradeisoi* and gardens in the region, the Sasanian kings sought
to legitimize their claim to territorial power.[95] The afterlife of the Persian
garden therefore re-emerged in later generations through carpets, friezes, and
decorated objects.[96]

The interweaving of stone and thread links this royal carpet tradition to
mosaic work, a relation that is particularly entrenched in the art of Syria

and the east, seen in the pavements of Antioch.[97] The decoration of wide expanses of floors in fifth century C.E. Near Eastern churches stimulated a trend in carpet-like configurations, in which simple geometric or vegetal designs were monotonously repeated. The floral carpet style included the *semis*, which is portrayed as a background strewn with floral motifs without an ordered arrangement. In the early sixth century C.E. House of the Phoenix at Daphne, in Antioch, an immense white floor is covered by rows of rosebuds.[98] The effect of a sea of thousands of rosebuds in abstract, two-dimensional arrangements reiterates the ways in which vegetal imagery and geometric patterns converge.

CONCLUSIONS

In this overview of ancient garden and landscape art, a variety of images, objects, and architectural constructions recovered from the built spaces of several ancient cultures of the Mediterranean and its surrounding landscapes reveals the polyvalency embedded within the act of representing these layered conceptions of nature. Beyond their capacity to evoke actual or imagined garden spaces, these visual artifices often served to legitimate, to historicize, to celebrate, to worship, or to propagate a plurality of ideas of landscape, environment, and man's control over the physical world. Some did this by challenging the apparent dichotomous relationship between art and nature, while others blurred any constructed distinction, embracing the ambiguity in the act of recreating "nature." Throughout this trajectory of garden and landscape impressions, the social, political, and cultural connections of these spaces and the people who created and enjoyed them are prevalent and emphasize the dynamics between image and viewer. Whether the view engendered static or active participation, these representations were integral to their multifunctional and meaningful contexts.

Modern interrogations will never recover the myriad meanings that garden representations afforded their specific audiences or the strategies involved in their production. We can appreciate, however, that different media, contexts, styles, and conventions operated in particular ways to evoke cultural responses to garden spaces and mediated the relationships between material objects and the people using or viewing them. These examples further show that gardens and their visual representations did not exist in isolation but were enmeshed in social and political practice and belonged to a long mnemonic current in the ancient world that struggled to capture the fleeting, transient character of the natural environment. Many of the examples above shifted some form of memory of past or contemporary landscapes into new and culturally different materializations. These images were therefore loaded with the concept of gardens seen, heard, and experienced. The ancient garden itself, like its modern counterpart, was a changing, ephemeral space, and its accompanying visual representations are the self-conscious records of that dynamic and transitory landscape.

CHAPTER EIGHT

Gardens and the Larger Landscape

KELLY D. COOK AND RACHEL FOULK

But you will cease to wonder, when I acquaint you with the villa, the advantages of its situation, and the extensive prospect of its sea-coast.

—Pliny, *Letters* 2.27

So begins Pliny the Younger, writing in the late first or early second century C.E., introducing his friend, Gallus, to the pleasures of his estate, Laurentinum.[1] The various aspects of his views, the villa's relationship to the landscape, and how the whole was designed in response to that landscape will be discussed below, but for now it serves as a midpoint of a millennium of garden development in the ancient world. Immense fortunes went into developing gardens, but also into creating architectural vistas that united one's domain as a whole composition. Nature came to take on a variety of meanings from 600 B.C.E. to 600 C.E., and the garden served as a mediating force in this development. How gardens were designed reflects the larger considerations of the landscape beyond and displays distinct social changes and ideals.

In the ancient Mediterranean, there were the physical spaces of gardens, in which plants and structures were combined to form a vision of perfected nature. Each garden reflected the larger scope of perceived nature: beyond the garden's boundaries, including other cultivated spaces, urban spaces, manipulated natural forms, such as canals and built lakes, and on to as yet untamed mountains and forests. The art and literature from this millennium attest to the dynamic interplay between controlled spaces and their antithesis, the wilderness. There were many gradations, operating within a fluid system of exchange between perception and representation. This chapter will consider the ways in which ancient cultures, particularly Greek and Roman, responded to the force of nature and the larger landscape, and how the multifaceted understanding of it transformed not only the built environment but the broader assortment of representational arts as well. What was the relationship between the garden and the larger landscape beyond its confines? What evidence exists for this? What might this evidence tell us about ancient ideas of nature?

Much of what we know about gardens and their surrounding landscapes comes through evidence offered by ancient Rome, which colonized large swathes of Europe, the Middle East, and Northern Africa. The Romans introduced distinct practices of land tenure over indigenous land uses. Cultural contact created a synthetic vision of gardens and their immediate surroundings. Rome, as with other Mediterranean cultures, did not have a monolithic

FIGURE 8.1: The Nile Mosaic from Praeneste (Palestrina), Italy. (Courtesy: Bridgeman Art Library)

concept of nature, nor did landscape have entirely the same meaning as the contemporary term. Localized conditions spawned multivalent relationships to land beyond what was bounded and cultivated, as famously represented in the Palestrina mosaic of the Nile. The Romans also responded to their Greek inheritance, if in ways more related to the values of an agricultural society than to a rich garden tradition.

GREEK LANDSCAPE PRACTICES

For the fifth century B.C.E. historian Herodotus, agriculture was the dividing line between civilized and uncivilized: "The Budini are indigenous; they are nomads, and the only people in these parts that eat fir-cones; the Geloni are farmers, eating grain and cultivating gardens; they are altogether unlike the Budini in form and in coloring. Yet the Greeks call the Budini too Geloni; but this is wrong (Herodotus, *Histories* 4.109.1)." Land was central to the Greek economy. Its cultivation became a marker for the development of regional and civic identities in the Greek world. The working of land represented a large proportion of most household wealth. The units of production—vineyards, orchards, vegetable gardens, and so on—were arranged within a larger estate or farm (*kleros*), generally quite modest in size and ranging from 55 to 300 *plethra* (1 hectare equals 11 plethra).[2] Greek gardens consisted of a vast patchwork of utilitarian spaces, with no one unit in particular made to be purely ornamental. Farmers established groves, vineyards, and gardens both vegetal and floral, but the terms for such spaces are often diffuse and occasionally interchangeable. These gardens (*kepoi*) were used to grow varieties of produce, to serve as sanctuaries or places for tomb markers, and to experiment with wild plants.[3] This last aspect of gardens is attested by Theophrastus in his *Enquiry into Plants*, compiled in the fourth through third centuries B.C.E., in which he describes the cultivation of herbs that are normally considered wild and suggests that gardens were not only meant to be productive in the short term, but could also be sites for experimentation and close observation of nature (Theophrastus 7.7.2).[4]

In Attica, most estates did not exceed the upper limit of 300 plethra, reflecting to some degree the desire to maintain equitable levels of wealth within the region.[5] There are, however, descriptions of properties in other areas in the Mediterranean that suggest a much grander scale. The Persians had a long history of large-scale development of landscapes, with elaborate parklands (*paradeisoi*), as chronicled in Xenophon's descriptions of King Cyrus's gardens. These settings would have enabled sweeping views of surrounding features, often from large terrace structures. Persian influence extended right up to

Greek dominions. In western Anatolia, at sites such as Sardis and Daskyleion, evidence for monumental terraces exists, which offered not only elaborate entrances to palace complexes but extensive views over surrounding landscapes.[6]

In the western Mediterranean, Persian influence may also have impacted the building of monumental projects under tyrants, such as that of Dionysios I (432–367 B.C.E.) at his palace at Rhegion. Like a Persian satrap, he orchestrated a vast complex that included a paradeisos, complete with imported plane trees.[7] Diodorus Siculus chronicles the luxury of Acragas on Sicily; one citizen, Tellias, outfitted 500 infantry soldiers from the resources of his property (which must have well exceeded 300 plethra); it also had a vast wine cellar (Diodorus Siculus, 13.83.1–3).[8] Land was essential to the rights and privileges of most Greeks, however, and conspicuously large holdings were often condemned, and were further demonized as being decidedly Eastern.[9]

A counterpoint can be found in Ptolemaic Egypt. When the generals of Alexander the Great's empire colonized Egypt, its older traditions of land tenure were not forsaken. The Ptolemaic Greeks opted to maintain the land tenure system of the pharaohs in which cultivated land was often tied to temple estates.[10] Basin irrigation served as the primary organizational system of cultivated units such as orchards and gardens. Individual gardens could often be found in private houses arranged alongside these irrigation systems, incorporating edible plants and palm and fruit trees.[11] As in Greece, gardens of Ptolemaic Egypt were only one part of a larger network of cultivated units. Ornamental gardens certainly could have been found, but in general even these would have had utilitarian functions such as the growing of medicinal herbs. The gardens and landscapes of Ptolemaic Egypt reflected the hierarchical nature of pharaonic and in turn Ptolemaic administration, unlike the Platonic view of land holding, which aimed to be more egalitarian.

Alexander the Great supposedly ordered the construction of the Palace of Alexandria. Strabo relates the vast wealth of this complex, its myriad rooms and outdoor spaces, which housed both official meeting places and private living quarters. The innermost complex was surrounded by a park (*alsos*) containing pavilions for private functions and entertainments.[12] In the city of Alexandria was the Paneion, an artificial hill renowned for its views of the city. Close to the Gymnasium and the official Court of Justice, the Paneion was the pinnacle of a large public parkland. The park at the palace and the parkland around the Paneion suggest two concurrent developments: first, an elaboration of the private, luxurious, cultivated space, growing evermore in its complex staging of entertainments and spectacles; and second, a mounting effort to establish public green spaces that contained the same potential for vistas as the private gardens. This civic motive for developing natural places is later manifested in Vitruvius's assertion of the health benefits of public greenery; it made for a healthier body and, hence, a healthier citizen (Vitruvius, 5.9.5).

REPRESENTATIONS OF THE GREEK LANDSCAPE

Beyond Theophrastus's *Enquiry into Plants* and his second treatise, *On the Causes of Plants*, a large number of agricultural treatises were produced in ancient Greece. Xenophon's *Oeconomicus* and Hesiod's *Works and Days* attest to the varieties of cultivation, close observation of plant and animal growth, and descriptive geographies of vegetative spaces. Such works may document agricultural and garden practices; however, Greek literature offers a host of allegorical renderings of nature, from Homer to Theocritus and beyond to Hellenistic prose and verse.

The state of mankind and his relation to land are of prime concern in Hesiod's epic poem *Works and Days*, written around 700 B.C.E. Within the context of multiple etiologies, Hesiod describes the toil of the farmer and his relation to the land in archaic Greece. As the poet explains to his brother Perses, the work of the current generation of man, the fifth in a series of ages of man, is agriculture. For the first, the golden, generation of mankind, who lived like the gods, "the fruitful grainland / yielded its harvest to them / of its own accord" (*Works and Days*, 117–18, trans. Lattimore). In the age of iron, men must constantly plow, plant, and tend to the land. The poet gives firm, specific advice on how to be productive and pious in order to enjoy the fruits of the life-sustaining land. This is not a description of a pleasure garden, but a field of labor, for "it is from work that men grow rich and own flocks and herds; by work, too, they become much better friends of the immortals" (*Works and Days*, 307–9, trans. Lattimore). Perses must live according to the rule of changing seasons, plowing, planting, tending, and reaping at the appropriate times, using the changing stars and weather as his guide. The work is difficult and requires many laborers to provide assistance. But this universally prescribed occupation is virtuous, keeping the farmer occupied and putting off idleness.

Works and Days cannot be read as a complete Greek farmer's almanac. Rather, it sheds light on general attitudes toward agricultural practice. The semi-arid, mountainous terrain of mainland Greece was not well suited to the large farming estates found elsewhere in the Mediterranean. Scholars have noted that the circumstances that inform *Works and Days* reflect the agrarian crisis that ultimately caused the Greek city-states to colonize more fertile land in the Mediterranean basin.[13]

THE ROMAN PARADIGM

Roman gardens reflected a relationship to the larger landscape informed by imperial modes of land tenure, as well as artistic representations of nature both visual and literary, and suggest an expression of human and political intent through an allegory. Roman landscapes came to be so deliberately designed that each view could encompass a complete unfolding of symbolic natures. Once established at its greatest breadth, the Roman Empire amassed vast new territories with its own distinctive traditions regarding the land and the concept of nature.

During the Roman Republic (508–27 B.C.E.), formal patterns of land tenure began to emerge on the Italian peninsula. The most drastic forms of land development were seen in those parcels obtained through military conquests. Conquered lands were added to the *ager publicus* (common lands). Roman identity was firmly bound to acquisition of land,[14] and these lands were a bone of contention between classes and of central concern to individuals' Roman rights. Saskia Roselaar argues that these lands consisted of arable tracts, pasture, and wilderness areas, and they were often turned over as private properties to Roman colonists. In the imperial era, Agennius Urbicus noted that sometimes towns owned lands far away, donated as gifts of emperors, signifying a form of ownership of a property without the benefit of actually seeing it (Agennius Urbicus 36.21–3). From the second century B.C.E., an increasing consolidation of lands into ever larger estates (*latifundia*) began. Elite landholders seized on pastoral literature and imagery to represent their wealth. Land holding could be controversial, but as the power of empire became more centralized, these elites fashioned a system of representation of nature and of land that formed the basis of their claims to ancestral holdings of their properties. In short, while poems of distant landscapes were certainly meant to entertain, elite Roman authority pivoted off this mastery of cultivated spaces. The Romans further elaborated the system of land survey, which gave a regimented and coherent base to these claims.

LAND SURVEY

Land survey and property demarcation date back nearly as far as the idea of land ownership. Boundary stones have been found in Babylonia, and Egyptian frescoes depict land surveyors, or rope-stretchers, as they were known, remeasuring areas around the Nile after an inundation. The Hellenistic Greeks learned much from the Egyptians in the way of land survey as their holdings expanded.[15]

The Romans were preeminent land surveyors. Aerial photography has shown evidence of Roman centuriation, the division of land into measured squares and defined by *limites* (balks) at sites around Italy and Mediterranean, including Alba Fucens, Cosa, and Luceria in Italy, as well as near El Djem in Tunisia. Figure 8.2 shows centuriation around Corinth, Greece, following its conquest by the Romans.[16] *Agrimensores*, literally the "measurers of land," were responsible for surveying. *Ager* implies a measured amount of land, not just a wild tract, and Roman surveying further involved two separate actions: the actual surveying or bounding of land and the laying out of a plan. Both operations demonstrate a profound sense of regulation of land and a denial of wildness: land was meant to be productive. Roman land survey perhaps dates back to the fourth century B.C.E., during a period of Latin colonization, but it is under the late republic and empire when territories were increasingly brought under Roman control that the profession of land surveyor grew. The *ager publicus* was surveyed, divided (preferably into squares, but also other rectangles), and allocated, with the survey enabling planning for observation and control of newly conquered populations. Ammianus Marcellinus (fourth century C.E.) names a surveyor, Innocentius, who while on campaign in Pannonia "had recommended the plan, in order that, if they should see the savages beginning disorder, they might attack them in the rear, when their attention was turned elsewhere" (Ammianus Marcellinus, *Res Gestae* 19.11.8).

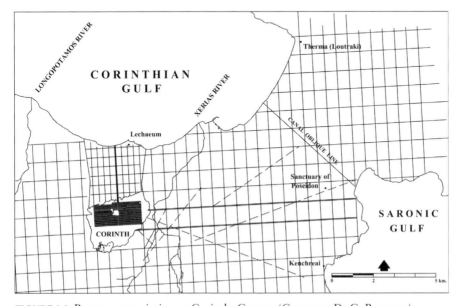

FIGURE 8.2: Roman centuriation at Corinth, Greece. (Courtesy: D. G. Romano)

When surveying a new colony, augurs who took auspices accompanied surveyors. Then they marked the axis of intersecting streets (the *cardo* and *decuma-
nus*), running respectively north-south and east-west, defining the center of a
town. Plots of land were then laid out from these initial lines in a square fashion.

The *Corpus Agrimensorum Romanorum* preserves writings of different
land surveyors, sometimes illuminating the Roman garden and its relation
to the larger landscape.[17] The authors indicate that in addition to boundary
stones, natural features such as trees, woods, ditches, and streams could be
used to identify boundaries, suggesting more generally that tending land can
create borders (for instance, see Siculus Flaccus, *De Condicionibus Agrorum*).
When the word *hortus*, or garden, is employed by the *agrimensor* Aggenius
Urbicus, it relates to the idea of private control and possession. He writes:

> Communities have places on the outskirts of town intended for funerals
> of the poor and they call these places *culinae*. They also have places set
> aside for the punishment of criminals. Private individuals without any
> respect for religious feeling are in the habit of appropriating parts of
> these places, since they are on the outskirt of town, and adding them to
> their own gardens (*hortis suis*). When a dispute has been initiated about

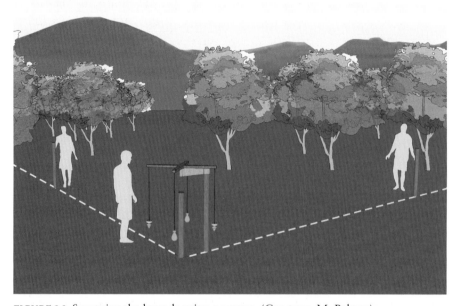

FIGURE 8.3: Surveying the bounds using a groma. (Courtesy: M. Palmer)

these places, if the community has maps, then he makes use of pieces of evidence and any other proof he can (use). (Agennius Urbicus, *De Controversiis Agrorum*)[18]

This indicates that in a legal sense the garden was a private holding distinguished from public lands and supports the idea of the garden as an enclosure separate from a wider landscape. But it also illustrates the rampant desire for the acquisition of land, even within communities, and the tensions that developed between corporate groups and private landholders.

REPRESENTATIONS OF THE ROMAN LANDSCAPE

The manuscripts of the *Corpus* preserve illustrations, but wall paintings provide further evidence for landscape representation. The best-preserved Roman paintings are wall frescoes from the Campania region of Italy, which were preserved by the eruption of Mt. Vesuvius in 79 C.E.[19] Pliny the Elder notes the first century B.C.E. development of painted landscape views, found on the walls of houses, that referenced the vistas over the surrounding territory. While these images were meant to create a visual system between outdoors and indoors, they also acted to demonstrate the harnessing of that environment by the householder:

> Nor must Studius also, of the period of his late lamented Majesty Augustus, be cheated of his due, who first introduced the most attractive fashion of painting walls with pictures of country houses and landscape gardens, groves, woods, hills, fish-ponds, canals, rivers, coasts, and whatever anybody could desire, together with various sketches of people going for a stroll or sailing in a boat or on land going to country houses riding on asses or in carriages, and also people fishing and fowling or hunting or even gathering the vintage. His works include splendid villas approached by roads across marshes, men tottering and staggering along carrying women on their shoulders for a bargain, and a number of humorous drawings of that sort besides, extremely wittily designed. He also introduced using pictures of seaside cities to decorate uncovered terraces, giving a most pleasing effect and at a very small expense. (Pliny, *Natural History*, 35.116–18)[20]

Pliny's description coincides with the archaeological evidence from Rome and Campania showing that landscape painting emerged in the middle of the first century B.C.E. The notoriety of Studius may suggest that he worked for the most elite patrons, namely the emperor Augustus and his family. Roger Ling proposes that the work of Studius or his circle can be observed on the properties of the imperial family, including the House of Livia on the Palatine, the Villa della Farnesina in Rome, and the Villa of Agrippa Postumus at Boscotrecase.[21] Though Pliny notes that these paintings were developed into their own genre by Studius sometime before the death of Augustus, they nonetheless have a close relationship to the conventions of pastoral literature, through their establishment of highly composed scenes of landscape prospects and elements and figures at leisure, and their close adherence to the dominant themes of frivolity and wit concurrent in art of the Hellenistic period. Pliny also addresses the vast range of landscape features that in one way or another came under the lathe of the Roman economy. The rivers and coasts reflect trade routes necessary to make elite fortunes. The gardens, groves, and fishponds were likewise necessary for the maintenance of elite households. These are also worldly scenes, contrived of distant prospects, recalling the imagery of the garden at the edge of the world.

The first century B.C.E. architect Vitruvius discusses the characteristics of landscape painting and its uses in decorating architectural space. He writes:

> In *ambulationes*, because of the length of the walls, they used for ornament the varieties of landscape gardening (*varietatibus topiorum*), finding subjects in the characteristics of particular places; for they paint harbors, headlands, shores, rivers, springs, straits, temples, groves, hills, cattle, shepherds. In places, some have the anatomy of statues, the images of gods, or the representations of legends; further the battles of Troy and the wanderings of Ulysses over the countryside with other subjects taken in like manner from nature. (Vitruvius 7.5.2, trans. Granger)

Vitruvius's use of the word "*ambulationes*" is especially important here, as he records a popular location for landscape imagery.[22] He makes clear that natural features such as shores, groves, hills, and rivers were especially suitable for rooms of ambulation, or walking. To Vitruvius's observation, we can add that it is the distant viewpoint from which these scenes are captured that makes them particularly appropriate for long and narrow passage architecture. While individual figures, monuments of architecture, and topographical features are rendered on a small scale, the overall impact is one of a wide, sprawling scene. The distant, panoramic perspective allowed the scenes to be stretched along the horizontal axis to fit the long and narrow space that defines hallways, corridors, and porticoes.

Roman landscape paintings evoked recognizable and contemporary environments to which viewers could bring their own experiences and interpretations, although few are thought to transcribe specific places. While the overarching subject of landscape imagery is the land itself, the figures or features that make up the views can be useful in establishing a typology.[23] Architectural landscapes depict monuments of human engineering, celebrating cityscapes as in the yellow monochrome near the window of cubiculum M from the Villa of P. Fannius Synistor at Boscoreale or seaside villa-scapes as in roundels with various maritime themes from the Villa San Marco at Stabiae.[24] So-called sacro-idyllic landscapes are more abbreviated scenes of a rural character, often combining a vertical element such as a column or tree with a shrine attended by small groups of worshippers.[25] For example, vertically aligned panels depicting sacred precincts, with either columns or baetylus at the center, surrounded by rocks, trees, and birds, are found in the Room of the Masks at the House of Augustus in Rome. Another sacro-idyllic scene is a painting with a herdsman and a ram from of a small shrine from Pompeii.[26]

Mythological figures might also populate landscape paintings, suggesting that contemporary environments, painted or real, are malleable and charged with legend.[27] When Vitruvius mentions possible subjects that might inhabit a landscape, he includes "the wanderings of Ulysses over the countryside" (*De Arch* 7.5.2, trans. Granger). Discovered on the Via Graziosa in Rome in the mid-nineteenth century, the so-called Odyssey landscapes of the mid-first century B.C.E. depict such wanderings. The paintings adorned an elite house on the Esquiline Hill, showing the hero's meetings with the Laestrygonians and Circe, as well as his experience in the underworld and his journey past the Sirens.[28] These paintings are regarded by many as the first true landscape paintings in the history of Western art. Odysseus and his adventures seem less important than the vast environment through which they moved. Rendered on a large scale, the artists have lavished great effort on the environment itself. Shorelines, mountains, promontories, caves, and vegetation are all surrounded by a sense of atmosphere. Greek inscriptions of the figures and other factors suggest that these paintings were inspired by Hellenistic traditions, but the context as well as the painted portico of pilasters indicates a Roman idiom. The illusionistic architectural frame points to the Roman interest in designed views of the larger landscape.[29]

FIGURE 8.4: The Odyssey fresco. (Courtesy: Kim Wilczak after painting in the Vatican Museum)

DESIGNING THE ROMAN VIEW

Pliny the Younger's letters describing his Laurentine and Tuscan villas of the late first or early second century C.E. contribute greatly to our understanding of elite Roman villa culture.[30] Carefully designed spaces bring nature into the human realm with tended gardens and planned vistas onto larger landscapes, facilitating the physical and mental exercise that Pliny and his contemporaries enjoyed. In the letter to Domitius Apollonaris, Pliny describes a view from his Tuscan villa, comparing the sight to a painting: "It is a great pleasure to look down on the countryside from the mountain, for the view seems to be a painted scene of unusual beauty rather than a real landscape, and the harmony to be found in this variety refreshes the eye wherever it turns" (*Ep* 5.6.13, trans. Radice). Pliny's evocative description suggests an intersection between art and nature, as he finds it delightfully difficult to distinguish picture from prospect. Such an account indicates that the ancient Romans were inclined to draw comparisons between painted and living panoramas, as Pliny celebrates the experience of viewing the natural world and its cultivation in varied media and forms. Paintings and actual landscapes reflect and inform each other, which argues for site-specific interpretations of painted landscape imagery.[31]

Urban landscape could also be compared to the beauty of a composed painting. The Greek geographer Strabo, for instance, writes of his travels in Rome at the turn of the first century, lavishing attention on the spectacle of the Campus Martius. Noting the size and beauty of the Field of Mars, which combines architecture and designed landscape, Strabo writes:

> The works of art situated on the Campus Martius, and the ground, which is covered with grass throughout the year, and the crowns of those hills which are above the river and extend as far as its bed, which present to

the eye the appearance of a stage-painting—all this, I say, affords a spectacle that one can hardly draw away from. (Strabo 5.3.8, trans. Jones)[32]

It seems no coincidence that the nearby (late first century B.C.E.) Villa della Farnesina, which has been associated with Julia, the daughter of Augustus, and her husband, Marcus Vipsanius Agrippa, is carefully decorated with landscape murals and ceiling stuccoes.[33] We see panoramic views painted in an impressionistic manner in the corridors (A and F–G). Mid-range views of a religious character are in the bedrooms (*cubicula* B, D, and E). Close-up garden paintings extend the space of the enclosed garden (*viridarium* L), while panoramic landscape vistas extend the walls of the dining room (*triclinium* C).[34] Interior wall paintings at this imperial residence simultaneously reflect and inform viewers' experiences of its architecture and grounds, suggesting a connection between public and private realms. Inside, the shifting perspectives of painted vistas coincide with architectural functions of rooms, encouraging movement in passageways and stationary contemplation in gathering spaces. Outside, the villa's spectacular prospect architecture framed vistas along the Tiber to the north and the Janiculum Hill to the south. This suburban villa was nestled within a luxurious garden zone and linked directly via a new bridge, the *Pons Agrippae*, to Augustus and Agrippa's major building projects in the Campus Martius, including the first Pantheon and Agrippa's Baths, surrounding gardens, an artificial lake, and a canal. As such, the villa's painted riverside scenes and garden spaces have particular resonance with the emerging urban landscape of Augustan Rome.

FIGURE 8.5: Panorama from Corridor F–G of the Villa della Farnesina, Rome. (Courtesy: Il Ministero per i Beni e le Attività Culturali—Sopritendenza Speciale per i Beni Archeologici di Roma)

FIGURE 8.6: Painting from garden room (L) from Villa della Farnesina. (Courtesy: Il Ministero per i Beni e le Attività Culturali—Soprintendenza Speciale per i Beni Archeologici di Roma)

Only recently have archaeologists begun to explore the promising field of landscape views as designed in villa and garden spaces. Many villas were arranged to maximize views of distant hills, the sea, or wooded glades, but how ancient designers may have actually orchestrated these views has been little understood. Growing knowledge of Roman land survey gives us some information, as well as literary descriptions of these views. In Campania, recent research has attempted to establish the designed views at the Villa Arianna. At Horace's Villa in the Sabine Hills, archaeologists have begun to unravel Horace's descriptions of that property and how these interface with excavation and radar findings. It appears that terracing allowed the site to maximize views as well as take advantage of climatic conditions.[35]

THE DOMUS AUREA, AN EMPEROR'S TRANSPLANTED LANDSCAPE

Nero's *Domus Aurea*, his Golden House, famously integrated an imperial palace, gardens, and a larger, designed landscape. After the great fire of 64 C.E., Nero was free to rebuild the landscape of the heart of Rome. The display of art and nature in its various guises was essential in the building complex and its surrounding grounds, which occupied the valley in between the Palatine, Esquiline, and Caelian hills.[36] Ancient sources indicate that Nero's construction brought the rustic comforts of a villa-estate, complete with woodlands, vineyards, and an artificial lake, into the urban center (Tacitus, *Annals* 15.42; Suetonius, *Nero* 31). Described in recent scholarship as the embodiment of *rus in urbe*, the country in the town, the complex combined these and other contrasting landscapes.[37] The Roman historian Tacitus openly criticized Nero for a construction that goes beyond the authority of nature:

> Nero, all the same, made use of the ruin of his country and built a palace in which the gems and gold were scarcely as much a cause for wonder (for they are familiar, and have long been vulgarized by luxury) as the fields and pools and, in one part, woods to provide solitude, and in an adjacent area, open spaces and vistas. The controllers and contrivers were Severus and Celer who had both the inventiveness and the audacity to attempt through art what even nature denied and to amuse themselves with the resources of an emperor. (*Annals* 15.42, trans. Pollitt)

Natural elements fell under the control of Severus and Celer, becoming media for artistic manipulation (*per artem*) much like precious materials.

The Roman biographer Suetonius's ekphrastic description of the Domus Aurea lavishes attention on its extravagance. He notes that the landscaped grounds were as diverse and impressive as the opulent architecture: "It also had a pool which resembled the sea and was surrounded by buildings which were to give the impression of cities; besides this there were rural areas varied with ploughed fields, vineyards, pastures, and woodlands, and filled with all types of domestic animals and wild beasts" (*Nero* 31, trans. Pollitt). Nero's estate combined different categories of landscape, offering the pleasures of comparison and variety. The constructed buildings, perhaps even the architecture of the preserved Esquiline suite, give the impression of cities (*ad urbem speciem*). Suetonius's differentiation between wild (*ferarem*) and domestic (*pecudum*) animals draws attention to the juxtaposition of natural and cultivated spaces. Flora and fauna are positioned together in the making of the living spectacle.

The architecture of the Domus Aurea's Esquiline suite functioned as both a viewing pavilion and stage-like backdrop for Nero, contrived for maximum impact, oriented on an east-west axis with its south façade opening directly onto the valley.[38] An open portico allows perhaps for a more subtle integration with the surrounding grounds in that the building becomes part of its landscape, rather than enclosing it, manipulating the visitor's view of the surrounding area. The orientation of the Esquiline suite framed the Caelian and Palatine hills, the orthogonal *stagnum*, or pool, and all of the other buildings in the valley, including the Temple of Divine Claudius.[39] Accordingly, each of these structures could be admired from the palace within the "natural" frame of the hills.[40]

With his constructed landscape, complete with the mountain of the Esquiline Hill and view of artificial sea, Nero was able to follow such traditions of rustic delights and seaside retreats as Baiae, Nero's favorite haunt on the Bay of Naples, in the center of Rome.[41] The transplanted landscape is a large part of what angered his critics because Nero had brought the villa and the villa-scape into the city, violating the rules of decorum as they applied to the construction of place.

THE SEASONAL LANDSCAPE—TWO ROMAN MOSAICS COMPARED

The large floor mosaic depicting the Nile River from the Sanctuary of Fortuna Primigenia at Palestrina, thirty-five kilometers east of Rome, is one of the earliest surviving landscapes from a Roman context.[42] Dated to the end of the second century B.C.E., the mosaic originally decorated the floor of an apse-shaped grotto-nymphaeum, opening onto a large hall at ancient Praeneste.[43] Representing the Nile River from above, the mosaicists portray, top to bottom, an expansive view of the river from its origins in Aethiopia to the delta. The raised vantage point makes the landscape seem to rise as it recedes into the distance.

Populated with buildings, boats, animals, and figures, each depicted in varied perspectives, the scene is an imaginative compendium of the vast territory through which the river runs in the season of inundation. Contemporary Hellenistic and Roman structures are integrated with a pharaonic temple suggesting the character of cosmopolitan Alexandria. Beyond, the rising terrain becomes more mountainous and lacks buildings. Darker-skinned African hunters chase

exotic animals, whose names are written in Greek, which is all representative of
the "Otherness" of Upper (southern) Egypt and Aethiopia. The mosaic's topography compares degrees of cultivation. While the foreground contains architecture and abundant vegetation, trellises, and enclosed gardens, the background is
less developed and rocky, and where more animals roam freely. This landscape
represents the importance, as well as the danger, of the annual flood, which bears
nutrient-rich silt that was integral to the success of agriculture, especially grain.
Probably inspired by the Hellenistic principles of *chorographia* and *topographia*
(the cartographic techniques of making views of small regions and much larger
areas respectively), this mosaic also points to Rome's interest in expansion.[44]

The relation of the villa garden and the larger landscape is suggested in the
late fourth or early fifth century C.E. Mosaic of Dominus Julius at Carthage.[45]
At the center of three registers, the fortified villa is depicted in profile. Numerous workers tend to cultivated lands or hunt in the surrounding wilderness to
serve the *domini*. Attendants bring each season's produce to the lord and lady
as they sit or stand in gardens, which connect the villa to the larger estate.

FIGURE 8.7: Dominus Julius Mosaic. (Courtesy: Centre Henri Stern)

In the uppermost register, directly above the villa, the *domina* sits enthroned between two pairs of tall cypress trees. On the left, the season is winter, and attendants bring her ducks and olives. To the right, the season is summer. A woman proudly presents the mistress with a lamb, and wheat is ready for harvest. Both the domina and *dominus* appear again in garden settings in the lower register. Set in a garden of blooming flowers, the mistress stands admiring herself in a hand mirror, while attendants offer roses and other gifts of springtime. To the right, the *dominus* sits enthroned in the garden between an orchard and a fenced vineyard where autumn is represented with the grape harvest and ripening fruit trees. Time has been collapsed in this scene, as the work and harvest of four seasons is presented in one landscape. As the lord and lady receive gifts from the wider landscape, their gardens serve as mediating spaces that indicate the privileged status of the villa owners.

The Nilotic mosaic at Praeneste represents a speculative view, one that closely allies close observation of nature with Rome's great debt to Hellenistic culture, and the curiosity and desire for Egyptian territory. Egypt's status as provider of grain and its offerings of diverse religious resources for the whole of the Mediterranean produced a popular imagery of fecundity and mysticism. The annual, methodical rising of the Nile, and Egypt's regulation by its ebb and flow signified a sort of primordial partnership between man and nature. The siting of the mosaic in a grotto-nymphaeum, laden with oracular intent, and designed on the monumental, cosmopolitan scale of Hellenistic prototypes intimates a project aimed at integrating Rome into a wider Mediterranean culture. The mosaic of Dominus Julius in Carthage, on the other hand, suggests the completion of that project, depicting a Romanized landscape now settled into the seasonal acts of cultivation and replicating the hierarchies of the Roman household. Placed within the domestic sphere, rather than at a sacred site, the mosaic reinforces the urban householder's tenure of the land and creates a simulacrum of his tended holdings.

ROME'S WORLD LANDSCAPE

Conceptually, the garden could represent *Romanitas*, and its presence could also be used to describe the character of larger territories under Roman rule. The metonymic status of the Roman garden in the context of political expansion is expressed by P. Aelius Aristides in his panegyric *Regarding Rome*, which he delivered in 155 c.e. to the imperial court in Rome under emperor Antoninus Pius. Aristides's praise of the capital city of Rome ultimately means praise of the whole empire, as he says, "The whole world is ruled by so great a city" (Aristides, *Regarding Rome* 9, trans. Behr). Comparing Rome's empire to the great empires that came before, including the Persian Empire and that of Alexander the Great, Aristides's panegyric is full of typically stylized yet illustrative examples that represent the reaches of Roman power and influence. Aristides makes the case that Rome is the greatest empire the world has ever seen. Toward the end of his speech, he describes the great significance of Roman influence in terms of physical monuments. He writes:

> Everything is full of gymnasiums, fountains, gateways, temples, handicrafts and schools . . . Indeed, the cities shine with radiance and grace, and *the whole earth has been adorned like a pleasure garden.* Gone beyond land and sea is the smoke rising from the fields and the signal fires of friend and foe, as is a breeze had fanned them away. There has been instead every kind of charming spectacle and a boundless number of games. (Aristides, *Regarding Rome* 97–99, trans. Behr; italics added for emphasis)

Discussing the garden alongside works of architecture associated with peacetime, education, and entertainment, Aristides indicates the cultural value of the garden as a place of leisure and learning. In this comparison, the garden contains markers of civilization: fountains, temples, and handicrafts. In this sense, the garden is a symbol that can encroach onto the larger landscape and indeed come to define the landscape of the known world. Whereas the physical garden is typically defined by its separation from the larger landscape, in this simile, the garden's replication according to the Roman type ultimately means the Romanization of the known world, the largest of landscapes. Aristides does not end his discussion of the Roman treatment of land with this comparison of the garden. He goes on to discuss more explicitly the wider landscape, writing:

> And what was said by Homer, "The earth was common to all", you have made a reality, by surveying the whole inhabited world, by bridging the rivers in various ways, by cutting carriage roads through the mountains, by filling desert places with post stations, and by civilizing everything with your way of life and good order. Therefore I conceive of life before your time as the life thought to exist before Triptolemus, harsh, rustic, and little different from living on a mountain; yet if not entirely so, still that while Athens initiated our present, cultivated existence, this has been confirmed by you "with second attempts better" as they say. (Aristides, *Regarding Rome* 101, trans. Behr)

According to the poetic account, land survey, technology, and infrastructure bring a better quality of life. As a Greek speaker from Anatolia, whose family had gained Roman citizenship in 123 C.E., Aristides perhaps fittingly reflects on the Greek past that contributed to the Roman present. By comparing the pre-Roman times to those that existed before Triptolemus, the demi-god who taught humans the art of agriculture, Aristides suggests that the Romans are themselves great cultivators. Invoking Homer and acknowledging the primacy of Athens, Aristides gives Rome great credit for its contribution to culture and civilization, and his praise is strengthened by such comparisons.

Building upon the idea of cultivation of land, Aristides links Roman rule with universal law, as he writes:

> And now, indeed there is no need to write a description of the whole world, nor to enumerate the laws of each people, but you have become universal geographers for all men by opening up all the gates of the inhabited world and by giving to all who wish it the power to be observers of everything and by assigning universal laws for all men. (Aristides, *Regarding Rome* 102, trans. Behr)

Aristides sees the Romans as cultivators not only of land but also of men. With Roman citizenship comes justice, a true indicator of civilization. Concluding with a reference to Hesiod's *Works and Days*, Aristides suggests that if Hesiod had known about the existence of Rome, the poet "would say that the iron race would perish on the earth when your leadership and empire were established, and then he would grant Justice and Reverence to return to mankind, and he would have pitied those before you" (Aristides, *Regarding Rome*, 106, trans. Behr). In this panegyric, the Roman Empire brings order to both land and citizens.

This Roman citizen, quoting Hesiod and Homer, collapses the large chronological gap between the Greeks and Romans, comparing them. Although serving different cultural, social, and artistic purposes, the garden and the larger landscape illustrate broader spheres of social change and influence. The garden and the larger landscape were ultimately part of the same fabric of nature, defined only by degrees of human intervention and vigilance.

NOTES

Introduction

I would like to thank the series editors, Michael Leslie and John Dixon Hunt, for the invitation to create this volume and the authors for their fine contributions and ideas for shaping the work. We are fortunate to have had the skills of Maureen Bolton, Kimberly Wilczak, and Michele Palmer in creating new images for the book, and the assistance of Jeffrey Carnes in the final editing and indexing of the volume. We are also grateful to Henry Ferry, executor of the Wilhelmina and Stanley Jashemski Trust for his assistance with photographs and plans.

1. So little is known of gardens in the late antique period that Petrarch's idea to "call 'ancient' whatever preceded the celebration and veneration of Christ's name in Rome [the reign of Constantine in the fourth century], 'modern' everything from then to our time" remains definitive. *Familiares* 6.2.16; trans. M. Bishop, *Letters from Petrarch* (Bloomington: Indiana University Press, 1966), 66.
2. B. G. Trigger, *The History of Archaeological Thought* (Cambridge: Cambridge University Press, 1989), 28.
3. D. Spenser, "Horace's Garden Thoughts," in *City, Countryside, and the Spatial Organization of Value in Classical Antiquity*, ed. R. M. Rosen and I. Sluiter, Mnemosyne Supplement 279 (Leiden: Brill, 2006), 246. M. Carroll, "Academies, Schools, and Gymnasia" and "Temple Gardens" in *Gardens of the Roman Empire*, vol. 1, ed. W. Jashemski, K. Gleason, K. Hartswick, and A.-A. Malek (New York: Cambridge University Press, in press). Carroll, through her research, has done much to solidify the material contribution of Greek academies, temple groves, and palaestra as the Greek contribution to public garden history.
4. Explored, for example by A. Spawforth, "Symbol of Unity: The Persian Wars Tradition in the Roman Empire," in *Greek Historiography*, ed. S. Hornblower

(Oxford: Clarendon Press, 1994), 233–47; and E. Bridges, E. Hall, and P. J. Rhodes, *Cultural Responses to the Persian Wars: Antiquity to the Third Millennium* (Oxford: Oxford University Press, 2007).

5. Most memorably, Athenaeus who cited the Xanthus, a pupil of Aristotle, as writing that "the Lydians in their luxury laid out paradeisoi, making them like parks because they thought it more luxurious not to have the rays of the sun fall up them at all." Athenaeus 12.515e–f (C.B. Gulick translation).

6. K. T. von Stackelberg, *The Roman Garden: Space, Sense, and Society* (London: Routledge, 2009), 50.

7. E. Panofsky, *Renaissance and Renascences in Western Art* (Stockholm: Almquist and Wiksell, 1960), 4.

8. N. Newton, *Design on the Land* (Cambridge MA: Belnap Press, 1971), 2.

9. M. Golden and Peter Toohey, eds., *Inventing Ancient Culture: Historicism, Periodization, and the Ancient World* (London: Routledge, 1997), 13.

10. E. Poehler, M. Flohr, and K. Cole, *Pompeii: Art, Industry and Infrastructure* (Oxford: Oxbow Books, 2011).

11. See J. Prest, *The Garden of Eden: the Botanic Garden and the Recreation of Paradise* (New Haven, CT: Yale University Press, 1988).

12. Prest, *The Garden of Eden.*

13. P. Du Prey, *The Villas of Pliny the Younger from Antiquity to Posterity* (Chicago: University of Chicago Press, 1995); H. H. Tanzer, *The Villas of Pliny the Younger* (New York: Columbia University Press, 1924); R. Förtsch, *Archäologischer Kommentar zu den Villenbriefen des jüngeren Plinius* (Mainz am Rhein: P. von Zabern, 1993).

14. Newton, *Design on the Land.* Compare with J. C. Shepherd and G. Jellicoe, *Italian Gardens of the Renaissance* (London: A. Tiranti, 1954).

15. D. Stronach's hypothesis that Pasargadae was a pre-Islamic *charbagh* in its fully built sense must remain conjectural after a recent inspection of the remains, although the garden clearly has a visual cross axis (see R. Boucharlat, per. comm., October 8, 2007; and I. Nielsen, "The Palace and the Royal Achaemid City: Two Case Studies—Pasargadae and Susa," in *The Royal Palace Institution in the First Millennium BC: Regional Development and Cultural Interchange between East and West*, ed. Nielsen [Athens: Danish Institute at Athens, 2001], 113–24).

16. D. Fairchild Ruggles, *Islamic Gardens and Landscapes* (Philadelphia: University of Pennsylvania Press, 2007); M. Carroll, *Earthly Paradises: Ancient Gardens in History and Archaeology* (Los Angeles: J. Paul Getty Museum, 2003), 124–29.

17. S. E. Alcock, *Archaeologies of the Past: Landscape, Monuments, and Memories* (Cambridge: Cambridge University Press, 2002), 41. Petrarch himself writes, "Among the many subjects which interested me, I dwelt especially upon antiquity, for our own age has always repelled me, so that had it not been for the love of those dear to me, I should have preferred to have been born in any other period than our own." Epistola ad Posteros. Trans. J. H. Robinson, *Petrarch: The First Modern Scholar and Man of Letters* (New York: G. P. Putnam, 1898), 64.

18. Alcock, *Archaeologies of the Past*, 41.

19. Seen in the recent conferences and books exploring East-West interconnections, as in Nielsen, "The Palace and the Royal Achaemid City." I first raised the topic at the conference "Past and Present Architectural and Garden Cultures in the Context of Constant Oriental-Occidental Interdependencies: Investigations of Cultural Origins and Identity" at the Leibniz Universität Hannover in 2007 and am grateful to the participants for their helpful feedback.

20. Alcock, *Archaeologies of the Past*, 19.

21. Alcock, *Archaeologies of the Past*, 35.

22. P. Horden and N. Purcell set the full Mediterranean context for the kind of gardens discussed here in *The Corrupting Sea: A Study of Mediterranean History* (Oxford: Blackwell Publishers, 2000), particularly 220–24.

23. R. Osborne, *Classical Landscape with Figures* (London: Sheridan House, 1987), 16.

24. C. Tuplin, *Achaemenid Studies* (Stuttgart: Franz Steiner Verlag, 1996), 98–131.

25. P. Grimal, *Les jardins romains*, 3rd ed. (Paris: Fayard, 1984), 79–86.

26. P. Grimal, *Les jardins romains* (Paris: Fayard, 1984), 78–85.

27. Xenophon, *Oeconomicus* 4.20ff. is the famous first use of the term *paradeisos*. Cicero, repeating the story in *De senectute* 59, chooses the phrase "et quenduam consaeptum agrum diligenter consitum ostendisse." On Lydian gardens, see Athenaeus, *Deipnosophistae* 12.515d–f.

28. A theme Xenophon develops in the *Cyropaedia*.

29. Later authors inveigh against the luxurious habits of other Asian kings as well.

30. Grimal, *Les jardins romains*, 78–80.

31. Here *park* is used in the common, modern sense of a large parcel of urban land made available to the public, rather than more strictly in its ancient sense of "an envelope of open space, planted or wild, with or without a focal complex of buildings, and surrounded by an enclosure wall" (Nicholas Purcell, "Dialectical Gardening," *Journal of Roman Archaeology* 14 [2001]: 551).

32. R. Lanciani, *Ancient and Modern Rome* (Boston: Marshall Jones, 1925), 69–82, devotes a chapter to Rome's porticoes, much of which is occupied by an assessment of Roman garden taste so scathing as to quell any interest in the subject. Grimal, *Les jardins romains*, 167–90, offers a more scholarly view of Rome's "promenades." Landscape architectural histories place the first publicly owned parks and gardens either with the Père Lachaise cemetery in Paris of 1804, the Square de l'Archeveché in Paris of 1844, Victoria Park in London and Birkenhead Park in Liverpool in 1847, the inspiration for Central Park, New York (Newton, *Design on the Land*, 223–25).

33. W. F. Jashemski, K. Gleason, K. Hartswick, A.-A. Malek, eds., *Gardens of the Roman Empire* (New York: Cambridge University Press, in press). Jashemski felt the irregularly laid-out peristyle of the House of Polybius to be more typical of Roman peristyles than might be expected. She associated increasing formality with the provision of aqueduct water (*The Gardens of Pompeii, Herculaneum and the Villas Destroyed by Vesuvius*, vol. 1. [New Rochelle: Caratzas Brothers, 1979], 53).

34. H. Yang, "An Archaeological Study of the Palace Garden of the Nanyue State," in *A Sourcebook for Garden Archaeology*, ed. A.-A. Malek (Bern: Peter Lang, 2013),

659–67; and *The Archaeological Study of Chinese Palaces* (Beijing: Forbidden City Publishing House, 2001). My thanks to Huicheng Zhong for his assistance in translating this second article source.

35. E. Leach, *The Rhetoric of Space: Literary and Artistic Representations of Landscape in Republican and Augustan Rome* (Princeton, NJ: Princeton University Press, 1988).

36. B. Bergmann, "Exploring the Grove: Pastoral Space on Roman Walls," in *The Pastoral Landscape*, ed. J. Dixon Hunt (Washington, D.C.: National Gallery of Art, 1992), 21–31.

37. Bergmann, "Exploring the Grove: Pastoral Space on Roman Walls," 39.

38. K.L. Gleason, J. Schryver, L. Passalacqua, "The Garden" in *The Horace's Villa Project, 1997–2003: Report on New Fieldwork and Research*, ed. B. Frischer, J. Crawford, and M. de Simone, 71–95 (Oxford: Archaeopress, 2006).

39. K. L Zachos, "The *Tropaeum* of the Sea-Battle of Actium at Nikopolis: Interim Report," *Journal of Roman Archaeology* 16 (2003): 65–92.

40. B. Campbell, *The Writings of the Roman Land Surveyors* (London: Society for the Promotion of Roman Studies, 2000), xlv–liii.

41. Agennius Urbicus, *De controveriis agrorum* 5–10, quoted in Campbell, *The Writings of the Roman Land Surveyors*, 22–23.

42. J. Frontinus, *De Agrorum qualitate* 5, quoted in Campbell, *The Writings of the Roman Land Surveyors*, 3.

43. Geary 1994: 8, quoted in Alcock, *Archaeologies of the Past*, 34.

44. K. L. Gleason and M. Leone, "Apprehending the Garden," in *A Sourcebook for Garden Archaeology*, ed. A. A. Malek 97–126 (Bern: Peter Lang, 2013).

45. M. Ciaraldi, *People and Plants in Ancient Pompeii: A New Approach from the Microscope Room* (London: Institute of Archaeology, 2007), 40–41.

46. Bergmann, 2002; J. R. Clarke, *The Houses of Roman Italy 100 BC –A.D. 250: Ritual, Space and Decoration* (Berkeley: University of California Press, 1991); K. J. Hartswick, *The Gardens of Sallust: A Changing Landscape* (Austin: University of Texas Press, 2004).

47. The history of the development of garden archaeology has been documented by A.-A. Malek, ed., *A Sourcebook for Garden Archaeology* (Bern: Peter Lang, 2013), 41–72.

48. I. Nielsen, *Hellenistic Palaces* (Aarhus: Aarhus University, 1994).

49. Jashemski et al., "Plants," in *Gardens of the Roman Empire*.

50. Panofsky, *Renaissance and Renascences in Western Art*, 11.

Chapter 1

This chapter is dedicated to two architects: Ehud Netzer (1934–2010). Eugenia Salza Prina Ricotti, whose architectural studies included the design of gardens and the larger landscape. Dai palazzi antichi alla vigna Barberini, sul monte Palatino, Scavi dell'École française de Rome 1985–1999. The translations of Vitruvius are from I. D. Rowland and T. N. Howe, *Vitruvius: Ten Books on Architecture* (Cambridge: Cambridge University Press, 1999). All other translations use the Loeb editions.

1. Of course, Vitruvius has his failings as a source for design process, well described by M. Wilson-Jones, *Principles of Roman Architecture* (New Haven, CT: Yale

University Press, 2000), 35; and R. Taylor, *Roman Builders: A Study in Architectural Process* (Cambridge: Cambridge University Press, 2003), 4.

2. On the terminology, see N. Purcell, "Town in Country, Country in Town," in *Ancient Roman Villa Gardens*, ed. E. B. MacDougall (Washington, D.C.: Dumbarton Oaks, 1987), 193, and "The Roman Garden as a Domestic Building," in *Roman Domestic Buildings*, ed. I. M. Barton (Exeter: University of Exeter Press, 1996), 121–51; L. Landgren, "Lauro, Myrto et Buxo Frequentata: A Study of the Roman Garden through Its Plants" (PhD diss., Lund University, 2004); K. von Stackelberg, *The Roman Garden: Space, Sense, and Society* (London: Routledge, 2009); on recent archaeological discoveries in and around Rome, see F. Villedieu, *Il Giardino dei Cesari* (Edizioni Quasar: Rome, 2001), 61–70, 84–97; B. S. Frizell and A. Klynne, *Roman Villas around the Urbs: Interaction with Landscape and Environment* (Proceedings from Swedish Institute in Rome Conference, September 17–18, 2004, Rome Swedish Institute, Rome, 2005); R. Meneghini, "Il Tempio o Foro della Pace," in *I Fori Imperiali: Gli scavi del Comune di Roma (1991–2007)*, ed. R. Meneghini and R. Santageli (Rome: Viviani Editori, 2007); B. Frischer, J. Crawford, and M. de Simone, *The Horace's Villa Project, 1997–2003*, 2 vols. (Oxford: Archaeopress, 2006); W. F. Jashemski, K. Gleason, K. Hartswick, and A.-A. Malek, eds., *Gardens of the Roman Empire* (New York: Cambridge University Press, forthcoming).

3. I. Rowland and T. N. Howe, *Vitruvius: The Ten Books on Architecture* (New York: Cambridge University Press, 1999), 13–17.

4. This chapter should be read in tandem with Chapter 3 (this volume) in which the role of horticulture in the agricultural treatises is discussed.

5. See N. Purcell, "The Roman Garden as a Domestic Building," in *Roman Domestic Buildings*, ed. I. M. Barton, 121–52 (Exeter: University of Exeter Press, 1996), and Lena Landgren's important dissertation research (note 1) on the frequency of specific garden terms.

6. Morris Hickey Morgan translation, commonly used by architects.

7. Von Stackelberg, *The Roman Garden*, 20.

8. Purcell, "The Roman Garden as a Domestic Building", 136; Von Stackelberg, *The Roman Garden*, 16–17.

9. See Langren, Chapter 3 (this volume).

10. Purcell, "The Roman Garden as a Domestic Building," 141.

11. Landgren, "Lauro, Myrto et Buxo Frequentata," 178–92.

12. See the reconstructions of Pliny the Younger's villa, discussed in the Introduction.

13. K. Gleason and M. Leone, "Apprehending the Garden," in *A Sourcebook for Garden Archaeology*, ed. A.-A. Malek, 97–126 (Bern: Peter Lang, 2013).

14. Vitruvius is writing his treatise for the emperor Augustus; thus, the discussion is focused on large projects requiring expertise. Existing garden histories have largely taken the perspective of the domestic gardener, which is useful for the study of gardens in villas and *domus* (W. F. Jashemski, *Gardens of Pompeii, Herculaneum, and the Villas Destroyed by Vesuvius*, vol. 1 [New Rochelle, NY: Caratzas, 1979]; L. Farrar, *Ancient Roman Gardens* (Stroud: Sutton Publishing, [1998] 2000). The more monumental forms of gardens discussed by Vitruvius are more comparable to the work of the landscape architect today.

15. In European design tradition, architects design the layout of gardens, engineers handle the water and structural engineering, and gardeners install and maintain the

plants according to the design of the architect. Vitruvius does not lay out these roles clearly enough to assume that this was the case in his day: his knowledge of water systems, for example, would be uncommon among architects today.

16. Rowland and Howe, *Vitruvius*, xv.

17. J. J. Coulton, *Ancient Greek Architects at Work: Problems of Structure and Design* (Ithaca, NY: Cornell University Press, 1977), 51. Also see Coulton, "Greek Architects and the Transmission of Design," *Architecture et société: De l'archaïsme grec à la fin de la république romaine* (Paris: Centre national de la recherche scientifique, 1983), 453–68.

18. Taylor, *Roman Builders*, 22–27; Wilson-Jones, *Principles of Roman Architecture*, 49–108

19. Rowland and Howe, *Vitruvius*, 14.

20. See, for example, E. Netzer, *The Architecture of Herod, the Great Builder* (Mohr Siebeck: Tübingen, 2006); J. DeLaine, "The Baths of Caracalla: A Study in the Design, Construction, and Economics of Large-scale Building Projects in Imperial Rome," *Journal of Roman Archaeology*, suppl. series no. 25 (1997); M. W. Jones *Principles of Roman Architecture* (New Haven, CT: Yale University Press, 2003); L. Lancaster, *Concrete Vaulted Construction in Imperial Rome: Innovations in Context* (Cambridge: Cambridge University Press, 2005).

21. Wilson-Jones, *Principles of Roman Architecture*, 59.

22. Wilson-Jones, *Principles of Roman Architecture*, 56–57; Taylor, *Roman Builders*, 27–36.

23. Louvre, A02.

24. Coulton, *Ancient Greek Architects at Work*, 52–53.

25. A. F. Shore, "Egyptian Cartography," in *Cartography in Prehistoric, Ancient, and Medieval Europe and the Middle East*, ed. B. Harley and D. Woodward (Chicago: University of Chicago Press, 1987), 118.

26. A. Badawy, *A History of Egyptian Architecture: The First Intermediate Period, The Middle Kingdom, and the Second Intermediate Period* (Berkeley: University of California Press, 1966), 236.

27. Coulton, *Ancient Greek Architects at Work*, 52–53.

28. L. Haselberger, "The Construction Plans for the Temple of Apollo at Didyma," *Scientific American* 253, no. 6 (1985): 126–32.

29. Wilson-Jones, *Principles of Roman Architecture*, 49–59.

30. G. F. Carettoni, *Forma Urbis Romae: La Pianta Marmorea di Roma Antica* (Rome: Danesi, 1960); on an earlier plan, see E. M. Steinby, "Il Frammento 18a della Forma Urbis Romae," *Lacus Iuturnae* I (1989): 24–33.

31. Wilson-Jones, *Principles of Roman Architecture*, 43.

32. Gleason, "Porticus Pompeiana: A New Perspective on the First Public Park of Ancient Rome," *Journal of Garden History* 14, no. 1 (1994): 13–27.

33. Rowland and Howe, *Vitruvius*, xvi, n6.

34. Again, Wilson-Jones, *Principles of Roman Architecture*, provides examples of ancient models.

35. A. Kuttner, "Culture and History at Pompey's Museum," *Transactions of the American Philological Association* 129 (1999): 350–51.

36. "Who can fail to be astonished . . . that a tree has been introduced from an alien world just for its shadow?" (Pliny, *HN* 12.6 in Purcell, "The Roman Garden as a Domestic Building," 136n21).

37. DeLaine, "The Baths of Caracalla"; Taylor, *Roman Builders*; M. Leone, *Critical Historical Archaeology* (Walnut Creek, CA: Left Coast Press, 2010).

38. Wilson-Jones, *Principles of Roman Architecture*, 7.

39. This has been summarized in Taylor, *Roman Builders*.

40. K. L. Gleason and M. Palmer, "Synthesis and Interpretation: The Garden as a Built Environment," in *A Sourcebook for Garden Archaeology*, ed. A.-A. Malek, 277–315 (Bern: Peter Lang, 2013).

41. Cf. Gleason, "A Garden Excavation in the Oasis Palace of Herod the Great at Jericho," *Landscape Journal* 12, no. 2 (1993): 158.

42. J. A. Hanson, *Roman Theater Temples* (Princeton, NJ: Princeton University Press, 1959); P. Gross, *Architecture et Societé à Rome et en Italie centro-meridionale aux deux derniers siècle de la République* (Bruxelles: Latomus, 1978), 44, 94, 168. The integration of temples into diverse complexes is common throughout the Mediterranean (see I. Nielsen, *Cultic Theaters and Ritual Drama* [Aarhus: Aarhus University Press, 2002], 172–211). Herod the Great, in close communication with Augustus and Marcus Agrippa, produced inventive, noncanonical combinations in this time period (see Netzer, *The Architecture of Herod*, 73–80).

43. S. Dalley, "Nineveh, Babylon and the Hanging Gardens: Cuneiform and Classical Sources Reconciled," *Iraq* 56 (1994): 45–58.

44. J. Reade, "Alexander the Great and the Hanging Gardens of Babylon," *Iraq* 62 (2000): 195–217.

45. Purcell, "Town in Country, Country in Town," 193.

46. Purcell, "Town in Country, Country in Town," 193.

47. The latter two texts were translated by Purcell, "Town in Country, Country in Town," 194n31.

48. Klynne, *Roman Villas around the Urbs*.

49. See Jashemski, Gleason, and Herchenbach, "Plants in the Garden," in *Gardens of the Roman Empire*, vol. 1, ed. W. F. Jashemski, K. L. Gleason, K. J. Hartswick, and A.-A. Malek (New York: Cambridge University Press, forthcoming).

50. P. Grimal, *Les jardins romains*, 3rd ed. (Paris: Presses universitaires de France, 1984), 173 ff.

51. T. O'Sullivan, "The Mind in Motion: Walking and Metaphorical Travel in the Roman Villa," *Classical Philology* 101, no. 2 (2006): 133–52. E. Macaulay-Lewis has expanded this study to an examination of archaeological remains and other forms of involvement in her doctoral thesis ("Political Museums: Porticos, Gardens and the Public Display of Art in Ancient Rome," in *Collecting and Dynastic Ambition*, ed. S. Bracken, A. Gáldy, and A. Turpin [Newcastle: Cambridge Scholars Publishing, 2009], 1–21).

52. Oriental Institute photographic archive P-125. P-207. P22263. Online at: http://oi.uchicago.edu/museum/collections/pa/persepolis/.

53. F. Villedieu, *Il Giardino dei Cesari. Dai pallazi antichi alla Vigna Barberini sul Monte Palatino. Scavi dell'École française de Rome, 1985-1999, Ministero per I Beni e le Attività Culturali Soprintendenza Archeologica di Roma* (Roma: Edizioni Quasar, 2001), 61–70, 84–97.

54. B. Bergmann, "Art and Nature in the Villa at Oplontis," in *Pompeian Brothels, Pompeii's Ancient History, Mirrors and Mysteries, Art and Nature at Oplontis, and*

the Herculaneum 'Basilica,' Journal of Roman Archaeology Supplemental Series 47 (Ann Arbor: University of Michigan, 2002), 87–120; and "Staging the Supernatural: Interior Gardens of Pompeian Houses," in *Pompeii and the Roman Villa: Art and Culture around the Bay of Naples*, ed. C. C. Mattusch (Washington, D.C.: National Gallery of Art, 2008), 53–69.

55. M. Beard and J. Henderson, *Classical Art: From Greece to Rome* (Oxford: Oxford University Press, 2001).

56. A. M. Ciarallo and M. M. Lippi, "The Garden of Casa dei Casti Amanti (Pompeii, Italy)," *Garden History* 21 (1993): 110–16.

57. K. L. Gleason, "Constructing Nature: With a Preliminary Notice of a New Environmental Garden at the Villa Arianna, Stabiae, Italy" in *Bollettino di Archeologia Online I 2010 Volume Speciale D/D9/3*. http://151.12.58.75/archeologia/bao_document/articoli/3_Gleason.pdf.

58. K. J. Hartswick, *The Gardens of Sallust: A Changing Landscape* (Austin: University of Texas Press, 2004); Haueber (1998).

59. The general Lucullus designed a triclinium aviary in which he could enjoy seeing the birds he was about to eat flying about him. The realities of the smell and frantic trapped birds proved less than pleasurable (Varro, *de re rustica* 3.4.3).

60. B. Kellum, "The Construction of Landscape in Augustan Rome: The Garden Room at the Villa ad Gallinas," *Art Bulletin* 76, no. 2 (1994): 211–24; J. C. Reeder, *The Villa of Livia Ad Gallinas Albas: A Study in the Augustan Villa and Garden* (Providence, RI: Center for Old World Archaeology and Art, Brown University, 2001); S. Settis, *La Villa di Livia: Le Pareti Ingannevoli* (Milan: Mondadori Electa, 2008); M. Gabriel, *Livia's Garden Room at Prima Porta* (New York: NYU Press, 1955), 7–8.

Chapter 2

1. Main works on ancient gardens: M. Gothein, "Der griechische Garten," *Athenische Mitteilungen* 34 (1909): 100–144; P. Grimal, *Les jardins romains*, 2nd ed. (Paris: Presses universitaires de France, 1969); M. Carroll-Spillecke, Κηπος: *Der antike griechische garten; Wohnen in der klassichen polis Band III* (München: Deutscher Kunstverlag, 1989); W. F. Jashemski, *The Gardens of Pompeii, Herculaneum and the Villas Destroyed by Vesuvius*, vol. 1 (New Rochelle, NY: Caratzas Brothers, 1979), and *The Gardens of Pompeii, Herculaneum and the Villas Destroyed by Vesuvius*, vol. 2: appendices (New Rochelle, NY: Caratzas Brothers, 1993); E. MacDougall and W. F. Jashemski, *Ancient Roman Gardens* (Washington, D.C.: Dunbarton Oaks, 1981); D. E. Birge, "Sacred Groves in the Ancient Greek World" (PhD diss., University of California, Berkeley, 1982); E. MacDougall, *Ancient Roman Villa Gardens* (Washington, D.C.: Dumbarton Oaks, 1987); M. Carroll-Spillecke, ed., *Der Garten von der Antike bis zum Mittelalter* (Mainz: Kulturgeschichte der antiken Welt 57, 1992); C. Tuplin, *Achaemenid Studies*, Historia Einzelschriften Heft 99 (Stuttgart: F. Steiner, 1996); B. Andreae, *Am Birnbaum: Gärten und Parks im antiken Rom, in den Vesuvstädten und in Ostia* (Mainz: v. Zabern, 1996); L. Farrar, *Ancient Roman Gardens* (Stroud: Sutton Publishing, 2000); L. Landgren, "Lauro

Myrto et Buxo Frequentata: A Study of the Roman Garden through its Plants" (PhD diss., Department of Archaeology and Ancient History, Lund University, 2004); J. Ganzert and J. Wolschke Bulmahn, *Bau- und Gartenkultur zwischen "Orient" und "Okzident": Fragen zu Herkunft, Identität und Legitimation* (München: Martin Meidenbauer, 2009).

2. This typology was first coined in an article treating the gardens of the Hellenistic palaces (I. Nielsen, "The Gardens of the Hellenistic Palaces," in *The Royal Palace Institution in the First Millennium BC: Regional Development and Cultural Interchange between East and West*, ed. I. Nielsen [Athens: Danish Institute at Athens, 2001], 165–87) but has proved to be useful also in a general treatment of ancient gardens.

3. *Paradeisos*, a Persian word, means enclosure but soon became used broadly. *Paradeisoi* could be sacred property, village land, or a high status pleasure garden. Although its original Persian meaning is uncertain, its later usage, especially in a biblical context, is very well-known (cf. D. Stronach, "The Royal Garden at Pasargadae. Evolution and Legacy," in *Archeologia Iranica et Orientalis: Miscellanea in Honorem Louis Vanden Berghe*, ed. L. De Meyer and E. Haerinck, 475–502 [Gent: Peters, 1989]). For paradeisoi in general, see, for example, Xenophon, who in *Oeconomicus* 4.13–14 emphasizes the interest that the Persian kings took in the layout of these parks and their cultivation. Cf. Ziegler (s.v. paradeisos, *Pauly's Real-Encyclopädie der classischen Altertumswissenschaft* 18, 1949, cols. 113–34), who deals mainly with the biblical meaning of the word, but also with the attitudes of the Greeks to the parks, which they identified with *kepoi* and *alsoi* (cf. Carroll-Spillecke, Κηπος: *Der antike griechische garten*). Important is Tuplin, *Achaemenid Studies*, 93ff., who reaches the conclusion that it is so broad in meaning that little definite may be concluded about size, contents, and location from the word alone. The word was also used in Ptolemaic and Roman Egypt, designating here an orchard subject to tax.

4. Tuplin, *Achaemenid Studies*, 104.

5. Tuplin, *Achaemenid Studies*, 115ff., for this *tryphe* character of the *paradeisos*. See I. Nielsen, "Royal Banquets: The Development of Royal Banquets and Banqueting Halls from Alexander to the Tetrarchs," in *Meals in a Social Context* (*Aarhus Studies in Mediterranean Antiquity* 1), ed. I. Nielsen and H. S. Nielsen (Aarhus: Aarhus University Press, 1998), 104–35, for al fresco dining, including the presence of *stibadia* and *triclinia* in gardens. During Alexander's campaign, *klinai* and a throne were placed in a paradeisos in Babylon (Athen. 12.537d, cit. Ephippus [126F4]). Comparison may be made with the Achaemenid kings, who often held court in their gardens. Hieron II of Syracuse used gardens near the city for audiences (Athen. 12.542a, cit. Selinus).

6. J.-C. Hugonot, "Ägyptische Gärten," in *Der Garten von der Antike bis zum Mittelalter*, ed. M. Carroll-Spillecke, Kulturgeschichte der antiken Welt 57 (Mainz: v. Zabern, 1992), 9–44.

7. W. M. Petrie, *The Palace of Apries* (London: School of Archaeology, 1909).

8. See J.-C. Margueron, "Die Gärten im Vorderen Orient," in *Der Garten von der Antike bis zum Mittelalter*, ed. M. Carroll-Spillecke, Kulturgeschichte der antiken Welt 57 (Mainz: v. Zabern, 1992), 45–80. In the Near East especially, though also

known from Egypt, a typical *topos* is the king as gardener, or gardeners becoming kings (Tuplin *Achaemenid Studies*, 118n125).

9. For the theory that the Hanging Gardens were instead situated in Niniveh, see S. Dalley, "Nineveh, Babylon and the Hanging Gardens: Cuneiform and Classical Sources Reconciled," *Iraq* 56 (1994): 45–58. For the park on the other side of the river, at Sittake, see Xenophon, *Anabasis* 2.4.14a; and Arrian, *Anabasis* 7.25. Cf. A. Kuhrt, "The Palace(s) of Babylon," in *The Royal Palace Institution in the First Millennium BC: Regional Development and Cultural Interchange between East and West*, ed. I. Nielsen (Athens: Danish Institute at Athens, 2001), 77–93. According to Diodorus 2.10.1f and Strabo 16.1.5, this garden was four *plethra* square—that is, 120 by 120 meters (approximately 394 by 394 ft), or 1.44 hectares (3.5 acres) and also other *paradeisoi* have this general size (see Tulpin, *Achaemenid Studies*, 97ff.)

10. For the sources to Achaemenid gardens, see Tuplin, *Achaemenid Studies*, 88ff. He sees three types of gardens here (*Achaemenid Studies*, 90): (1) buildings in an unenclosed mixture of formal garden and parkland; (2) buildings within an enclosed garden of some 3.5 hectare (8.6 acres); (3) small gardens enclosed by buildings. This typology may partly be correlated with our types 1–3 for ancient gardens. In contrast to the Assyrian gardens, the Achaemenid ones were seldom depicted on the reliefs.

11. D. Stronach, *Pasargadae* (Oxford: Oxford University Press, 1978); R. Boucharlat, "Pasargadai," *Reallexikon der Assyriologie* 10, nos. 5/6 (2004): 359f.

12. R. Boucharlat and A. Labrousse, "Le palais d'Artaxerxes II sur la rive droite du Chaour à Suse," *Cahiers de la Délégation Archéologique Francaise en Iran* 10 (1979): 19–136.

13. E. F. Schmidt, *Persepolis* (Chicago: University of Chicago, Oriental Institute Publications 68, 1953). Also in the Sassanid period this tradition was continued, for example in a hunting park or paradeisos near Taq-I Bustan (T. S. Kawami, "Antike persische Gärten," in *Garten von der Antike bis zum Mittelalter*, ed. M. Carroll-Spillecke [Mainz: v. Zabern, 1992], 93ff.).

14. Kelainai (Xen., *An.* 1.2.7–9); Daskyleion (Xenophon, *Hellenica* 4.1.15–16); North Syria (Xen., *An.* 1.4.9–11). Cf. Sidon: Diodor. 16.41–45. Jerusalem, Nehemias 2.8–9. Bazaira, Curtius Rufus 8.1.11f, Diodorus 17 *prologue* 26. Ramat Rahel: Y. Aharoni, "Excavations at Ramath rahel, 1954: Preliminary Report," *Israel Exploration Journal* 6 (1956): 102–11, 137–57; O. Lipschits, "The 2006 and 2007 Excavation Seasons at Ramat Rahel: Preliminary Report," *Israel Exploration Journal* 59 (2009): 1–20. Royal parks are also mentioned in connection with the Babylonian destruction (*II Kings* 25.4).

15. For Gelon's garden, Athen. 12.541c–542a. For the park (*kepos*) laid out by Dionysius in Syracuse, Plato, *Epinomis* 2.313a, 3.319a, 7.347a, 7.348e. For Rhegion, see Pliny, *HN* 12.7; Theophrastus, *De Causis Plantarum* Pl. 4.5.9. Cf. Grimal, *Les jardins romains*, 2nd ed., 77; I. Nielsen, *Hellenistic Palaces: Tradition and Renewal*, 2nd ed. (Aarhus: Aarhus University Press, 1999), 79f.

16. For *alsos, sema, museion*, see Strabo 17.1.8; for *palaestra*, Polyb. 15.25.3, 15.28.4, 15.30.6, 15.31.2–4; for *maiandros*, Polyb. 15.30.6.

17. See G. Downey, *A History of Antioch in Syria from Seleucus to the Arab Conquest*, (Princeton, NJ: Princeton University Press, 1961), 640–50; Nielsen, *Hellenistic Palaces*, 2nd ed., 112ff., cat. no. 15.

18. These late sources are Libanius, *Orationes* 11.206; Theodoretus, *Historia Eccle-siastica* 4.26.1–3; and Evagrius 2.12. For Daphne and the road to it, see Strab. 16.750; Liban., *Or.* 11. 356ff. A combination of a palatial and a sacred function is also documented in Daphne. One of them surrounded the temple of Apollo and Artemis and had a range of c. 16 km (10 miles), according to Strabo (16.2.6).

19. See P. Bernard, *Fouilles d'Aï Khanoum I* (Mémoires DAFA XXI) (Paris: Klincks-ieck, 1973); Nielsen, *Hellenistic Palaces*, 2nd ed., cat. no.19.

20. See E. Will and F. Larche. *Iraq el Emir—Le château du Tobiade Hyrcan* (Paris: Librairie orientaliste Paul Geuthner, 1991); cf. E. Netzer, "Il palazzo riflesso," *Archeo* 13, no. 7 (1997): 50–54, who draws attention to the mirror effect of the lake; Nielsen, *Hellenistic Palaces*, 2nd ed., cat. no. 21.

21. Netzer, *Hasmonean and Herodian Palaces at Jericho, Final Reports of the 1973–1987 Excavations*, vol. 1, *Stratigraphy and Architecture* (Jerusalem: Israel Explora-tion Society: Institute of Archaeology, Hebrew University of Jerusalem, 2001), 11ff.

22. For these Herodian palaces, Netzer, *Hasmonean and Herodian Palaces at Jericho*; Nielsen, *Hellenistic Palaces*, 2nd ed., 180ff., and cat. nos. 26–31.

23. L.-A. Bedal, *The Petra Pool-Complex: A Hellenistic Paradeisos in the Nabataean Capital* (Piscataway, NJ: Gorgias Press, 2004).

24. See E. La Rocca, "Il lusso come espressione di potere," in *Le tranquille dimore degli dei*, ed. M. Cima and E. La Rocca (Venice: Marsilio, 1986), 3–35; C. Häuber, "Endlich lebe ich wie ein Mensch: Zu domus, horti und villae in Rom," in *Das Wrack: Der antike Schiffsfund von Mahdia*, ed. G. Hellenkemper Salies (Köln: Rheinland-Verlag GmbH, 1994), 911–26.

25. E.S.P. Ricotti, "The Importance of Water in Roman Garden Triclinia," in *Ancient Roman Gardens*, ed. E. B. MacDougall (Washington, D.C.: Dumbarton Oaks, 1987), 135–84.

26. One may compare with the specialized gardens of the Victorians. We know that Greek plants were introduced into the East in connection with Alexander's con-quests, and according to a Zenon papyrus (*P. Cairo Zeno* 59075, 257 B.C.E.), the Ptolemaic official Tobias of Transjordania sent rare animals to Ptolemy II for his zoo. We hear also that Ptolemy VIII Physcon wrote a treatise on the breeding of birds in the palace area (Plutarch, *Alexander* 35.8; Athen. 14.653c). One is re-minded of the old Egyptian palaces, especially the proposed aviary in the palace of Tell el Amarna (Hugonot, "Ägyptische Gärten"), but they also formed part of palaces in the Near East—for example, in Assur (Margueron, "Die Gärten im Vor-deren Orient").

27. See Birge, "Sacred Groves in the Ancient Greek World," for sacred groves in Greece. Cf. Tuplin, *Achaemenid Studies*, 120, for sources. The Scholium to Aeschylus (*Sep-tem contra Thebas* 272) mentions that citizens set aside *alsoi kai paradeisous* for the gods.

28. From D. L. Page, *Greek Literary Papyri* (London: Heinemann, 1942).

29. D. B. Thompson, "The Garden of Hephaistos," *Hesperia* 6 (1937): 401–25.

30. Corinth: C. Roebuck, *The Asklepieion and Lerna* (Corinth v. 14) (Princeton, NJ: American School of Classical Studies at Athens, 1951); Nemea: S. G. Miller, "Ex-cavations at Nemea," *Hesperia* 46 (1977): 1–26.

31. Cf. D. Soren, *The Sanctuary of Apollo Hylates at Kourion, Cyprus* (Tucson: Uni-versity of Arizona Press, 1987); V. Karageorghis and M. Carroll-Spillecke, "Die

heiligen Haine und Gärten Zyperns," in *Garten von der Antike bis zum Mittelalter 1992*, ed. M. Carroll-Spillecke (Mainz: v. Zabern, 1992), 146ff.

32. B. Bergquist, *Herakles on Thasos: The Archaeological, Literary, and Epigraphic Evidence for his Sanctuary; Status and Cult Reconsidered* (Uppsala: Almqvist & Wiksell, 1973).

33. J. H. Kent, "The Temple Estates of Delos, Rheneia and Mykonos," *Hesperia* 17 (1948): 243ff.

34. For Nemi, F. Coarelli, *I santuari del Lazio in età Repubblicana* (Rome: La Nuova Italia Scientifica, 1987). For Gabii, H. Lauter, "Ein Tempelgarten?" *Archäologischer Anzeiger* (1968): 626–31; M. Almagro-Gorbea, *El Santuario de Juno en Gabii* (Rome: Escuela espanola de historia y arquelogía en Roma, Bibliotheca italica 17, 1982); Coarelli, "I *luci* del Lazio: la documentazione archeologica," in *Les Bois Sacrés: Actes du colloque international* (Neaples: Centre Jean Bérard, 1993), 45–52.

35. Jashemski, "Antike römische Gärten in Campanien," in *Der Garten von der Antike bis zum Mittelalter*, ed. M. Carroll-Spillecke (Mainz: Kulturgeschichte der antiken Welt 57, 1992), 199f.

36. K. Lembke, *Das Iseum Campense in Rom: Studien über den Isiskult unter Domitian* (Heidelberg: Verlag Archäologie und Geschichte, 1994).

37. For the early porticus gardens in Rome, see Coarelli, *Il campo Marzio dale origini alla fine della Repubblica* (Rome: Quasar, 1997), 515ff.; for the porticus of Pompey, see also Coarelli, *Il campo Marzio dale origini alla fine della Repubblica*, 539ff.; for the new excavations in the Templum Pacis, see R. Meneghini and R. S. Valenziani, *I Fori Imperiali: Gli scavi del Comune di Roma (1991–2007)* (Rome: Viriani Editore, 2007); for the recent excavations in the Adoneia on the Palatine, see M. A. Tomei, "Nota sui giardini antichi del Palatino," *Mélanges d'Archéologie et d'Histoire de l'École Francaise de Rome, Antiquité* 104 (1992): 938ff.; J. P. Morel, "Stratigraphie et histoire sur le Palatin: la zone centrale de la Vigna Barberini," *Comptes rendus des séances de l'Académie des inscriptions et belles-lettres* (1996): 173–206. Cf. R. B. Lloyd, "Three Monumental Gardens on the Marble Plan," *American Journal of Archaeology* 86 (1982): 91–100.

38. The so-called Adonis gardens (*kepoi*) known in a private context the Greek area, especially from Athens, were in fact only potted plants that were placed on the roof of the house during the Adoneia festival (see B. Soyez, *Byblos et la Fete des Adonies* [Leiden: Brill, 1977]).

39. Jashemski, "Roman Gardens in Tunisia: Preliminary Excavations in the House of Bacchus and Ariadne and in the East Temple at Thuburbo Maius," *American Journal of Archaeology* 99 (1995): 573.

40. Coarelli, "I *luci* del Lazio: la documentazione archeological."

41. S. de Caro, "Sculpture from Oplontis" in *Ancient Roman Villa Gardens*, ed. E. MacDougall, (Washington, D.C.: Dumbarton Oaks, 1987), 78–113; B. Bergmann, "Art and Nature in the Villa at Oplontis," in *Pompeian Brothels, Pompeii's Ancient History, Mirrors and Mysteries, Art and Nature at Oplontis, and the Herculaneum 'Basilica,' Journal of Roman Archaeology, Supplemental Series* 47 (Ann Arbor: University of Michigan, 2002), 87–120. A. Wallace-Hadrill, "Horti and Hellenization," in *Horti Romani*, ed. M. Cima and E. La Rocca, 1–12 (Rome: "L'Erma" di

Bretschneider, 1998). J. R. Clarke, *The Houses of Roman Italy, 100 B.C.-A.D. 250: Ritual, Space, and Decoration* (Berkeley: University of California Press, 1991). Lloyd, "Three Monumental Gardens on the Marble Plan," 95.

42. For these gymnasia and their gardens, see Gotheim, "Der griechische Garten"; J. Delorme, *Gymnasion* (Paris: Bibliotheéque des Écoles françaises d'Athenes et de Rome, 1960), 51ff., and *passim*; Grimal, *Les jardins romains*, 2nd ed., 69ff. and *passim*; Carroll-Spillecke, *Der Garten von der Antike bis zum Mittelalter*, 161ff.

43. Gotheim, "Der griechische Garten."

44. Cf. Varro (*RR*, Proem), who says that while in the old days there were no *gymnasia* of the Greek type, now they (the elite) are not satisfied unless their villas teem with Greek names.

45. See Jashemski, *The Gardens of Pompeii*, vol. 1; "Antike römische Gärten in Campanien," 198f.

46. See for this development and the Roman *thermae* in general, I. Nielsen, *Thermae et Balnea: The Architecture and Cultural History of Roman Public Baths*, 2nd ed. (Aarhus: Aarhus University Press, 1993).

47. E. Netzer, *Die Paläste der Hasmonäer und Herodes' des Grossen* (Mainz: v. Zabern, 1999).

48. J. Alarcao and R. Etienne, "Les jardins à Conimbriga (Portugal)," in *Ancient Roman Garden*, ed. E. B. MacDougall and W. F. Jashemski (Washington, D.C.: Dumbarton Oaks, 1981), 77ff.

49. For this famous theatre complex, see J. A. Hanson, *Roman Theater Temples* (Princeton, NJ: Princeton University Press, 1959), 43f.; K. L. Gleason, "Porticus Pompeiana: A New Perspective on the First Public Park of Ancient Rome," *Journal of Garden History* 14, no. 1 (1994): 13–27; I. Nielsen, *Cultic Theaters and Ritual Drama* (Aarhus: Aarhus University Press, 2002), 197ff.

50. J. Travlos, *Pictorial Dictionary of Athens* (London: Thames and Hudson, 1971), 244ff.

51. This park is mentioned by Ovidius, *Ars Amatoria* I.72; Martial, *Epigrammaton Libri* III 20.8; Pliny, *HN* XIV 3.11.

52. Stronach, "The Royal Garden at Pasargadae: Evolution and Legacy"; Kawami, "Antike persische Gärten"; Tuplin, *Achaemenid Studies*, 88f., and R. Boucharlat, "The Palace and the Royal Achaemenid City: Two Case Studies—Pasargadae and Susa," *The Royal Palace Institution in the First Millennium BC: Regional Development and Cultural Interchange between East and West*, ed. I. Nielsen (Athens: Danish Institute at Athens, 2001), 113–23; Boucharlat, "Pasargadai." Unfortunately, we do not know what grew in this garden. Stronach ("The Garden as a Political Statement: Some Case Studies from the Near East in the First Millennium B.C.," *Bulletin of the Asia institute* 4 [1990]: 176) has suggested that a fourfold royal garden might have been intended to symbolize the "four quarters" of the universe—that is, the Achaemenid Empire in microcosm, but this has not been proven in the excavations (Boucharlat, "Pasargadai").

53. Boucharlat and Labrousse, "Le palais d'Artaxerxes II."

54. A. B. Tilia, "Discovery of an Achaemenian Palace Near Takht-I Rustam to the North of the Terrace of Persepolis," *Iran* 12 (1974): 200–204.

55. Tuplin, *Achaemenid Studies*, 88f.
56. For Alcinous's garden, Homer's *Odyssey* 7.112–132, cf. D. Braund, "Palace and Polis: Dionysus, Scythia and Plutarch's Alexander," *The Royal Palace Institution in the First Millennium BC: Regional Development and Cultural Interchange between East and West*, ed. I. Nielsen (Athens: Danish Institute at Athens, 2001), 15–31.

    For Laertes' garden, *Od.* Book 24, 205ff. See also for these gardens, Gotheim, "Der griechische Garten." For Homeric and archaic gardens, Carroll-Spillecke, Κηπος; *Der Garten von der Antike bis zum Mittelalter*, 154f. One may compare with the description of the Palace of Aeetes in Colchis, given in the *Argonautica* of Apollonius Rhodius (3.164ff.), a contemporary of Ptolemy II and from Alexandria. Here, a wide vestibule led to a garden with fountains, which led to the palace proper, the *messaulos*, used in the Homeric sense of the word.
57. Bernard, *Fouilles d'Aï Khanoum I*.
58. Netzer, *Hasmonean and Herodian Palaces at Jericho*.
59. One may compare with the stibadia seen in the Nile Mosaics found in Italy (see Nielsen, "Royal Banquets"; K.M.D. Dunbabin, "Triclinium and Stibadium," in *Dining in a Classical Context*, ed. W. J. Slater, 121–48 (Ann Arbor: University of Michigan Press, 1991).
60. Netzer, *Hasmonean and Herodian Palaces at Jericho*, 287ff.
61. Liljenstolpe and Klynne 1997–98; Klynne and Liljenstolpe 2000
62. Tomei, "Nota sui giardini antichi del Palatino."
63. G. Lugli, "La villa di Domiziano sui Colli Albani," *Bullettino della Commissione Archeologica Comunale di Roma* (1918): 64–65.
64. For gardens in Villa Adriana, see A. Hoffmann, *Das Gartenstadion in der Villa Hadriana* (Mainz: v. Zabern, 1980); Ricotti, "The Importance of Water."
65. For the villa in Tusculum, *Ep.* 5.6; for that in Laurentum, *Ep.* 2.17. For the *otium* villas of the Roman elite in general, J. H. D'Arms, *Romans on the Bay of Naples. A Social and Cultural Study of the Villas and Their Owners from 150 B.C. to A.D. 400* (Cambridge, MA: Harvard University Press, 1970); H. Mielsch, *Die romische Villa: Architektur und lebensform* (Munich: Beck, 1987); N. Purcell, "The Roman Garden as a Domestic Building," in *Roman Domestic Buildings*, ed. I. M. Barton (Exeter: University of Exeter Press, 1996), 121–52; Farrar, *Ancient Roman Gardens*, 12ff.
66. Jashemski, "Antike römische Gärten in Campanien."
67. B. Bergmann, "Art and Nature in the Villa at Oplontis," *Journal of Roman Archaeology* 16 (2002): 87–120, 93ff.
68. B. Cunliffe, "Roman Gardens in Britain: A Review of the Evidence," *Ancient Roman Gardens*, ed. E. B. MacDougall and W. F. Jashemski (Washington, D.C.: Dumbarton Oaks, 1981), 95–108; "Fishbourne Revisited: The Site in Its Context," *Journal of Roman Archaeology* 4 (1991): 160–69; *Fishbourne Roman Palace* (Stroud: Tempus, 1998).
69. In fact, an area free from buildings is often set out in Greek cities and colonies for this purpose. That the same was the case in Italy is amply documented in Pompeii. Outside the Athenian city walls, we hear of luxurious gardens referred to by Thucydides 2.62.3. For Greek gardens, see Carroll-Spillecke, Κηπος: *Der antike*

griechische garten, and *Der Garten von der Antike bis zum Mittelalter*; for Roman house gardens, Jashemski, *The Gardens of Pompeii*, vol. 1, and *The Gardens of Pompeii*, vol. 2; Farrar, *Ancient Roman Gardens*.

70. G. Vallet, F. Villard, and P. Auberson, *Megara Hyblaea I, Le quartier de l'agora archaique* (Rome: École Francaise, 1976).

71. F. Brown, *Cosa: The Making of a Roman Town* (Ann Arbor: University of Michigan Press, 1979).

72. Jashemski, *The Gardens of Pompeii*, vol. 1; *The Gardens of Pompeii*, vol. 2.

73. Jashemski, "The Discovery of a Market-Garden Orchard at Pompeii: The Garden of the House of the Ship Europa," *American Journal of Archaeology* 78 (1974): 391–404; "Antike römische Gärten in Campanien," 187ff.

74. The standard numbering system for houses at Pompeii; for example, Regio II Insula II.8.6 number 6.

75. Jashemski, "Antike römische Gärten in Campanien," 193ff.

76. Jashemski, "Antike römische Gärten in Campanien," 192f.

77. Carroll-Spillecke, "Antike römische Gärten in Campanien," 164.

78. Jashemski, "Antike römische Gärten in Campanien," 201f.

79. J.M.C. Toynbee, *Death and Burial in the Roman World* (London: Thames and Hudson, 1971), 81f.

80. See L. Bek, "*Questiones Convivales*: The Idea of the *Triclinium* and the Staging of Convival Ceremony from Rome to Byzantium," *Analecta romana Instituti Danici* 12 (1983): 81–107; Ricotti, "The Importance of Water"; Nielsen, "Royal Banquets"; Bergmann, "Art and Nature in the Villa at Oplontis."

81. Hugonot, "Ägyptische Gärten."

82. Margueron, "Die Gärten im Vorderen Orient," 71ff.

83. See Nielsen, *Hellenistic Palaces*, 2nd ed., 77f.

84. For this theory, see Carroll-Spillecke, Κηπος: *Der antike griechische garten*, contra, Nielsen, *Hellenistic Palaces*, 2nd ed.

85. See G. Clarke, "The Governor's Palace, Acropolis, Jebel Khalid," in *The Royal Palace Institution in the First Millennium BC: Regional Development and Cultural Interchange between East and West*, ed. I. Nielsen (Athens: Danish Institute at Athens, 2001), 215–47.

86. See Nielsen, *Hellenistic Palaces*, 2nd ed., cat. no. 12. See Livy (40.7.8) also cited by M. P. Hatzopoulos, "Macedonian Palaces: Where King and City Meet," in *The Royal Palace Institution in the First Millennium BC: Regional Development and Cultural Interchange between East and West*, ed. I. Nielsen (Athens: Danish Institute at Athens, 2001), 189–200, in which Philip V walks up and down (*inambulavit*) in his palace, which suggests that an *ambulatio* was often associated with gardens.

87. G. Pesce, *Il "Palazzo delle Colonne" in Tolemaide di Cirenaica* (Rome: L'Erma di Bretschneider, 1950).

88. McKenzie (*The Architecture of Petra* [Oxford: Oxford University Press, 1990], 85ff.) argues convincingly that many of the gardens seen on the second style paintings were inspired by Egyptian gardens, just as the fantastic architecture of these paintings were probably inspired from Alexandria.

89. This is mentioned in the *Book of Esther* (1:3–8).

90. Cf. Nielsen, *Hellenistic Palaces*, 2nd ed., 182ff. Netzer, *Die Paläste der Hasmonäer und Herodes des Grossen*, 15ff.

91. See Gleason, "A Garden Excavation in the Oasis Palace of Herod the Great at Jericho," *Landscape Journal* 12, no. 2 (1993): 156–67.

92. K. L. Gleason, B. Burrell, and E. Netzer, "The Promotory Palace at Caesarea Maritima: Preliminary Evidence for Herod's Praetorium," *Journal of Roman Archaeology* 11 (1998): 23–52.

93. Thus they are included in Vitruvius's description of these houses (6.5.2): "For persons of high rank who hold office and magistracies, and whose duty it is to serve the state, we must provide princely vestibules, lofty halls and very spacious peristyles, plantations and broad avenues finished in a majestic manner."

94. Nielsen, *Hellenistic Palaces*, 2nd ed., 171ff.

95. Tomei, "Nota sui giardini antichi del Palatino," 944ff.

96. Bek, "*Questiones Convivales*."

97. Tomei, "Nota sui giardini antichi del Palatino," 950.

98. W. F. Jashemski and E.S.P. Ricotti, "1992 Preliminary Excavations in the Gardens of Hadrian's Villa: The Canopus Area and the Piazza d'Oro," *American Journal of Archaeology* 96 (1996): 593–95.

99. Thompson cited in A. Frantz, *Late Antiquity: AD 267–700. The Athenian Agora*, vol. 24 (Princeton, NJ: Princeton University Press, 1988), 95–116, pl. 54–55.

100. Jashemski, "The Campanian Peristyle Garden," in *Ancient Roman Gardens*, eds. E. B. MacDougall and W. Jashemski (Washington, D.C.: Dumbarton Oaks, 1981), 31. The conditions in the Vesuvian area and especially in Pompeii were perfect, since it was possible to trace the garden as it looked at the time of the destruction 79 C.E. In the earlier excavations, only a few roots had been ascertained and no garden excavated (the evidence is collected in Jashemski, *The Gardens of Pompeii*, vol. 1; *The Gardens of Pompeii*, vol. 2; "The Campanian Peristyle Garden," 37).

101. Jashemski, "The Campanian Peristyle Garden," 32ff.

102. Jashemski, "The Campanian Peristyle Garden," 33ff.

103. Jashemski, "The Campanian Peristyle Garden," 37.

104. Jashemski, "The Campanian Peristyle Garden," 37ff.

105. Jashemski, *The Gardens of Pompeii*, vol. 1, 135–37.

106. Garden sculpture: Farrar, *Ancient Roman Gardens*, 97ff.; sculpture in the House of the Vettii: Jashemski, *The Gardens of Pompeii*, vol. 1, 35ff.; pool types in the Pompeian gardens: Jashemski, *The Gardens of Pompeii*, 41–43; mosaic fountains: Jashemski, *The Gardens of* Pompeii, vol. 1, 41–43; garden paintings: Jashemski, *The Gardens of Pompeii*, vol. 2, Appendix 2. Such a luxurious garden with sculptures was reconstructed in the Museum of Bonn based on the contents of the sunken Mahdia ship (G. Hellenkemper Salies, ed., *Das Wrack: Der antike Schiffsfund von Mahdia* (Köln: Rheinland Verlag GmbH, 1994).

107. Jashemski, "The Campanian Peristyle Garden," 41.

108. M. Robinson, "Evidence for Garden Cultivation and the Use of Bedding-Out Plants in the Peristyle Garden of the House of the Greek Epigrams (V 1,18i) at Pompeii," *Opuscula Romana* 31–32 (2006–07): 155–59.

109. Jashemski, "Roman Gardens in Tunisia."

110. Alarcao and Etienne, "Les jardins à Conimbriga (Portugal)."

111. Caissons are attested since the first century B.C.E. in the public porticoes: Porticus Pompeia and Porticus Philippi, in Rome (P. Gros, *Aurea Templa: recherches sur l'architecture religieuse de Rome à l'Époque d'Auguste* [Rome: École Francaise de Rome, 1976], 90). Flavian gardens featured caissons in a peristyle (C) of the Flavian palace on the Palatine and the Templum Pacis. But outside Rome and Conimbriga, such pools with caissons are very seldom seen, and then mostly in villas in Spain.

112. M. LeGlay, "Les jardins à Vienne," in *Ancient Roman Gardens 1981*, ed. E.B. MacDougall and W. Jashemski (Washington, D.C.: Dumbarton Oaks, 1981), 49–65.

113. A. Desbat, *La Maison des Dieux Océan à Saint-romain-en-Gal*, 55th suppl. (Paris: Gallia, 1994), esp. 199–200.

114. Desbat, *La Maison des Dieux*, 176.

115. Le Glay, "Les jardins à Vienne."

116. A. Dreliossi-Herakleidou, "Späthellenistische palastartige Gebäude in der Nähe der Akropolis von Rhodos," in *Basileia: Die Paläste der hellenistischen Könige*, ed. W. Hoepfner und G. Brands (Mainz: v. Zabern, 1996), 182–92.

117. Thompson, "The Garden of Hephaistos," 69.

118. See Jashemski, *The Gardens of Pompeii*, vol. 1, 289–314; *Ancient Roman Gardens*; "Antike römische Gärten in Campanien."

119. Jashemski, *The Gardens of Pompeii*, vol. 1, 322, 326–28.

120. Also Jashemski, *The Gardens of Pompeii*, vol. 1, 544, 271.

121. R. Tölle-Kastenbein, *Samos 14. Das Kastro Tigrani. Die Bauten und Funde griechischer, römischer und byzantinischer Zeit* (Bonn: R. Habelt, 1974).

122. T. Spyropoulos, "Prächtige Villa, Refugium und Musenstätte: Die Villa des Herodes Atticus in arkadischen Euá," *Antike Welt* 34 (2003): 463–70.

123. Piazza Armerina: G. Gentili, *Die Kaiserliche Villa bei Piazza Armerina* (Rome: Libreria dello Stato, 1971). Montmaurin: G. Fouet, *La villa gallo-romaine de Montmaurin vers le milieu de 4e siécle* (Paris: Saint-Gaudens, 1983); J.-M. Pailler, "Montmaurin: A Garden Villa," in *Ancient Roman Villa Gardens*, ed. E.B. MacDougall (Washington, D.C.: Dumbarton Oaks, 1987), 205–21.

124. Jashemski, *The Gardens of Pompeii*, vol. 1, 135–37.

125. A. Mallwitz, *Olympia und seine Bauten* (München: Beck, 1972), 206–10, fig. 167.

126. Mallwitz, *Olympia und seine Bauten*, 252–54; Tölle-Kastenbein, *Samos 14*, 192.

127. Mallwitz, *Olympia und seine Bauten*, 276–77.

128. Frantz, *Late Antiquity*, 40–48.

Chapter 3

1. This text is in part a summary of the author's unpublished doctoral thesis "Lauro Myrto et Buxo Frequentata: A Study of the Roman Garden through Its Plants" (Lund University, 2004).

2. The letters by Pliny have recently received attention (*Arethusa, Re-Imagining Pliny the Younger*, special issue 36, no. 2 [2003]). Questions are raised regarding earlier uses of Pliny's texts as sources for solid "information" on Roman society

(with references to A. N. Sherwin-White, *The Letters of Pliny: A Historical and Social Commentary* [Oxford: Clarendon Press, 1966]; R. Förtsch, *Archäologischer Kommentar zu den Villenbriefen des Jüngeren Plinius* [Mainz am Rhein: Philip von Zabern, 1993]). Nonetheless, throughout the present study, the letters of Pliny will figure as a source of information. Even if Pliny himself never walked around in those gardens he describes, the various references to handling the plants, experiences of shapes and contours of leaves, and descriptions of various elements such as pergolas, walls, and fountains must have some bearing on reality. Thus, Pliny's letters are used as testimonies on gardening and on views on gardening in vogue in the first century C.E.

3. Before Carl Linnaeus created the binary name classification, botanists had no systemized nomenclature for plants. Thus, there are cases in ancient Latin literature of specific plant names, for example *viola*, that are used for a number of plants with various characteristics. This study employs the identifications of J. André, *Les noms de plantes dans la Rome antique* (Paris: Les Belles Lettres 1985).

4. W. F. Jashemski, *Gardens of Pompeii, Herculaneum, and the Villas Destroyed by Vesuvius*, vol. 1 (New Rochelle, NY: Caratzas Brothers, 1979); Jashemski, "The Contribution of Archaeology to the Study of Ancient Roman Gardens," in *Garden History: Issues, Approaches, Methods*, Colloquium on the History of Landscape Architecture 13, ed. J. Dixon Hunt (Washington, D.C.: Dumbarton Oaks, 1992), 5–30; *The Gardens of Pompeii, Herculaneum and the Villas Destroyed by Vesuvius*, vol. 2 (New Rochelle, NY: Caratzas,1993).

5. B. Bergmann, "Art and Nature in the Villa at Oplontis," *Journal of Roman Archaeology* 47 (2002): 87–120.

6. For archaeological recovery of garden evidence, see A.-A. Malek, ed., *A Sourcebook for Garden Archaeology* (Bern: Peter Lang, 2012).

7. S. Hales, *The Roman House and Social Identity* (Cambridge: Cambridge University Press, 2003), 159.

8. See H. Caneva, "Ipotsi sul significato simbolico del giardino dipinto della Villa di Livia (Prima Porta, Roma)," *Bullettino della commissione archeologica comunale di Roma* 100 (1999): 63–80, for an extensive summary of earlier research on Roman garden paintings.

9. K.L. Gleason. "Constructing Nature: With a Preliminary Notice of a New Monumental Garden at the Villa Arianna, Stabiae, Italy," in *Bollettino di Archeologia Online I 2010/Volume Speciale D/D9/3*: 8–15. http://151.12.58.75/archeologia/bao_document/ articoli/3_Gleason.pdf.

10. These are, regarding trees, *cupressus, laurus, picea, pinus, platanus*, and regarding fruit trees, *arbutus, citrus, ficus, lotos, morus, tubur*, and *ziziphus*. Shrubs and flowers referred to are *acanthus, adianthus, buxus, cynoglossum, hedera, Iovis barba, lilium, murtus, rhododendron, rosa, rosmarinus, vicapervica*, and *viola*.

11. Scholars do not agree as to the identification of *lapis specularis* in Latin literature. It has been identified with selenite as well as muscovite. Various characteristics of lapis specularis fit both selenite and muscovite (L. Landgren, "Lauro, Myrto et Buxo Frequentata, 83).

12. For a detailed discussion of the evidence of *topiarius* in Roman literature and epigraphy, see Landgren, "Lauro, Myrto et Buxo Frequentata," ch. 5.

13. For example *Corpus Inscriptionum Latinarum* VI 4360, VI 6369, VI 7300, VI 8638.

14. See, for example, H. L. Royden, *The Magistrates of the Roman Professional Collegia in Italy from the First to the Third Century A.D.* (Pisa: 1988), ch. 1, for an introduction to the *collegium*.

15. Carlsen 1995, 64.

16. For a thorough discussion of *viridia* and *viridarium* in the literary and epigraphical records, see Landgren, "Lauro, Myrto et Buxo Frequentata," ch. 5.

17. Cicero, *Epistulae ad Quintum fratrem* 3.1.5: *ita omnia convestivit hedera, qua basim villae, qua intercolumnia ambulationis, ut denique illi palliati topiariam facere videantur et hederam vendere.* This passage provides the earliest literary use of the words *topiarius* and *topiaria* to denote the gardener and his special qualities and tasks.

18. Cf. the description of Pliny the Elder of the acanthus that "clothes" (*vestire*) the border and the raised part of (garden) beds (Pliny the Elder, *Historia Naturalis* 22.76).

19. *Ambulatio* refers to an open walk as well as a covered walk, a portico (*Oxford Latin Dictionary*, s.v. "ambulatio" 2, 116). In this instance, the latter is usually preferred.

20. For *basis villa*, see H. Mielsch, *Die romische Villa: Architektur und lebensform* (Munich: Beck, 1987), 40.

21. Pliny, *HN* 14.11: *totas villas et domos ambiri singularum palmitibus ac sequacibus loris.*

22. Pliny, *Epistulae* 5.6 38–39: *zothecula . . . obscurum umbra . . . nam laetissima vitis per omne tectum in culmen nititur et adscendit.* For *zothecula*, see Förtsch, *Archäologischer Kommentar*, 55–56.

23. A. Ciarallo and M. Mariotti Lippi, "The Garden of 'Casa dei Casti Amanti' (Pompeii, Italy)," *Garden History* 21 (1993): 115. As the authors themselves state, the identification as vine is not secured by the single vine pollen recovered from the garden, but no other plant is suggested.

24. Jashemski, *Gardens of Pompeii*, vol. 1, 29; W. F. Jashemski and F. G. Meyer, *The Natural History of Pompeii* (Cambridge: Cambridge University Press, 2002), 102. We should note that similar arrangements as to the growing of lemon or citron is found along one wall in the garden of Hercules (II.7.6) in Pompeii (Jashemski, *Gardens of Pompeii*, vol. 1, 285). See also L. Farrar, *Ancient Roman Gardens* (Stroud: Sutton Publishing, [1998] 2000), 81–82, suggesting trained plants growing in plant boxes discovered in close affinity to a wall in a garden at the House of Europa, at Cuicul, in Algeria.

25. K. D. White, *Roman Farming* (Ithaca, NY: Cornell University Press 1970), 231–36, with good illustrations.

26. Another possibility is of course that the ivy was employed as garlands, hung between the columns. Ivy garlands are occasionally found in garden paintings; for example, in the House of the Fruit Orchard (1.9.5) and in the House of the Wedding

of Alexander (VI. Insula occcid. 42) in Pompeii (Jashemski, *Gardens of Pompeii*, vol. 2, ills. 363 on 318, 418 on 354).

27. Jashemski, *Gardens of Pompeii*, vol. 1, 32.

28. Jashemski, *Gardens of Pompeii*, vol. 1, 295.

29. Jashemski *Gardens of Pompeii*, vol. 2, 375.

30. S. De Caro, "The Sculptures of the Villa of Poppaea at Oplontis: A Preliminary Report," in *Ancient Roman Villa Gardens*, ed. E. B. MacDougall (Washington, D.C.: Dumbarton Oaks, 1987), 120. The columns were not found in any of the gardens, however, but in rooms twenty-nine and thirty-nine respectively.

31. Bergmann, "Art and Nature in the Villa at Oplontis," 112. See also M. Mathea-Förtsch, *Römische Rankenpfeiler und -pilaster: Schmuckstutzen mit vegetabilem Dekor, vornehmlich aus Italien und der westlichen Provinzen* (Mainz: Von Zabern, 1999), who has clearly shown the widespread use of sculpted columns, in public as well as in private architecture, on house fronts as well as in gardens. Pompeii also presents objects with climbing ivy in the House of Menander (I.10.4) and columns in a garden painting are depicted with ivy (E. De Carolis, "La pittura di giardino a Ercolano e Pompei," in *Domus—viridaria—horti picti* [Napoli: Bibliopolis, 1992], 33n8).

32. Bergmann, "Art and Nature in the Villa at Oplontis." The organization of Roman landscaped areas, such as gardens, has only occasionally been observed in modern research. Beside Bergmann's Oplontis study, see the study on the villa descriptions of Pliny the Younger by Förtsch, *Archäologischer Kommentar*, who also analyses the gardens from a design point of view (especially chapter 6).

33. In the House of the Golden Cupids (VI.16.7), a pinax support in the shape of a tree trunk entwined with ivy is preserved (Jashemski, *Gardens of Pompeii*, vol. 1, 40).

34. Jashemski, *Gardens of Pompeii*, vol. 1, 304.

35. B. Cunliffe, "Roman Gardens in Britain: A Review of the Evidence," in *Ancient Roman Gardens*, Colloquium on the History of Landscape Architecture, ed. E. B. Macdougall and W. F. Jashemski (Washington, D.C.: Dumbarton Oaks, 1981), 103–5.

36. The bedding trenches were filled with marled loam to create alkaline conditions; these would suit a lime-loving plant as the box. However, pollen analysis has not yielded any positive results. The reason may be that if cut, the plant does not flourish and consequently does not produce any pollen. In addition, box gives very little pollen even in a natural growth. Box clippings have been found in other Roman villas in Britain. See Cunliffe, "Roman Gardens in Britain," 105 with further references.

37. Pliny, *HN* 16.140: *Cupressus . . ., nunc vero tonsilis facta in densitatem parietum.*

38. K. D. White, *Farm Equipment of the Roman World* (Cambridge: Cambridge University Press, 1975), 24, discusses the relevant terms for fencing in agricultural contexts.

39. Jashemski, *Gardens of Pompeii*, vol. 2, 116; Jashemski and Meyer, *The Natural History of Pompeii*, 21.

40. *Tondere* is used for several different cutting actions; the cutting of hair or beard, the shearing of sheep, the shearing of carpeting and the lopping of trees and bushes (*OLD*, s.v. "tondeo," 1948). The adjective *tonsilis*, however, is mainly applied to

fabrics and topiary plants (*OLD*, s.v. "tonsilis," 1949). *Tonsilis* was chosen when an aspect of trimming and cutting neat was to be expressed; *tapetes* were closely cut to get rid of any roughness of the fabric, and the nap of new-woven cloth was trimmed (L. Larsson Lovén, "The Imagery of Textile Making: Gender and Status in the Funerary Iconography of Textile Manufacture in Roman Italy and Gaul," PhD diss., Göteborg, 2002, 75) Since a similar action was applied to topiary plants, the same word as in textile terminology was employed. Further, with all possibility similar tools were used in topiary as in certain textile handlings (Landgren, "Lauro, Myrto et Buxo Frequentata," 112–16).

41. Landgren, "Lauro, Myrto et Buxo Frequentata," 104–11.
42. Pliny, *HN* 12.13: *Primus C. Matius ex equestri ordine, divi Augusti amicus, invenit nemora tonsilia intra hos LXXX annos.*
43. Landgren, "The Roman Pleasure Garden—Foundations for Future Studies," *Opuscula Romana* 20 (1996): 44.
44. A. M. Clevely, *Topiary: The Art of Clipping Trees and Ornamental Hedges* (London: Salem House Publishers, 1988), 11.
45. Clevely, *Topiary*, 12.
46. Pliny, *HN.* 15.49 and Columella 5.10.19 on the apple; Col. 12.4.2 and 12.46.1 for cookbooks; Tacitus, Annales 12.60 for his relationship with Augustus.
47. A. Kuttner, "Looking Outside Inside: Ancient Roman Garden Rooms," *Studies in the History of Gardens and Designed Landscapes* 19, no. 1 (1999): 35n93, interprets Pliny as if C. Matius "perfected and popularised" the topiary.
48. Pliny, *HN* 16.140: *Cupressus . . . nunc . . . etiam in picturas operis topiarii, venatus classesve et imaginesrerum . . .*
49. Martial also mentions *tonsilis* in connection with leek (10.48: *lactuca sedens et tonsile porrum*, "squat lettuce and clipped leek") referring to the use of serving cut leek. It is usually denoted *porrum sectivum*, but in this instance, tonsilis might have been used for metrical reasons.
50. Pliny, *Ep.* 5.6.16: *Ante porticum xystus concisus in plurimas species distinctusque buxo.*
51. Pliny, *Ep.* 5.6.16–17: *bestiarium effigies invicem adversas buxus inscripsit . . . buxum multiformem.*
52. Pliny, *Ep.* 5.6.35: *. . . buxus intervenit in formas mille descripta, litteras interdum, quae modo nomen domini dicunt modo artifices.*
53. Apuleius, *Apologia* 61.6: *multas geometricas formas e buxo.*
54. V. Hunink, ed., *Pro de se magia* (Apologia) (Amsterdam: Gieben, 1997), 164.
55. C. Lazarro, *Italian Renaissance Garden: From the Conventions of Planting, Design, and Ornament to the Grand Gardens of Sixteenth-Century Central Italy* (New Haven, CT: Yale University Press, 1990), esp. 49–51.
56. See Landgren, "Lauro, Myrto et Buxo Frequentata," 112–16, for a discussion of possible tools used for topiary shaping.
57. Jashemski and Meyer, *The Natural History of Pompeii*, 113.
58. For example, in the house of L. Ceius Secundus (Jashemski and Meyer, *The Natural History of Pompeii*, fig. 94). There is also one example of a rose, tied to a stake.
59. For example, Cicero, *De Oratore* 1.7.28–29, *Legatus* 2.7; Virgil, *Georgics* 4.146; Martial 9.61.5–6.

60. Among others, Horace, *Odes* 2.15.4.

61. R. Meiggs, *Trees and Timber in the Ancient Mediterranean World* (Oxford: Clarendon Press, 1982), 267.

62. Meiggs, *Trees and Timber*, 267.

63. The majority of the Latin plant names on *chamae* are direct translations from Greek names. For a complete list of all the plants with the prefix chamae together with a collection of testimonies, see André, *Les noms de plantes*, 59–61.

64. *Chamaeplatanus* is classified as *nomen herbae* in *ThLL*. However, as the relevant text is found in the twelfth book of the *Historia Naturalis*, dealing with exotic trees, and since Pliny very clearly states that chamaeplatanus is part of the tree class, the identification of the plant with a plane tree is unquestionable.

65. Pliny, *HN* 12.12–13: *Durantque et in Italia portenta terrarum praeter illa scilicet quae ipsa excogitavit Italia. Namque et chamaeplatani vocantur coactae brevitatis, quoniam arborum etiam abortus invenimus; hoc quoque ergo in genere pumilionum infelicitas dicta erit. fit autem et serendi genere et recidendi.*

66. See Landgren, "Lauro, Myrto et Buxo Frequentata," 97–99.

67. But see *Thesaurus linguae latinae*, where this passage is listed under *cogo* IV.1, *densus, solidus*. Pliny shows his displeasure by comparing the stunting to abortion and the look of the trees to dwarfs. The significance of the use of *abortus* in referring to the stunted trees has been pointed out; these are just another example of the interruption of a natural cycle, which Pliny comments on also in other passages (M. Beagon, *Roman Nature: The Thought of Pliny the Elder* [Oxford: Clarendon Press, 1992], 83). However, in contrast to the natural phenomenon of, for example, figs that do not mature and fall off (Pliny, *HN* 16.95), a *chamaeplatanus* represents a deliberate and unnatural "abortion." Further, the allusion to *pumiliones*, dwarfs, might seem odd, but Pliny also tells of pruning methods for vines that make the plants dwarf-like in growth (Pliny, *HN* 17.176).

68. So, in some modern commentaries, for example Rackham (LOEB edition, 1944), André (Budé edition, 1949), and König & Winkler (Heimeran Verlag, 1977).

69. L. Piacente, "L'ars topiaria e l'arte bonsai," in *L'uomo e natura* (Genova: P. Barboni, 1996), 79.

70. P. Skydsgaard, *Varro the Scholar: Studies in the First Book of Varro's De re Rustica* (Copenhagen: Munksgaard, 1968), 56.

71. *OLD*, s.v. "recido" 1, 1581: to cut back (trees, etc.) to the base or the stock.

72. *Recidere* is not found in the appendix of main terms used in the cultivation of vines, olives, and trees, listed by White, *Roman Farming*, 263–66.

73. According to Pliny the Younger, in a portico in his Tuscan villa planted with four planes, the water from a *labrum*, a large basin, ran over the edges and thus watered the surrounding trees (Pliny, *Ep.* 5.6.20.). It has been suggested that the planes must have been too large for a portico such as this and in this instance rather refer to dwarf planes (Jashemski, *Gardens of Pompeii*, vol. 1, 53). This is an interesting thought. However, we must recall some of the archaeological findings from Pompeii, showing that rather big trees sometimes were growing inside peristyle gardens. We do not know the size of the portico, or it can just as well be that Pliny refers to plane trees as popular garden trees, without any thought of an exact place for them. Thus, this text cannot be taken as a testimony for *chamaeplatani*.

74. Pliny, *Ep.* 5.6.17: *Humiles et retentas manu arbusculas.*

75. W. Melmoth, *Letters by Pliny the Younger*, trans. W. Melmoth (New York: P. F. Collier & Son, 1909–14). B. Radice, *Letters, and Panegyricus*, 2 vols. (Cambridge, MA: Harvard University Press, 1969), translates *arbusculae* as bushes. However, there is nothing that speaks against the interpretation of *arbusculae* as small trees (*OLD*, s.v. "arbuscula," 161: a small or young tree, shrub).

76. In describing his aviary, Varro refers to a portico in which low-growing trees, *arbusculae humiles*, are planted instead of a row of columns (Varro, Res Rusticae 3.5.11).

77. Cf. Var. *R.* 3.5.12, mentioning a *silva manu sata*—that is, an artificially planted wood—as part of his aviary. Cf. also, Fronto p.5 N., *in pomariis hortulisque arbusculae manu cultae rigataeque* (so in orchard and gardens the growth of trees, reared and watered by hand), where we also find *arbuscula* together with *manu* in a context that favors an identification of arbuscula with a tree.

78. See Gleason, "Constructing Nature"; Jashemski, *Gardens of Pompeii*, vol. 2, 348–56, fig. 406.

79. P. Grimal, *Les jardins romains*, 3rd ed. (Paris: Fayard, 1984), 279. Grimal mentions the *chamaecyparissos* as another example of a stunted species, but there are no reasons to doubt the identification to the santoline (André, *Les noms de plantes*, 59).

80. Jashemski, *Gardens of Pompeii*, vol. 2, 305–6.

81. A. Barbet and P. Miniero, eds., *La villa di San Marco a Stabiae* (Napoli: Centre Jean Bérard, 1999).

82. The other plant referred to as an *herba topiaria* is the evergreen *vicapervica*, identified as the periwinkle (Pliny, *HN* 21.68).

83. Pliny, *Ep.* 5.6.35: *alternis metulae surgunt, alternis inserta sunt poma.*

84. Grimal takes the *metulae*, cone shaped objects, as manufactured in stone, and *poma* referring to actual fruit-trees (Grimal, *Les jardins romains*, 254). However, Sherwin-White argues that Pliny describes even more topiary work in the shape of obelisks and fruit-trees (Sherwin-White, *The Letters of Pliny*, 328), and has a follower in E. Stärk ("Vindemia: Drei Szenen zu den Römern auf dem Lande," *Gymnasium* 97 [1990]: 209). Förtsch, on his side, is dubious about this interpretation (*Archäologischer Kommentar*, 67), and Kasten (*Epistularum libri decem*, trans. H. Kasten [Munich: Heimeran, 1968]) is not explicit, giving *kleine Pyramiden und . . . Obstbäume* (in his commentary of 1968).

85. A third alternative, *metula* cut out of box together with real fruit trees, is suggested by Radice, *Letters and Panegyricus*.

86. Pliny, *HN* 36.25: *quorum pares in Asini monimentis sunt.*

87. For the collection of Asinius Pollio, see J. Isager, *Pliny on Art and Society: The Elder Pliny's Chapters on the History of Art* (Odense: Routledge, Chapman and Hall 1991), 163–67.

88. E. Bartmann, "Sculptural Collection and Display in the Private Realm," in *Roman Art in the Private Sphere: New Perspectives on the Architecture and Decor of the Domus, Villa, and Insulae*, ed. E.K. Gazda (Ann Arbor: University of Michigan Press, 1991), 76 for examples.

89. See Förtsch, *Archäologischer Kommentar*, 75 for similar ideas.
90. Förtsch, *Archäologischer Kommentar*, 81.

Chapter 4

Many thanks to Rona Evyasaf, Kathryn Gleason, George Lewis, and Saskia Stevens who read versions of this paper. Their comments greatly improved it; all errors remain my own.

1. The *toparius*, a landscape architect or master gardener, was often a slave. In his letter to Calvisius Rufus (*Epistulae* 3.19.3), Pliny lists a topiarius, alongside stewards and workmen, as some of the staff on his estates. In his description of elaborate box hedges in the shapes of animals and letters and names, Pliny (*Ep.* 5.6.) does not even give his gardener a title but calls him *artifex*, a professional artist. Pliny the Elder also mentions *topiarii* in his *Natural History* in his discussion of cultivated myrtle (*Historia Naturalis* 15.37.122) and of cultivated trees (*HN* 18.68.265). For an early, but still relevant discussion, see P. Grimal, *Les jardins romains*, 2nd ed. (Paris: Presses universitaires de France, 1969), 88–95.
2. Vitruvius's *De Architectura* is the only surviving complete work on architecture, and gardens are not a focus. Likewise, the writings of the *agromensores*, the land surveyors, do not deal with garden design. See B. Campbell, *The Writings of the Roman Land Surveyors: Introduction, Text, Translation and Commentary* (London: Society for the Promotion of Roman Studies, 2000), for a translation of their writings. The *Forma Urbis Romae*, or Severan marble plan, of 210 C.E. records several known gardens, of which only the *Templum Pacis* has been excavated.
3. A. L. Giesecke, *The Epic City: Urbanism, Utopia and the Garden in Ancient Greece and Rome* (Washington, D.C.: Center for Hellenic Studies, Trustees for Harvard University, 2007), 73–74; M. Carroll-Spillecke, Κηπος: *Der antike griechische garten; Wohnen in der klassichen polis Band III* (München: Deutscher Kunstverlag, 1989).
4. Aristotle reports that he did not allow everyone in, only members from his deme (Arist., *Constitution of Athens* 27.3), but he also notes that Kimon's farm was unfenced and that people were allowed in to take whatever they liked from his fields.
5. N. Purcell, "The Roman Garden as a Domestic Building," in *Roman Domestic Buildings*, ed. I. M. Barton (Exeter: University of Exeter Press, 1996), 135–36.
6. For example, archaeological remains of impressive and unique architecture have been found in the Horti Sallustiani, the Horti Lucullani, the Horti Maecenatiani, the Horti Lamiani and in the *horti* under the Villa Farnesina. See K. J. Hartswick, *The Gardens of Sallust: A Changing Landscape* (Austin: University of Texas Press, 2004); M. Cima and E. La Rocca, eds., *Le tranquille dimore degli dei: la residenza imperiali degli horti Lamiani* (Venice: C. Marsilio, 1986), and Cima and La Rocca, eds., *Horti Romani: atti del Convegno internazionale, Roma, 4–6 maggio 1995* (Rome: L'Erma di Bretschneider,1998); C. Häuber, "Zur Topographie der Horti Maecenatis und der Horti Lamiani auf dem Esquilin in Rome," *Kölner Jahrbuch* 23 (1990): 11–107; C. Häuber and F. Schütz, "The Sanctuary *Isis et Serapis* in *Regio III* in Rome: Preliminary Reconstruction and Visualization of the Ancient

Landscape Using 3/4D-GIS-Technology," *Bollettino di Archeologia on line I 2010/ Volume speciale D/D3/7* (2011): 82–94, http://www.archeologia.beniculturali.it/ pages/pubblicazioni.html; H. Broise and V. Jolivet, "Horti Lucullani," in *Lexicon topographicum urbis Romae*, vol. 3, H–O (Roma: Ed. Quasar, 1996), 67–70, for a summary of their results and a more extensively bibliography.

7. J. D'Arms, "Between Public and Private: The *Epulum Publicum* and Caesar's *Horti Trans Tiberim*," in *Horti Romani*, ed. M. Cima and E. La Rocca (Rome: L'Erma di Bretschneider, 1998), 33–34.

8. J. D'Arms, "Between Public and Private," 34.

9. Grimal, *Les jardins romains*, 116–17; N. Purcell, "The Roman Garden as a Domestic Building," 132; D'Arms, "Between Public and Private," 33–43; K. T. von Stackelberg, *The Roman Garden: Space, Sense and Society* (London: Routledge, 2009), 73–80.

10. He had hosted the public feast before, but it seems to have taken place elsewhere in the city, perhaps in a series of public spaces (D'Arms, "Between Public and Private," 39–40).

11. Purcell, "The Roman Garden as a Domestic Building," 132.

12. This trend of private residences taking on public functions continued throughout the empire. When Augustus assumed the office of Pontifex Maximus, he did not live in the Domus Publica in the Roman Forum, but remained in his home on the Palatine, thereby making his *domus* a public space.

13. Purcell, "The Roman Garden as a Domestic Building," 132.

14. von Stackelberg, *The Roman Garden*, 134–40.

15. von Stackelberg, *The Roman Garden*, 134–40, esp. 137–40.

16. von Stackelberg, *The Roman Garden*, 138.

17. Cima and La Rocca, *Le tranquille dimore degli dei*.

18. Purcell, "The Roman Garden as a Domestic Building," 129–30.

19. E. Macaulay-Lewis, "The City in Motion" (PhD diss., School of Archaeology, Oxford University, Oxford, 2008), 153–94.

20. On his Sabine estate and on the dichotomy between town and country, see Horace, *Epistulae* 1.7, 1.10, 1.14, 1.16, 1.18; *Epodi* 2; *Odes* 1.17, 1.22, 2.13, 2.17, 2.18, 3.1, 3.4, 3.8, 3.13, 3.18, 3.22, 3.23, 3.29; *Satirae* 2.3, 2.6, 2.7.

21. Horace does not use a consistent vocabulary to describe his Sabine estate. He refers to it as a *domus*, which is generally a word used to describe an urban residence (*Carm.* 2.18.2). He also calls it a *villa*, which seems a more accurate name (*Carm.* 3.22.5), since *villa* is the term that typically describes a rural residence of a certain scale that generally had some part dedicated to agricultural production. He also calls it *fundus meus* (*Epist.* 1.16.1).

22. Many other republican and imperial authors echo Horace's sentiments. For example, both Senecas and Pliny the Elder comment upon the extravagant folly of villas and their gardens. Cf. Seneca the Elder, *Controversiae* 2.1.13, 5.5; Seneca the Younger, *Quaestiones naturales* 3.17.2; *Epistulae* 122.8; Pliny, *HN* 12.6.

23. Porphyry an extremely expensive type of granite that was very popular for imperial sculpture in the late empire.

24. B. Frischer, J. W. Crawford, and M. de Simone, *The Horace's Villa Project, 1997–2003: Report on New Fieldwork and Research* (Oxford: Archaeopress, 2006).

25. K. L. Gleason, J. Schryver, and L. Passalacqua, "The Garden," in *The Horace's Villa Project, 1997–2003: Report on New Fieldwork and Research*, ed. B. Frischer, J. Crawford, and M. de Simone (Oxford: Archaeopress, 2006), 72–73.

26. Frischer, Crawford, and De Simone, *The Horace's Villa Project.*

27. Gleason, Schryver, and Passalacqua, "The Garden," 72.

28. Cf. to the villas on the Bay of Naples. For example, the large peristyle garden of Villa Arianna in *Stabiae* was positioned around a view of Vesuvius.

29. Gleason, Schryver, and Passalacqua, "The Garden," 73.

30. C. Bruun, "Inscriptions on Lead Pipes," in *The Horace's Villa Project, 1997–2003: Report on New Fieldwork and Research*, ed. B. Frischer, J. Crawford, and M. de Simone (Oxford: Archaeopress, 2006), 296n16; V. Rudlich, "The Ownership of the Licenza Villa," in *The Horace's Villa Project, 1997–2003: Report on New Fieldwork and Research*, ed. B. Frischer, J. Crawford, and M. de Simone (Oxford: Archaeopress, 2006), 315–26.

31. Gleason, Schryver and Passalacqua, "The Garden," 83.

32. Gleason, Schryver and Passalacqua, "The Garden," 86.

33. Gleason, Schryver and Passalacqua, "The Garden," 91.

34. Gleason, Schryver and Passalacqua, "The Garden," 91–92.

35. Purcell, "The Roman Garden as a Domestic Building," 121–22.

36. Grimal, *Les jardins romains*, 171.

37. The form of the Porticus Pompei is known from fragments of the Forma Urbis Romae, or Severan Marble Plan, (fragments 37*b* [missing], 37*de*, 37*l*, 39*acb*, 39*d* [missing], and 39g), Renaissance drawings, and archaeological excavations. There is a considerable bibliography on the Porticus Pompei and the theatre of Pompei, which the *porticus* adjoined. On the Porticus Pompei, see K. Gleason, "Porticus Pompeiana: A New Perspective on the First Public Park of Ancient Rome," *Journal of Garden History* 14, no. 1 (1994): 13–27; A. Kuttner, "Culture and History at Pompey's Museum," *Transactions of the American Philological Association* 129 (1999): 343–73; Kuttner, "Republican Rome looks at Pergamon," *Harvard Studies in Classical Philology* 97 (1995):157–78. For recent work on the theater, including the relationship between the theatre and the portico, see M. C. Gagliardo and J. E. Packer, "A New Look at Pompey's Theater: History, Documentation, and Recent Excavation," *American Journal of Archaeology* 110, no. 1 (2006): 93–122; J. E. Packer, J. Burge, and M. C. Gagliardo, "Looking Again at Pompey's Theatre: The 2005 Excavation Season," *American Journal of Archaeology* 111, no. 3 (2007): 505–22; F. Sear, *Roman Theatres: An Architectural Study* (Oxford: Oxford University Press, 2006), 57–61. For a history of the rebuilding of the theatre, see Gagliardo and Packer, "A New Look at Pompey's Theater," 96, table 1; and on the dating of the image of the theatre-portico on the *FUR*, see F. Sear, "The Scaenae Frons of the Theater of Pompey," *American Journal of Archaeology* 97, no. 4 (1993): 687–701, esp. 687, 690.

38. Kuttner, "Culture and History at Pompey's Museum," 345.

39. Gleason "Porticus Pompeiana," 14; Prop. 2.32.20.

40. Gleason, "Porticus Pompeiana," 19. The grove was later built over as the *FUR* shows two sets of two rows of columns raised on bases (dots enclosed by squares) rather than plantings, probably from the Domitianic rebuilding of the complex.

41. E. Gatti, "Saepta Iulia," *Lexicon Topographicum Urbis Romae* IV (1999): 228–29, for an outline of the range of activities which were accommodated in the "Saepta Iulia," which seems to be more of a complex that developed organically than one that a consciously designed one. Horace provides another example of a man strolling around the Circus Maximus, window shopping all day (Horace, *Satirae* 1.6.111–131).

42. Kuttner, "Culture and History at Pompey's Museum," 346; P. Gros, "Porticus Pompei," in *Lexicon topographicum urbis Romae*, vol. 4, P–S (Roma: Edizioni Quasar, 1999), 148–49.

43. Kuttner, "Republican Rome looks at Pergamon," 172; Gros, "Porticus Pompei," 148–49.

44. Gros, "Porticus Pompei," 149.

45. Kuttner, "Republican Rome looks at Pergamon," 172; Gleason, "Porticus Pompeiana," 19.

46. Kuttner, "Republican Rome looks at Pergamon," 173–74.

47. Kuttner, "Republican Rome looks at Pergamon," 159. Pergamene-inspired art was prominently displayed in the portico. The muse group, as Ann Kuttner has argued ("Republican Rome looks at Pergamon," 171–72) was an imitation of the "cave group [near] the Great Altar [of Pergamon.]" The paintings of male and female poets and intellectuals, the first such set in Rome, expanded on the Pergamene Polias Library portraits. Like the Attalid Polias portico, the colonnade of the portico was draped with tapestries made of the golden Pergamene fabric, Attaleia.

48. See T. O'Sullivan, "Mind in Motion: The Cultural Significance of Walking in the Roman World" (PhD thesis, Department of the Classics, Harvard University, 2003), 97–100, for an interesting discussion of this passage.

49. P. Zanker, *The Power of Images in the Age of Augustus* (Ann Arbor: University of Michigan Press, 1988), 139–43.

50. O'Sullivan, "Mind in Motion," 89, noted that the love poets are not all interested in the political symbolism of Rome's *porticus*.

51. K.M.D. Dunbabin, *Mosaics of the Greek and Roman World* (Cambridge: Cambridge University Press, 1999). For a discussion of dining in a private garden, see D'Arms, "Between Public and Private," 33–43. Pompey also bribed voters in the gardens of his *horti*, see Plutarch, *Vitae Parallelae Pompeius* 44.3.

52. R. E. Prior, "Going Around Hungry: Topography and Poetics in Martial 2.14," *American Journal of Philology* 117, no. 1 (1996): 122.

53. Prior, "Going Around Hungry," 121–41, gives this poem excellent treatment. Selius appears in several of Martial's other epigrams: 2.11, 2.27, and 2.64.

54. For a discussion of the topographical issues, see Prior, "Going Around Hungry," 124–28.

55. In another poem, 11.1, Martial implies that idle crowds would gather in the Porticus Pompei.

56. Prior, "Going Around Hungry," 135.

57. Gleason, "Porticus Pompeiana," 15.

58. In 48 B.C.E., at the battle of Pharsalus, Julius Caesar also vowed a temple to Venus Genetrix, his ancestor, to be constructed in his Forum (Appian, *Bella civilia* 2.68.281, 2.69.284).

59. Gardens in and around the city of Rome were often used as political staging grounds, as a location for murder and conspiracy. The gardens of the *horti* were used in particular; see M. T. Boatwright, "Luxuriant Garden and Extravagant Women: The *Horti* of Rome between Republic and Empire," in *Horti Romani*, ed. M. Cima and E. L. Rocca (Rome: L'Erma di Bretschneider, 1998), 71–82; M. Beard, "Imaginary *Horti*; or, Up the Garden Path," in *Horti Romani*, ed. M. Cima and E. L. Rocca (Rome: L'Erma di Bretschneider, 1998), 23–33.

60. Packer's recent explorations of the theatre of Pompeii, still unpublished, has led him to suggest that there was always a *scaenae frons* in the complex (J. Packer, per. comm., 2009).

61. Sear, "The Scaenae Frons of the Theater of Pompey," 687–701.

62. The Porticus Liviae still served as a park until the sixth century C.E. when it was converted into a cemetery (C. Panella, "Porticus Liviae," in *Lexicon topographicum urbis Romae*, vol. 4, P–S [Roma: Edizione Quasar, 1999], 128–29).

63. The debate over Christianity in the *Octavius* by Minucius Felix dates to the late second or early third century C.E., and it occurs while the protagonists are walking in Ostia, suggesting that walking for leisure and for philosophical discussions was still popular at this time.

64. Gros, "Porticus Pompei," 148–49.

65. Purcell, "The Roman Garden as a Domestic Building," 123.

66. On Porticus Liviae, see E. Macaulay-Lewis, "Political Museums: Porticos, Gardens and the Public Display of Art in Ancient Rome," in *Collecting and Dynastic Ambition*, ed. S. Bracken, A. Gáldy, and A. Turpin (Newcastle: Cambridge Scholars Publishing, 2009), 1–21; on the Mausoleum of Augustus and the northern Campus Martius, see P. Rehak, *Imperium and Cosmos: Augustus and the Northern Campus Martius*, ed. J. G. Younger (Madison: University of Wisconsin Press, 2006).

Chapter 5

1. See, for example, M. Gothein, *A History of Garden Art*, 2nd ed. (New York: Hacker, [1928] 1979); and P. Grimal, *Les jardins romains*, 2nd ed. (Paris: Presses universitaires de France, 1969).

2. For Herodotus, see Cyrus's speech to the Persians warning of the dangers of conquest (Herodotus 9.122). A more positive sentiment was expressed by Horace (*Epistulae* 2.1.156): "*Graecia capta ferum victorem cepit et artes intulit agresti Latio*" ("Captured Greece captivated her savage victor and brought the arts to rustic Latium").

3. M. L. West, *The East Face of Helicon: West Asiatic Elements in Greek Poetry and Myth* (Oxford: Oxford University Press, 1997), 467–69.

4. It also means "underworld" (*Kur-nu-gi*, the land of no return). See S. N. Kramer, *From the Poetry of Sumer: Creation, Glorification, Adoration* (London: University of California Press, 1979), 24n9; M. L. West, *The East Face of Helicon: West Asiatic Elements in Greek Poetry and Myth* (Oxford: Oxford University Press, 1997), 154.

5. J. A. Black, "Some Structural Features of Sumerian Narrative Poetry," in *Mesopotamian Epic Literature: Oral or Aural?* ed. M. E. Vogelzang and H.J.L. Vantisphout (Lampeter: Mellen, 1992), 77–79; Kramer, *From the Poetry of Sumer*, 38.

6. A highly scented tree, possibly juniper.

7. Kramer, *From the Poetry of Sumer*, 39.

8. For original Sumerian text of the *Lugale*, see J. A. Black, G. Cunningham, J. Ebling, E. Fluckiger-Hawker, E. Robson, J. Taylor, and G. Zólyomi, *The Electronic Text Corpus of Sumerian Literature* (Oxford: Oxford University Press, 1998), http://www-etcsl.orient.ox.ac.uk. The lines quoted can be found in "The Exploits of Ninurta" 1.6.2, 397–400. Definitions are taken from J. A. Halloran's *Sumerian Lexicon: A Dictionary Guide to the Ancient Sumerian Language* (Los Angeles: Logogram, 2006). I am grateful to the late professor John Healey for his assistance in identifying *kiri$_6$*. For *kirû* and *kirimāhu*, see D. J. Wiseman, "Mesopotamian Gardens," *Anatolian Studies* 33 (1983): 137; for *kar*, *karmel*, and *kerem*, see F. Brown, R. Driver, and C. Briggs, *Brown-Driver-Briggs Hebrew and English Lexicon* (Peabody, MA: Hendrickson, 1996).

9. R. Higgins, *Minoan and Mycenean Art*, 3rd ed. (London: Thames and Hudson, 1997), 94–102; C. Boulotis "Mycenean Wall Painting," in *The Mycenean World: Five Centuries of Early Greek Culture 1600–1100 BC*, ed. K. Demakopolou (Athens: Ministry of Culture, National Hellenic Committee, 1988), 35–37.

10. Probably examples of *L. chalcedonicum*, a wild lily found today only on mainland Greece, although an alternative identification is *L. martagon*, a common cultivated lily (see J. E. Raven, *Plants and Plant Lore in Ancient Greece* [Oxford: Faith Raven, 2000], 27–30).

11. L. Morgan, *The Miniature Wall Paintings of Thera. A Study in Aegean Culture and Iconography* (Cambridge: Cambridge University Press, 1988), 147–49.

12. M. Shaw, "The Aegean Garden," *American Journal of Archaeology* 97, no. 4 (1993): 661–85.

13. M.A.S. Cameron, "Unpublished Paintings from the 'House of the Frescoes' at Knossos," *Annual of the British School at Athens* 63 (1968): 5, 19; Morgan, *The Miniature Wall Paintings of Thera*, 39–40.

14. For general aspects of this interchange, see W. V. Davies and L. Schofield, eds., *Egypt, the Aegean and the Levant* (London: British Museum Press, 1995); for the landscape representations in particular, see Morgan, "Minoan Painting and Egypt: The Case of Tell el-Dab'a," in *Egypt, the Aegean and the Levant*, ed. W. V. Davies and L. Schofield (London: British Museum Press, 1995), 29–53.

15. J. H. Breasted, *Ancient Records of Egypt* (Chicago: University of Chicago Press, 1906), vol. 2, 293.

16. The dates of Tuthmosis III's reign traditionally include Hatshepsut's regency.

17. A. Wilkinson, *The Garden of Ancient Egypt* (London: Rubicon Press 1998), 137–39.

18. A. Grayson, *Assyrian Royal Inscriptions: Pt. 2, From Tiglath-Pileser I to Ashur-nasir-apli II* (Wiesbaden: Otto Harrassowitz, 1976), 17.

19. S. Dalley, "Ancient Mesopotamian Gardens and the Identification of the Hanging Gardens of Babylon Resolved," *Garden History* 21, no. 1 (1993): 4.

20. A. Oppenheim, "On the Royal Gardens in Mesopotamia," *Journal of Near Eastern Studies* 24 (1965): 331–32; Wiseman, "Mesopotamian Gardens," 137–39; S. Dalley, "Ancient Mesopotamian Gardens and the Identification of the Hanging Gardens of Babylon Revealed," *Garden History* 21 (1993): 4–5. This may be the garden represented on the relief panel from the North Palace of Ashurbanipal, now in the British Museum (ME 124939A).

21. A tradition later extended to Cyrus the Great; see R. Drews, "Sargon, Cyrus and Mesopotamian Folk History," in *Journal of Near Eastern Studies* 33 (1973): 387–93.

22. Dalley, "Ancient Mesopotamian Gardens," 4.

23. K. L. Gleason, "Towards an Archaeology of Landscape Architecture in the Roman World" (PhD diss., Oxford University, 1989), 265.

24. R. O. Faulkner, *Ancient Egyptian Coffin Texts* (Warminster: Aris and Phillips, 1973), vol. 2, texts 134 and 144, and vol. 3, texts 171 and 173.

25. S. Morenz, *Egyptian Religion* (London: Methuen, 1973), 174–80.

26. Wilkinson, *The Garden of Ancient Egypt*, 25, 97, 142.

27. F. Villedieu, ed., *Il Giardino dei Cesari. Dai pallazi antichi alla Vigna Barberini sul Monte Palatino. Scavi dell'École française de Rome, 1985–1999, Ministero per I Beni e le Attività Culturali Soprintendenza Archeologica di Roma* (Rome: Quasar, 2001), 84–97.

28. G. A. Gaballa, "Three Documents from the Reign of Rameses III," *Journal Egyptian Archaeology* 59 (1973): 113.

29. Morgan, *The Miniature Wall Paintings of Thera*, 40.

30. E. Cook, "Near Eastern Sources for the Palace of Alkinoos," *American Journal of Archaeology* 108 (2004): 43.

31. B. Sergent, "Les Phéaciens avant l'Odyssée," in *La Mythologie et l'Odyssée. Hommage à Gabriel Germain*, ed. A. Hurst and F. Létoublon (Geneva: Actes du colloque international de Grenoble 20–22 mai 1991, 2002), 199–219; M. Dickie, "Phaeacian Athletes," *Papers of the Liverpool Latin Seminar* 4 (1983): 237–76.

32. For commentaries on this episode of the *Odyssey*, see W. B. Stanford, *The Odyssey of Homer* (London: Macmillan, 1959), 325; A. Heubeck, S. West, and J. B. Hainsworth, *A Commentary on Homer's Odyssey: Books I–VIII* (Oxford: Oxford University Press, 1988), 329–30; A. F. Garvie, *Homer Odyssey Books VI–VIII* (Cambridge: Cambridge University Press, 1994). Stanford sees the ordered and symmetrical appearance of the garden as an indication of an "Oriental or Minoan influence." R. D. Dawe, *The Odyssey: Translation and Analysis* (Lewes, Sussex: The Book Guild, 1993), 286–87, sees the garden as an irrelevant curiosity to the main events.

33. Although *Odyssey* translator Fagles uses "orchard" throughout the passage, I refer to it as a garden since Homer is careful to distinguish three different parts (the

orchard, the vineyard, and the beds of greens) and pointedly refers to the whole as a *kēpos*.

34. M. V. Ferriolo, "Homer's Garden," *Journal of Garden History* 9 (1989): 88–89; Sergent, "Les Phéaciens avant l'Odyssée," 201–9. Stanford, *The Odyssey of Homer*, 325, calls the garden "a fairyland" (for similar sentiments, see Grimal, *Les jardins romains*, 66, 84). In contrast, Garvie, *Homer Odyssey Books VI–VIII*, 186–91, perceives the garden of Alcinous as "useful" and not wholly idealized, as well as a vegetative expression of the Phaeacians' ambivalent status.

35. A. Motte, *Prairies et jardins de la Grèce antique: de la religion à la philosophie* (Brussels: Académie Royale de Belgique, 1973), 233–79.

36. P. Horden and N. Purcell, *The Corrupting Sea: A Study of Mediterranean History* (Oxford: Wiley-Blackwell, 2000), 210.

37. E. Cook, "Near Eastern Sources for the Palace of Alkinoos," *American Journal of Archaeology* 108 (2004): 57–61, 67–8; Grayson, *Assyrian Royal Inscriptions*, 154.

38. F. Chamoux, "Une évocation littéraire d'un palais Macédonien (Argonautiques III, 215 sq.)," *Ancient Macedonia Vth International Symposium (10–15th October 1989)* (Thessaloniki: Institute for Balkan Studies, 1993), 337–42.

39. E. B. Moynihan, *Paradise as a Garden in Persia and Mughal India* (New York: George Braziller, 1979).

40. D. Stronach, "Parterres and Stone Watercourses at Pasargadae: Notes on Achaemenid Contribution to Garden Design," *Journal of Garden History* 14 (1994): 5–9.

41. It is used in opposition to *sitos* (grain or food fit for man) in Herodotus 9.41 and Xenophon, *Cyropaedia* 8.6.12. In the Homeric sense, it is used to designate the area of the courtyard where cattle were kept (Homer, *Iliad* 11.774, 24.640). For subsequent Latin terminology, see K. T. von Stackelberg, *The Roman Garden. Space, Sense and Society* (London: Routledge, 2009), 9–21.

42. J. Dillon, "What Happened to Plato's Garden," *Hermathena* 84 (1983): 51–9; Motte, *Prairies et jardins de la Grèce antique*, 411–29; M. Morford, "The Stoic Garden," *Journal of Garden History* 7 (1987): 155. The Stoic Zeno also compared the study of philosophy to a walled garden of fruit trees (Diogenes Laertius 7.40).

43. For the intersection of philosophical and political concepts of the polis with the idea of garden space, see A. L. Giesecke, *The Epic City: Urbanism, Utopia and the Garden in Ancient Greece and* Rome (Washington, D.C.: Center for Hellenic Studies, 2007).

44. R. Osborne, "Classical Greek Gardens: Between Farm and Paradise," in *Garden History: Issues, Approaches, Methods*, ed. J. Dixon Hunt (Washington, D.C.: Dumbarton Oaks, 1992), 384; M. Beard, "Imaginary *Horti*; or, Up the Garden Path," in *Horti Romani*, ed. M. Cima and E. L. Rocca (Rome: L'Erma di Bretschneider, 1998), 29.

45. For example, Sir William Temple's essay *Upon the Gardens of Epicurus; or, Of Gardening in the Year 1685*.

46. R. Osborne, *Classical Landscape with Figures: The Ancient Greek City and Its Countryside* (London: George Philip, 1987), 46–48, and "Classical Greek Gardens: Between Farm and Paradise," in *Garden History: Issues, Approaches, Methods*, Colloquium on the History of Landscape Architecture 13, ed. J. D. Hunt

(Washington D.C.: Dumbarton Oaks, 1992), 380–81; Motte, *Prairies et jardins de la Grèce antique*, 5–25.

47. For example, Zeus's grove of plane trees at Labraunda (Hdt. 5. 119) and Herakles's laurel grove at Olympia (Pindar, *Olympian* 3. 13–18, 23–26, 31–34). Pausanias mentions a grove of holm oaks dedicated to the Eumenides, of cypress to Hebe, of plane trees to Demeter and Dionysus, and of ash to Apollo (Paus. 2.11.4, 2.13.3, 2.36.8, 7.5.10).

48. The best example of an urban temple *kēpos* is attached to the temple of Hephaistos at Athens, excavated by D.B. Thompson. Dated to the third century B.C.E., this consisted of rows of trees, probably laurel and pomegranate, planted around three sides of the temple in plant pots set into rock-cut holes (D. B. Thompson, "The Garden of Hephaistos," *Hesperia* 6 [1937]: 416–25).

49. For the uncertain date of the Adonia, see M.P.J. Dillon, " 'Woe for Adonis'—but in Spring, not Summer," *Hermes* 131 (2003): 1–16.

50. Alcphr. 4. 14; Plato, *Ph.* 276B; Simpl. *in Cael.* 269 a 9 ff.; Plut., *De sera numinis vindicta* 17.560 B-C; Thphr., *HP* 6.7.3; Suda, s.v. *Adōneios kēpoi.*

51. M. Detienne, *The Gardens of Adonis: Spices in Greek Mythology* (Hassocks, Sussex: Harvester Press, 1977), 65, 99–110, believes that the gardens were allowed to wilt in the summer heat. Dillon, " 'Woe for Adonis,' " 9, points out that there is no mention of this in ancient sources; instead, the pots are thrown into the sea or wells.

52. The Garden Party relief in the British Museum (ME 124920).

53. Wilkinson, *The Garden of Ancient Egypt*, 100.

54. See also, Osborne, "Classical Greek Gardens," 388. Greek Anthology 712.8 and 885, 2. In addition to the play between *hortus/cunnus*, *hortus* could also signify *culus* (Priapeia 5.4): see J. N. Adams, *The Latin Sexual Vocabulary* (London: Duckworth, 1982), 84, 96, 113, 228–29.

55. Propertius 2.32.20; Catullus 55.6; Ovid, *Ars amatoria* 1.67, *Epistulae ex ponto* 1.8.36; Martial, *Epigrams* 11.1.11, 11.47.3.

Chapter 6

1. See Chapter 5, "Meaning."

2. A. R. Littlewood, "Romantic Paradises: the Role of the Garden in the Byzantine Romance," *Byzantine and Modern Greek Studies* 5 (1979): 108–9; C. Barber, "Reading the Garden in Byzantium: Nature and Sexuality," *Byzantine and Modern Greek Studies* 16 (1992): 6–17.

3. The pirate stronghold at Corycia was eliminated by Pompey's campaign of 67/66 B.C. For the identification of the old man as a resettled refugee from this campaign, see R. F. Thomas, ed., *Virgil, Georgics, vol. 2, Books III–IV* (Cambridge: Cambridge University Press, 1988), 167–75; R.A.B. Mynors, ed., *Virgil, Georgics* (Oxford: Clarendon Press, 1990), 273–78. This garden was later adopted by Renaissance poets celebrating life under the Medici government (see J. Ijsewijn, "Poetry in a Roman Garden: The *Coryciana*," in *Latin Poetry and the Classical*

Traditions: Essays in Medieval and Renaissance Literature, ed. M. Goodman and O. Murray [Oxford: Clarendon Press, 1990], 211–16).

4. P. Thibodeau, "The Old Man and his Garden (Verg. *Georg.* 4, 116–148)," *Materiali e discussioni per l'analisi dei testi classici* 47 (2001): 175–89.

5. E. R. Curtius, *European Literature and the Latin Middle Ages* (New York: Pantheon Books, 1953), 186, 195–200. Curtius sees the *locus amoenus* in Virgil's Corcyrian garden (Vir., *Georgics* 4.125–146) and Ovid's garden of Flora (Ovid, *Fasti* 5.311–324). See also C. E. Newlands, *Statius' Silvae and the Poetics of Empire* (Cambridge: Cambridge University Press, 2002), 130–37; K. S. Myers, "*Miranda fides*: Poet and Patrons in Paradoxographical Landscapes in Statius' *Silvae*," *Materiali e Discussioni* 44 (2000): 109; E. Langlois, *Origines et sources du roman de la Rose* (Paris: E. Thorin, 1891).

6. For other mythical couplings in meadows, orchards, and gardens, see C. Calame, *The Poetics of Eros in Ancient Greece* (Princeton, NJ: Princeton University Press, 1999), 153–64.

7. R. F. Thomas, "The Old Man Revisited: Memory, Reference and Genre in Virg., *Georg.* 4, 116–48," *Materiali e discussioni per l'analisi dei testi classici* 29 (1992): 36–44; E. L. Bowie, "Theocritus' Seventh Idyll, Philetas and Longus," *Classical Quarterly* 35 (1985): 67–91.

8. Even earlier the Republican poet Lucretius had expressed his preference for men enjoying themselves on soft grass amid flowers by a stream in the shade of a tree rather than reveling within gold-lacquered halls (2.22–33).

9. A. Richlin, *The Garden of Priapus: Sexuality and Aggression in Roman Humor* (New York: Oxford University Press, 1992); V. E. Pagán, *Rome and the Literature of Gardens* (London: Duckworth, 2006).

10. In general for Propertius, see M. Hubbard, *Propertius* (Bristol: Bristol University Press, 1974); for Tibullus, see F. Cairns, *Tibullus: A Hellenistic Poet at Rome* (Cambridge: Cambridge University Press, 1979); P. Lee-Stecum, *Powerplay in Tibullus: Reading Elegies Book 1* (Cambridge: Cambridge University Press, 1998): 36–37.

11. Apples have a lengthy association with sexuality and eroticism in Greek and Latin literature from the time of Hesiod, both as a means of promoting fertility by sympathetic magic and as a mere symbol. See M. Lugauer, *Untersuchungen zur Symbolik des Apfels in der Antike* (Erlangen-Nürnberg: Faculty of Philosophy, Friedrich-Alexander-Universität, 1967); A. R. Littlewood, "The Symbolism of the Apple in Greek and Roman Literature," *Harvard Studies in Classical Philology* 72 (1967): 147–81; Littlewood, "The Symbolism of the Apple in Byzantine Literature," *Jahrbuch der österreichischen Byzantinistik* 23 (1974): 33–59; Littlewood, "The Apple in the Sexual Imagery of Kazantzakis: A Study in the Continuity of a Greek Tradition," *Neo-Hellenika* 3 (1978): 37–55; Littlewood, "The Erotic Symbolism of the Apple in Late Byzantine and Meta-Byzantine Demotic Literature," *Byzantine and Modern Greek Studies* 17 (1993): 83–103; M. K. Brazda, *Zur Bedeutung des Apfels in der antiken Kultur* (Bonn: Faculty of Philosophy, Rheinische Friedrich-Wilhelms-Universität, 1977); Cairns, *Tibullus*, 51–54; J.C.B. Petropoulos, *Eroticism in Ancient and Medieval Greek Poetry* (London: Duckworth, 2003): 61–73.

12. See generally on this topic, Z. Pavlovskis, *Man in an Artificial Landscape: the Marvels of Civilization in Imperial Roman Literature* (Leiden: Brill, 1973).

13. All references to the *Anthologia Latina* are to the edition of F. Buecheler and A. Riese, Teubner, Leipzig, 1894–1906, reprinted by Hakkert, Amsterdam, 1964.

14. For Sidonius's prose description of his own estate at Avitacum, see p. XX.

15. Luxorius is backed up by the historian Procopius, who remarks on the well-watered pleasure gardens encountered by the Byzantine army under Belisarius in 533 C.E. (*Carmina ad Vandalos spectantia* 2.6.9).

16. D. Davies, "The Evocative Symbolism of Trees," in *The Iconography of Landscape: Essays on the Symbolic Representation, Design, and Use of Past Environments*, ed. D. Cosgrove and S. Daniels (Cambridge: Cambridge University Press, 1988), 32–42; A. Ponte, "Architecture and Phallocentrism in Richard Payne Knight's Theory," in *Sexuality and Space*, ed. B. Colomina (New York: Princeton Architectural Press 1992), 296–97.

17. F. I. Zeitlin, "Gardens of Desire in Longus's *Daphnis and Chloe*: Nature, Art, and Imitation," in *The Search for the Ancient Novel*, ed. J. Tatum (Baltimore, MD: Johns Hopkins University Press, 1994), 160.

18. A. R. Littlewood, "Romantic Paradises: the Role of the Garden in the Byzantine Romance," *Byzantine and Modern Greek Studies* 5 (1979): 95–114; C. Barber, "Reading the Garden in Byzantium: Nature and Sexuality," *Byzantine and Modern Greek Studies* 16 (1992): 14–17.

19. For examples of topiary work in the shape of "hunts, fleets of ships and images of real objects," see *Historia Naturalis* 16.60.143. His nephew, the Younger Pliny, describes box cut into the forms of animals and letters to spell the gardener's and his own name on his Tuscan estate (*Epistulae* 5.6.16, 35).

20. Mention should be made also of the lost Georgics by Decimus Claudius Albinus, a man best known for his unsuccessful coup d'état in 197 C.E. (Scriptores Historia Augustae, *Clodius* 11.7).

21. Although this is an eminently practical agricultural work, it does include chapters on kitchen gardens and one (3.21) devoted to flowers.

22. For a survey of its history and summary of its hortulan content, see R. Rodgers, "*Kepopoiía*: Garden Making and Garden Culture in the *Geoponika*," in *Byzantine Garden Culture*, ed. A. R. Littlewood, H. Maguire, and J. Wolschke-Bulmahn (Washington, D.C.: Dumbarton Oaks Research Library and Collection, 2002): 159–75, and for some details of its range of plants and their manipulation, both possible and impossible, see A. R. Littlewood, "Gardens of Byzantium," *Journal of Garden History* 12, no. 2 (1992): 133–38.

23. This insult became popular, being mentioned by no fewer than three historians: Plutarch, who attributes it to the Stoic philosopher Tubero; Velleius Paterculus (2.33.4); and the Elder Pliny (*HN* 9.80.170), who attributes it to Pompey.

24. This was the subject of a treatise by a certain Moschion, according to Athenaeus, who quotes extensively from it (5.206d–209e).

25. Pliny indicates his contempt by the exaggerated claim that part of the tree's shade was in fact caused by the emperor's own bulk.

26. In the tenth century, the Byzantines added to the imperial garden's symbolism when it came to represent also renewal as a "New Eden" and a reflection of the emperor's virtues (see H. Maguire, "Imperial Gardens and the Rhetoric of Renewal," in *New*

Constantines: The Rhythm of Imperial Renewal in Byzantium, 4th–13th Centuries, ed. P. Magdalino [Aldershot: Variorum, 1994], 181–97). On the whole subject of the garden as a symbol of power in the Near East, Rome, and Byzantium, see A. R. Littlewood, "Gardens of the Palaces," in *Byzantine Court Culture from 829 to 1204*, ed. H. Maguire (Washington, D.C.: Dumbarton Oaks, 1997), 13–38.

27. K. L. Gleason, "Towards an Archaeology of Landscape Architecture in the Roman World" (D.Phil. diss., Oxford University, 1989).

28. Littlewood, "Gardens of the Palaces," 32–33.

29. Cicero, *Epistulae as Atticum* 4.12, 7.7.6, 8.2.3, 12.19, 12.21.2, 12.23.2, 12.23.3, 12.25.2, 12.40.2, 12 43.3, 12.52.2, 13.12.2, 13.46.3, 14.16.1, 15.15.3; *Pro Caelio* 36, 38, 49; *Cato* 54, 56; *De domo sua* 112; *De finibus* 5.3; *Pro Milone* 74; *De natura deorum* 2.4.11; *Orationes Philippicae* 2.67, 2.71, 2.109, 8.9, 13.11; *Epistulae ad Quintum fratrem* 2.9.8, 3.1.14; *Rabirio Postumo* 26; *In Verrem* 2.87, 4.121.

30. Particularly in his letters to Atticus and the Philippics, which comprise nineteen instances where *horti* are objects of desire. Most egregiously, he claims that it is legitimate to buy a house, which in the context must have been one to include grand gardens, with funds borrowed from friends "in order to reach a certain position in society" (*Att.* 1.13.6).

31. Compare, for example, Cicero's own interest in acquiring *horti* in his letters to Atticus about the behavior of Verres and Clodia in theirs: *Cael.* 36, 38, 49; *Verr.* 2.87, 4.121.

32. For commentaries on these letters and the villas they describe, see A. N. Sherwin-White, *The Letters of Pliny: A Historical and Social Commentary*, 2nd ed. (Oxford: Clarendon Press, 1985): 186–99, 321–30; E. Lefèvre, "Plinius Studien I: Römische Baugesinnung und Landschaft Auffassung in den Villenbriefen (2.17, 5.6)," *Gymnasium* 34 (1977): 34; R. Förtsch, *Archäologischer Kommentar zu den Villenbriefen des Jüngeren Plinius* (Mainz am Rhein: Philip von Zabern, 1993).

33. See, for example, C. Lazarro, *Italian Renaissance Garden: From the Conventions of Planting, Design, and Ornament to the Grand Gardens of Sixteenth-Century Central Italy* (New Haven, CT: Yale University Press, 1990); L. Farrar, *Ancient Roman Gardens* (Stroud: Sutton Publishing, 1998), 54–57; W. F. Jashemski, *The Gardens of Pompeii, Herculaneum and the Villas Destroyed by Vesuvius*, vol. 1 (New Rochelle, NY: Caratzas Brothers, 1979), 53–54. The canonical role of Pliny's letters in shaping perceptions of Roman villas can be seen in the widespread application of Pliny's neologism "cryptoportico" to covered walkways by nineteenth century excavators: see B. Bergmann, "Visualizing Pliny's Villas," *Journal of Roman Archaeology* 8 (1995): 411. Du Prey gives an account of Pliny's influence on Italian villas: P. Du Prey, *The Villas of Pliny the Younger from Antiquity to Posterity* (Chicago: University of Chicago Press 1995), 16–29 (Palladio and Peruzzi), and 40–73 (Medici villas). The grounds of the Villa D'Este at Tivoli draw on both Hadrian's villa and Pliny's letters. For the eighteenth century landscape garden at Rousham, which was designed to recreate in part the experience of Pliny's garden, see J.D. Hunt, ed., *Garden History: Issues, Approaches, Methods* (Washington, D.C.: Dumbarton Oaks, 1992), 178.

34. An attitude exemplified by Jefferson's descriptions of Monticello, which are strongly Plinian in tone; see Du Prey, *The Villas of Pliny the Younger*, 23–25; R. Strong, *A*

Celebration of Gardens (London: Harper Collins, 1991), xi. For this attitude in Byzantium see Littlewood, "Gardens of Byzantium," 128–29, "Gardens of the Palaces," 16–18.

35. M. Trapp, ed., *Greek and Latin Letters: An Anthology with Translation* (Cambridge: Cambridge University Press, 2003), 12; J. Henderson, *Pliny's Statue. The Letters, Self-Portraiture and Classical Art* (Exeter: University of Exeter Press, 2002), 2–14, 37.

36. He and his father owned no fewer than three suburban villas and twelve country villas (see J. H. D'Arms, *Romans on the Bay of Naples: A Social and Cultural Study of the Villas and Their Owners from 150 B.C. to A.D. 400* [Cambridge, MA: Harvard University Press, 1970], 226–29).

37. This stricture is, of course, also pagan: John's coeval Eunapius (*Vitae sophistarum* 464) and his older contemporaries, the emperor Julian (*Orationes* 1.13D, 2.101D) and the great rhetorician Libanius (*Epistulae* 419), have similar comments. The *locus classicus* is much earlier in Plutarch's criticism of Lucullus (*Lucullus* 39.4–5).

38. H. Maguire, *Earth and Ocean: The Terrestrial World in Early Byzantine Art* (University Park: Penn State University Press, 1987).

39. Accounts of the Annunciation were later indebted to the tradition when Anastasius of Antioch had asserted in the sixth century that it had taken place on the same day of the year as the first spring (*In Annuntiationem* [PG 89.1380D-1386A]), and even more hortulan motifs became legitimate through the Virgin's association with the enclosed garden of Canticles.

40. The word *garden* is significantly an addition to the text in the Greek (and Latin) versions.

41. For instance, in Eusebios (*Historia ecclesiastica* 2.17.5). On monastic gardening in Byzantium, see A. M. Talbot, "Byzantine Monastic Horticulture: the Textual Evidence", in *Byzantine Garden Culture*, ed. A. R. Littlewood, H. Maguire, and J. Wolschke-Bulmahn (Washington, D.C.: Dumbarton Oaks Research Library and Collection, 2002): 37–67.

42. Descriptions of the delights of country estates may be found at *Var.* 8.31, 11.10, 11.14, 12.22. His emphasis on water and fish reflects not only his own predilection but also the reality of his age.

43. There is a pun in the Latin, for *deliciae* may mean both "darlings" and "table-delicacies."

Chapter 7

I would like to express my thanks foremost to Kathryn Gleason for the opportunity to write this chapter and for her continual advice and support. My thanks and appreciation also go to Annetta Alexandridis, Kim Hartswick, Verity Platt, James Schryver, and Maria Shaw for the generous time that they afforded to reading and editing numerous drafts. Any omissions or errors are my own.

1. B. St-Denis, "Just What Is a Garden?" *Studies in the History of Gardens and Designed Landscapes* 27, no. 1 (2007): 62.

2. Garden representations, although depicting "physicality," are arbitrary constructions (D. Cosgrove and S. Daniels, eds., *The Iconography of Landscape: Essays on the Symbolic Representation, Design, and Use of Past Environments* [Cambridge: Cambridge University Press, 1988]). See also C. J. Glacken, *Traces on the Rhodian Shore* (Berkeley: University of California Press, 1967).

3. For active viewing, see B. Bergmann, "Painted Perspectives of a Villa Visit: Landscape as Status and Metaphor," in *Roman Art in the Private Sphere*, ed. E. K. Gazda (Ann Arbor: University of Michigan Press, 1991), 49–70; Bergmann, "Rhythms of Recognition: Mythological Encounters in Roman Landscape Painting," in *Im Spiegel des Mythos: Bilderwelt und Lebenswelt*, ed. F. De Angelis and S. Muth, (Wiesbaden: Reichert, 1999), 81–107; Bergmann, "Meanwhile, back in Italy . . . ," in *Pausanias and His Periegesis, the Traveler and Text*, ed. S. E. Alcock, J. Cherry, and J. Elsner (Oxford: Oxford University Press, 2001), 154–66; Bergmann, "Art and Nature in the Villa at Oplontis," *Journal of Roman Archaeology* 16 (2003): 87–120; A. Kuttner, "Delight and Danger in the Roman Water Garden: Sperlonga and Tivoli," in *Landscape Design and the Experience of Motion*, ed. M. Conan (Washington, D.C.: Dumbarton Oaks, 2003), 103–56; A.-A. Malek, "De la mosaïque à la Jonchée à la mosaïque à la treille: la sentiment de la nature en Afrique romaine," in *Ancient Roman Mosaics: Paths through the Classical Mind, Acta of Conference Held in March, 2000 in Luxembourg*, ed. C.-M. Ternes with the collaboration of the Worcester Art Museum and Rheinisches Landesmuseum, Trier (Luxembourg: Imprimerie Linden, 2002); T. O'Sullivan, "Walking with Odysseus: The Portico Frame of the Odyssey Landscapes," *American Journal of Philology* 128, no. 4 (2007): 497–532; M. Conan, ed., *Landscape Design and the Experience of Motion* (Washington, D.C.: Dumbarton Oaks, 2003).

4. Perspective in the Greco-Roman world was conceived of as the physical background for performative action: *skaenographia*, or "stage painting" (Plato, *Critias* 107a–d). Scenery was generated from *topia*, the painted representations of place and land (Vitruvius, *De Architectura* 5.6.9). See also E. La Rocca, *Lo spazio negate: La pittura di paesaggio nella cultura artistica greca e romana* (Milan: Mondadori Electa S.p.A, 2008).

5. The Roman eye in particular was considered active (Kuttner, "Delight and Danger," 103). See also J. Elsner, *Roman Eyes: Visuality & Subjectivity in Art & Text* (Princeton, NJ: Princeton University Press, 2007).

6. W.J.T. Mitchell, "Imperial Landscape," in *Landscape and Power*, ed. W.J.T. Mitchell (Chicago: University of Chicago Press, 1994), 5–34.

7. For example, M. Helms, *Ulysses' Sail: An Ethnographic Odyssey or Power, Knowledge and Geographic Distance* (Princeton, NJ: Princeton University Press, 1988); Mitchell, "Imperial Landscape."

8. See J. D. Hunt, *Greater Perfections: The Practice of Garden Theory* (Philadelphia: University of Pennsylvania Press, 2000), and *The Afterlife of Gardens* (Philadelphia: University of Pennsylvania Press, 2004).

9. See L. C. Halpern, "The Uses of Paintings in Garden History," in *Garden History: Issues, Approaches, Methods*, ed. J. D. Hunt (Washington, D.C.: Dumbarton Oaks, 1992), 183–202; Hunt, *Greater Perfections*, 143; A. Kuttner, "Looking Outside Inside: Ancient Roman Garden Rooms," *Studies in the History of Gardens and Designed Landscapes* 19, no. 1 (1999): 7–35.

10. See Mitchell, "Imperial Landscape."

11. See Helms, *Ulysses' Sail*; A. K. Thomason, "Representations of the North Syrian Landscape in Neo-Assyrian Art," *Bulletin of the American Schools of Oriental Research* 323 (2001): 63–96.

12. Thomason, "Representations of the North Syrian Landscape," 65.

13. Room S_1 (Thomason, "Representations of the North Syrian Landscape," 89–91, fig. 27).

14. See P. Albenda, "Grapevines in Ashurbanipal's Garden," *Bulletin of the American Schools of Oriental Research* 215 (1974): 5–17, for a discussion of the plant depictions in Ashurbanipal's reliefs.

15. See preceding chapters for discussion of the Persian *pairadaeza/paradeisos*. See E. B. Moynihan, *Paradise as a Garden in Persia and Mughal India* (New York: George Braziller, 1979); C. Tuplin, *Achaemenid Studies*, Historia Einzelschriften Heft 99 (Stuttgart: F. Steiner, 1996); K. L. Gleason, "Gardens," in *The Oxford Encyclopedia of Archaeology in the Near East*, vol. 2., ed. E. M. Myers (New York: Oxford University Press, 1997), 383–87.

16. For the principal excavated *pairadaeza* at Pasargadae, see D. Stronach, "Parterres and Stone Water Courses at Pasargadae: Notes on the Achaemenid Contribution to Garden Design," *Journal of Garden History* 4, no. 1 (1994): 3–12.

17. For the Hellenistic palace *paradeisos*, see I. Nielsen, *Hellenistic Palaces* (Aarhus: Aarhus University, 1994).

18. C. D. Sheppard, "A Note on the Date of Taq-i-Bustan and Its Relevance to Early Christian Art in the Near East," *Gesta* 20, no. 1 (1981): 9–13.

19. E. B. Moynihan, *Paradise as a Garden*, 35.

20. G. Herrman, "The Rock Reliefs of Sasanian Iran," in *Mesopotamia and Iran in the Parthian and Sasanian Periods: Rejection and Revival 238 BCE-CE642*, ed. J. Curtis (London: British Museum Press, 2000), 35–45.

21. See M. Shaw, "The Aegean Garden," *American Journal of Archaeology* 97, no. 4 (1993): 661–85.

22. A. P. Chapin, "Power, Privilege and Landscape in Minoan Art," in *ΞΑΡΙΣ: Essays in Honor of Sara A. Immerwahr*, ed. A. Chapin (Princeton, NJ: American School of Classical Studies at Athens, Supplement 33, 2004), 47–64. For the religious significance of the plants, see N. Marinatos, *Minoan Religion: Ritual, Image and Symbol* (Columbia: University of South Carolina Press, 1993).

23. Chapin, "The Fresco with Multi-Colored Rocks and Olive Branches from the Northwest Slope Plaster Dump at Pylos Re-examined," in *Aegean Wall Painting: A Tribute to Mark Cameron*, ed. L. Morgan, British School at Athens Studies, 13 (London: British School at Athens, 2005), 123–30.

24. J. Hurwit, "The Representation of Nature in Early Greek Art," in *New Perspectives in Early Greek Art*, ed. D. Buitron-Oliver (Washington, D.C.: Studies in the History of Art, 1991), 33–62.

25. M. Carroll, *Earthly Paradises. Ancient Gardens in History and Archaeology* (Los Angeles: Getty Publications, 2003).

26. Hurwit, "The Representation of Nature in Early Greek Art."

27. P. Bowe, "The Sacred Groves of Ancient Greece," *Studies in the History of Gardens and Designed Landscapes* 29, no. 4 (2009): 233–45.

28. See M. Carroll-Spillecke, *Landscape Depictions in Greek Relief Sculpture* (Frankfurt am Main: P. Lang, 1985).

29. W. Atallah, *Adonis dans la literature et l'art grecs* (Paris: C. Klincksieck, 1966).

30. Now in the Archaeological Museum at Athens (Carroll, *Earthly Paradises*, 67, fig. 51). Aphrodite (and later Venus) became heavily associated with gardens, and many examples of garden art with the goddess survive.

31. See Carroll, *Earthly Paradises*.

32. Such as the laurel of Apollo and the cypress of Hades; S. Steingräber, *Abundance of Life: Etruscan Wall Painting* (Los Angeles: J. Paul Getty, 2006), 70.

33. For an example, see the antechamber paintings in the Tomb of Hunting and Fishing, Steingräber, *Abundance of Life*, 96–97. Ribbons in trees were associated with mythic ritual in the classical Greek period; see B. S. Ridgway, "Greek Antecedents of Garden Sculpture," in *Ancient Roman Gardens*, ed. E. B. MacDougall and W. Jashemski (Washington, D.C.: Dumbarton Oaks, 1981), 27–28.

34. Pliny (*Historia Naturalis* 35.17–18) mentions Etruscan paintings in Caere (Cerveteri) and in Latium.

35. Carroll, *Earthly Paradises*, 22, fig. 11.

36. Carroll, *Earthly Paradises*, 8–9, figs. 1, 9.

37. R. Parkinson, *The Painted Tomb-Chapel of Nebamun* (London: British Museum Press, 2008).

38. P.G.P. Meyboom, *The Nile Mosaic of Palestrina: Early Evidence of Egyptian Religion in Italy* (Leiden: E. J. Brill, 1995), 96n4.

39. Herodotus (2.109.3) believed that the Egyptians, who had to perform annual land surveying because of the flooding of the Nile, invented geometry. On the Persian *pairadaeza* and symmetry: Stronach, "Parterres and Stone Water Courses at Pasargadae," op. cit., n12.

40. The taste for botanical illustration continued, and during the reign of the pharaoh Akhenaten (fourteenth century B.C.E.), artists under royal order began to "make the visual perception the actual appearance of nature" (A. Wilkinson, *The Gardens of Ancient Egypt* [London: Rubicon Press, 1998]).

41. Bergmann, "Meanwhile, back in Italy . . . ," 157. See Propertius (first-century B.C.E.) in an elegiac poem to Cynthia about traveling to other gardens (2.32.1–16).

42. For example, the *euripus* from the House of Octavius Quartio at Pompeii (K. T. von Stackelberg, *The Roman Garden: Space, Sense and Society* [London: Routledge, 2009], 120–22; V. Platt, "Viewing, Desiring, Believing: Confronting the Divine in a Pompeian House," *Art History* 25, no. 1: [2002]: 87–112); statues of crocodiles around the Canopus at Hadrian's villa at Tivoli (Kuttner, "Delight and Danger"). See *Egittomania: l'immaginario dell' antico Egitto e l'Occidente*, ed. C. R. Redda (Turin: Ananke, 2006).

43. J. J. Pollitt, *Art in the Hellenistic Age* (Cambridge: Cambridge University Press, 1986), 250ff.

44. The site is known colloquially as "Little Petra"; F. Zayadine "Decorative Stucco at Petra and Other Hellenistic Sites," in *Studies in the History and Archaeology of Jordan III*, ed. A. Hadidi (New York: Routledge & Kegan Paul, 1987), 142.

45. C. Lilyquist, "Egyptian Art," *Notable Acquisitions (Metropolitan Museum of Art)* [newsletter] (1984–85): 4–5.

46. Pollitt, *Art in the Hellenistic Age.*

47. Glacken, *Traces on the Rhodian Shore.*

48. La Rocca, *Lo spazio negate*, 17–24. The Mouseion of Alexandria specialized in the study of natural history and led the early fields of geographic research (Meyboom, *The Nile Mosaic of Palestrina*, 104).

49. Other important examples include the tomb paintings from Vergina, in Macedon, and to a lesser extent, the Telephos Frieze from Pergamon; Pollitt, *Art in the Hellenistic Age*, 185–209.

50. Meyboom, *The Nile Mosaic of Palestrina*, 8.

51. Meyboom, *The Nile Mosaic of Palestrina*, 34.

52. Meyboom, *The Nile Mosaic of Palestrina*, 96–106; Pollitt, *Art in the Hellenistic Age*, 205–8.

53. O'Sullivan, "Walking with Odysseus"; Pollitt, *Art in the Hellenistic Age*, 185–209; R. Biering, *Die Odyssee-Fresken vom Esquilin* (Munich: Biering and Brinkmann, 1995).

54. See Pollitt, *Art in the Hellenistic Age*, 208.

55. O'Sullivan "Walking with Odysseus."

56. Bergmann, "Meanwhile, back in Italy . . . "; La Rocca, *Lo spazio negato.*

57. M. Gabriel, *Livia's Garden Room at Prima Porta* (New York: NYU Press, 1955); B. Kellum, "The Construction of Landscape in Augustan Rome: The Garden Room at the Villa ad Gallinas," *The Art Bulletin* 76, no. 2 (1994): 211–24.

58. Kuttner, "Looking Outside Inside."

59. However, this grotto is ambiguous: an ornate stucco ceiling floats above, while nothing painted on the walls suggests any sort of support. The blending of garden imagery without substantial architecture afforded an unusual viewing experience. I would like to thank Verity Platt for this note.

60. Kellum, "The Construction of Landscape in Augustan Rome."

61. S. Hales, *The Roman House and Social Identity* (Cambridge: Cambridge University Press, 2003), 221–31.

62. Bergmann, "Art and Nature in the Villa at Oplontis." See also the "Auditorium" of Maecenas in Rome: W. F. Jashemski, *The Gardens of Pompeii, Herculaneum and the Villas Destroyed by Vesuvius*, vol. 2: appendices (New Rochelle, NY:Caratzas Brothers, 1993), cat. 128, figs.

63. W. F. Jashemski, *The Gardens of Pompeii, Herculaneum and the Villas Destroyed by Vesuvius*, vol. 1 (New Rochelle, NY: Caratzas Brothers, 1979), 56; see for

example Jashemski, *The Gardens of Pompeii*, vol. 2 (New Rochelle, NY: Caratzas Brothers, 1993), 327, fig. 379.

64. Jashemski, *The Gardens of Pompeii*, vol. 1, 79; see for example, Jashemski, *The Gardens of Pompeii*, vol. 2, 398–99, fig. 491.

65. For example, Bergmann, "Painted Perspectives of a Villa Visit," n10; J. R. Clarke, *The Houses of Roman Italy 100 B.C.–A.D. 250: Ritual, Space, and Decoration* (Berkeley: University of California Press, 1991), 171–73.

66. Bergmann, "Painted Perspectives of a Villa Visit."

67. A "*paradeisos*-inspired" genre of landscape paintings also emerged; see Clarke, *The Houses of Roman Italy 100 B.C.–A.D. 250*; Bergmann, "Painted Perspectives of a Villa Visit."

68. Bergmann, "Painted Perspectives of a Villa Visit."

69. The topic of garden sculpture has been treated in a number of works, ranging from analyses of specific sites such as Tivoli (S. Dillon, "Subject Selection and Viewer Reception of Greek Portraits from Herculaneum and Tivoli," *Journal of Roman Archaeology* 13 [2000]: 21–40) and Oplontis (S. De Caro, "The Sculptures of the Villa of Poppaea at Oplontis: A Preliminary Report," in *Ancient Roman Villa Gardens*, ed. E.B. MacDougall [Washington, D.C.: Dumbarton Oaks, 1987], 77–134) to syntheses (Ridgway, "Greek Antecedents of Garden Sculpture"; E. Bartmann, "Sculptural Collection and Display in the Private Realm," in *Roman Art in the Private Sphere: New Perspectives on the Architecture and Decor of the Domus, Villa, and Insulae*, ed. E.K. Gazda [Ann Arbor: University of Michigan Press, 1991], 71–88; von Stackelberg, *The Roman Garden*).

70. Hales, *The Roman House and Social Identity*, 147, fig. 54.

71. R. Paribeni, "Roma," *Notizie degli Scavi di Antichitá* 51 (1926): 284; Dillon, "Subject Selection and Viewer Reception," my translation.

72. See Clarke, *The Houses of Roman Italy 100 B.C.–A.D. 250*, fig. 122 for a life-size Priapus in the garden of the Vettii. On Priapus in art, see P. Stewart, "Fine Art and Coarse Art: The Image of Roman Priapus," *Art History* 20, no. 4 (1994): 575–88.

73. Platt, "Viewing, Desiring, Believing"; von Stackelberg, *The Roman Garden*, 121–22.

74. L. Farrar, *Ancient Roman Gardens* (Stroud: Sutton Publishing, 1998), 125–27. *Oscilla* are carved stone images that were usually round, could depict several motifs, and were designed to list and wave in the breeze; cf. R. Taylor, "Roman Oscilla: An Assessment," *RES: Anthropology and Aesthetics* 48 (2005): 83–105.

75. E. Moorman, *La pittura parietale romana come fonte di conoscenza per la scultura antica* (Assen: van Gorcum, 1988).

76. Kuttner, "Looking Outside Inside," 349. For art collections in gardens, see K. J. Hartswick, *The Gardens of Sallust: A Changing Landscape* (Austin: University of Texas Press, 2004), 16–17. Cicero, *In Verrem* 2.4.126; Pliny, *HN* 36.23, 25.

77. De Caro, "The Sculptures of the Villa of Poppaea at Oplontis," 99–101, figs. 15a–b, 16a–b.

78. For example, the statue of Aphrodite in D. K. Hill, "Some Sculpture from Roman Domestic Gardens," in *Ancient Roman Gardens*, eds. E.B. MacDougall and

W. Jashemski (Washington, D.C.: Dumbarton Oaks, 1981): 93, fig. 16; L. Mariani, "Aphrodite di Cirene" *Bolletino d'Arte* 8 (1914): 180–81.

79. K.M.D. Dunbabin, *Mosaics of the Greek and Roman World* (Cambridge: Cambridge University Press, 1999), 236.

80. See for example the House of the Wedding of Alexander: Jashemski, *The Gardens of Pompeii*, vol. 2, 268n550; Dunbabin, *Mosaics of the Greek and Roman World*, 243.

81. T. Budetta, ed., *The Garden: Reality and Imagination in Ancient Art, Museo Archeologico della Penisola Sorrentina "Georges Vallet," July 17–December 22 2005* (Castellamare di Stabia: Nicola Longobardi Editore, 2006).

82. See for example M. Blanchard-Lemée, M. Ennaïfer, H. Slim, and L. Slim, *Mosaics of Roman Africa* (New York: George Braziller, 1995), fig. 51.

83. M. Blanchard-Lemée, M. Ennaïfer, H. Slim, and L. Slim, *Mosaics of Roman Africa* (New York: George Braziller, 1995), figs. 69–71. The mosaic, Silenus Bound, dates to the second half of the third century C.E.

84. See Malek, "De la mosaïque à la Jonchée à la mosaïque à la treille." On the vine motif in other Roman mosaics, see Chapter 7 ("Dining in an Arbor") in C. Kondoleon, *Domestic and Divine: Roman Mosaics in the House of Dionysos* (Ithaca, NY: Cornell, 1995).

85. Known as the Doves of Sosos (Dunbabin, *Mosaics of the Greek and Roman World*, 26–7); N. Büttner, *The History of Gardens in Painting* (New York: Abbeville Press Publishers, 2008), 26; C. Riccardi, ed., *Il mausoleo di Galla Placidia a Ravenna* (Modena: F. C. Panini, 1996).

86. J. Elsner, *Imperial Rome and Christian Triumph: The Art of the Roman Empire AD 100–450* (Oxford: Oxford University Press, 1998), fig. 103.

87. For an example, see the painting from the early fourth century C.E. Christian necropolis at Tipasa, in North Africa: S. Lancel, *L'Algèrie antique: de Massinissa à Saint Augustin* (Paris: Mengés, 2003), 162, fig. 160.

88. The vault mosaics share a remarkable similarity to contemporary mosaics from Carthage, found in the Maison de la Volière: see A. Ennabli and W.B. Osman, "Etude des pavements de la villa de la Volière," in *Mosaïque: Recueil d'Hommages a Henri Stern* (Paris: Editions Recherches sur les civilisations, 1983), plates 35–37; H. Stern, "Les mosaïques de l'église de Sainte-Constance à Rome," *Dumbarton Oaks Papers* 12 (1957): 202.

89. Stern, "Les mosaïques de l'église de Sainte-Constance à Rome," 202.

90. John 15:1, "I am the true vine, and my Father is the gardener."

91. The "Sevso" Treasure, taken from a name inscribed on the rim of the "Hunting Plate," has no known provenience: M. Mundell Mango and A. Bennett, "The Sevso Treasure: Part One," *Journal of Roman Archaeology* [special issue], Supplementary Series 12 (1994); K. M. Dunbabin, *The Roman Banquet: Images of Conviviality* (Cambridge: Cambridge University Press, 2003).

92. Mundell Mango and Bennett, "The Sevso Treasure," 441, fig. 13–14a, 13–15.

93. M. Conway, "A Persian Garden Carpet," *Burlington Magazine for Connoisseurs* 23, no. 122 (1913): 95–99; Moynihan, *Paradise as a Garden*, 32–35. Chosroe I reigned from 531–79 C.E.

94. Although Chosroe's carpet is lost, an example of a carpet does survive from the fifth century B.C.E.: the Pazyryk carpet found in the ice of Siberia shows a royal hunting scene in its border: S. Dalley, "Ancient Assyrian Textiles and the Origins of Carpet Design," *Iran* 29 (1991): 117–35; Moynihan, *Paradise as a Garden*, 34.

95. The first Sasanian king, Arsacid, chose his name from "Artaxerxes," one of the kings in the fifth century Achaemenid dynasty.

96. Moynihan, *Paradise as a Garden*, 33.

97. Dunbabin, *Mosaics of the Greek and Roman World*, 176–78. The question of whether these mosaics were influenced by contemporary carpets is frustrated by the lack of textile evidence from the period.

98. Dunbabin, *Mosaics of the Greek and Roman World*, 178, figs. 191, 192.

Chapter 8

1. See Pliny, *Letters, and Panegyricus*, vol. 2, trans. B. Radice (Cambridge, MA: Harvard University Press, 1969), 151.

2. A. Burford, *Land and Labor in the Greek World* (Baltimore: Johns Hopkins University Press, 1993), 66–69.

3. M. Carroll-Spillecke, "The Gardens of Greece from Homeric to Roman Times," *Journal of Garden History* 12 (1992): 84–101.

4. See also A. Hort, *Enquiry into Plants and Minor Works on Odours and Weather Signs* (London: W. Heinemann, 1948), 7.7.2.

5. Note Plato's expression of ratios appropriate for ownership of the land.

6. I. Nielsen, *Hellenistic Palaces: Tradition and Renewal* (Aarhus: Aarhus University Press, 1994), 63.

7. Nielsen, *Hellenistic Palaces*, 79.

8. See also Burford's analysis of this text, *Land and Labor*, 66–69.

9. See Demosthenes, "An Unknown Pleader Against Phaenippus in the Matter of an Exchange of Properties," in *Private Orations*, vol. 2, ed. Demosthenes and A. T. Murray (Cambridge, MA: Harvard University Press, 1936), 28–53.

10. J. G. Manning, *Land and Power in Ptolemaic Egypt: The Structure of Land Tenure* (Cambridge: Cambridge University Press, 2003), 65

11. Manning, *Land and Power in Ptolemaic Egypt*, 73.

12. Nielsen, *Hellenistic Palaces*, 131.

13. For example, M. Carroll-Spillecke, "The Gardens of Greece from Homeric to Roman Times," *Journal of Garden History* 12 (1992): 84–85.

14. T. Roselaar, *Public Land in the Roman Republic: A Social and Economic History of Ager Publicus in Italy, 396–89 B.C.* (Oxford: Oxford University Press, 2010), 65, 138–42.

15. A. W. Oswald, *The Roman Land Surveyors: An Introduction to the Agrimensores* (New York: Barnes and Noble, 1971), 19–30.

16. D. G. Romano, "City Planning, Centuriation and Land Division in Roman Corinth: *Colonia Laus Iulia Corinthiensis* and *Colonia Iulia Flavia Augusta Corinthiensis*,"

in *Corinth XX, The Centenary, 1896–1996*, ed. C. K. Williams and N. Bookidis (Princeton, NJ: ASCSA, 2003).

17. See B. Campbell, *The Writings of the Roman Land Surveyors* (London: Society for the Promotion of Roman Studies, 2000).

18. See also Campbell, *The Writings of the Roman Land Surveyors*, 42–45.

19. Bettina Bergmann has established the importance of landscape in Roman art in seminal articles, including "Painted Perspectives of a Villa Visit: Landscape as Status and Metaphor," in *Roman Art in the Private Sphere*, 2nd ed., ed. E. K. Gazda (Ann Arbor: University of Michigan Press, 1994), 49–70.

20. See also H. Rackham, *Natural History*, vol. 9 (Cambridge, MA: Harvard University Press, 1938), 347; R. Ling, "Studius and the Beginnings of Roman Landscape Painting," *Journal of Roman Studies* 67 (1977): 1–16, is fundamental regarding the interpretation of this passage.

21. Ling, "Studius," 7–10.

22. T. O'Sullivan, "Walking with Odysseus: The Portico Frame of the Odyssey Landscapes," *American Journal of Philology* 128, no. 4 (2007): 497–532.

23. The authors emphasize that these paintings are ultimately part of a broader tradition and are best considered together. The important study by A. Mau (*Geschichte der decorativen Wandmalerei in Pompeji* [Berlin: G. Reimer, 1882]) established the four styles of Pompeian painting, a chronological system that helps to define the field.

24. On architectural landscapes, see the synthetic study of M. Rostovtzeff, "Die hellenistisch-roemische Architekturlandschaft," *Mitteilungen des Deutschen Archäologischen Instituts: Römische Abteilung* 26 (1911): 1–186. Paintings: New York, Metropolitan Museum of Art 1903 (03.14.13); Naples, Museo Archelogico Nazionale, inv. 9408.

25. The term *sacro-idyllic* (or *sacral-idyllic*) is introduced by M. Rostovtzeff, "Die hellenistisch-roemische Architekturlandschaft." On the relation between Augustan literature, which revives the ideals of the rustic farmer with small land holdings, and sacro-idyllic landscape paintings, see S. Silberberg-Peirce, "Politics and Private Imagery: The Sacral-Idyllic Landscapes in Augustan Art," *Art History* 3 (1989): 241–51; S. Silberberg, "A Corpus of the Sacral-Idyllic Landscape Paintings in Roman Art" (PhD diss., University of California, Los Angeles, 1980).

26. Naples, Museo Archeologico Nazionale, inv. 9418.

27. On mythological landscape, see C. M. Dawson, *Romano-Campanian Mythological Landscape Painting* (New Haven, CT: Yale University Press, 1944); B. Bergmann, "Rhythms of Recognition: Mythological Encounters in Roman Landscape Painting," in *Im Spiegel des Mythos. Bilderwelt und Lebenswelt*, ed. F. De Angelis and S. Muth (Wiesbaden: Reichert, 1999), 81–107.

28. Vatican, Sala delle Nozze Aldobrandine. One fragmentary panel depicting the Sirens, in Rome, Museo Nazionale Romano, Palazzo Massimo alle Terme. P. H. von Blanckenhagen, "The Odyssey Frieze," *Mitteilungen des Deutschen Archäologischen Instituts: Römische Abteilung* 70 (1963): 100–146; R. Biering, *Die Odysseefresken vom Esquilin* (Munich: Biering and Brinkmann, 1995).

29. O'Sullivan, "Walking with Odysseus."

30. B. Bergmann, "Visualizing Pliny's Villas," *Journal of Roman Archaeology* 8 (1995): 406–20; P. Du Prey, *The Villas of Pliny the Younger from Antiquity to Posterity* (Chicago: University of Chicago Press, 1995); R. Förtsch, *Archäologischer Kommentar zu den Villenbriefen des Jüngeren Plinius* (Mainz am Rhein: Philip von Zabern, 1993).

31. Pliny likewise compares garden paintings to his living garden (*Ep.* 5.6.19–23).

32. On this passage, see T. P. Wiseman, "*Strabo* on the Campus Martius: *5.3.8. c236*," *Liverpool Classical Monthly* 4 (1979): 129–34.

33. H. G. Beyen, "Les *domini* de la villa de la Farnesine," in *Studia Varia Carolo Guilielmo Vollgraff a Discipulis Oblata* (Amsterdam: North Holland Pub., 1948), 3–21.

34. Rome, Museo Nazionale Romano: Palazzo Massimo alle Terme, inv. 1078–84, 1088–89; Bragantini and de Vos 1982, 234–39, tavv. 122–65; Ling, "Studius," 9.

35. B. Frischer, J. W. Crawford, and Monica De Simone, *The Horace's Villa Project, 1997–2003: Report on New Fieldwork and Research* (Oxford: Archaeopress, 2006), see vol. 1, 72–74.

36. L. Fabbrini, "Domus Aurea: Il piano superior del quartiere orientale," *Memorie della Pontificia accademia romana di archeologia* 14 (1982): 5–24. C. Panella, "Domus Aurea: Area dello Stagnum," in *Lexicon Topographicum Urbis Romae*, ed. E.M. Steinby (Rome: Edizioni Quasar, 1995), 51–55; L. Ball, *The Domus Aurea and the Roman Architectural Revolution* (Cambridge: Cambridge University Press, 2003). A. Cassatella and S. Panella, "Domus Aurea," in *Lexicon Topographicum Urbis Romae*, ed. E.M. Steinby (Rome: Edizioni Quasar, 1995), 49–51.

37. See N. Purcell "Town in Country, Country in Town" in *Ancient Roman Villa Gardens*, ed. E. B. MacDougall (Washington, D.C.: Dumbarton Oaks Research Library and Collection, 1987), 187–203. See also Martial 12.57.

38. On the Esquiline wing as pavilion, see L. Ball, *The Domus Aurea and the Roman Architectural Revolution* (Cambridge: Cambridge University Press, 2003), 8–11; A. Boëthius, *The Golden House of Nero: Some Aspects of Roman Architecture* (Ann Arbor: University of Michigan Press, 1960), 113–17. On the stage-like function, see E. Champlin, "God and Man in the Golden House," in *Horti Romani: atti del Convegno internazionale, Roma, 4–6 maggio 1995*, ed. M. Cima and E. La Rocca (Rome: L'Erma di Bretschneider,1998), 339–41.

39. C. Panella, *Meta Sudans, 1. Un'area sacra "in Palatio" e la valle del Colosseo prima e dopo Nerone* (Rome: Istituto poligrafico e Zecca dello Stato, 1996).

40. Fabbrini's excavations (1982) of the second floor at the eastern section of the building, which faced to the north, indicate that the Gardens of Maecenas could be admired over the Esquiline Hill in the opposite direction.

41. Champlin, *Nero* (Cambridge, MA: Belknap Press of Harvard University Press, 2003), 156–60; F. Zevi, "Nero, Baiae, e la Domus Aurea," *Ulisse: il mito e la memoria*, ed. B. Andreae and C. Parisi Presicee (Rome: Progetti Museali, 1996), 320–31.

42. Palestrina, Museo Nazionale Prenestino. On the mosaic, P.G.P. Meyboom, *The Nile Mosaic of Palestrina: Early Evidence of Egyptian Religion in Italy* (Leiden: E. J. Brill, 1995).

43. The mosaic's modern reconstructions recommend a cautious reading of its composition, especially at the top where it has been most heavily restored.

44. See Meyboom, *The Nile Mosaic of Palestrina*, 185–90.

45. Tunis, Musée National du Bardo, inv. I. D. Parrish, *Season Mosaics of Roman North Africa* (Rome: Archeologica, 1984), 111–13, cat. no. 9.

BIBLIOGRAPHY

Adams, J. N. *The Latin Sexual Vocabulary*. London: Duckworth, 1982.

Aharoni, Y. "Excavations at Ramat Rahel, 1954: Preliminary Report." *Israel Exploration Journal* 6 (1956): 102–11, 137–57.

Alarcao, J., and R. Etienne. "Les jardins à Conimbriga (Portugal)." In *Ancient Roman Gardens*, ed. E. B. Macdougall and W. F. Jashemski, 67–80. Washington, D.C.: Dumbarton Oaks, 1981.

Albenda, P. "Assyrian Sacred Trees in the Brooklyn Museum." *Iraq* 36 (1994): 123–33.

Albenda, P. "Grapevines in Ashurbanipal's Garden." *Bulletin of the American Schools of Oriental Research* 215 (1974): 5–17.

Alcock, S. E. *Archaeologies of the Past: Landscape, Monuments, and Memories*. Cambridge: Cambridge University Press, 2002.

Almagro-Gorbea, M. *El Santuario de Juno en Gabii*. Rome: Escuela espanola de historia y arquelogía en Roma, Bibliotheca italica 17, 1982.

Anderson, M. L. "Pompeian Frescoes in the Metropolitan Museum of Art." *Metropolitan Museum of Art Bulletin* 45, no. 3 (1987).

André, J. *Les noms de plantes dans la Rome antique*. Paris: Les Belles Lettres, 1985.

Andreae, B. *Am Birnbaum: Gärten und Parks im antiken Rom, in den Vesuvstädten und in Ostia*. Mainz: v. Zabern, 1996.

Arnold, D. *The Temple of Mentuhotep at Deir el-Bahari: From the Notes of H. E. Winlock*. New York: Metropolitan Museum of Art, 1979.

Ashmore, W., and Knapp, A. B. "Archaeological Landscapes: Constructed, Conceptualized, Ideational." *Archaeologies of Landscape: Contemporary Perspectives*, ed. W. Ashmore and A. B. Knapp, 1–30. Hoboken, NJ: Wiley, 1999.

Atallah, W. *Adonis dans la literature et l'art grecs*. Paris: C. Klincksieck, 1966.

Badawy, A. *A History of Egyptian Architecture: The First Intermediate Period, The Middle Kingdom, and the Second Intermediate Period*. Berkeley: University of California Press, 1966.

Ball, L. *The Domus Aurea and the Roman Architectural Revolution*. Cambridge: Cambridge University Press, 2003.

Barber, C. "Reading the Garden in Byzantium: Nature and Sexuality." *Byzantine and Modern Greek Studies* 16 (1992): 1–19.

Barbet, A., and P. Miniero. *La villa di San Marco a Stabiae*. Napoli: Centre Jean Bérard 1999.

Bartmann, E. "Sculptural Collection and Display in the Private Realm." In *Roman Art in the Private Sphere: New Perspectives on the Architecture and Decor of the Domus, Villa, and Insulae*, ed. E.K. Gazda, 71–88. Ann Arbor: University of Michigan Press, 1991.

Beagon, M. *Roman Nature: The Thought of Pliny the Elder*. Oxford: Clarendon Press, 1992.

Beard, M. "Imaginary *Horti*; or, Up the Garden Path." In *Horti Romani*, ed. M. Cima and E.L. Rocca, 23–32. Rome: L'Erma di Bretschneider, 1998.

Beard, M., and J. Henderson. *Classical Art: From Greece to Rome*. Oxford: Oxford University Press, 2001.

Bedal, L.-A. *The Petra Pool-Complex: A Hellenistic Paradeisos in the Nabataean Capital*. Piscataway, NJ: Gorgias Press, 2004.

Bedal, L.-A., and G. Schryver. "Nabataean Landscape and Power." In *Crossing Jordan: North American Contributions to the Archaeology of Jordan*, ed. T. Levy, M. Daviau, R. Younker, and M. Shaer, 375–84. London: Equinox, 2007.

Behr, C. A. *P. Aelius Aristides: The Complete Works*. Leiden: Brill, 1981.

Bek, L. "*Questiones Convivales:* The Idea of the *Triclinium* and the Staging of Convival Ceremony from Rome to Byzantium." *Analecta romana Instituti Danici* 12 (1983): 81–107.

Bergmann, B. "Art and Nature in the Villa at Oplontis." In *Pompeiian Brothels, Pompeii's Ancient History, Mirrors and Mysteries, Art and Nature at Oplontis, and the Herculaneum Basilica*, ed. C. Stein and J. Humphrey, *Journal of Roman Archaeology Supplemental Series* 47: 87–120, 406–20. Ann Arbor: University of Michigan, 2002.

Bergmann, B. "Exploring the Grove: Pastoral Space on Roman Walls." In *The Pastoral Landscape*, ed. J. Dixon Hunt, 21–48. Washington, D.C.: National Gallery of Art, 1992.

Bergmann, B. "Meanwhile, Back in Italy . . . " In *Pausanias and His Periegesis, the Traveler and Text*, ed. S. E. Alcock, J. Cherry, and J. Elsner, 154–66. Oxford: Oxford University Press, 2001.

Bergmann, B. "Painted Perspectives of a Villa Visit: Landscape as Status and Metaphor." In *Roman Art in the Private Sphere*, ed. E.K. Gazda, 49–70. Ann Arbor: University of Michigan Press, 1991.

Bergmann, B. "Painted Perspectives of a Villa Visit: Landscape as Status and Metaphor." In *Roman Art in the Private Sphere: New Perspectives on the Architecture and Décor of the Domus, Villa and Insula*, 2nd ed., ed. E. K. Gazda, 49–70. Ann Arbor: University of Michigan Press, 1994.

Bergmann, B. "Rhythms of Recognition: Mythological Encounters in Roman Landscape Painting." In *Im Spiegel des Mythos: Bilderwelt und Lebenswelt/Lo specchio del mito: Immaginario e realtà. Symposium, Rome, February 19–20, 1998*, 81–107. Deutsches Archäologisches Institut Rom. Dr. Ludwig Reichart Verlag Wiesbaden, 1999.

Bergmann, B. "Staging the Supernatural: Interior Gardens of Pompeian Houses." In *Pompeii and the Roman Villa: Art and Culture around the Bay of Naples*, ed. Carol C. Mattusch, 53–69. Washington, D.C.: National Gallery of Art, 2008.

Bergmann, B. "Visualizing Pliny's Villas." *Journal of Roman Archaeology* 8 (1995): 406–20.

Bergquist, B. *Herakles on Thasos: The Archaeological, Literary, and Epigraphic Evidence for his Sanctuary; Status and Cult Reconsidered.* Uppsala: Almqvist & Wiksell, 1973.

Bernard, P. *Fouilles d'Aï Khanoum I* (Mémoires DAFA XXI). Paris: Klincksieck, 1973.

Beyen, H. G. "Les *domini* de la villa de la Farnesine." In *Studia Varia Carolo Guilielmo Vollgraff a Discipulis Oblata*, 3–21. Amsterdam: North Holland Pub., 1948.

Biering, G. *Die Odysseefresken vom Esquilin.* Munich: Biering and Brinkmann, 1995.

Bietak, M. "Connections between Egypt and the Minoan World: New Results from Tell el-Dab'a/Avaris." In *Egypt, the Aegean and the Levant*, ed. W. V. Davies and L. Schofield, 19–28. London: British Museum Press, 1995.

Birge, D. E. "Sacred Groves in the Ancient Greek World." PhD diss., University of California, Berkeley, 1982.

Black, J.A. "Some Structural Features of Sumerian Narrative Poetry." In *Mesopotamian Epic Literature: Oral or Aural?* ed. M. E. Vogelzang and H.J.L. Vantisphout, 71–101. Lampeter: Mellen, 1992.

Black, J.A., G. Cunnigham, J. Ebling, E. Fluckiger-Hawker, E. Robson, J. Taylor, and G. Zólyomi. *The Electronic Text Corpus of Sumerian Literature.* Oxford: Oxford University Press, 1998.

Blaison, M. "Suétone et l'ekphrasis de la Domus Aurea (Suét. Ner. 31)." *Latomus* 57 (1998): 617–24.

Blanchard-Lemée, M., M. Ennaïfer, H. Slim, and L. Slim. *Mosaics of Roman Africa.* New York: George Braziller, 1995.

Boatwright, M.T. "Luxuriant Garden and Extravagant Women: The *Horti* of Rome between Republic and Empire." In *Horti Romani*, ed. M. Cima and E.L. Rocca, 71–82. Rome: L'Erma di Bretschneider, 1998.

Boëthius, A. *The Golden House of Nero: Some Aspects of Roman Architecture.* Ann Arbor: University of Michigan Press, 1960.

Boucharlat, R. "The Palace and the Royal Achaemenid City: Two Case Studies—Pasargadae and Susa." In *The Royal Palace Institution in the First Millennium BC: Regional Development and Cultural Interchange between East and West*, ed. I. Nielsen, 113–23. Athens: Danish Institute at Athens, 2001.

Boucharlat, R., and A. Labrousse. "Le palais d'Artaxerxes II sur la rive droite du Chaour à Suse." *Cahiers de la Délégation Archéologique Francaise en Iran* 10 (1979): 19–136.

Boucharlat, S. V. "Pasargadai." In Reallexikon der Assyriologie und Vorderasiatischen Archäologie, Bd 10, Lfg. 3/4, ed. D. O. Edzard, E. Ebeling, B. Meissner, 293–302. Walter de Gruyter, 2004.

Boulotis, C. "Mycenean Wall Painting." In *The Mycenean World: Five Centuries of Early Greek Culture 1600–1100 BC*, ed. K. Demakopolou, 35–37. Athens: Ministry of Culture, Naational Hellenic Committee, December, 1988.

Bowe, P. "The Sacred Groves of Ancient Greece." *Studies in the History of Gardens and Designed Landscapes* 29, no. 4 (2009): 233–45.

Bowie, E.L. "Theocritus' Seventh Idyll, Philetas and Longus." *Classical Quarterly* 35 (1985): 67–91.

Bragantini, I., and M. de Vos. *Museo Nazionale Romano: Le Pitture II, 1. Le decorazioni della villa romana della Farnesina*. Rome, Leonardo Arte 1982.

Braund, D. "Palace and Polis: Dionysus, Scythia and Plutarch's Alexander." *The Royal Palace Institution in the First Millennium BC: Regional Development and Cultural Interchange between East and West*, ed. I. Nielsen, 15–31. Athens: Danish Institute at Athens, 2001.

Brazda, M.K. *Zur Bedeutung des Apfels in der antiken Kultur*. Bonn: Faculty of Philosophy, Rheinische Friedrich-Wilhelms-Universität, 1977.

Breasted, J.H. *Ancient Records of Egypt*. Chicago: University of Chicago Press, 1906.

Bridges, E., E. Hall, and P. J. Rhodes. *Cultural Responses to the Persian Wars: Antiquity to the Third Millennium*. Oxford: Oxford University Press, 2007.

Broise, H., and V. Jolivet. "Horti Lucullani." In *Lexicon topographicum urbis Romae*, vol. 3, H–O, 67–70. Roma: Ed. Quasar, 1996.

Brown, F. *Cosa: The Making of a Roman Town*. Ann Arbor: University of Michigan Press, 1979.

Brown, F., R. Driver, and C. Briggs. *Brown-Driver-Briggs Hebrew and English Lexicon*. Peabody, MA: Hendrickson, 1996.

Bruun, C. "Inscriptions on Lead Pipes." In *The Horace's Villa Project, 1997–2003: Report on New Fieldwork and Research*, ed. B. Frischer, J. Crawford, and M. de Simone, 295–301. Oxford: Archaeopress, 2006.

Budetta, T., ed. *The Garden: Reality and Imagination in Ancient Art, Museo Archeologico della Penisola Sorrentina "Georges Vallet," July 17–December 22 2005*. Castellamare di Stabia: Nicola Longobardi Editore, 2006.

Burford, A. *Land and Labor in the Greek World*. Baltimore: Johns Hopkins University Press, 1993.

Büttner, N. *The History of Gardens in Painting*. New York: Abbeville Press Publishers, 2008.

Cairns, F. *Tibullus: A Hellenistic Poet at Rome*. Cambridge: Cambridge University Press, 1979.

Calame, C. *The Poetics of Eros in Ancient Greece*. Princeton, NJ: Princeton University Press, 1999.

Cameron, M.A.S. "Unpublished Paintings from the 'House of the Frescoes' at Knossos." *Annual of the British School at Athens* 63 (1968): 1–31.

Campbell, B. *The Writings of the Roman Land Surveyors: Introduction, Text, Translation and Commentary*. London: Society for the Promotion of Roman Studies, 2000.

Caneva, H. "Ipotsi sul significato simbolico del giardino dipinto della Villa di Livia (Prima Porta, Roma)." *Bullettino della commissione archeologica comunale di Roma* 100 (1999): 63–80.

Carettoni, G.F. *Forma Urbis Romae: La Pianta Marmorea di Roma Antica*. Rome: Danesi, 1960.

Carroll, M. *Earthly Paradises: Ancient Gardens in History and Archaeology*. Los Angeles: Getty Publications, 2003.

Carroll-Spillecke, M., ed. *Der Garten von der Antike bis zum Mittelalter*. Mainz: Kulturgeschichte der antiken Welt 57, 1992.

Carroll-Spillecke, M. "The Gardens of Greece from Homeric to Roman Times." *Journal of Garden History* 12 (1992): 84–101.

Carroll-Spillecke, M. "Griechische Gärten." *Garten von der Antike bis zum Mittelalter* 7, no. 2 (1992): 153–75.

Carroll-Spillecke, M. Κηπος: *Der antike griechische garten: Wohnen in der klassichen polis Band III*. München: Deutscher Kunstverlag, 1989.

Carroll-Spillecke, M. *Landscape Depictions in Greek Relief Sculpture*. Frankfurt am Main: P. Lang, 1985.

Cassatella, A., and S. Panella. "Domus Aurea." In *Lexicon Topographicum Urbis Romae*, ed. E. M. Steinby, 49–51. Rome: Edizioni Quasar, 1995.

Casson, L. *The Periplus Maris Erythraei*. Princeton, NJ: Princeton University Press, 1989.

Chamoux, F. "Une évocation littéraire d'un palais Macédonien (Argonautiques III, 215 sq.)." *Ancient Macedonia Vth International Symposium (10–15th October 1989)*. Thessaloniki: Institute for Balkan Studies, 1993.

Champlin, E. "God and Man in the Golden House." In *Horti Romani: atti del Convegno internazionale, Roma, 4–6 maggio 1995*, ed. M. Cima and E. La Rocca, 333–44. Rome: L'Erma di Bretschneider, 1998.

Champlin, E. *Nero*. Cambridge, MA: Belknap Press of Harvard University Press, 2003.

Chapin, A. P. "The Fresco with Multi-Colored Rocks and Olive Branches from the Northwest Slope Plaster Dump at Pylos Re-Examined." In *Aegean Wall Painting: A Tribute to Mark Cameron*, ed. L. Morgan, 123–30. British School at Athens Studies, 13. London: British School at Athens, 2005.

Chapin, A.P. "Power, Privilege and Landscape in Minoan Art." In *ΞΑΡΙΣ: Essays in Honor of Sara A. Immerwahr*, ed. A. Chapin, 47–64. Princeton, NJ: American School of Classical Studies at Athens, 2004.

Ciaraldi, M. *People and Plants in Ancient Pompeii: A New Approach to Urbanism from the Microscope Room*. London: Accordia Research Institute, University of London, 2007.

Ciarallo, A. M., and M. Manotti Lippi. "The Garden of "Casa dei Casti Amanti (Pompeii, Italy)." *Garden History* 21 (1993): 110–16.

Cima, M., and E. La Rocca, eds. *Horti Romani: atti del Convegno internazionale, Roma, 4–6 maggio 1995*. Rome: L'Erma di Bretschneider, 1998.

Cima, M., and E. La Rocca, eds. *Le tranquille dimore degli dei: la residenza imperiali degli horti Lamiani*. Venice: C. Marsilio, 1986.

Clarke, G. "The Governor's Palace, Acropolis, Jebel Khalid." In *The Royal Palace Institution in the First Millennium BC: Regional Development and Cultural Interchange between East and West*, ed. I. Nielsen, 215–47. Athens: Danish Institute at Athens, 2001.

Clarke, J. R. *The Houses of Roman Italy 100 B.C.–A.D. 250: Ritual, Space, and Decoration*. Berkeley: University of California Press, 1991.

Clarke, J. R. "Landscape Paintings in the Villa of Oplontis." *Journal of Roman Archaeology* 9 (1996): 81–107.

Clevely, A. M. *Topiary: The Art of Clipping Trees and Ornamental Hedges.* London: Salem House Publishers, 1988.

Cline, E. H. " 'Rich beyond the Dreams of Avaris' Tell El-Dab'a and the Aegean World— A Guide for the Perplexed." *Annual of the British School at Athens* 93 (1998): 100–219.

Coarelli, F. *Il campo Marzio dale origini alla fine della Repubblica.* Rome: Quasar, 1997.

Coarelli, F. "Il Campo Marzio: Storia e topografia." *Mélanges de l'Ecole française de Rome: Antiquité* 89 (1977): 807–46.

Coarelli, F. "Il complesso pompeiano del Campo Marzio e la sua decorazione scultorea." *RendPontAcc* 44 (1979): 99–110.

Coarelli, F. "I *luci* del Lazio: la documentazione archeological." In *Les Bois Sacrés: Actes du colloque international,* 45–52. Naples: Centre Jean Bérard, 1993.

Coarelli, F. *I santuari del Lazio in età Repubblicana.* Rome: La Nuova Italia Scientifica, 1987.

Colomina, B., ed. *Sexuality and Space.* New York: Princeton Architectural Press, 1992.

Conan, M., ed. *Landscape Design and the Experience of Motion.* Washington, D.C.: Dumbarton Oaks, 2003.

Conan, M. "Nature into Art: Gardens and Landscapes in the Everyday Life of Ancient Rome." *Journal of Garden History* 6, no. 4 (1986): 348–56.

Conway, M. "A Persian Garden Carpet." *Burlington Magazine for Connoisseurs* 23, no. 122 (1913): 95–99.

Cook, E. "Near Eastern Sources for the Palace of Alkinoos." *American Journal of Archaeology* 108 (2004): 43–77.

Cosgrove, D. *Social Formation and Symbolic Landscapes.* London: Croon Helm, 1984.

Cosgrove, D., and S. Daniels, eds. *The Iconography of Landscape: Essays on the Symbolic Representation, Design, and Use of Past Environments.* Cambridge: Cambridge University Press, 1988.

Coulton, J. J. *Ancient Greek Architects at Work: Problems of Structure and Design.* Ithaca, NY: Cornell University Press, 1977.

Coulton, J. J. "Greek Architects and the Transmission of Design." *Architecture et société: De l'archaïsme grec à la fin de la république romaine,* 453–68. Paris: Centre national de la recherche scientifique, 1983.

Crane, G. "The 'Odyssey' and Conventions of the Heroic Quest." *Classical Antiquity* 6 (1987): 11–37.

Cunliffe, B. *Excavations at Fishbourne.* 2 vols. London: Society of Antiquaries, 1971.

Cunliffe, B. "Fishbourne Revisited: The Site in Its Context." *Journal of Roman Archaeology* 4 (1991): 160–69.

Cunliffe, B. *Fishbourne Roman Palace.* Stroud: Tempus, 1998.

Cunliffe, B. "Roman Gardens in Britain: A Review of the Evidence." *Ancient Roman Gardens,* ed. E. B. Macdougall and W. F. Jashemski, 95–108. Washington, D.C.: Dumbarton Oaks, 1981.

Curtius, E. R. *European Literature and the Latin Middle Ages.* New York: Pantheon Books, 1953.

Dalley, S. "Ancient Assyrian Textiles and the Origins of Carpet Design." *Iran* 29 (1991) 117–35.

Dalley, S. "Ancient Mesopotamian Gardens and the Identification of the Hanging Gardens of Babylon Resolved." *Garden History* 21, no. 1 (1993): 1–13.

Dalley, S. "Nineveh, Babylon and the Hanging Gardens: Cuneiform and Classical Sources Reconciled." *Iraq* 56 (1994): 45–58.

Danzig, G. "Why Socrates Was Not a Farmer: Xenophon's *Oeconomicus* as a Philosophical Dialogue." *Greece and Rome* 50 (2003): 57–76.

Darling, J. K. "Sacro-Idyllic Landscapes of the Antonine Dynasty in Rome." PhD diss., University of Illinois, Urbana-Champaign, 1979.

D'Arms, J. "Between Public and Private: The *Epulum Publicum* and Caesar's *Horti Trans Tiberim*." In *Horti Romani*, ed. M. Cima and E. La Rocca, 33–43. Rome: L'Erma di Bretschneider, 1998.

D'Arms, J. H. *Romans on the Bay of Naples: A Social and Cultural Study of the Villas and Their Owners from 150 B.C. to A.D. 400*. Cambridge, MA: Harvard University Press, 1970.

Davies, D. "The Evocative Symbolism of Trees." In *The Iconography of Landscape: Essays on the Symbolic Representation, Design, and Use of Past Environments*, ed. D. Cosgrove and S. Daniels, 32–42. Cambridge: Cambridge University Press, 1988.

Davies, W. V., and L. Schofield, eds. *Egypt, the Aegean and the Levant*. London: British Museum Press, 1995.

Dawe, R. D. *The Odyssey: Translation and Analysis*. Lewes, Sussex: The Book Guild, 1993.

Dawson, C. M. *Romano-Campanian Mythological Landscape Painting*. New Haven, CT: Yale University Press, 1944.

De Caro, S. "The Sculptures of the Villa of Poppaea at Oplontis: A Preliminary Report." In *Ancient Roman Villa Gardens*, ed. E. B. MacDougall, 77–134. Washington, D.C.: Dumbarton Oaks, 1987.

De Carolis, E., "La pittura di giardino a Ercolano e Pompei." In *Domus—viridaria—horti picti*, 29–33. Napoli: Bibliopolis, 1992.

De Cazanove, O., and J. Scheid, eds. *Les Bois Sacrés*. Naples: Centre Jean Bérard, 1993.

De Pretis, A., ed. "Re-Imagining Pliny the Younger." Special issue, *Arethusa* 36, no. 2 (2003).

DeLaine, J. "The Baths of Caracalla: A Study in the Design, Construction, and Economics of Large-Scale Building Projects in Imperial Rome." *Journal of Roman Archaeology*, suppl. series 25 (1997).

Delorme, J. *Gymnasion*. Paris: Bibliotheéque des Écoles françaises d'Athenes et de Rome, 1960.

Demakopolou, K., ed. *The Mycenean World: Five Centuries of Early Greek Culture 1600–1100 BC*. Athens: Ministry of Culture, Naational Hellenic Committee, December, 1988.

Demosthenes. "An Unknown Pleader against Phaenippus in the Matter of an Exchange of Properties." In *Private Orations*, vol. 2, ed. Demosthenes and A. T. Murray, 28–53. Cambridge, MA: Harvard University Press, 1936.

Desbat, A. *La Maison des Dieux Océan à Saint-romain-en-Gal*, 55th suppl. Paris: Gallia, 1994.

De Simone, M., S. Nerucci, and L. Passalacque. "Quadriporticus." In *The Horace's Villa Project, 1997–2003: Report on New Fieldwork and Research*, ed. B. Frischer, J. Crawford, and M. de Simone, 97–103. Oxford: Archaeopress, 2006.

Detienne, M. *The Gardens of Adonis: Spices in Greek Mythology*. Hassocks, Sussex: Harvester Press, 1977.

Dickie, M. "Phaeacian Athletes." *Papers of the Liverpool Latin Seminar* 4 (1983): 237–76.

Dilke, O.A.W. *The Roman Land Surveyors: An Introduction to the Agrimensores*. New York: David and Charles, 1971.

Dillon, J. "What Happened to Plato's Garden." *Hermathena* 84 (1983): 51–59.

Dillon, M.P.J. " 'Woe for Adonis'—but in Spring, not Summer." *Hermes* 131 (2003): 1–16.

Dillon, S. "Subject Selection and Viewer Reception of Greek Portraits from Herculaneum and Tivoli." *Journal of Roman Archaeology* 13 (2000): 21–40.

Doumas, C. *The Wall Paintings of Thera*. London: The Thera Foundation, 1992.

Downey, G. *A History of Antioch in Syria from Seleucus to the Arab Conquest*. Princeton, NJ: Princeton University Press, 1961.

Dreliossi-Herakleidou, A. "Späthellenistische palastartige Gebäude in der Nähe der Akropolis von Rhodos." In *Basileia. Die Paläste der hellenistischen Könige*, ed. W. Hoepfner und G. Brands, 182–92. Mainz: v. Zabern, 1996.

Drews, R. "Sargon, Cyrus and Mesopotamian Folk History." *Journal of Near Eastern Studies* 33 (1974): 387–93.

Dunbabin, K.M. *Mosaics of the Greek and Roman World*. Cambridge: Cambridge University Press, 1999.

Dunbabin, K. M. *The Roman Banquet: Images of Conviviality*. Cambridge: Cambridge University Press, 2003.

Dunbabin, K. M. "Triclinium and Stibadium." In *Dining in a Classical Context*, ed. W. J. Slater, 121–48. Ann Arbor: University of Michigan Press, 1991.

Du Prey, P. *The Villas of Pliny the Younger from Antiquity to Posterity*. Chicago: University of Chicago Press, 1995.

Elsner, J. *Imperial Rome and Christian Triumph: The Art of the Roman Empire AD 100–450*. Oxford: Oxford University Press, 1998.

Elsner, J. *Roman Eyes: Visuality & Subjectivity in Art & Text*. Princeton, NJ: Princeton University Press, 2007.

Ennabli, A., and W.B. Osman. "Etude des pavements de la villa de la Volière." In *Mosaïque: Recueil d'Hommages a Henri Stern*. Paris: Editions Recherches sur les civilisations, 1983.

Evyasaf, R. S. "Gardens at a Crossroads: The Influence of Persian and Egyptian Gardens on the Hellenistic Royal Gardens of Judea," 27–37. *AIAC Congress Publication*. Rome: Bollettino di Archeologia, 2008.

Fabbrini, L. "Domus Aurea: Il Palazzo sul Esquilino." In *Lexicon Topographicum Urbis Romae*, ed. E. M. Steinby, 56–63. Rome: Edizioni Quasar, 1995.

Fabbrini, L. "Domus Aurea: Il piano superiore del quartiere orientale." *Memorie della Pontificia Academia diarcheologia* 15 (1982): 5–24.

Fabbrini, L. "Domus Aurea: una nuova lettura planimetria del palazzo sul colle Oppio." In *Analecta Romana*, supp. X, 169–89. Rome: Danish Institute, 1983.

Fabbrini, L. "I Corpi Edilizi che Condizionarono L'Attuazione del Progetto del Palazzo Esquilino di Nerone." *Rendiconti della Pontificia Academia dell'archeologia* 58 (1986): 129–79.

Farrar, L. *Ancient Roman Gardens*. Stroud: Sutton Publishing, [1998] 2000.

Faulkner, R. O. *Ancient Egyptian Coffin Texts*. Warminster: Aris and Phillips, 1973.

Ferriolo, M. V. "Homer's Garden." *Journal of Garden History* 9 (1989): 86–94.

Foresta, S. "La Villa della Farnesina: un punto di vista private. Ricezione rielaborazione di modelli ellenistici a Roma." *Incidenza dell'Antico: dialoghi di storia greca* 2 (2004): 113–35.

Förtsch, R. *Archäologischer Kommentar zu den Villenbriefen des Jüngeren Plinius*. Mainz am Rhein: Philip von Zabern, 1993.

Fouet, G. *La villa gallo-romaine de Montmaurin vers le milieu de 4e siècle*. Paris: Saint-Gaudens, 1983.

Foulk, R. "Politics of Place: Landscape Painting in Imperial Rome and its Environs." PhD diss., Emory University, Atlanta, 2011

Frantz, A. *Late Antiquity: AD 267–700; The Athenian Agora*, vol. 24. Princeton, NJ: Princeton University Press, 1988.

Frischer, B., J. W. Crawford, and M. de Simone. *The Horace's Villa Project, 1997–2003: Report on New Fieldwork and Research*. Oxford: Archaeopress, 2006.

Frizell, B. S., and A. Klynne. *Roman Villas around the Urbs: Interaction with Landscape and Environment*. Proceedings from Swedish Institute in Rome Conference, September 17–18, 2004, Rome Swedish Institute, Rome, 2005.

Gaballa, G. A. "Three Documents from the Reign of Rameses III." *Journal Egyptian Archaeology* 59 (1973): 109–13.

Gabriel, M. *Livia's Garden Room at Prima Porta*. New York: NYU Press, 1955.

Gagliardo, M. C., and J. E. Packer. "A New Look at Pompey's Theater: History, Documentation, and Recent Excavation." *American Journal of Archaeology* 110, no. 1 (2006): 93–122.

Ganzert, J., and J. Wolschke-Bulmahn, eds. *Bau- und Gartenkultur zwischen "Orient" und "Okzident": Fragen zu Herkunft, Identität und Legitimation*. München: Martin Meidenbauer, 2009.

Garvie, A. F. *Homer Odyssey Books VI–VIII*. Cambridge: Cambridge University Press, 1994.

Gatti, E. "Saepta Iulia." *Lexicon Topographicum Urbis Romae* IV (1999): 228–29.

Gentili, G. *Die Kaiserliche Villa bei Piazza Armerina*. Rome: Libreria dello Stato, 1971.

Giesecke, A. L. *The Epic City: Urbanism, Utopia and the Garden in Ancient Greece and Rome*. Washington, D.C.: Center for Hellenic Studies, Trustees for Harvard University, 2007.

Glacken, C. J. *Traces on the Rhodian Shore*. Berkeley: University of California Press, 1967.

Gleason, K. L. "Constructing Nature: With a Preliminary Notice of a New Monumental Garden at the Villa Arianna, Stabiae, Italy." *Bollettino di Archeologia online I 2010/Volume speciale D/D9/3*: 8–15. http://151.12.58.75/archeologia/bao_document/articoli/3_Gleason.pdf.

Gleason, K. L. "A Garden Excavation in the Oasis Palace of Herod the Great at Jericho." *Landscape Journal* 12, no. 2 (1993): 156–67.

Gleason, K. L. "Gardens." In *The Oxford Encyclopedia of Archaeology in the Near East*, vol. 2, ed. E. M. Myers, 383–87. New York: Oxford University Press, 1997.

Gleason, K. L. "Porticus Pompeiana: A New Perspective on the First Public Park of Ancient Rome." *Journal of Garden History* 14, no. 1 (1994): 13–27.

Gleason, K. L. "The Promotory Palace at Caesarea Maritima: Preliminary Evidence for Herod's Praetorium." *Journal of Roman Archaeology* 11 (1998): 23–52.

Gleason, K. L. "Towards an Archaeology of Landscape Architecture in the Roman World." PhD diss., Oxford University, 1989.

Gleason, K. L., B. Burrell, and E. Netzer. "The Promotory Palace at Caesarea Maritima: Preliminary Evidence for Herod's Praetorium." *Journal of Roman Archaeology* 11 (1998): 23–52.

Gleason, K. L., and M. Leone. "Apprehending the Garden." In *A Sourcebook for Garden Archaeology*, ed. A.-A. Malek, 97–126. Bern: Peter Lang, 2013.

Gleason, K. L., and M. Palmer. "Synthesis and Interpretation: The Garden as a Built Environment." In *A Sourcebook for Garden Archaeology*, ed. A.-A. Malek, 277–315. Berg: Peter Lang, 2013.

Gleason, K. L., J. Schryver, and L. Passalacqua. "The Garden." In *The Horace's Villa Project, 1997–2003: Report on New Fieldwork and Research*, ed. B. Frischer, J. Crawford, and M. de Simone, 71–95, 659–78. Oxford: Archaeopress, 2006.

Golden, M., and P. Toohey, eds. *Inventing Ancient Culture: Historicism, Periodization, and the Ancient World*. London: Routledge, 1997.

Goodman, P., and O. Murray, eds. *Latin Poetry and the Classical Traditions: Essays in Medieval and Renaissance Literature*. Oxford: Clarendon Press, 1990.

Gothein, M. "Der griechische Garten." *Athenische Mitteilungen* 34 (1909): 100–144.

Gothein, M. L. *A History of Garden Art*. 2nd ed. New York: Hacker, [1928] 1979.

Granger, F. *Vitruvius: De Architectura*. Cambridge, MA: Harvard University Press, 1931.

Grayson, A. *Assyrian Royal Inscriptions: Pt. 2, From Tiglath-Pileser I to Ashur-nasir-apli II*. Wiesbaden: Otto Harrassowitz, 1976.

Grimal, P. *Les jardins romains*. 2nd ed. Paris: Presses universitaires de France, 1969.

Grimal, P. *Les jardins romains*. 3rd ed. Paris: Fayard, 1984.

Gros, P. *Architecture et Societé à Rome et en Italie centro-meridionale aux deux derniers siècle de la République*. Bruxelles: Latomus, 1978.

Gros, P. *Aurea Templa: recherches sur l'architecture religieuse de Rome à l'Époque d'Auguste*. Rome: École Francaise de Rome, 1976.

Gros, P. "Porticus Pompei." In *Lexicon topographicum urbis Romae*, vol. 4, P–S, 148–49. Roma: Ed. Quasar, 1999.

Gulick, C. B. *Athenaeus: The Deipnosophists*, 7 vols. Cambridge, MA: Harvard University Press, 1927–41.

Hales, S. *The Roman House and Social Identity*. Cambridge: Cambridge University Press, 2003.

Halloran, J.A. *Sumerian Lexicon: A Dictionary Guide to the Ancient Sumerian Language*. Los Angeles: Logogram, 2006.

Halpern, L.C. "The Uses of Paintings in Garden History." In *Garden History: Issues, Approaches, Methods*, ed. J.D. Hunt, 183–202. Washington, D.C.: Dumbarton Oaks, 1992.

Hanson, J. A. *Roman Theater Temples*. Princeton, NJ: Princeton University Press, 1959.

Hartswick, K.J. *The Gardens of Sallust: A Changing Landscape*. Austin: University of Texas Press, 2004.

Haselberger, L. "The Construction Plans for the Temple of Apollo at Didyma." *Scientific American* 253, no. 6 (1985): 126–32.

Hatzopoulos, M. P. "Macedonian Palaces: Where King and City Meet." In *The Royal Palace Institution in the First Millennium BC: Regional Development and Cultural Interchange between East and West*, ed. I. Nielsen, 189–200. Athens: Danish Institute at Athens, 2001.

Häuber, C. "Endlich lebe ich wie ein Mensch: Zu domus, horti und villae in Rom." In *Das Wrack: Der antike Schiffsfund von Mahdia*, ed. G. Hellenkemper Salies. Köln: Rheinland-Verlag GmbH, 1994.

Häuber, C. "Zur Topographie der Horti Maecenatis und der Horti Lamiani auf dem Esquilin in Rome." *Kölner Jahrbuch* 23 (1990): 11–107.

Häuber, C., and F. Schütz. "The Sanctuary *Isis et Serapis* in *Regio III* in Rome: Preliminary Reconstruction and Visualization of the Ancient Landscape Using 3/4D-GIS-Technology." *Bollettino di Archeologia online I 2010/Volume speciale D/D3/7* (2011): 82–94. http://www.archeologia.beniculturali.it/pages/pubblicazioni.html.

Hellenkemper Salies, G., ed. *Das Wrack: Der antike Schiffsfund von Mahdia*. Köln: Rheinland Verlag GmbH, 1994.

Helms, M. *Ulysses' Sail: An Ethnographic Odyssey or Power, Knowledge and Geographic Distance*. Princeton, NJ: Princeton University Press, 1988.

Henderson, J. *Pliny's Statue: The Letters, Self-Portraiture and Classical Art*. Exeter: University of Exeter Press, 2002.

Hepper, N.F. *Pharaoh's Flowers: The Botanical Treasures of Tutankhamun*. London: HMSO, 1990.

Herrman, G. "The Rock Reliefs of Sasanian Iran." In *Mesopotamia and Iran in the Parthian and Sasanian Periods: Rejection and Revival 238 BCE–CE642*, ed. J. Curtis, 35–45. London: British Museum Press, 2000.

Heubeck, A., S. West, and J. B. Hainsworth. *A Commentary on Homer's Odyssey: Books I–VIII*. Oxford: Oxford University Press, 1988.

Higgins, R. *Minoan and Mycenean Art*. 3rd ed. London: Thames and Hudson, 1997.

Hill, D.K. "Some Sculpture from Roman Domestic Gardens." In *Ancient Roman Gardens*, ed. E.B. MacDougall and W. Jashemski, 81–94. Washington, D.C.: Dumbarton Oaks, 1981.

Hoffmann, A. *Das Gartenstadion in der Villa Hadriana*. Mainz: v. Zabern, 1980.

Horden, P., and N. Purcell. *The Corrupting Sea: A Study of Mediterranean History.* Oxford: Wiley-Blackwell, 2000.

Hort, A. *Enquiry into Plants and Minor Works on Odours and Weather Signs.* London: W. Heinemann, 1948.

Houlihan, P. G. *The Animal World of the Pharaohs.* London: Thames and Hudson, 1996.

Hubbard, M. *Propertius.* Bristol: Bristol University Press, 1974.

Hugonot, J.-C. "Ägyptische Gärten." In *Der Garten von der Antike bis zum Mittelalter,* ed. M. Carroll-Spillecke, 9–44. Kulturgeschichte der antiken Welt 57. Mainz: v. Zabern, 1992.

Hugonot, J.-C. *Le jardin dans L'Egypte ancienne.* Paris: Peter Lang, 1989.

Hunink, V., ed. *Pro de se magia* (Apologia). Amsterdam: J. C. Gieben, 1997.

Hunt, J.D. *The Afterlife of Gardens.* Philadelphia: University of Pennsylvania Press, 2004.

Hunt, J. D., ed. *Garden History: Issues, Approaches, Methods.* Washington, D.C.: Dumbarton Oaks, 1992.

Hunt, J. D. *Greater Perfections: The Practice of Garden Theory.* Philadelphia: University of Pennsylvania, 2000.

Hunt, J. D., ed. *The Pastoral Landscape.* London: National Gallery of Art, 1992.

Hunt, J. D. "Verbal Versus Visual Meanings in Garden History: the Case of Rousham." In *Garden History: Issues, Approaches, Methods,* ed. Dixon Hunt, 151–81. Washington, D.C.: Dumbarton Oaks, 1992.

Hurst, A., and F. Létoublon, eds. *La Mythologie et l'Odyssée. Hommage à Gabriel Germain.* Geneva: Actes du colloque international de Grenoble, May 20–22, 1991, 2002.

Hurwit, J. "The Representation of Nature in Early Greek Art." In *New Perspectives in Early Greek Art,* ed. D. Buitron-Oliver, 32, 33–62. Washington, D.C.: Studies in the History of Art, 1991.

Ijsewijn, J. "Poetry in a Roman Garden: The *Coryciana.*" In *Latin Poetry and the Classical Traditions: Essays in Medieval and Renaissance Literature,* ed. P. Goodman and O. Murray, 211–31. Oxford: Clarendon Press, 1990.

Isager, J. *Pliny on Art and Society: The Elder Pliny's Chapters on the History of Art.* Odense: Routledge, Chapman and Hall, 1991.

Jashemski, W. F. "Antike römische Gärten in Campanien." In *Der Garten von der Antike bis zum Mittelalter,* ed. M. Carroll-Spillecke, 177–212. Mainz: Kulturgeschichte der antiken Welt 57, 1992.

Jashemski, W. F. "The Campanian Peristyle Garden." In *Ancient Roman Gardens,* eds. E. B. MacDougall and W. Jashemski, 29–49. Washington, D.C.: Dumbarton Oaks, 1981.

Jashemski, W. F., "The Contribution of Archaeology to the Study of Ancient Roman Gardens." In *Garden History: Issues, Approaches, Methods,* ed. J. Dixon Hunt, 5–30. Washington, D.C.: Dumbarton Oaks, 1992.

Jashemski, W. F. "The Discovery of a Market-Garden Orchard at Pompeii: The Garden of the House of the Ship Europa." *American Journal of Archaeology* 78 (1974): 391–404.

Jashemski, W. F. *The Gardens of Pompeii, Herculaneum and the Villas Destroyed by Vesuvius,* vol. 1. New Rochelle: Caratzas Brothers, 1979.

Jashemski, W. F. *The Gardens of Pompeii, Herculaneum and the Villas Destroyed by Vesuvius*, vol. 2. New Rochelle, NY: Caratzas Brothers, 1993.

Jashemski, W. F. "The Gardens of Pompeii, Herculaneum and the Villas Destroyed by Vesuvius." *Journal of Garden History* 12 (1992): 102–25.

Jashemski, W. F. "Roman Gardens in Tunisia: Preliminary Excavations in the House of Bacchus and Ariadne and in the East Temple at Thuburbo Maius." *American Journal of Archaeology* 99 (1995): 559–76.

Jashemski, W. F., K. Gleason, K. Hartswick, and A.-A. Malek, eds. *Gardens of the Roman Empire*. New York: Cambridge University Press, forthcoming.

Jashemski, W. F., and F. G. Meyer, eds. *The Natural History of Pompeii*. Cambridge: Cambridge University Press, 2002.

Jashemski, W. F., and E.S.P. Ricotti. "1992 Preliminary Excavations in the Gardens of Hadrian's Villa: The Canopus Area and the Piazza d'Oro." *American Journal of Archaeology* 96 (1996): 593–95.

Jones, H. L. *The Geography of Strabo*. Cambridge, MA: Harvard University Press, 1917–32.

Jones, M. W. *Principles of Roman Architecture*. New Haven, CT: Yale University Press 2003.

Jonker, G. *The Topography of Remembrance: The Dead, Tradition, and Collective Memory in Mesopotamia*. Leiden: E. J. Brill, 1975.

Karageorghis, V., and M. Carroll-Spillecke. "Die heiligen Haine und Gärten Zyperns." In *Garten von der Antike bis zum Mittelalter 1992*, ed. M. Carroll-Spillecke, 141–52. Mainz: v. Zabern, 1992.

Kawami, T. S. "Antike persische Gärten." In *Garten von der Antike bis zum Mittelalter 1992*, ed. M. Carroll-Spillecke, 81–99. Mainz: v. Zabern, 1992.

Kellum, B. "The Construction of Landscape in Augustan Rome: The Garden Room at the Villa ad Gallinas." *The Art Bulletin* 76, no. 2 (1994): 211–24.

Kent, J. H. "The Temple Estates of Delos, Rheneia and Mykonos." *Hesperia* 17 (1948): 243ff.

Klynne, A., and Liljenstolpe, P. "Investigating the Gardens of the Villa of Livia." *Journal of Roman Archaeology* 13 (2000): 220–33.

Kondoleon, C. *Domestic and Divine: Roman Mosaics in the House of Dionysos*. Ithaca, NY: Cornell, 1995.

Kramer, S. N. *From the Poetry of Sumer: Creation, Glorification, Adoration*. London: University of California Press, 1979.

Kuhrt, A. "The Palace(s) of Babylon." In *The Royal Palace Institution in the First Millennium BC*, ed. I. Nielsen, 77–93. Monographs of the Danish Institute at Athens, vol. 4. Athens: Danish Institute, 2001.

Kuttner, A. "Culture and History at Pompey's Museum." *Transactions of the American Philological Association* 129 (1999): 343–73.

Kuttner, A. "Delight and Danger in the Roman Water Garden: Sperlonga and Tivoli." In *Landscape Design and the Experience of Motion*, ed. M. Conan, 103–56. Washington, D.C.: Dumbarton Oaks, 2003.

Kuttner, A. "Looking Outside Inside: Ancient Roman Garden Rooms." *Studies in the History of Gardens and Designed Landscapes* 19, no. 1 (1999): 7–35.

Kuttner, A. "Republican Rome looks at Pergamon." *Harvard Studies in Classical Philology* 97 (1995): 157–78.

Lancaster, L. *Concrete Vaulted Construction in Imperial Rome: Innovations in Context.* Cambridge: Cambridge University Press, 2005.

Lancel, S. *L'Algèrie antique: de Massinissa à Saint Augustin.* Paris: Mengés, 2003.

Lanciani, R. *Ancient and Modern Rome.* Boston: Marshall Jones, 1925.

Landgren, L. "Lauro Myrto et Buxo Frequentata: A Study of the Roman Garden through Its Plants." PhD diss., Lund University, 2004.

Landgren, L. "The Roman Pleasure Garden—Foundations for Future Studies." *Opuscula Romana* 20 (1996): 40–46.

Langlois, E. *Origines et sources du roman de la Rose.* Paris: E. Thorin, 1891.

Lapp, N.L., ed. *The Excavation at Araq el-Emir: Volume 1, Annual of the American Schools of Oriental Research* 47 (1980): iii–158.

La Rocca, E. "Il lusso come espressione di potere." In *Le tranquille dimore degli dei*, ed. M. Cima and E. La Rocca, 3–35. Venice: Marsilio, 1986.

La Rocca, E. *Lo spazio negate: La pittura di paesaggio nella cultura artistica greca e romana.* Milan: Mondadori Electa S.p.A., 2008.

Larsson Lovén, L. "The Imagery of Textile Making: Gender and Status in the Funerary Iconography of Textile Manufacture in Roman Italy and Gaul." PhD diss., Göteborg, 2002.

Lattimore, R. *Hesiod: The Works and Days; Theogony; The Shield of Herakles.* Ann Arbor: Ann Arbor Paperbacks, 1991.

Lauter, H. "Ein Tempelgarten?" *Archäologischer Anzeiger* (1968): 626–31.

Lazarro, C. *Italian Renaissance Garden: From the Conventions of Planting, Design, and Ornament to the Grand Gardens of Sixteenth-Century Central Italy.* New Haven, CT: Yale University Press, 1990.

Leach, E. "Landscape and the Prosperous Life: The Discrimination of Genre in Augustan Literature and Painting." *The Age of Augustus: Interdisciplinary Conference Held at Brown University, Providence April 30–May 2, 1982*, ed. R. Winkes, 189–95. Providence, RI: Brown University, 1985.

Leach, E. *The Rhetoric of Space: Literary and Artistic Representations of Landscape in Republican and Augustan Roman.* Princeton, NJ: Princeton University Press, 1998.

Leach, E. "A Roman Design for Nature." In *Vergil's Eclogues: Landscapes of Experience.* Ithaca, NY: Cornell University Press, 1974.

Leach, E. *The Social Life of Painting in Ancient Rome and on the Bay of Naples.* Cambridge: Cambridge University Press, 2004.

Lee-Stecum, P. *Powerplay in Tibullus: Reading Elegies Book 1.* Cambridge: Cambridge University Press, 1998.

Lefèvre E. "Plinius Studien I: Römische Baugesinnung und Landschaft Auffassung in den Villenbriefen (2.17, 5.6)." *Gymnasium* 34 (1977): 519–41.

LeGlay, M. "Les jardins à Vienne." In *Ancient Roman Gardens*, ed. E. B. Macdougall and W. F. Jashemski, 49–65. Washington, D.C.: Dumbarton Oaks, 1981.

Lembke, K. *Das Iseum Campense in Rom: Studien über den Isiskult unter Domitian.* Heidelberg: Verlag Archäologie und Geschichte, 1994.

Leone, M. *Critical Historical Archaeology.* Walnut Creek, CA: Left Coast Press, 2010.

Les Bois sacrés: Acte du colloque International organisé par le centre Jean Bérard à L'École pratique des Hautes etudes. Naples: Centre Jean Bérard 1993.

Liljenstolpe, P., and A. Klynne. "The Imperial Gardens of the Villa of Livia at Prima Porta: A Preliminary Report on the 1997 Campaign." *OpusculaRomana* 22–23 (1997–98): 127–47.

Lilyquist, C. "Egyptian Art." *Notable Acquisitions (Metropolitan Museum of Art)* [newsletter] (1984–85): 4–5.

Lipschits, O., Y. Gadot, M. Oeming, and B. Arubas. "The 2006 and 2007 Excavation Seasons at Ramat Rahel: Preliminary Report." *Israel Exploration Journal* 59 (2009): 1–20.

Ling, R. *Roman Painting*. Cambridge: Cambridge University Press, 1991.

Ling, R. "Studius and the Beginnings of Roman Landscape Painting." *Journal of Roman Studies* 67 (1997): 1–16.

Littlewood, A. R. "Ancient Literary Evidence for the Pleasure Gardens of Roman Country Villas." In *Ancient Roman Villa Gardens*, ed. E. B. MacDougall, 7–30. Washington, D.C.: Dumbarton Oaks, 1987.

Littlewood, A. R. "The Apple in the Sexual Imagery of Kazantzakis: A Study in the Continuity of a Greek Tradition." *Neo-Hellenika* 3 (1978): 37–55.

Littlewood, A. R. "The Erotic Symbolism of the Apple in Late Byzantine and Meta-Byzantine Demotic Literature." *Byzantine and Modern Greek Studies* 17 (1993): 83–103.

Littlewood, A. R. "Gardens of Byzantium." *Journal of Garden History* 12, no. 2 (1992): 126–53.

Littlewood, A. R. "Gardens of the Palaces." In *Byzantine Court Culture from 829 to 1204*, ed. H. Maguire, 13–38. Washington, D.C.: Dumbarton Oaks, 1997.

Littlewood, A. R. "Romantic Paradises: The Role of the Garden in the Byzantine Romance." *Byzantine and Modern Greek Studies* 5 (1979): 95–114.

Littlewood, A. R. "The Symbolism of the Apple in Byzantine Literature." *Jahrbuch der österreichischen Byzantinistik* 23 (1974): 33–59.

Littlewood, A. R. "The Symbolism of the Apple in Greek and Roman Literature." *Harvard Studies in Classical Philology* 72 (1967): 147–81.

Littlewood, A. R., H. Maguire, and J. Wolschke-Bulmahn, eds. *Byzantine Garden Culture*. Washington, D.C.: Dumbarton Oaks, 2002.

Lloyd, R. B. "Three Monumental Gardens on the Marble Plan." *American Journal of Archaeology* 86 (1982): 91–100.

Lugauer, M. *Untersuchungen zur Symbolik des Apfels in der Antike*. Erlangen-Nürnberg: Friedrich-Alexander-Universität, 1967.

Lugli, G. "La villa di Domiziano sui Colli Albani." *Bullettino della Commissione Archeologica Comunale di Roma* (1918): 64–65.

Luschin, E. M. "Römische Gartenanlagen. Studien zu Gartenkunst und Städtebau in der römischen Antike." PhD thesis, University of Vienna, Vienna, 2010.

Macaulay-Lewis, E. "The City in Motion." DPhil thesis, Oxford University, 2008.

Macauley-Lewis, E. "Movement and Space in Roman Architecture and Gardens 100BC–150AD." DPhil thesis, Oxford University, 2009.

Macaulay-Lewis, E. "Political Museums: Porticos, Gardens and the Public Display of Art in Ancient Rome." In *Collecting and Dynastic Ambition*, ed. S. Bracken, A. Gáldy, and A. Turpin, 1–21. Newcastle: Cambridge Scholars Publishing, 2009.

MacDougall, E. *Ancient Roman Villa Gardens*. Washington, D.C.: Dumbarton Oaks, 1987.

MacDougall, E., and W.F. Jashemski. *Ancient Roman Gardens*. Washington, D.C.: Dunbarton Oaks, 1981.

Maguire, H. *Earth and Ocean: The Terrestrial World in Early Byzantine Art*. University Park: Penn State University Press, 1987.

Maguire, H. "Imperial Gardens and the Rhetoric of Renewal." In *New Constantines: the Rhythm of Imperial Renewal in Byzantium, 4th–13th Centuries*, ed. P. Magdalino, 181–97. Aldershot: Variorum, 1994.

Malek, A.-A. "De la mosaïque à la Jonchée à la mosaïque à la treille: la sentiment de la nature en Afrique romaine." In *Ancient Roman Mosaics: Paths through the Classical Mind, Acta of Conference Held in March, 2000 in Luxembourg*, ed. C.-M. Ternes with the collaboration of the Worcester Art Museum and Rheinisches Landesmuseum, Trier. Luxembourg: Imprimerie Linden, 2002.

Malek, A.-A., ed. *A Sourcebook for Garden Archaeology*. Bern: Peter Lang, 2012.

Mallwitz, A. *Olympia und seine Bauten*. München: Beck, 1972.

Manning, J.G. *Land and Power in Ptolemaic Egypt: The Structure of Land Tenure*. Cambridge: Cambridge University Press, 2003.

Margueron, J.-C. "Die Gärten im Vorderen Orient." In *Der Garten von der Antike bis zum Mittelalter*, ed. M. Carroll-Spillecke, 45–80. Kulturgeschichte der antiken Welt 57. Mainz: v. Zabern, 1992.

Mariani, L. "Aphrodite di Cirene." *Bolletino d'Arte* 8 (1914): 180–81

Marinatos, N. *Minoan Religion: Ritual, Image and Symbol*. Columbia: University of South Carolina Press, 1993.

Masson, G. *Italian Gardens*, New York: Abrams, 1961.

Mathea-Förtsch, M. *Römische Rankenpfeiler und -pilaster: Schmuckstutzen mit vegetabilem Dekor, vornehmlich aus Italien und der westlichen Provinzen*. Mainz: P. von Zabern 1999.

Mattern, T. "Review of M.W. Jones, Principles of Roman Architecture." *Gnomon* 75, no. 4 (2003): 349–53.

Mau, A. *Geschichte der decorativen Wandmalerei in Pompeji*. Berlin: G. Reimer, 1882.

Mckenzie, J. *The Architecture of Petra*. Oxford: Oxford University Press, 1990.

Medri, M. "Suet, *Nero* 31.1: Elementi e Proposite per la Ricostruzione del Progetto della Domus Aurea." In *Meta Sudans, 1. Un'area sacra 'in Palatio' e la valle del Colosseo prima e dopo Nerone*, ed. C. Panella, 165–88. Rome, 1996.

Meiggs, R. *Trees and Timber in the Ancient Mediterranean World*. Oxford: Clarendon Press, 1982.

Melmoth, W. *Letters by Pliny the Younger*. New York: P. F. Collier & Son, 1909–14.

Meneghini, R. "Il Tempio o Foro della Pace." In *I Fori Imperiali: Gli scavi del Comune di Roma (1991–2007)*, ed. R. Meneghini and R. Santageli. Rome: Viviani Editori, 2007.

Meneghini, R., and R. S. Valenziani. *I Fori Imperiali: Gli scavi del Comune di Roma (1991–2007)*. Rome: Viriani Editore, 2007.

Messineo, G. *Ad Gallinas Albas: Villa di Livia*. Rome: L'Erma di Bretschneider 2001.

Meyboom, P.G.P. *The Nile Mosaic of Palestrina: Early Evidence of Egyptian Religion in Italy*. Leiden: E. J. Brill, 1995.

Mielsch, H. *Die romische Villa: Architektur und lebensform*. Munich: Beck, 1987.

Miller, N. F., and Gleason, K. L., eds. *The Archaeology of Garden and Field*. Philadelphia: University of Pennsylvania Press, 1994.

Miller, S. G. "Excavations at Nemea." *Hesperia* 46 (1977): 9ff., 1–26.

Mitchell, W.J.T. "Imperial Landscape." In *Landscape and Power*, ed. W.J.T. Mitchell, 5–34. Chicago: University of Chicago Press, 1994.

Mols, S.T.A.M., and E. M. Moormann. *La Villa della Farnesina: le pitture*. Milan: Mondadori Electa, 2008.

Moorman, E. *La pittura parietale romana come fonte di conoscenza per la scultura antica*. Assen: van Gorcum, 1988.

Morel, J. P. "Stratigraphie et histoire sur le Palatin: la zone centrale de la Vigna Barberini." *Comptes rendus des séances de l'Académie des inscriptions et belles-lettres* (1996): 173–206.

Morenz, S. *Egyptian Religion*. London: Methuen, 1973.

Morford, M. "The Stoic Garden." *Journal of Garden History* 7 (1987): 151–75.

Morgan, L. *The Miniature Wall Paintings of Thera: A Study in Aegean Culture and Iconography*. Cambridge: Cambridge University Press, 1988.

Morgan, L. "Minoan Painting and Egypt: The Case of Tell el-Dab'a." In *Egypt, the Aegean and the Levant*, ed. W. V. Davies and L. Schofield, 29–53. London: British Museum Press, 1995.

Morgan, M.H. *Vitruvius, the Ten Books on Architecture*. New York: Dover Publications, 1960.

Motte, A. *Prairies et jardins de la Grèce antique: de la religion à la philosophie*. Brussels: Académie Royale de Belgique, 1973.

Moynihan, E.B. *Paradise as a Garden in Persia and Mughal India*. New York: George Braziller, 1979.

Mundell Mango, M., and A. Bennett. "The Sevso Treasure: Part One." *Journal of Roman Archaeology* [special issue], suppl. series 12 (1994).

Myers, K.S. "*Docta otia*: Garden Ownership and Configurations of Leisure in Statius and Pliny the Younger." *Arethusa* 38 (2005): 103–29.

Myers, K.S. "*Miranda fides*: Poet and Patrons in Paradoxographical Landscapes in Statius' *Silvae*." *Materiali e discussioni per l'analisi dei testi classici* 44 (2000): 103–38.

Myers, S. Review of K.J. Hartswick, *The Gardens of Sallust: A Changing Landscape*. Austin: University of Texas Press, 2004. *The Journal of Roman Studies* 98 (2008): 258–60.

Mynors, R.A.B., ed. *Virgil, Georgics*. Oxford: Clarendon Press, 1990.

Na'aman, N. "An Assyrian residence at Ramat Rahel?" *Tel Aviv* 28 (2001): 260–80.

Netzer, E. *The Architecture of Herod, the Great Builder*. Tübingen: Mohr Siebeck, 2006.

Netzer, E. *Die Paläste der Hasmonäer und Herodes' des Grossen.* Mainz: v. Zabern, 1999.

Netzer, E. *Hasmonean and Herodian Palaces at Jericho, Final Reports of the 1973–1987 Excavations.* Vol. 1, *Stratigraphy and Architecture.* Jerusalem: Israel Exploration Society: Institute of Archaeology, Hebrew University of Jerusalem, 2001.

Netzer, E. "Il palazzo riflesso." *Archeo* 13, no. 7 (1997): 50–54.

Netzer, E. *The Palaces of the Hasmoneans and Herod the Great.* Jerusalem: Yad Ben-Zvi Press, 2001.

Netzer, E. "Tyros, the 'Floating Palace.'" In *Text and Artefact in the Religions of Mediterranean Antiquity, Essays in Honour of Peter Richardson*, ed. S. G. Wilson and M. Desjardins, 340–53. Waterloo: Wilfrid Laurier University Press, 2000.

Newlands, C. E. "*Naturae mirabor opus*: Ausonius' Challenge to Statius in the *Mosella.*" *TAPA* 118 (1988): 403–19.

Newlands, C. E. "Statius and Ovid: Transforming the Landscape." *Transactions of the American Philological Association* 134 (2004): 133–55.

Newlands, C. E. *Statius' Silvae and the Poetics of Empire.* Cambridge: Cambridge University Press, 2002.

Newton, N. *Design on the Land.* Cambridge, MA: Belnap, 1971.

Nicolet, C. *Space, Geography, and Politics in the Early Roman Empire.* Ann Arbor: University of Michigan Press, Jerome Lectures 19, 1991.

Nielsen, I. *Cultic Theaters and Ritual Drama.* Aarhus: Aarhus University Press, 2002.

Nielsen, I. "The Gardens of the Hellenistic Palaces." In *The Royal Palace Institution in the First Millennium BC: Regional Development and Cultural Interchange between East and West*, ed. I. Nielsen, 165–87. Athens: Danish Institute at Athens, 2001.

Nielsen, I. *Hellenistic Palaces.* Aarhus: University of Aarhus, 1994.

Nielsen, I. *Hellenistic Palaces: Tradition and Renewal.* 2nd ed. Aarhus: Aarhus University Press, 1999.

Nielsen, I. "Royal Banquets: The Development of Royal Banquets and Banqueting Halls from Alexander to the Tetrarchs." In *Meals in a Social Context (Aarhus Studies in Mediterranean Antiquity 1)*, ed. I. Nielsen and H. S. Nielsen, 104–35. Aarhus: Aarhus University Press, 1998.

Nielsen, I., ed. *The Royal Palace Institution in the First Millennium BC*, monographs of the Danish Institute at Athens, vol. 4. Aarhus: Aarhus University Press, 2001.

Nielsen, I. *Thermae et Balnea: The Architecture and Cultural History of Roman Public Baths.* 2nd ed. Aarhus: Aarhus University Press, 1993.

Oppenheim, A. "On the Royal Gardens in Mesopotamia." *Journal of Near Eastern Studies* 24 (1965): 328–33.

Osborne, R. "Classical Greek Gardens: Between Farm and Paradise." In *Garden History: Issues, Approaches, Methods*, ed. J. Dixon Hunt, 373–91. Washington, D.C.: Dumbarton Oaks, 1992.

Osborne, R. *Classical Landscape with Figures: The Ancient Greek City and Its Countryside.* London: George Philip, 1987.

O'Sullivan, T. "Mind in Motion: The Cultural Significance of Walking in the Roman World." PhD thesis, Department of the Classics, Harvard University, 2003.

O'Sullivan, T. "The Mind in Motion: Walking and Metaphorical Travel in the Roman Villa." *Classical Philology* 101, no. 2 (2006): 133–52.

O'Sullivan, T. *Walking in Roman Culture*. New York: Cambridge University Press, 2011.

O'Sullivan, T. "Walking with Odysseus: The Portico Frame of the Odyssey Landscapes." *American Journal of Philology* 128, no. 4 (2007): 497–532.

Oswald, A. W. *The Roman Land Surveyors: An Introduction to the Agrimensores*. New York: Barnes and Noble, 1971.

Packer, J. E., J. Burge, and M. C. Gagliardo. "Looking Again at Pompey's Theatre: The 2005 Excavation Season." *American Journal of Archaeology* 111, no. 3 (2007): 505–22.

Pagán, V. E. *Rome and the Literature of Gardens*. London: Duckworth, 2006.

Pailler, J.-M. "Montmaurin: A Garden Villa." In *Ancient Roman Villa Gardens*, ed. E. B. MacDougall, 205–21. Washington, D.C.: Dumbarton Oaks, 1987.

Panella, C. "Domus Aurea: Area dello Stagnum." In *Lexicon topographicum urbis Romae*, 51–55. Roma: Edizioni Quasar, 1995.

Panella, C. *Meta Sudans, 1. Un'area sacra 'in Palatio' e la valle del Colosseo prima e dopo Nerone*. Rome: Istituto poligrafico e Zecca dello Stato, 1996.

Panella, C. "Porticus Liviae." In *Lexicon topographicum urbis Romae*, vol. 4, P–S, 127–9. Roma: Ed. Quasar, 1999.

Panofsky, E. *Renaissance and Renascences in Western Art*. Stockholm: Almquist and Wiksell, 1960.

Paribeni, R. "Roma." *Notizie degli Scavi di Antichità* 51 (1926): 284.

Parker, W. H. *Priapea: Poems for a Phallic God*. London: Croom Helm, 1988.

Parkinson, R. *The Painted Tomb-Chapel of Nebamun*. London: British Museum Press, 2008.

Parrish, D. *Season Mosaics of Roman North Africa*. Rome: Archeologica, 1984.

Pavlovskis, Z. *Man in an Artificial Landscape: the Marvels of Civilization in Imperial Roman Literature*. Leiden: Brill, 1973.

Pesce, G. *Il "Palazzo delle Colonne" in Tolemaide di Cirenaica*. Rome: L'Erma di Bretschneider, 1950.

Peters, W.J.T. "Die Landschaftsbilder in den Wand- und Deckenmalereien der Domus Aurea." *Bulletin antieke beschaving* 57 (1982): 52–62.

Peters, W.J.T. *Landscape in Romano-Campanian Mural Painting*. Assen: University of Groningen, 1963.

Peters, W.J.T. "Tacitus en Suetonius over het Park van Nero's Domus Aurea." In *Noctes Noviomagenses J.C.F. Nuchelmans XIII lustris pr. Kal. Sept. anno Domini MCMLXXXV feliciter peractis rude donato ab amicis oblatae*, ed. G.J.M. Bartelink and J. H. Brouwers, 105–17. Weesp, 1985.

Petrie, W. M. *The Palace of Apries*. London: School of Archaeology, 1909.

Petropoulos, J.C.B. *Eroticism in Ancient and Medieval Greek Poetry*. London: Duckworth, 2003.

Piacente, L. "L'ars topiaria e l'arte bonsai." In *L'uomo e natura*, ed. P. Barboni, 65–82. Genova: Compagnia dei Librai, 1996.

Platt, V. "Viewing, Desiring, Believing: Confronting the Divine in a Pompeian House." *Art History* 25, no. 1 (2002): 87–112.

Poehler, E., M. Flohr, and K. Cole. *Pompeii: Art, Industry and Infrastructure.* Oxford: Oxbow Books, 2011.

Poggioli, R. *The Oaten Flute: Essays on Pastoral Poetry and the Pastoral Ideal.* Cambridge: Harvard University Press, 1975.

Pollitt, J.J. *Art in the Hellenistic Age.* Cambridge: Cambridge University Press, 1986.

Pollitt, J. J. *The Art of Rome c. 753 B.C.–337 A.D.: Sources and Documents in the History of Art.* Englewood Cliffs, NJ: Prentice Hall, 1966.

Ponte, A. "Architecture and Phallocentrism in Richard Payne Knight's Theory." In *Sexuality and Space*, ed. B. Colomina, 272–305. New York: Princeton Architectural Press, 1992.

Prest, J. *The Garden of Eden: the Botanic Garden and the Recreation of Paradise.* New Haven, CT: Yale University Press, 1988.

Preus, A. "Some Ancient Ecological Myths and Metaphors." In *The Greeks and the Environment*, ed. L. Westra and M. R. Thomas, 11–18. Oxford: Rowman and Littleford, 1997.

Prior, R. E. "Going Around Hungry: Topography and Poetics in Martial 2.14." *American Journal of Philology* 117, no. 1 (1996): 121–41.

Purcell, N. "Dialectical Gardening." *Journal of Roman Archaeology* 14 (2001): 546–56.

Purcell, N. "The Roman Garden as a Domestic Building." In *Roman Domestic Buildings*, ed. I. M. Barton, 121–52. Exeter: University of Exeter Press, 1996.

Purcell, N. "The Roman Villa and the Landscape of Production." In *Urban Society in Roman Italy*, ed. T. Cornell and K. Lomas, 151–79. New York: University College London Press, 1995.

Purcell, N. "Town in Country, Country in Town." In *Ancient Roman Villa Gardens*, ed. E. B. MacDougall, 187–203. Washington, D.C.: Dumbarton Oaks, 1987.

Rackham, H. *Natural History*, vol. 9. Cambridge, MA: Harvard University Press, 1938.

Radice, B. *Letters, and Panegyricus*, vol. 2. Cambridge, MA: Harvard University Press, 1969.

Raven, J. E. *Plants and Plant Lore in Ancient Greece.* Oxford: Faith Raven, 2000.

Reade, J. "Alexander the Great and the Hanging Gardens of Babylon." *Iraq* 62 (2000): 195–217.

Redda, C. R., ed. *Egittomania: l'immaginario dell' antico Egitto e l'Occidente.* Turin: Ananke, 2006.

Reeder, J. C. *The Villa of Livia Ad Gallinas Albas: A Study in the Augustan Villa and Garden. Archaeologica Transatlantica XX.* Providence, RI: Center for Old World Archaeology and Art, 2001.

Rehak, P. *Imperium and Cosmos: Augustus and the Northern Campus Martius*, ed. J. G. Younger. Madison: University of Wisconsin Press, 2006.

Riccardi, C. ed. *Il mausoleo di Galla Placidia a Ravenna.* Modena: F. C. Panini, 1996.

Richards, J. "Conceptual Landscapes in the Egyptian Nile Valley." *Archaeologies of Landscape: Contemporary Perspectives* 4 (1999): 83–100.

Richardson, L. *A New Topographical Dictionary of Ancient Rome.* Baltimore: Johns Hopkins University Press, 1992.

Richlin, A. *The Garden of Priapus: Sexuality and Aggression in Roman Humor.* New York: Oxford University Press, 1992.

Ricotti, E.S.P. "The Importance of Water in Roman Garden Triclinia." In *Ancient Roman Gardens*, ed. E. B. MacDougall, 135–84. Washington, D.C.: Dumbarton Oaks, 1987.

Ricotti, E.S.P. "Le ville di Silin." *Rendiconti della Pontificia Accademia di Archeologia* XLIII (1970–71): 135–63.

Ridgway, B.S. "Greek Antecedents of Garden Sculpture." In *Ancient Roman Gardens*, ed. E.B. MacDougall and W. Jashemski, 7–28. Washington, D.C.: Dumbarton Oaks, 1981.

Rizzo, S. "Indagini nei Fori Imperiali." *Römische Mitteilungen* 108 (2001): 215–44.

Robinson. J.H. *Petrarch: The First Modern Scholar and Man of Letters.* New York: G. P. Putnam, 1898.

Robinson, M. "Evidence for Garden Cultivation and the Use of Bedding-Out Plants in the Peristyle Garden of the House of the Greek Epigrams (V 1,18i) at Pompeii." *Opuscula Romana* 31–32 (2006–07): 155–59.

Rodgers, R. "*Kepopoiía*: Garden Making and Garden Culture in the *Geoponika*." In *Byzantine Garden Culture*, ed. A. R. Littlewood, H. Maguire, and J. Wolschke-Bulmann, 159–75. Washington, D.C.: Dumbarton Oaks, 2002.

Roebuck, C. *The Asklepieion and Lerna* (Corinth v. 14). Princeton, NJ: American School of Classical Studies at Athens, 1951.

Romano, D. G. "City Planning, Centuriation and Land Division in Roman Corinth: *Colonia Laus Iulia Corinthiensis* and *Colonia Iulia Flavia Augusta Corinthiensis*." In *Corinth XX, The Centenary, 1896–1996*, ed. C. K. Williams and N. Bookidis. Princeton, NJ: ASCSA, 2003.

Roselaar, S.T. *Public Land in the Roman Republic: A Social and Economic History of Ager Publicus in Italy, 396–89 B.C.* Oxford: Oxford University Press, 2010.

Rostovtzeff, M. "Die hellenistisch-roemische Architekturlandschaft." *Mitteilungen des Deutschen Archäologischen Instituts: Römische Abteilung* 26 (1911): 1–186.

Rowland, I., and T. N. Howe. *Vitruvius: The Ten Books on Architecture.* New York: Cambridge University Press, 1999.

Royden, H. L. *The Magistrates of the Roman Professional Collegia in Italy from the First to the Third Century A.D.* Pisa: Giardini editori e stampatori, 1988.

Rudlich, V. "The Ownership of the Licenza Villa." In *The Horace's Villa Project, 1997–2003: Report on New Fieldwork and Research*, ed. B. Frischer, J. Crawford, and M. de Simone, 315–26. Oxford: Archaeopress, 2006.

Ruggles, D. F. *Islamic Gardens and Landscapes.* Philadelphia: University of Pennsylvania Press, 2007.

Schäfer, J. "The Role of 'Gardens' in Minoan Civilization (Plates XIV–XVI)." In *The Civilizations of the Aegean and their Diffusion in Cyprus and the Eastern Mediterranean, 2000-600 B.C.*, ed. V. Karageorghis, 85–87. Larnaca: Pierides Foundation, 1989.

Schefold, K. "Origins of Roman Landscape Painting." *Art Bulletin* 42 (1960): 87–96.

Schmidt, E. F. *Persepolis.* Chicago: University of Chicago, Oriental Institute Publications 68, 1953.

Sear, F. *Roman Theatres: An Architectural Study*. Oxford: Oxford University Press, 2006.

Sear, F. "The Scaenae Frons of the Theater of Pompey." *American Journal of Archaeology* 97, no. 4 (1993): 687–701.

Sergent, B. "Les Phéaciens avant l'Odyssée." In *La Mythologie et l'Odyssée. Hommage à Gabriel Germain*, ed. A. Hurst and F. Létoublon, 199–219. Geneva: Actes du colloque international de Grenoble, May 20–22, 1991, 2002.

Settis, S. *La villa di livia: la pareti ingannevoli*. Milan: Mondadori Electa, 2008.

Shaw, M. "The Aegean Garden." *American Journal of Archaeology*, 97, no. 4 (1993): 661–85.

Shepherd, J. C., and G. Jellicoe. *Italian Gardens of the Renaissance*. London: A. Tiranti, 1954.

Sheppard, C. D. "A Note on the Date of Taq-i-Bustan and Its Relevance to Early Christian Art in the Near East." *Gesta*, 20, no. 1 (1981): 9–13.

Sherwin-White, A. N. *The Letters of Pliny: A Historical and Social Commentary*. 2nd ed. Oxford: Clarendon Press, 1985.

Shipley, G., and J. Salmon, eds. *Human Landscapes in Classical Antiquity*. London: Routledge, 1996.

Shore, A. F. "Egyptian Cartography." In *Cartography in Prehistoric, Ancient, and Medieval Europe and the Middle East*, ed. B. Harley and D. Woodward, 117–29. Chicago: University of Chicago Press, 1987.

Sichtermann, H. "Mythology and Landscape." *Essays in Memory of Karl Kerényi*, ed. E. C. Polomé, 49–65. Washington, D.C.: Institute for the Study of Man, 1984.

Silberberg, S. "A Corpus of the Sacral-Idyllic Landscape Paintings in Roman Art." PhD diss., University of California Los Angeles, Los Angeles, 1980.

Silberberg-Peirce, S. "Politics and Private Imagery: The Sacral-Idyllic Landscapes in Augustan Art." *Art History* 3 (1989): 241–51.

Skydsgaard, P. *Varro the Scholar: Studies in the First Book of Varro's De re rustica*. Copenhagen: Munksgaard, 1968.

Smith, C. D. "Where Was the 'Wilderness' in Roman Times?" In *Human Landscapes in Classical Antiquity*, ed. G. Shipley and J. Salmon, 154–79. London: Routledge, 1996.

Soren, D. *The Sanctuary of Apollo Hylates at Kourion, Cyprus*. Tucson: University of Arizona Press, 1987.

Soyez, B. *Byblos et la Fete des Adonies*. Leiden: Brill, 1977.

Spawforth, A. "Symbol of Unity: The Persian Wars Tradition in the Roman Empire." In *Greek Historiography*, ed. S. Hornblower, 233–47. Oxford, Clarendon Press, 1994.

Spenser, D. "Horace's Garden Thoughts." In *City, Countryside, and the Spatial Organization of Value in Classical Antiquity*, ed. R. Rosen and I Sluiter, 239–74. Mnemosyne Supplement 279. Leiden: Brill, 2006.

Spyropoulos, T. "Prächtige Villa, Refugium und Musenstätte: Die Villa des Herodes Atticus in arkadischen Euá." *Antike Welt* 34 (2003): 463–70.

Stanford, W. B. *The Odyssey of Homer*. London: Macmillan, 1959.

Stärk, E. "Vindemia: Drei Szenen zu den Römern auf dem Lande." *Gymnasium* 97 (1990): 193–211.

St-Denis, B. "Just What Is a Garden?" *Studies in the History of Gardens and Designed Landscapes* 27, no. 1 (2007): 61–76.

Steinby, E. M. "Il Frammento 18a della Forma Urbis Romae." *Lacus Iuturnae* I (1989): 24–33.

Steinby, E. M., ed. *Lexicon Topigraphicum Urbis Romae*. Rome: Edizioni Quasar, 1993.

Steingräber, S. *Abundance of Life: Etruscan Wall Painting*. Los Angeles: J. Paul Getty, 2006.

Stern, H. "Les mosaïques de l'église de Sainte-Constance à Rome." *Dumbarton Oaks Papers* 12 (1957): 157–218.

Stewart, P. "Fine Art and Coarse Art: The Image of Roman Priapus." *Art History* 20.4 (1994): 575–88.

Stronach, D. "The Garden as a Political Statement: Some Case Studies from the Near East in the First Millennium B.C." *Bulletin of the Asia institute* 4 (1990): 171–80.

Stronach, D. "Parterres and Stone Watercourses at Pasargadae: Notes on the Achaemenid Contribution to Garden Design." *Journal of Garden History* 14 (1994): 3–12.

Stronach, D. *Pasargadae*. Oxford: Oxford University Press, 1978.

Stronach, D. "The Royal Garden at Pasargadae: Evolution and Legacy." In *Archeologia Iranica et Orientalis: Miscellanea in Honorem Louis Vanden Berghe*, ed. L. De Meyer and E. Haerinck, 475–502. Gent: Peters, 1989.

Strong, R. *A Celebration of Gardens*. London: Harper Collins, 1991.

Talbot, A.-M. "Byzantine Monastic Horticulture: The Textual Evidence." In *Byzantine Garden Culture*, ed. A. R. Littlewood, H. Maguire, and J. Wolschke-Bulmahn, 37–67. Washington, D.C.: Dumbarton Oaks, 2002.

Tanzer, H. H. *The Villas of Pliny the Younger*. New York: Columbia University Press, 1924.

Tatum, J., ed. *The Search for the Ancient Novel*. Baltimore: Johns Hopkins University Press, 1994.

Taylor, R. *Roman Builders: A Study in Architectural Process*. Cambridge: Cambridge University Press, 2003.

Taylor, R. "Roman Oscilla: An Assessment." *RES: Anthropology and Aesthetics*, 48 (2005): 83–105.

Thibodeau, P. "The Old Man and His Garden (Verg. *Georg.* 4, 116–148)." *Materiali e discussioni per l'analisi dei testi classici* 47 (2001): 175–95.

Thomas, R.F. "The Old Man Revisited: Memory, Reference and Genre in Virg., *Georg.* 4, 116–48." *Materiali e discussioni per l'analisi dei testi classici* 29 (1992): 35–70.

Thomas, R.F. "Tree Violation and Ambivalence in Virgil." *Transactions of the American Philological Association* 118 (1988): 261–73.

Thomas, R.F., ed. *Virgil, Georgics V.2 Books III–IV*. Cambridge: Cambridge University Press, 1988.

Thomason, A.K. "Representations of the North Syrian Landscape in Neo-Assyrian Art." *Bulletin of the American Schools of Oriental Research* 323 (2001): 63–96.

Thompson, D. B. *Garden Lore of Ancient Athens*. Princeton, NJ: American School of Classical Studies at Athens, 1963.

Thompson, D. B. "The Garden of Hephaistos." *Hesperia* 6 (1937): 396–425.

Thompson, H. A. "Activity in the Athenian Agora 1966–67." *Hesperia* 37 (1968): 36–72.

Tilia, A. B. "Discovery of an Achaemenian Palace Near Takht-I Rustam to the North of the Terrace of Persepolis." *Iran* 12 (1974): 200–204.

Tölle-Kastenbein, R. *Antike Wasserkultur*. München: C. H. Beck, 1990.

Tölle-Kastenbein, R. *Samos 14. Das Kastro Tigrani. Die Bauten und Funde griechischer, römischer und byzantinischer Zeit*. Bonn: R. Habelt, 1974.

Tomei, M. A. "Nota sui giardini antichi del Palatino." *Mélanges d'Archéologie et d'Histoire de l'École Francaise de Rome, Antiquité* 104 (1992): 917–51.

Toynbee, J.M.C. *Death and Burial in the Roman World*. London: Thames and Hudson, 1971.

Trapp, M., ed. *Greek and Latin Letters: An Anthology with Translation*. Cambridge: Cambridge University Press, 2003.

Travlos, J. *Pictorial Dictionary of Athens*. London: Thames and Hudson, 1971.

Trigger, B. G. *The History of Archaeological Thought*. Cambridge: Cambridge University Press, 1989.

Tuplin, C. *Achaemenid Studies*. Historia Einzelschriften Heft 99. Stuttgart: F. Steiner, 1996.

Vallet, G., F. Villard, and P. Auberson. *Megara Hyblaea I, Le quartier de l'agora archaïque*. Rome: École Francaise, 1976.

Villedieu, F., ed. *Il Giardino dei Cesari. Dai pallazi antichi alla Vigna Barberini sul Monte Palatino. Scavi dell'École française de Rome, 1985–1999, Ministero per I Beni e le Attività Culturali Soprintendenza Archeologica di Roma*. Rome: Edizioni Quasar, 2001.

Vogelzang, M. E., and H.L.J. Vantisphout, eds. *Mesopotamian Epic Literature: Oral or Aural?* Lampeter: Mellen, 1992.

von Blanckenhagen, P. H. "The Odyssey Frieze." *Mitteilungen des Deutschen Archäologischen Instituts: Römische Abteilung* 70 (1963): 100–146.

von Blanckenhagen, P. H., and C. Alexander. *The Augustan Villa at Boscotrecase*. Mainz: P. von Zabern 2009.

von Stackelberg, K. T. *The Roman Garden: Space, Sense and Society*. London: Routledge, 2009.

Wallace-Hadrill, A. *Houses and Society in Pompeii and Herculaneum*. Princeton, NJ: Princeton University Press, 1994.

Ward-Perkins, J. B. "Nero's Golden House." *Antiquity* 30, no. 120 (1956): 209–19.

Warden, P. G. "The Domus Aurea Reconsidered." *The Journal of the Society of Architectural Historians* 40, no. 4 (1981): 271–78.

West, M. L. *The East Face of Helicon: West Asiatic Elements in Greek Poetry and Myth*. Oxford: Oxford University Press, 1997.

White, K. D. *Farm Equipment of the Roman World*. Cambridge: Cambridge University Press, 1975.

White, K. D. *Roman Farming*. Ithaca, NY: Cornell University Press, 1970.

Wilkinson, A. *The Garden of Ancient Egypt.* London: Rubicon Press, 1998.

Wilkinson, A. "Symbolism and Design in Ancient Egyptian Gardens." *Garden History* 22, no. 1 (1994).

Will, E., and F. Larche. *Iraq el Emir—Le château du Tobiade Hyrcan.* Paris: Librairie orientaliste Paul Geuthner, 1991.

Wilson-Jones, M. *Principles of Roman Architecture.* New Haven, CT: Yale University Press, 2000.

Wiseman, D. J. "Mesopotamian Gardens." *Anatolian Studies* 33 (1983): 137–45.

Wiseman, T. P. "*Strabo* on the Campus Martius: 5.3.8. c236." *Liverpool Classical Monthly* 4 (1979): 129–34.

Yang, H. *The Archaeological Study of Chinese Palaces.* Beijing: Forbidden City Publishing House, 2001.

Yang, H. "An Archaeological Study of the Palace Garden of the Nanyue State." In *A Sourcebook for Garden Archaeology*, ed. A.-A. Malek, 659–67. Bern: Peter Lang, 2013.

Zachos, K. L. "The *Tropaeum* of the Sea-Battle of Actium at Nikopolis: Interim Report." *Journal of Roman Archaeology* 16 (2003): 65–92.

Zanker, P. *The Power of Images in the Age of Augustus.* Ann Arbor: University of Michigan Press, 1988.

Zarmakoupi, M. "Designing the landscapes of the Villa of Livia at Prima Porta." In *Essays in Classical Archaeology for Eleni Hatzivassiliou 1977–2007*, ed. D. Kurtz, 269–76. Oxford: Archaeopress, 2008.

Zayadine, F. "Decorative Stucco at Petra and other Hellenistic Sites." In *Studies in the History and Archaeology of Jordan III,* ed. A. Hadidi, 131–42. New York: Routledge & Kegan Paul, 1987.

Zeitlin, F. I. "Gardens of Desire in Longus's *Daphnis and Chloe*: Nature, Art, and Imitation." In *The Search for the Ancient Novel*, ed. J. Tatum, 148–70. Baltimore: Johns Hopkins University Press, 1994.

Zevi, F. "Nero, Baiae, e la Domus Aurea." In *Ulisse: il mito e la memoria*, ed. B. Andreae and C. Parisi Presicee, 320–31. Rome: Progetti Museali, 1996.

CONTRIBUTORS

Kelly D. Cook is a lecturer in landscape architecture at the University of Maryland. She recently completed her PhD in the history of art from Cornell University (2012) and holds her master of landscape architecture degree from SUNY/ESF in Syracuse, New York. Her research interests include ancient Roman gardens and viewed landscapes, as well as early modern landscape representation and concepts of nature, the subject of her doctoral thesis, "Sex and Stones: Grotesque Ornament as Form and Space in Early Modern France." Her fieldwork includes the Scandinavian excavations at Lago di Nemi, restoring Ancient Stabia, Caesarea Maritima, Israel, and the Petra Pool and Garden Project.

Rachel Foulk is assistant professor of art history at Ferris State University, Big Rapids, Michigan. She recently completed her PhD at Emory University (2011), where she was the recipient of the Emory University Woman's Club Memorial Award in Graduate Research. Her dissertation, "Politics of Place: Landscape Painting in Imperial Rome" argues that imperial painted landscapes must be viewed within the context of the city's topography in order to fully interpret their political and cultural expression. She is currently preparing her dissertation for publication.

Kathryn Gleason is associate professor of landscape architecture and archaeology at Cornell University. Known for her work on the archaeological recovery of ancient Roman-era gardens, her investigations include the palaces of Herod the Great of Judaea, the villa of Horace at Licenza, and the

Villa Arianna at Stabia, Italy, as well as the emerging Nabataean garden and pool complex at Petra, Jordan. Her doctoral degree in Roman archaeology is from Oxford University. She is a Fellow of the American Society of Landscape Architects, as well as the American Academy in Rome and the Albright Institute for Archaeological Research in Jerusalem. In addition to numerous field reports and articles, she is coeditor of *The Archaeology of Garden and Field* with Naomi F. Miller (University of Pennsylvania Press, 1994), a major contributor to *A Sourcebook of Garden Archaeology* (Peter Lang, 2013), and is executive editor of the late Wilhelmina Jashemski's *Gardens of the Roman Empire* (Cambridge University Press, in press). She is also the founding president of the international Society for Garden Archaeology.

Catherine Kearns is a PhD student in classical archaeology at Cornell University. Her research is on the landscape archaeology of Cyprus in the first millennium B.C.E., and she is a Fulbright Scholar at CAARI on Cyprus in 2012–2013. Her master's thesis at the University of Arizona was on ancient Roman gardens, and she is a regional editor for *Gardens of the Roman Empire*. An active field archaeologist, she has worked on monumental gardens at the Villa Arianna, Stabiae, and the Petra Pool and Garden Project, as well as urban/landscape sites on the Tsaghkahovit plain of Armenia and on the Kalavasos and Maroni Built Environments Project (KAMBE) on Cyprus.

Lena Landgren holds her PhD in classics and ancient history from Lund University, Sweden. Excerpts from her important doctoral dissertation, "Lauro Myrto et Buxo Frequentata: A Study of the Roman Garden Through Its Plants" (2004), are published here for the first time. She is a founding member of the Forum for Garden History Research.

Antony R. Littlewood is emeritus professor of classical studies at the University of Western Ontario (Canada). He is the leading expert on Byzantine gardens, with research interests in Byzantine literature and Greek palaeography. In addition to his continuing research on Byzantine gardens, he is currently working on the *Rhetorical and Grammatical Treatises of Michael Psellos*. A recent fellow at the Swedish Collegium for Advanced Study at Uppsala and a permanent research fellow of the Centre for Late Antique and Byzantine Studies at the University of Reading, he has published extensively on classical Roman and Byzantine gardens for a range of Dumbarton Oaks projects and publications, assessing the future directions for scholarship in A. Littlewood, H. Maguire and J. Wolschke-Bulmahn's (eds.) *Byzantine Garden Culture* (Dumbarton Oaks Research Library and Collection, 2002).

He has also published a biography for the Association of Cricket Statisticians and Historians, is writing another, and plans to work on a third when the calls of Byzantine manuscripts and the lure of travel to wild and out-of-the-way countries permit.

Elizabeth Macaulay-Lewis is a visiting assisting professor at the Graduate Center, City University of New York. She is a classical archaeologist whose interests lie in the study of Roman gardens, architecture, and their reception. Her fieldwork includes the gardens of Horace's Villa, Licenza, the Petra Pool and Garden Project, Jordan, and an ancient plant nursery in the western Nile Delta, Egypt. She is currently working on digital reconstructions of the gardens at Hadrian's Villa, as well as ancient plant trade and nurseries. She holds an A.B. from Cornell University in classics, archaeology, and history and MSt and DPhil degrees in classical archaeology from Oxford University. She has published numerous articles and field reports on gardens in Rome, *ollae Perforatae* (planting pots), and ancient plant trade. She also serves on the governing board of the Archaeological Institute of America.

Inge Nielsen is a professor of classical archaeology at the University of Hamburg, Germany. Author of numerous important books on ancient baths, palaces, dining, and cultic theatres, her work is notable for including discussions of gardens and the broader designed landscape. She has been active in numerous excavations: Ficana and Ostia (Italy), Gadara/Umm Qays (Jordan), the Scandinavian excavations of the Temple of Castor and Pollux in the Roman Forum in Rome, and, most recently, the German excavations at Lilybaeum/ Marsala in Sicily. She is a member of the Royal Danish Academy of Sciences, a full member of the German Archaeological Institute (DAI), and, was for ten years a member of the Central Directorate of the DAI. Her publications on gardens include *Hellenistic Palaces. Tradition and Renewal* (University Press, Aarhus, 1990, 1999) and an article on the gardens of the Hellenistic palaces for the conference volume that she edited, *The Royal Palace Institution in the First Millennium BC.*

Katharine T. von Stackelberg is an associate professor of classics at Brock University, Ontario. Author of *Roman Gardens: Space, Sense, and Society* (Routledge, 2009), her research interests focus on the ways in which gardens and landscapes have been used as vehicles of cultural communication, indoctrination and resistance. She is currently working on project concerning the reception of Greco-Roman Villa Gardens in Europe and America 1873–1974.

INDEX

References to figures appear in bold.